# iOS GAME DEVELOPMENT

## DEVELOPING GAMES FOR iPAD, iPHONE, AND iPOD TOUCH

# iOS GAME DEVELOPMENT

## DEVELOPING GAMES FOR iPAD, iPHONE, AND iPOD TOUCH

**THOMAS LUCKA**

CRC Press
Taylor & Francis Group
Boca Raton London New York

CRC Press is an imprint of the
Taylor & Francis Group, an **informa** business

AN A K PETERS BOOK

CRC Press
Taylor & Francis Group
6000 Broken Sound Parkway NW, Suite 300
Boca Raton, FL 33487-2742

Printed on acid-free paper
Version Date: 20130610

Printed and bound in India by Replika Press Pvt. Ltd.

International Standard Book Number-13: 978-1-4665-6993-5 (Paperback)

**Library of Congress Cataloging-in-Publication Data**

Lucka, Thomas.
    iOS game development : developing games for iPad, iPhone, and iPod Touch / author, Thomas Lucka.
      pages cm
    Includes bibliographical references and index.
    ISBN 978-1-4665-6993-5 (pbk. : acid-free paper)
      1. Computer games--Programming. 2. iPhone (Smartphone)--Programming. 3. iOS (Electronic resource) I. Title.

    QA76.76.C672L75 2013
    794.8'15265--dc23

2012048337

**Visit the Taylor & Francis Web site at**
**http://www.taylorandfrancis.com**

**and the CRC Press Web site at**
**http://www.crcpress.com**

*For my father, Horst Lucka (1935–2007)*

# Contents

# 6. The Third Dimension 3D Games        237

# Preface

Ironically, it was Microsoft that in 1997 saved Apple from collapse with an investment of $150 million. Thirteen years later, the value of Apple's shares had increased more than 10-fold and, for the first time, the software giant Microsoft had lost its position as the world's largest technology company (based on market value)—replaced by the company headquartered in Cupertino, California.

When, in 2007, Steve Jobs took the microphone onstage in San Francisco to introduce a new, "revolutionary" cell phone and claimed that its technology was 2 years ahead of anything its competitors had to offer, one could hardly have guessed that he was actually being a bit too modest. Today, iPhone, iPod touch, and iPad have become symbols of technological progress.

A few years ago, the mobile device market was highly fragmented, with more than 1,200 different cell phones equipped with the J2ME development environment; now, OS fragmentation has arrived. In the course of a few months, Android attained a mass market with ever cheaper models, iOS held its ground as a high-end product, and fresh new operating systems such as the innovative Windows Phone from Microsoft and Nokia increasingly conquered markets throughout the world.

Yet, Apple's iPhone still stands for innovation and represents nothing less than a paradigm shift in the mobile phone industry. No wonder, then, that Apple has recently replied to these developments with iOS 5/6, the largest and most comprehensive update since the invention of the iPhone. For the first time, the new operating system will not run on all devices of the iOS family, and never before have so many innovations been presented to developers—and to users as well. In the field of game development, we should mention especially the GLKit and Game Center Services.

And even though other manufacturers, such as Nokia, Samsung, Sony Ericsson, and Google, have brought much more powerful handheld devices to market, the major reason for Apple's outstanding position is found less in the hardware than in the seamless economic system around the App Store, which to date has offered more than half a million games and programs, making it the largest download market in the mobile industry.

Apple laid the foundation for the App Store several years earlier with the iTunes portal. Through its combination of hardware (MP3 player) and software (iTunes), it was always a beat ahead of other music download platforms.

When in the summer of 2008 (1 year after the introduction of the iPhone), the iPhone software development kit (SDK) gave independent developers access to the iPhone's hardware, it quickly became clear that a small revolution had taken place.

With small apps, the functionality of the native operating system could be expanded arbitrarily, and the (at the time) unique touch-sensor control allowed for a completely new gaming experience. It is not the case that Apple invented this thing with apps; however, Apple's strictly prescribed interplay linking development, deployment, and distribution made it possible for even the smallest hobby developers to share in the benefits of digital distribution. And, yes, it is indeed still possible—despite the overwhelming numbers—to make a lot of money with App Store games. If you understand the example programs presented in this book and implement the basics of game development in some smaller game projects, you should be able at least to earn back the cost of this book. So let us proceed without delay!

A book like this does not arise in a vacuum, so here I would like to express my heartfelt thanks to several individuals:

Fernando Schneider, who approached me with the idea for an iPhone game book, an idea that fell on more than sympathetic ears

Holger Patz, without whom the games in this book would not have looked nearly as good, especially the 3D game Spaceflight, the pixel zombies, and the 360° shooter in the chapter on OpenGL ES 2D (Holger created most of the graphics, but I take responsibility for those game graphics that were less than successful.)

Janina Sieslack, who, hardworking (and often perplexed) as ever, toiled over the first edition of the manuscript

Markus Maaßen and Juan Pao, without whose enthusiasm for Apple products I would not have bought a MacBook in 2008

Another big thank-you goes to the AK Peters team behind Rick Adams, who brought this edition that you hold in your hands right now to life, and to David Kramer for his excellent translation. Contributors of essential input to the book include Jörg Büttner, Sandra Gottmann, Bernd Hein, Patrick Hennies, Alexander Hüsgen, Sascha Kolewa, Marco Kraus, Anita Nagy, Julia Stepp, Szymon Ulewicz, and Marcus Weidl. Finally, I wish to thank my mother, who showed understanding whenever my road took me from Berlin to Kassel and writing took precedence over the usual work in the parental garden.

I hope that you enjoy reading this book, and I wish you, of course, great success with your first games in the App Store. With this book, you have taken the first step. Happy coding! (^^)/

**Thomas Lucka**

# 1 Introduction—Let There Be ... Games!

## ■ 1.1 Why Program Games for the iPhone?

At first glance, the iPhone, iPod touch, and iPad do not look like your typical gaming device. There is no joystick, no gamepad, not even any buttons (other than the home button, the on/off switch, and the volume control). And yet games are the leading source of sales in the App Store. A full 28% of iPad users reported in a recent study by *Resolve Market Research* that they use the device primarily for gaming. This is all the more astonishing when one considers that games make up only 17% of the App Store. The web catalog Apptism, which offered a nearly complete Internet listing of the contents of the App Store (before it was bought out by ngmoco), showed 2 years ago a total of 213,292 apps, of which only 36,008 were games. Meanwhile, the number of apps, according to Apple, has grown to over half a million, and every month users download more than a billion apps onto their personal devices. Thus, the App Store still offers in comparison to other mobile operating systems both the largest selection and a very active download community.[*]

The absence of classical input options certainly complicates the playing of typical genre games as represented by, for example, Jump'n'Runs or Shoot'em Ups. Nevertheless, the touch-sensitive surface of iOS devices offers the possibility of emulating the missing joystick or game pad: Both variants are used, in addition to others, in the C64 emulator from Manomio (*http://c64.manomio.com*). Nonetheless, particularly for new editions

---

[*] For comparison: The Flurry Tech Blog gives only 350,000 available apps for the Android market for October 2011 (*http://blog.flurry.com*).

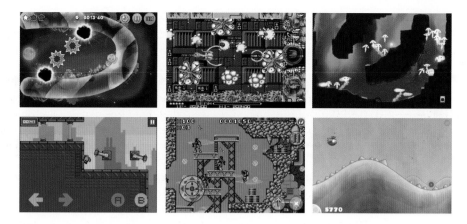

**Figure 1.1** Upper row (left to right): Magnetic Baby (Bravery), R-Type (Electronic Arts), Spirits (Spaces of Play). Lower row: League of Evil (Ravenous Games), Dark Void Zero (Beeline Interactive), Tiny Wings (Andreas Illiger).

of older retro titles from the 1980s, which often require the player's rapid and precise reaction, the touch control remains inferior to the controls borrowed from the arcade: it is too notchy, too imprecise, and, in addition, part of the screen is obscured by the virtual control (see Figure 1.1).

But it is precisely in this shortcoming that the challenge lies: The operating concept of iPhone & Co. forces game developers to think in new ways and requires new ideas and innovative control options. There are by now plenty of successful examples that show how the touch display and motion sensor can be used for games.* Since games have to be tailored to the iPhone iOS, the platform of necessity provides for new and unique gaming experiences that cannot be readily transferred to other gaming consoles or, conversely, adapted from other platforms to the iPhone.

## ▮▮ 1.2 Welcome to the World of Apple—the iPhone Phenomenon

In the beginning was … Snake! Snake? The road from the first black-and-white cell phone game (Nokia 6110, 1997) to the iPhone is not very long: By 2003, one could play three-dimensional (3D) multiplayer games on the first Nokia smartphones and, a short time later, one could begin to experience touch-sensitive displays and motion sensors (sometimes even emulated via the camera input of Symbian devices). But it was the iPhone that cleverly brought together the sum of the parts—joined to a catchy marketing campaign ("there's an app for everything")—to achieve the requisite market penetration. A single device with several million users that offers a complete development platform; this was a novelty in the mobile industry, which had previously been highly fragmented with numerous models.

---

* A good overview is offered by webzines such as *Touch Arcade* (*http://toucharcade.com*) and *Pocket Gamer* (*http://www.pocketgamer.co.uk/latest.asp?sec=7*).

Meanwhile, the successful iPhone concept was transferred to devices not enabled for telephony, such as the iPod MP3 player and the iPad. This put Apple's devices in direct competition with dedicated mobile gaming devices such as GameBoy, Nintendo DS, and Sony PSP Portable.

The digital sales channel for games via the App Store gave Apple and, of course, also developers a much more cost-effective and efficient alternative to the traditional game cartridges or disks and store sales. It could be argued that more freedom demands more responsibility, but the more likely reality is that Apple controlled all facets of the business in order to increase sales. But the user experience will also benefit from these restrictions:

- The purchase of new games takes place exclusively within the confines of the device itself. Even free games can be installed only via the App Store.

- The installation process is completely hidden from the user (no popups or installation instructions); only a bar under the app icon indicates the progress of the download.

- Developers need to supply only a single distribution channel.

- Apple controls what software reaches the App Store, and what software does not.

- Since new software is (officially) sold only through the App Store, Apple profits directly from sales (currently 30% of the sales price of an app).

- Apple determines the look and feel of its own shops.

- Users have a single reliable and stable entry point to search for new software.

Other manufacturers, in contrast, offer completely open platforms, such as Nokia, for example, with the Linux-based N900 or the N9 (MeeGo): Here, users have a variety of ways to install new software from the Nokia store or from independent third parties or even self-installation. And the development tools, too, can be chosen practically without restriction, while Apple, in contrast, permits only apps based on Objective-C, which in turn can be created only with IDE Xcode on a Mac OS X computer.

But success appears to have proven Apple right; Apple products have become a cult. When the iPhone 3GS was introduced in 2009 in eight countries, 1.6 million devices were sold within a week. In an equal period of time, Google sold only 20,000 units of its Android cell phone Nexus One (Flurry 2010, *http://blog.flurry.com*). In autumn 2011, the iOS market share among smartphone operating systems stood at 15% according to Gartner market research (worldwide for the third quarter, 2011), placing it in third place, just behind Symbian, with 16.9%, and the numerous low-end Android devices, whose total market share stood at 52.5%, divided among various manufacturers. This trend still continues. As IDC Worldwide Mobile Phone Tracker reports for August 2012, the market share for Android has risen to 68.1%, whereas iOS still is around 16.9%, followed by Blackberry (4.8%), Symbian (4.4%), and Windows Phone (3.5%).

The biggest year-by-year change, however, is that of the Windows Phone, at 115.3%. An interesting fact is that most app stores generate most of their revenue through games. (For example, ZDNet reports that for the Windows Phone platform, 57% of all sales are from games. Even more interesting is that, despite this success, only 14% of the products available in the store are games—it seems that games may not be so easy to develop as most bread-and-butter apps. Of course, we hope that this book proves the opposite!).

At the beginning of 2010, GigaOM reported 58 million active App Store users (iPhone: 34 million; iPod touch: 24 million), who inside of a month downloaded approximately 280 million apps, one-fourth of which contained paid content. In just the 2009/2010 holiday shopping season, 500 new apps were added from among the community of about 28,000 iOS developers.* In the meantime, the number of developers has continued to rise; perhaps on account of this book, an additional few more will be added.

# ▌ 1.3 The iPhone Family—Specifications

The fragmentation within iOS compatible devices continues to increase. Every summer, a new iPhone version appears, and it is not improbable that, in the future, Apple will introduce new product categories in addition to the iPad.

The good news is that all devices are (conditionally) mutually compatible if you take into account the specific device properties. All examples in this book will run on all devices in the iPhone family and have been extensively tested with various iOS versions.

Currently, there are 16 different devices in three categories:

- **iPhone:** iPhone (1st Gen), iPhone 3G, iPhone 3GS, iPhone 4, iPhone 4S, iPhone 5

- **iPod touch:** iPod touch (1st Gen), iPod touch 2G, iPod touch 3G, iPod touch 4, iPod touch 5

- **iPad:** iPad (1st Gen), iPad 2, iPad 3rd Gen, iPad 4th Gen, iPad Mini

Aside from the iPad models, the iPhone 4/4S/5, and iPod touch 5, the devices have the following common features:

- Capacitive multitouch screen

- 320 × 480 pixel LCD screen, 18 bit (262,144 colors), 163 pixels per inch

- Working memory (RAM): at least 128 MB eDRAM

- Flash storage: at least 8 GB NAND

- In addition to the main CPU, all devices have a 3D graphics chip that supports at least OpenGL ES 1.1†

---

* The App Store sales figures are likely to constitute a great part of the success story of the iPhone. At *http://www.distimo.com/appstores* you can find a comparison of the four largest download stores (App Store from Apple, Windows Marketplace from Microsoft, Nokia Store from Nokia, and Android Market from Google).
† Main CPU: iPhone 3GS and iPod touch 3G: 833 MHz (underclocked at 600 MHz), ARM Cortex-A8, other models: 620 MHz (underclocked at 400–412 MHz) Samsung 32 Bit RISC ARM, except for iPod touch 2G, which is minimally faster (underclocked at 532 MHz); 3D graphics CPU: iPhone 3GS and iPod touch 3G: PowerVR MBX Lite 3D GPU, iPhone 4: A4, iPhone 4S / iPad 2: DualCore A5; the other models run with the minimally slower PowerVR SGX GPU.

- Sensors: acceleration sensor (accelerometer), ambient light sensor, proximity sensor (iPhone only)

- WLAN 802.11b/g.

- At least Bluetooth 2.0+EDR (all models except 1st Gen iPod touch)

The iPad 1 and 2 and iPad Mini have a 1024 × 768 pixel display (iPad 3/4: retina resolution of 2048 × 1536 pixels), and iPhone 4/4S and iPod touch 4 have 960 × 640 pixels (iPhone 5/iPod 5: 1136 × 640 pixels, which is basically retina resolution with additional space at the bottom). All five devices run with at least an A4 processor with 1 GHz (iPad 2 and iPhone 4S with A5 dual core processor) and are much faster than the remaining devices. While the iPhone 3GS, iPod touch 3G, and iPad have 256 MB working memory, iPad 2, iPhone 4/4S, and iPod touch 4 offer a comfortable 512 MB. iPhone 5 and iPod 5 use an A6 processor, which is supposed to be twice as fast as the A5 of the iPhone 4S, but since Apple builds the processors itself, it is impossible to compare them to those used by other manufacturers.

All devices can freely update their latest iOS version via iTunes. From iOS 5, however, only devices from the second generation are fully updated. However, anyone wishing to consider the various iOS versions can find the "SDK-based Development" guide at the Apple Dev Center: *https://developer.apple.com/iphone/prerelease/library/documentation/DeveloperTools/Conceptual/cross_development/Introduction/Introduction.html*.

Since iOS 6, backward compatibility has been further reduced. Although the OS supports all iPad variants, iOS 6 apps can run only on iPhone 3GS/iPod fourth generation and newer.

In practice this means that there are still millions of devices out on the market that cannot be updated. As most developers like to target the newest iOS and skip support for previous versions, there will be a reasonable demand for new games that support older iOS versions. Statistics show that most apps are bought from customers with new devices. On the other hand, getting new software for older devices will become harder and harder; this makes up new opportunities, especially for independent developers.

The examples in this book were developed and tested for iOS 6.x, but in most cases are backward compatible to earlier iOS versions and will even run on the 1st Gen iPhone. Especially regarding game performance (this counts even more on older devices), it is recommended by Apple to make use of OpenGL ES (2D/3D graphics) and OpenAL (sound), which will be the main focus of this book. And although we will cover new APIs like the GLKit, most of the work is done with frameworks available on the iOS platform since its very first launch. Relevant information can be found in subsequent chapters.

## ▍ 1.4 All Beginnings Are Easy …

So, what do you need to get started developing games for iPhone iOS? Ideally, we would love to answer, "This book, and nothing else!" On the other hand, every reader will have different requirements, and we have no desire to fill this book with redundant information that can easily be found elsewhere.

To follow the examples in this book, you should have knowledge of at least one object-oriented language (Java, C#, C++). If concepts such as object, inheritance, class, and method seem like so much gobbledygook, you might want to begin by working through a Java tutorial. Why Java? Although Java is not the language of the iPhone, it is best suited for imparting the basics of programming, and for this reason it is the first programming language taught in most colleges and universities today. Deeper knowledge of object-oriented programming will not be necessary for this book. We have tried to make the source code as simple and straightforward as possible.

Rudimentary programming experience is the only theoretical knowledge you need as a prerequisite. Since it is through the iPhone that most readers have their first contact with a Mac or Objective-C 2.0 (the language of Mac OS), we have added a concise crash course to bring all readers to the same level.

You will observe that we (intentionally) do not employ the entire range of the language, so the basics can be quickly internalized. We therefore assume no extensive knowledge of iPhone iOS and its framework. However, we will not go into any great depth and will keep our focus on the essential components for game development. Anyone looking for extensive explanations of the numerous APIs, the use of Xcode, or even Interface Builder and the design of GUIs can read in parallel any one of a number of books on application development. In this book, games are developed and, therefore, we shall focus on the Cocoa Touch framework, Core Graphics, and especially OpenGL ES—always with practical reference to the concrete requirements of the game developer.

So that you can follow the examples of this book not only in theory but also in practice, you will need the following:

- An Intel-based Mac computer (or MacBook or Mac Mini) running either Mac OS X Snow Leopard 10.6.2 or higher or Lion 10.7.x or higher.

- If you want to try out the examples in real life and not just in the simulator, you will also need an iPhone, iPod touch, or iPad, which you can update for free via iTunes to the newest OS version. (This is not, however, a requirement; most of the examples in this book run on iOS 3.2 or later.)

- To install the examples on an iPhone, iPod, or iPad, you will also need access to the Apple Developer Program (current price, $99 a year).[*]

- You will need an Internet connection to download the iPhone software development kit (SDK) and the examples in this book.

## 1.4.1 Downloading the Examples in This Book

Numerous larger and smaller apps have been developed for this book: over 30 different iOS projects (including four larger games). Each app represents a small piece of the

---

[*] Those unwilling to bow to the dictates of Apple can alternatively begin with the development of WebApps (JavaScript, HTML, and CSS); cf. Stark (2010). The iPhone iOS makes use of a powerful WebKit browser. After installation over the Internet, WebApps act like native apps. However, you cannot distribute them through the App Store without an Objective-C wrapper (Apple officially forbids even this possibility). There remains only the path via the Internet or through Apple's WebApp homepage (*http://www.apple. com/webapps*). With Dashcode, Apple actually provides a development environment. But be warned: The performance of WebApps is insufficient for game development other than very simple games with only a few animated graphics.

complex field of game development in a straightforward fashion. In the respective chapters, reference will be made to the underlying example project. To better understand the explanations, it is recommended that you have the examples at hand to run on a computer in parallel with your reading.

### Download Link

You can find the examples on the accompanying website to the book: *www.qioo. de/projects/book/iosgames*.

The examples have been stored as a zip archive. You will find the password in this book. Simply follow the instructions on the website.

## 1.4.2 Feedback

Books like this are aimed at a select and limited group of interested readers. Your opinion is therefore very important to us. Please do not hesitate to contact the author or the publisher. You can reach us at *iphonebook@qioo.de*.

The examples developed for this book come out of real-world experience, but they have been customized from a pedagogical point of view to make them understandable to as wide an audience as possible. Code optimization has taken precedence over readability only in places where it was truly unavoidable. Because the iOS platform is still young, this book offers a wealth of exclusive information that has not appeared in print before now.

Please let us know if you find any errors, and support us in our effort to publish even better books in the future: What expectations did you have for this book? Were they fulfilled? Were there topics that should have been covered or topics that you thought were superfluous? At what points of the book would you have liked to see more extensive explanations? Was the level of difficulty too high? Was it too low? Using the book, were you able to complete the example programs without difficulty? Were they of help in the completion of your own projects?

We are always interested in receiving constructive criticism and in solving problems connected with the book. Please feel free to contact us at any time. And look at the book's website from time to time (see preceding address) to obtain information on updates.

# 2 The Basics—How Does It All Work?

## 2.1 The Source of Power—The iOS Dev Center

In addition to the development environment Xcode, Apple provides a host of tutorials and sample codes on the web pages of the Apple Developer Center. You can find iOS-specific topics at http://developer.apple.com/devcenter/ios/index.action.

There you will find extensive information on the important iOS libraries such as Cocoa Touch, Core Graphics, and Core Audio, as well as external libraries such as OpenGL ES and OpenAL. In addition, the Apple Developer Center offers support for Objective-C in general and for distribution via iTunes Connect, in case you plan on testing your app later on a device or publishing it through the App Store.

To obtain access to the individual areas, you will need to get a free Apple ID. Simply click on the link "Register" on the homepage (Figure 2.1).

## 2.2 Downloading and Installing Xcode and the iOS SDK

Before we can begin developing apps, we must first download the iOS SDK (earlier called simply "iPhone SDK"). This usually comes already bundled with the Xcode development environment. You can find the current version at *http://developer.apple.com /iphone/index. action#downloads*.

There is only one file that you have to download. If possible, always choose the most recent version of Xcode and iOS.

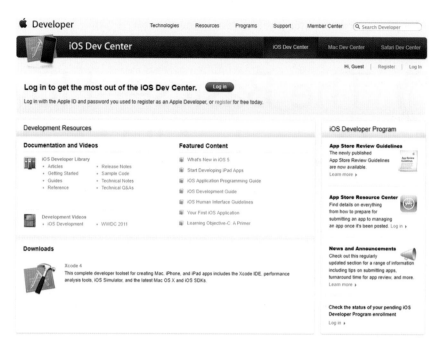

Figure 2.1 Homepage of the Apple Developer Center.

After clicking on the *.dmg installation package and completing a successful installation, you will find Xcode on your Mac in the following directory: */Developer/Applications/Xcode.app*.

In addition to Xcode, the iOS SDK contains additional tools such as Interface Builder, Instrument, and the iPhone/iPad emulator.

## 2.2.1 Download and Try Out Example Codes from Apple

To test whether the installation was successful, try out the example code from this book or one from the Apple Dev Center. A good overview of the Core Graphics drawing methods is provided by QuartzDemo: *http://developer.apple.com/iphone/library/samplecode/QuartzDemo/index.html*.

Download the file QuartzDemo.zip and unpack it by double clicking on its icon. In the applications folder, click on "QuartzDemo.xcodeproj" to start the project within Xcode. You compile and start the emulator by clicking on the "Run" button. The iPhone emulator begins automatically in the foreground.

## 2.2.2 Using the iPhone Simulator

The iPhone simulator supports all devices in the iOS family. As soon as the emulator comes into the foreground, you can simulate hardware behavior via the background window. Just click on the "Hardware" tab:

- Turn left: simulator is turned to the left (keyboard shortcut: cmd + left arrow).

- Turn right: simulator is turned to the right (keyboard shortcut: cmd + right arrow).

- Minimize the simulator (keyboard shortcut: cmd + H).

- Close the simulator (keyboard shortcut: cmd + Q).

Using HARDWARE > DEVICE, you can select the desired emulator:

- iPad

- iPad (Retina)

- iPhone

- iPhone (Retina 3.5 inch)

- iPhone (Retina 4 inch)

Since your computer's screen may not offer enough space for the iPad or the Retina variant of the iPhone, using WINDOW > SCALE you can resize the window from 100% to, for example, 50%. On the iPhone 4-inch simulator running games designed for 3.5-inch iPhone resolution, the extra space—on the real device—will be shown simply as a blacked-out area unless you specifically create a UIView supporting the 4-inch ratio.

The simulator also provides support for life cycle events. We shall look at these in greater detail later.

## ▌ 2.3  Using Xcode Templates

Xcode provides a number of preinstalled templates that you can use as the basis for your own projects, such as the "Empty Application" and the Open GL ES app "OpenGL Game." The templates can be found under FILE > NEW > NEW PROJECT; note that IOS > APPLICATION must be selected in the upper left-hand corner of the window. You can give the project a name of your own choosing when you save it. You can save to any location and, later, you can start the project along with Xcode by clicking on "MyiPhoneTestApp.xcodeproj."

## ▌ 2.4  Hello World with Console Output

In this chapter we want to jump directly into app development, so your basic programming skills will be required. We begin with the basic sequence of creating and developing iOS apps. We will save actual game development for a later chapter. So do not worry if everything is not 100% clear at first. As soon as you have learned how to create an app, execute it, and edit the source code, we will introduce the peculiarities of the programming language Objective-C in a brief course so that you can experiment on your own.[*]

In any case, we already know what a program written in Xcode looks like and how it is launched. Therefore, as our very first program, let us create a "Hello World" app.

Create a new project by launching IDE Xcode and selecting FILE > NEW > NEW PROJECT in the menu. The template selection window, which was introduced earlier, opens.

---

[*] If you are encountering Objective-C for the first time, you might wish to work through the minicourse first and then return to this chapter.

On the left-hand side, select "iOS" and "Application" in order to access the existing iOS template projects. For our template, let us choose "Empty Application," which represents the minimal starting point for applications. For older Xcode versions, choose here "Window-based Application." Click on NEXT to assign a file name, such as "HelloWorld," and specify a location for the project (this project, like all the examples in this book, can be found at the download site given at the front of the book). To enable the project to run on all iOS devices, you should choose iPhone under "Device Family." As "Class Prefix" please choose "HelloWorld"; this name will then be automatically prefixed to your delegate classes. The "Company Identifier" will become important later if you wish to offer your game through the App Store. It would be a good idea at this point to choose a unique name—for example, the address of your website domain. You should deactivate the checks for "Core Data," "Automatic Reference Counting (ARC)," and "Unit Tests." ARC has been available only since iOS 5; we shall discuss it in our Objective-C minicourse. You can also create an optional Git repository if you are planning to manage the project later using the Git version control.

## 2.4.1 Delegates and the Main() Method

After the project has been created, it is presented in Xcode as follows: On the left is the project view with the associated source code, resources ("Supporting Files"), and frameworks; on the right can be found information on the currently selected file; and in the middle is the editor window. The template first provides two text files for us—namely, the class `HelloWorldAppDelegate`, or `AppDelegate` if you have omitted the "Class Prefix," consisting of header (*.h, declaration) and implementation (*.m):

```
HelloWorldAppDelegate.h
HelloWorldAppDelegate.m
```

This is, as can be seen from the name, the delegate of the app. The two text files containing the source code have been filled with content for us by Xcode.

Listing 2.1 HelloWorldAppDelegate.h

```
#import <UIKit/UIKit.h>

@interface HelloWorldAppDelegate : UIResponder <UIApplicationDelegate>

@property (strong, nonatomic) UIWindow *window;

@end
```

Listing 2.2 HelloWorldAppDelegate.m

```
#import "HelloWorldAppDelegate.h"

@implementation HelloWorldAppDelegate
```

```
@synthesize window = _window;

- (BOOL) application: (UIApplication *) application
    didFinishLaunchingWithOptions: (NSDictionary *) launchOptions {
    self.window = [[[UIWindow alloc] initWithFrame:
        [[UIScreen mainScreen] bounds]] autorelease];
    self.window.backgroundColor = [UIColor whiteColor];
    [self.window makeKeyAndVisible];
    return YES;
}

- (void) applicationWillResignActive: (UIApplication *) application {}
- (void) applicationDidEnterBackground: (UIApplication *) application {}
- (void) applicationWillEnterForeground: (UIApplication *) application {}
- (void) applicationDidBecomeActive: (UIApplication *) application {}
- (void) applicationWillTerminate: (UIApplication *) application {}

- (void) dealloc {
    [_window release];
    [super dealloc];
}

@end
```

We shall describe these files in more detail later, but first we should learn a bit of theory. (If you are interested only in practical implementation, you may skip the following introduction.)

We have already mentioned the concept of delegate. What, then, is a delegate? A delegate is a sort of middleman that, on the one hand, offers the developer access to the more complicated application object UIApplication, while, on the other hand, being able to process messages as a representative of this object. A delegate class implements the <UIApplicationDelegate> protocol and thereby has a set of predefined interfaces that allow the UIApplication instance to send messages to the delegate—if certain events occur whose processing should be delegated.

What sorts of events are we talking about? It could be, for example, an incoming telephone call that interrupts the running application, or the user has pressed the home button to shut down the app. But the launch of our application by the app icon also represents such an event. Later, we shall consider the life cycle of an app in greater detail and discuss additional messages of the protocol.

Objects that send a message to the UIApplication instance do not need to know that this instance will not be handling the message itself but instead will pass it to the app delegate. In computer science, this delegate pattern is widely used in software design:

- The delegator (UIApplication) receives a request (for example, "app launched") and delegates it to the delegate instance.

- The delegate (app delegate) eventually executes the request (for example, what should happen when the app is started).

- Since the delegate contains a reference to the delegator, messages can also be sent in the opposite direction.

Every iOS app has such a delegate class, which from the viewpoint of the developer marks the actual beginning of program execution. The `application: didFinishLaunchingWithOptions:` method, which was stipulated via the `<UIApplicationDelegate>` protocol, will be called precisely when our app has been placed in a state that allows for the processing of the program instructions (among other things, the *Sandbox*, an area of memory in which the currently running app can cause no harm, is created; this protects the data of other programs from unauthorized access).

Those interested in what goes on before entry into program flow can have a look in the folder "Supporting Files." There can be found the `main()` method, which, as in C/C++, is called by the operating system as soon as the program is started. There is usually no reason to make any changes to `main.m`.

## 2.4.2 Program Flow, Frameworks, and the App File

Do not let the host of new terms confuse you; the basic structure of an app is always the same, so in the future, we shall have to make very few changes to it. What is important at this point is the Plist file `HelloWorld-Info.plist`, which is also an XML file. "Plist" stands for property list. This file represents a sort of project manifest, giving the operating system information that it needs before execution, such as, for example, the current version number and the name of the program.

Before we turn again to the delegate, we would like to refer again to the Framework folder inside Xcode. The basic frameworks are already included:

- **UIKit.framework**—window management, UI elements, touch handling, etc.

- **Foundation.framework**—basic functionality (e.g., strings, threads)

- **CoreGraphics.framework**—interface to Quartz 2D (graphics)

Later, we shall show how additional frameworks, such as those for audio playback and OpenGL ES, can be added. If you click on the check to the left of the file name, you can see the individual components of the associated framework in the form of header files.

Under "Products," you will find a reference to the executable program:

`HelloWorld.app`

To launch the app, click the "Run" button. The iPhone simulator window should open automatically and display an empty white screen.

If you now click on the home button, you can close the app, just like on a real device.

## 2.4.3 The Structure of the Delegate Class and Implementation of Console Output

Since our Hello World app is supposed to output a text to the console, we have to program this, of course. But first let us revisit the structure of the delegate.

The following line sets certain properties of the instance variable `window` from the template:

```
@property (strong, nonatomic) UIWindow *window;
```

Moreover, implicitly generated setter/getter methods can be requisitioned via the directive `@property`. The `@synthesize` directive makes available the properties and setter/getter pairs called for in the header.*

Thus, in the header, only the `window` instance is declared. Since this is part of the `UIKit` framework, the `UIKit` header must also be imported. This is done via

```
#import <UIKit/UIKit.h>
```

Moreover, with

```
HelloWorldAppDelegate : UIResponder <UIApplicationDelegate>
```

it is determined that our delegate is derived from the superclass `UIResponder` (optional alternative: NSObject), and the `UIApplicationDelegate` protocol is implemented (protocols are integrated into Java as "interfaces"; in Objective-C it suffices to use angle brackets). A protocol is nothing more than an implementation direction. Let us take a look at the delegate method `application:didFinishLaunchingWithOptions:` (only slightly altered):

```
- (BOOL) application: (UIApplication *) application
    didFinishLaunchingWithOptions: (NSDictionary *) launchOptions {
    self.window = [[[UIWindow alloc]
        initWithFrame: [[UIScreen mainScreen] bounds]] autorelease];
    self.window.backgroundColor = [UIColor whiteColor];
    [self.window makeKeyAndVisible];
    NSLog(@"Hello World!");
    return YES;
}
```

As can be seen from the name of this method, it is called as soon as the loading process of our application has finished. Thus, the method creates the starting point of an iPhone app and is therefore the ideal place for our "Hello World" text.

To write a text to the console, we use the `NSLog()` function:

```
NSLog(@"Hello World!")
```

One can pass a string as well as several parameters to the function, similarly to the `printf()` function. Strings in Objective-C are always introduced with the @ directive.

In the delegate class you will also find the `dealloc` method, which our class has inherited from `NSObject`. Here it will be overwritten in order to free up memory for

---

* If you want simply to generate setter/getter methods and can live otherwise with the default properties of a member, a call from `@property NSString* text` suffices. The default properties are `readwrite` (that is, setter *and* getter; a getter alone is `readonly`; if custom names are to be used for setter/getter, one can specify this explicitly as a property—for example, `setter = mySetterMethod`, `getter = myGetterMethod`), `assign` (behavior under assignment; other possible values are `retain`, `copy`), `atomic` (behavior under thread accessing; with `atomic`, accesses are processed sequentially; the alternative, non-atomic, allows for parallel accesses).

the window with `[window release]`;. After this comes the deallocation of the instance of our delegate class via `[super dealloc]`.

Do not be worried if the syntax of Objective-C still seems somewhat strange. Fear not! We shall soon provide a brief tutorial.

To see our console output in action, we must rebuild the project and start it using the run button. The iPhone simulator starts our program anew, and in the console there appears, as expected, the text "Hello World":

```
[Session started at 2011-11-18 21:20:12 +0200.]
2011-11-18 21:20:14.866 HelloWorld[3167:207] Hello World!
```

Of course, for debugging an application you can start the debugger that is integrated into Xcode after setting a breakpoint by right-clicking (or ctrl-click) on the sidebar of the code window. Sometimes, a simple console output can be used to locate an error in program output.

For example, to output an integer value, you program as follows:

```
int value = 22;
NSLog(@"value equals:%i", value);
```

This yields the following output:

```
2011-11-18 21:28:38.192 HelloWorld[3241:207] value equals: 22
```

You can pass several comma-separated values:

```
NSString *myString = @"a string";
float fvalue = 22.7;
NSLog(@"output:%f, String:%@, Window:%@", fvalue, myString, self.window);
```

You then obtain the following output:

```
2011-11-18 21:33:26.446 HelloWorld[3283:207] output: 22.700001, String: a
    string, Window: <UIWindow: 0x3b11170; frame = (0 0; 320 480); opaque =
    NO; autoresize = RM+BM; layer = <CALayer: 0x3b11f30>>
```

In a string, variables are always indicated by a percent sign as placeholder followed by the variable type—thus, i for int, f for float, and @ for an object (strings are also objects).[*]

After the string, all variables are passed in the order in which they stand in the string. The number of variables is unlimited, but make sure to use the correct format specifier.

As you can see from the console output, the window object has already been prepared for console output, and it outputs a few meaningful fields:

```
<UIWindow: 0x3b11170;
frame = (0 0; 320 480);
opaque = NO;
autoresize = RM+BM;
layer = <CALayer: 0x3b11f30>>
```

---

[*] An overview of all format specifiers can be found at *http://developer.apple.com/iphone/library/documentation/ Cocoa/Conceptual/Strings/ index.html*.

Thus, for example, `frame` contains the size of the window: 320 × 480 pixels. In the case of objects not thus prepared, the console outputs simply the memory address—for example, `<Classname: 0xf090e0>`.

# ▌ 2.5 Hello World with Text in a View Instance

Before we enter into some of the peculiarities of Objective-C in the next chapter (What is the meaning of the angle brackets? Why do I have to release memory? What is a view instance?), we show in this chapter how to write a "Hello World" announcement on the screen of an iPhone.[*]

In order to display anything at all on the screen, you have to access the screen context to obtain a sort of canvas on which to draw. The UIKit framework provides the `UIView` class for this purpose.

Using FILE > NEW FILE > IOS > COCOA TOUCH > OBJECTIVE-C CLASS, we create a new class. As a name for the view, we choose "MainView."

To make a `UIView` out of the new class, we alter the template provided by Xcode as follows.

---

**Listing 2.3** MainView.h

```
#import <UIKit/UIKit.h>

@interface MainView : UIView {
}

@end
```

We make sure that the class is derived from `UIView`, and we import the `UIKit` header in which the `UIView` class is declared.

The implementation of the class is straightforward. We simply overwrite the `drawRect:` method inherited from `UIView`. This method is then called whenever an event occurs that informs the `UIView` instance that there is something new to draw in the view.

---

**Listing 2.4** MainView.m

```
#import "MainView.h"

@implementation MainView

- (void) drawRect: (CGRect) rect {
    //the text will be drawn here
}

@end
```

---

[*] If you are encountering Objective-C for the first time, you might want to read the Objective-C minicourse in Section 2.6. There you will find links to further tutorials.

The drawing process must therefore be triggered by an event. But how do we trigger this event? For this, there is a variety of possibilities. Since we have to execute the drawRect: method only once, it suffices to "trigger" the rendering process via the MainView class. To do so, we have to modify the delegate.

Listing 2.5 HelloWorldAppDelegate.h

```
#import <UIKit/UIKit.h>
#import "MainView.h"

@interface HelloWorldAppDelegate : UIResponder <UIApplicationDelegate>

{
    MainView *mainView;
}

@property (strong, nonatomic) UIWindow *window;

@end
```

Listing 2.6 application:didFinishLaunchingWithOptions: Method

```
- (BOOL) application: (UIApplication *)application
    didFinishLaunchingWithOptions:(NSDictionary *)launchOptions {
    self.window = [[[UIWindow alloc] initWithFrame:
        [[UIScreen mainScreen] bounds]] autorelease];
    self.window.backgroundColor = [UIColor whiteColor];
    mainView = [[MainView alloc] initWithFrame:
        [UIScreen mainScreen].applicationFrame];
    [self.window addSubview: mainView];
    [self.window makeKeyAndVisible];
    return YES;
}
```

While in the header file we simply declare MainView, a bit more takes place in the implementation. We ensure that mainView is allocated and finally is implemented at the size of the current screen with

```
mainView = [[MainView alloc] initWithFrame:
    [UIScreen mainScreen].applicationFrame];
```

Instead of writing the preceding call in one line, we could alternatively have done the following:

```
id viewId = [MainView alloc];
mainView = [viewId initWithFrame: CGRectMake(0,0,320,480)];
```

With id we are dealing with an Objective-C generic object data type that can stand for any type of object. First, the alloc instruction sees to it that the object viewId is assigned memory. In the next step, the actual initialization of the object takes place (Objective-C has no class name constructor like that in Java). The initWith- Frame: method comes from the UIView class and expects as parameter a rectangle of type CGRect. We thus directly create a rectangle with 320 × 480 pixels. In fact, the screen area will be a bit smaller, since the status bar at the top of the screen requires a few pixels (we will, of course, see later how to hide the status bar).

Since the release of the iPad and iPhone/iPod 4/4S, which have a larger screen, it is advisable to query the available screen size of the device using [UIScreen main-Screen].applicationFrame.

After the MainView instance has been created, we have only to make it *visible,* which is done by making mainView a subview of the main window window:

```
[self.window addSubview: mainView];
[self.window makeKeyAndVisible];
```

If you create the window as a property and make it available in the implementation via the @synthesize directive, you need to address the variable via self—that is, [self. window addSubview: mainView]; otherwise, a call without self would suffice.

Instead of a UIView, we could alternatively implement a UIViewController, which conveniently has a UIView member. The controller would then be assigned to the window instance as a rootViewController, and the MainView to the controller as a view member. Such an example can be found in the "GameKitBasics" project, which is created in Chapter 4. For a UIView without an additional controller, the implementation is a bit shorter.

The makeKeyAndVisible method ensures that the parent window is activated and can contain touch events. In addition, the addSubview: triggers the drawRect: method a single time so that we can begin the actual drawing process of the "Hello World" text:

```
- (void) drawRect: (CGRect) rect {
    CGContextRef gc = UIGraphicsGetCurrentContext();
    CGContextSetRGBFillColor(gc, 1, 1, 1, 1);

    NSString *str = @"Hello World II";
    UIFont *uif = [UIFont systemFontOfSize: 40];
    [str drawAtPoint: CGPointMake(50, 200) withFont: uif];
}
```

To render content to a view, we use the Core Graphics framework. Therefore, we next obtain the current graphics context from the function UIGraphicsGetCurrent Context() and then call on this the function CGContextSetRGBFillColor() to set the color for drawing. We specify the color as an RGB (red, green, blue) triple plus an alpha value in the range from 0 to 1:

- **Red, Green, Blue:** 0.0 (black) to 1.0 (white)

- **Alpha:** 0.0 (transparent) to 1.0 (opaque)

Since a view is preset with a black background, we choose white for the foreground color. The next step allows us to display the string on the screen: the NSString class has the drawAtPoint:withFont: method for this purpose. It expects a CGPoint

Figure 2.2 The HelloWorld app started under Xcode.

structure as its first parameter, which determines that the string is to be drawn at the position

```
x = 40
y = 200
```

The font can be specified in a second parameter. We are not fussy, so we simply choose the iPhone's preset system font. We have created a UIFont object using the systemFontOfSize: method with a font size of 40 (see Figure 2.2).

Regarding game development, we have made another step forward with this second Hello World variant: We now know how to render something to the screen, even if it is nothing more elaborate than a simple text. For our future game projects, we shall also use the UIView class as a painting surface. In the process, we shall delve rather deeply into Core Graphics concepts, which in this initial overview have been given insufficient attention.

And for all those who are encountering Objective-C for the first time, we are now going to discuss the core language of iOS and introduce a few of its special features so that you will be fully equipped to tackle the upcoming chapters.

## ■ 2.6  Who's Afraid of Objective-C? A 15-Minute Crash Course

Granted, at first sight, Objective-C may look rather strange. But on a second look, you will find that all the concepts and patterns found in other languages are present in Objective-C as well, only with a somewhat different syntax. If you are familiar with Java, C#, or C/C++, you should have no difficulties after this minicourse in understanding Objective-C source code. Of course, we are not going to present the entire language, instead restricting our survey to the areas that will be required in developing the games and projects in this book.

### 2.6.1 Help Getting Started

If you are interested in a more thorough introduction and/or have no programming experience to speak of, you can find numerous Internet tutorials on Objective-C, such as the following: *http://www.cocoadevcentral.com/d/learn_objectivec.*

A more demanding presentation is the introduction "The Objective-C Programming Language" offered by Apple: *http://developer.apple.com/mac/library/documentation/cocoa/ conceptual/ObjectiveC /Introduction/introObjectiveC.html.*

But be careful! Before getting too deeply involved in Objective-C, you should be sure that you are familiar with the concepts of object-oriented programming (OOP), since most tutorials make such an assumption. You can find numerous tutorials on the web, or you can purchase any one of a number of books on Java, since the OOP concepts, in our opinion, can be most easily taught in terms of that language.

### 2.6.2 How Objective-C Was Born

Objective-C was developed in the early 1980s, based on the C language, but extended, as the name implies, to include object-oriented language elements deriving from the language Smalltalk. Moreover, C++ classes can be incorporated into Xcode projects (*.mm for C++ classes, instead of *.m for Objective-C classes, suffices for the compiler). Since Objective-C was implemented as the standard language of the operating system NeXTStep, the language also formed the basis of its successor, Mac OS X, and therefore has been employed primarily in Mac programming and, of course, for iOS.

### 2.6.3 Method Syntax

Perhaps the most unusual feature at first glance is the bracket syntax of Objective-C. A typical method call might look like this:

```
[myObject printString: @"Objective-C is cool!"];
```

First, you give the name of the object instance whose method is to be called. Here, the object instance is myObject, and the method name is printString:. After the colon comes the parameter that is to be passed to the method. The colon is a part of the method name if the method expects a parameter. Parameterless methods do not have a colon. In Objective-C, one speaks sometimes of messages instead of methods. Thus, the message "output this string" is sent to the object myObject.

As in other languages, an arbitrary number of parameters can be passed. Here is the syntax:

```
int result = [myObject multiplyFirstValue: 2
                      withSecondValue: 4
                      andAddThirdValue: 8];
```

The square brackets form a sort of frame for the method call. In contrast to Java and C/C++, additional parameters require an extension of the method name. The preceding method is thus called

```
multiplyFirstValue:withSecondValue:andAddThirdValue:
```

It returns an integer value. The readability of source code can be improved by the use of meaningful method names. Indeed, without even looking at the declaration, we can see that the method multiplies the value 2 by 4 and then adds 8. The return value is therefore 16. Whether you write the individual components of the method name in a column or a row (separated by a space) is entirely up to you (and the amount of space on the line).

## 2.6.4 Declaration of Classes

The second important feature of Objective-C is the use of @ directives. These are control commands for the compiler that begin with the character @. Thus, strings are always preceded by an @ directive, and they are also used in class declaration.

**Listing 2.7** MyObject.h

```
@interface MyObject : NSObject {
    float member1;
    float member2;
}

- (id) init;

- (void) printString: (NSString *) string;

- (int) multiplyFirstValue: (int) value1
            withSecondValue: (int) value2
            andAddThirdValue: (int) value3;

@end
```

The header begins with @interface, and it ends with @end. Member variables (also called instance variables) are declared inside curly braces. Methods are declared without curly braces and hence without an implementation block. After the minus sign (hyphen), which identifies the method as an instance method, comes the return value and then the method signature.

Member variables may not be initialized. For example, float member1 = 0.2; would lead to a compiler error. Instance variables are automatically declared as @protected. Other possible types of visibility are, for example, @public and @private.

The colon in the first line indicates that MyObject is derived from NSObject (the parent class of all objects). Hence, MyObject "inherits" all members and methods of NSObject.

**Listing 2.8** MyObject.m

```
#import "MyObject.h"

@implementation MyObject

- (id) init {
```

```
        member1 = 0.1;
        member2 = 0.2;
        return self;
}

- (void) printString: (NSString *) string {
        NSLog(@"output:%@", string);
}

- (int) multiplyFirstValue: (int) value1
            withSecondValue: (int) value2
            andAddThirdValue: (int) value3 {

        return value1*value2+value3;
}

@end
```

Similarly, the implementation of methods is introduced by @implementation and again ended with @end. Referenced classes and variables must be imported into both the header and implementation files; to do so, the header in which such classes or variables are declared must be specified by #import "MyObject.h". In contrast to self-defined classes, the libraries supplied with the SDK must be surrounded by angle brackets: #import <UIKit/UIKit.h>.

## 2.6.5  Creating Objects

We have already seen some methods in action and have introduced the associated class. But how is an object instance created from the class? It is easy:

```
MyObject *myObject = [[MyObject alloc] init];
    //object was created and can now process messages
    [myObject printString: @"Objective-C is cool!"];
```

Let us now look a bit at the implementation of the class:

```
- (id) init {
    member1 = 0.1;
    member2 = 0.2;
    return self;
}
```

First the object is allocated via alloc; memory is assigned and we obtain an object instance on which we then call the init method. Objective-C does not use constructors; instead, you have to ensure that instance variables are initialized with the desired values. This is done by the init method. We could, however, have chosen a different name and passed parameters. In this case, however, we choose init and thereby overwrite the init method of the NSObject.

Since we have already created the object with alloc, we have already, with self, a reference to ourselves. If something goes wrong in the allocation (for instance, insufficient memory), we can play it safe and check again in the `init` method whether the reference* in fact exists:

```
if (self) {
    //everything is OK
} else {
    //error: self = nil
}
```

Here, `nil` means that the object is not present and therefore has the truth value `false` (note that `nil` is not the same as `NULL` and thus can be used as a valid parameter). The return value of `self` (= our object reference) is id; an id is a typeless object—a wild card for objects, so to speak. Since we are creating the object with

```
MyObject *myObject = [[MyObject alloc] init];
```

we shall make a typed object of type `MyObject` out of the typeless id object that the `init` method returned to us. The star * indicates that the variable is a *pointer*. Usually, objects are referenced by their memory location. Since `myObject` is a pointer variable, it points to a memory location, `0x5366a09`.

## 2.6.6  Instance and Class Methods

As you have seen earlier, the minus sign marks our methods as instance methods. Therefore, these can be applied only to an object. Now the question arises how the `alloc` method, which is not called on an object, actually works. You perhaps already suspect what the answer is: `alloc` is declared as a class method. Class methods can be called directly without there being an associated object; such methods are indicated by a prefixed plus sign. (Please do not confuse it with the `static` keyword, which we shall meet later.) A glance at the declaration of the `alloc` method (right-click on the method name in the source code and > JUMP TO DEFINITION) confirms this:

```
+ (id) alloc;
```

The method is implemented in `NSObject` and can be called directly for every class derived from it.

[`MyObject alloc`] consequently returns an id object. Alternatively, we could have created the `myObject` instance as follows:

```
id myObject2Id = [MyObject alloc];
MyObject *myObject2 = [myObject2Id init];
[myObject2 printString: @"Alternative call."];
```

The id data type is already defined as a pointer structure.† Therefore, the asterisk * character must be omitted from id. However, for object creation, one usually uses the preceding nested call.

---

\* In the event that you do not derive from `NSObject` and wish to include the constructor of the parent class, you can also use the following construct: if (self = [super init]) {...}.
† typedef struct objc_object { Class isa; } *id;

And now a quick little example to show how a class method is created. The declaration is made in the header:

```
+ (int) multiply: (int) value1 with: (int) value2;
```

The implementation is

```
+ (int) multiply: (int) value1 with: (int) value2 {
    return value1*value2;
}
```

And, finally, how it is used is

```
int multiplyResult = [MyObject multiply: 16 with: 2];
NSLog(@"multiplyResult :%i", multiplyResult);//32
```

You can use the `multiply:by:` method at any time without having first to access the object instance. But you are not required to do so. In contrast to the case of static methods in Java, in Objective-C you cannot class methods on an object instance without the compiler issuing a complaint (this is true for C++ as well).

## 2.6.7 Memory Management

An important topic for novices is the absence of *garbage collection,* which has been available only since iOS 5 via ARC. In contrast to Mac OS X development and programming languages such as Java, in iOS, the memory required for objects is not automatically released when it is no longer required. This can lead to memory leaks—that is, holes in memory. Using the performance tool (in Xcode: RUN > RUN WITH PERFORMANCE TOOL > LEAKS), it is possible to analyze memory usage while a program is running. This point cannot be overemphasized: If your program continually requests new memory and then does not release it, in the worst case the application will be shut down by the iPhone OS. Then the user will have to restart the app, and the game will begin from the beginning. Before your application is forcibly closed, you obtain the friendly warning `applicationDid-ReceiveMemoryWarning:`. If you wish to implement this method in the delegate class, you can then make a last attempt to save the situation by releasing some memory.

But for smaller games, you would find it difficult to use up the existing 80 to 128 MB of memory (part of it is used by iOS). Even with small memory holes, your app should continue to run for several minutes without any problems.

For professional applications, it is, of course, recommended not to let things get so far out of hand. But how, then, is memory released, and when must one take care to do so?

The most likely case that arises in game development is the creation of objects while a game is running. New adversaries appear on the screen and are about to attack the player; they are defeated, and new waves of adversaries swarm forward. If you decide to create objects during a game, then you should, of course, take care to clear them away when they are no longer needed.

The release of memory can be initiated at once with the `release` message

```
MyObject *myObject = [[MyObject alloc] init];
...
[myObject release];
```

---

As a rule of thumb, note that for every object that is created with `alloc`, a call to `release` should follow at some point. In this regard, you may have encountered the `deallocate` method, which is inherited from `NSObject`.

If some object derived from `NSObject` receives a `release` message, then the object's `dealloc` method is called, and the memory occupied by the object is released. For larger classes, you can collect the `release` calls and call them all together in the overwritten `dealloc` method:

```
- (void)dealloc {//overwrite dealloc
    [window release];//clean up
    [super dealloc];//release memory
}
```

Thus, the `window` object in the delegate class is released as soon as the delegate object is released. With [super dealloc], you then call the parent version of the method, which destroys the object. If you overwrite the `dealloc` method, you must also call the super method; otherwise, the memory will not be released.

There is, however, a minor flaw in this: `dealloc` is called only when there are no more references to an object. Therefore, Objective-C provides a reference counter, `retainCount`.

With a `retainCount` message, you obtain at all times the current number of references to your object. The `release` message does not immediately provide for memory release, but simply reduces the reference counter by 1. You can also increase the reference counter manually; with the `retain` message, the value increases by 1. As soon as the reference counter contains the value 0, the `dealloc` method is automatically called. Here is an example:

1. Object `obj` is created with `alloc`: `retainCount = 1`

2. `[obj release];//retainCount = 0;`

3. The `dealloc` method of `obj` is called; the object is destroyed

Thus, the following code fragment produces the displayed console output:

```
MyObject *test1 = [[MyObject alloc] init];
MyObject *test2 = [[MyObject alloc] init];
[test2 retain];//increase by 1
NSLog(@"retainCount test1:%i", [test1 retainCount]);
NSLog(@"retainCount test2:%i", [test2 retainCount]);
[test1 release];
[test2 release];//decrease by 1
NSLog(@"retainCount test2:%i", [test2 retainCount]);
[test2 release];//only now is test2 deallocated
```

Console output is

```
2010-04-26 11:31:15.358 ObjCCrashcourse[600:207] retainCount test1: 1
2010-04-26 11:31:15.359 ObjCCrashcourse[600:207] retainCount test2: 2
2010-04-26 11:31:15.359 ObjCCrashcourse[600:207] MyObject instance is
    deallocated.
```

2. The Basics—How Does It All Work?

```
2010-04-26 11:31:15.360 ObjCCrashcourse[600:207] retainCount test2: 1
2010-04-26 11:31:15.361 ObjCCrashcourse[600:207] MyObject instance is
   deallocated.
```

Here is a hint regarding arrays. If you are working with NSArray and add objects to an array, the object's retainCount will be increased by 1. You must therefore immediately afterward send the release method to the object. If the NSArray again receives a release message, it reduces the retainCount of the stored object by 1.*

### 2.6.8  Automatic Reference Counting (ARC)

As you may have noticed already when you were creating a new Xcode project, you can select the option "Use Automatic Reference Counting" (ARC). Since we earlier showed how you can implement memory management manually, so to speak, you might feel a small burden being lifted from your shoulders when you discover that, with the ARC option, you can let Xcode worry about memory management. More precisely, the new LLVM 3.0 compiler automatically takes care of reference counting, so that in your source code you will no longer need any retain, release, or autorelease calls. However, this feature assumes at least Xcode 4.2.x, available since iOS 5; even if the compiler is capable of upgrading *garbage collection* for older versions of iOS, it cannot hurt to maintain control over this and take responsibility yourself for memory optimization. For the following examples, the ARC option is not required.

We would like to end for the time being our little discussion of matters related to Objective-C. We have omitted important topics such as properties, protocols, and categories, since we will not be needing them in the remainder of the book. We have omitted other questions in this chapter, such as, for example, *how are global constants created? What is the preprocessor good for? How do arrays work?* However, we will answer them when the time comes in the context of concrete example projects.

## ▌ 2.7  The Life Cycle of an App

The main task of the delegate class is to react to changes in an app's state with the desired behavior. It is up to you how much you want to make use of this opportunity. For example, you can interrupt a game that is running on an iPhone that has just received an incoming call or short message service (SMS; text message) or has switched into sleep mode (for example, during a chess game if there has been no user input for a long time).

An iOS application can be in any one of a number of states (see Figure 2.3), two of which are generally of no interest to the app developer: We can ignore the cases "App is being initialized" and "App has terminated." We have already dealt with the transition into the state "App is active" in the previous examples. A possible alternative to the application:didFinishLaunchingWithOptions: method is the older version applicationDidFinishLaunching:. If an iPhone user receives a call or SMS during a game, a popup window will appear on the screen asking whether the player wishes to

---

* Sometimes—for example, when you are working with threads—you do not know precisely when the life of an object should be ended. For this case, Objective-C provides NSAutoreleasePool.

Figure 2.3  Life cycle of an iOS application.

take the call or read the text message. Under iOS 3.x or earlier versions, if the answer is yes, then the application is terminated. If the answer is no, the popup simply disappears. Each of these two possible events has its corresponding message:

- App is interrupted -> `applicationWillResignActive:`

- App is resumed -> `applicationDidBecomeActive:`

While the popup is being displayed, the app continues to run in the background, with the user unable to provide any input. We must take care of this situation ourselves—for example, by halting a running game and saving the game state just to be on the safe side.

Since the iPhone beginning with iOS 4.0 allows for applications that can execute certain tasks in the background while other apps are active (multitasking), two additional messages have been introduced: `applicationWillEnterBackground:` and, in the reverse direction, `applicationWillEnterForeground`. Multitasking of applications can be considered a special case in game programming, and therefore we shall not consider it further here.

The message `applicationWillTerminate:` is sent for the state "the App will be closed." We now have about 5 seconds in which to store important data, such as the current game state.

A further message is related not to a state, but to an important note: `application-DidReceiveMemoryWarning:`. Although Apple recommends that this message be implemented so that an appropriate response of memory release can be given, game developers should not let things get to such a point. During a running game, you cannot, say, suddenly decrease the number of adversaries just because you are running short of memory. The only solution is careful advance testing and adjusting of the game's design as necessary.

Altogether, then, there are six relevant methods that we have implemented in our example games.

**Listing 2.9** Lifecycle-App

```objc
@implementation LifecycleAppDelegate

//…

//App is ready for use, variant 1
- (BOOL) application: (UIApplication *) application
    didFinishLaunchingWithOptions: (NSDictionary *) launchOptions {
    NSLog(@"application:didFinishLaunchingWithOptions: called.");
    [window makeKeyAndVisible];
    return YES;
}

//App is ready for use, variant 2
- (void) applicationDidFinishLaunching: (UIApplication *) application
    {
    NSLog(@"applicationDidFinishLaunching: called.");
}

//App has been interrupted but continues to run in the background
- (void) applicationWillResignActive: (UIApplication *) application {
    NSLog(@"applicationWillResignActive: called.");
}

//App has been interrupted but the interruption has passed
- (void) applicationDidBecomeActive: (UIApplication *) application {
    NSLog(@"applicationDidBecomeActive: called.");
}

//Memory is running short
- (void) applicationDidReceiveMemoryWarning: (UIApplication *)
application {
    NSLog(@"applicationDidReceiveMemoryWarning: called.");
}

//App will terminate (for example, the home button has been pressed)
- (void) applicationWillTerminate:(UIApplication *) application {
    NSLog(@"applicationWillTerminate: called.");
}

//…

@end
```

The iPhone simulator allows for the simulation of individual states. Consider in this regard the following console output:

1. Application is activated:

```
2011-11-26 22:20:05.780 Lifecycle[1617:207]

application:didFinishLaunchingWithOptions: called.
2011-11-26 22:20:05.781 Lifecycle[1617:207] applicationDidBecomeActive:
  called.
```

2. Limited memory is simulated. In the iPhone simulator menu, go to HARDWARE and then to SIMULATE MEMORY WARNING:

```
2011-11-26 22:20:16.289 Lifecycle[1617:207] Received simulated memory
    warning.
2011-11-26 22:20:16.290 Lifecycle[1617:207] applicationDidReceiveMemory-
    Warning: called.
```

3. The interruption of an application can be simulated with LOCK. For this, click on Hardware > LOCK:

```
2011-11-26 22:20:21.932 Lifecycle[1617:207] applicationWillResignActive:
    called.
```

4. To unlock, move the slider to the right, to SLIDE TO UNLOCK:

```
2011-11-26 22:20:23.743 Lifecycle[1617:207] applicationDidBecomeActive:
    called.
```

5. Press the Home key of the iPhone simulator:

```
2011-11-26 22:20:27.118 Lifecycle[1617:207] applicationWillTerminate: called.
```

Before we can fill the respective methods with useful code, we need some knowledge that we still lack: How, for example, do we store data permanently? How can a running game be interrupted? We shall deal with both these questions in later chapters. Just have a bit of patience, for first we shall take a look at the no less important "universal" subject of iPhone versus iPod touch versus iPad.

## ■ 2.8 Broad Support: Universal Apps

Compared to other mobile platforms, the iOS SDK covers only a handful of devices. Nevertheless, with the introduction of the iPad, Apple introduced the notion of "universal app" to describe a technology whereby all devices of the iPhone family can be supported using a single binary.* You will find an introduction to universal apps at *http://devimages. apple.com/iphone/resources/introductiontouniversalapps.pdf.*

While the iPhone and iPod touch models currently have three different resolutions (320 × 480, 640 × 960, and 640 × 1136 pixels), the iPad 1 and 2 have a single resolution of 1024 × 768 pixels (iPad 3rd gen: 2048 × 1536 pixels). Universal apps currently make sense only in relation to the higher iPad resolution, since this uses a different aspect ratio. One can switch between 320 × 480 and 640 × 960 pixels (retina) without any loss, since the aspect ratio is the same and the scale factor is 2. Retina displays are supported via the @2x suffix (see the following pages; things do not work so easily if you are switching between the iPad and iPhone/iPod touch.

There are three different strategies available for publishing an app in the App Store:

1. **As an iPhone app:** The game has been optimized for the various iPhone and iPod touch versions or else is oriented to the weakest of the iOS devices—namely,

---

* We will not go into game-specific topics in this section. The content is also not necessary for an understanding of the later sections, so you can postpone reading this section until later.

the iPhone of the first generation. This will make it upwardly compatible with all other models. Support for iPad 1 and 2 or iPhone 4/4S and iPod touch 4 happens automatically without any further adaptation: Games run in 320 × 480 pixel resolution centered on the screen. Optionally, the user can double the resolution by pressing a button that displays the game in full-screen mode. (The individual pixels are made larger.)

2. **As an iPad app:** Of course, you can decide to develop your app exclusively for the iPad. This has been possible since the iPhone SDK 3.2. The other devices of the iPhone family must be explicitly excluded if the game is published over iTunes Connect. This is mandatory; otherwise, Apple will not allow the app into the App Store. A screen resolution optimized for 1024 × 768 pixels is incompatible with smaller models.

3. **As a universal application:** With the iPhone SDK 3.2 you can support both iPad and iPhone/iPod touch devices with a single binary. This allows you to combine the results of variants 1 and 2. This is accomplished via a variety of techniques that make it possible to determine at runtime the device on which the game is running. We shall show an example of how this works (Figure 2.4).

Since variant 2 covers only the iPad, it should be used for games that make sense only with the higher resolution (such as a four-person iPad game with all four players sitting around the device). Because fewer devices are covered, however, this variant is not necessarily to be recommended. Variant 1 is the most uncomplicated solution, although you thereby lose the advantages of the larger screen. Variant 3, on the other hand, should be considered only if you are prepared to deal with the higher overhead (larger graphics, different screen allocation, fewer/more game elements on the screen, etc.).

Figure 2.4 A game in the iPad simulator 3.2: left, original size; right, enlarged by a factor of 2.

Also, in your planning you should, without fail, take into account explicit iPad support requirements as well as landscape and portrait formats. For iPhone and iPod touch apps, Apple does not currently make any such recommendation.

So as not to burden the code in the later example projects unnecessarily, we shall use variant 1 as much as possible in the examples in this book and develop code for the target resolution of 320 × 480 pixels and support only one screen orientation. The examples will be as straightforward and readable as possible and oriented toward beginning game developers. Finally, variant 1 guarantees that our games will run on all iOS devices without the need for adjustment.

## 2.8.1 What Advantages Does the iPad Offer for Game Development?

While games for the 320 × 480 pixel iPhone simply have the number of pixels multiplied by a factor of 4 for the larger display of the iPhone 4, the increase in size to the iPad is more complex, since the screen has a different aspect ratio and is of significantly larger dimensions. This has an effect on the way apps are conceived, and from the point of view of game development, the iPad's screen dimensions offer some advantages[*]:

- Board games, strategy games, and simulation games all can profit from the larger screen, since more information can be placed directly on the display. There is still plenty of room for the actual game.

- The touch control is more precise and, with it, more complex gestures can be incorporated, using four or five fingers at once (even both hands).

- Split screen, such as with Nintendo DS, allows for the simultaneous display of an interactive map and the game's live action.

- In multiplayer games, the larger screen offers sufficient space to accommodate two to four persons at the device. This is not only for creators of classical board games (such as Monopoly, Trivial Pursuit, Parcheesi, chess); here you can find new distribution channels for games.

- For strategy games with many onscreen interface elements there is more space available, so you can avoid having to use nested submenus. Moreover, there are new iPad-specific UI elements available, such as, for instance, *Split View* and *Popover*.

## 2.8.2 Platform-Independent Programming

Now comes the question about how universal apps are developed. The following requirements must be fulfilled:

- The game runs on an iPhone, iPod touch/iPhone 4, iPod touch 4 automatically in 320 × 480 resolution. (All devices use the same screen dimensions; for iPhone 4S/iPod 4, the number of pixels is increased by a factor of 4.)

---

[*] Further information on iPad-specific app development can be found at *http://developer.apple.com/ipad/sdk*, including the "iPad Programming Guide," iPad sample code, and the "iPad Human Interface Guidelines" (HIG).

- On an iPad, the game is not optionally scaled up, but rather runs directly after it is launched with a 1024 × 768 pixel screen resolution (iPad 3rd gen: pixels are multiplied by 4).

- On an iPhone 5 or iPod 5, the screen resolution is 640 × 1136 (portrait) or 1136 × 640 pixels (landscape) and therefore will be treated as retina resolution as with iPhone 4S, but with additional space at the bottom (portrait) or at one side (landscape).

- Both landscape and portrait modes should be supported (because the iPad has no default orientation, whereas the iPhone and iPod have portrait mode as the default).

## 2.8.3 Conditional Coding

Different platforms bring with them not only different hardware specifications, but also different APIs (application programming interfaces). This is where *conditional programming* comes into the picture. At the program's runtime, it is decided whether a particular interface is available. Depending on what is available, one or another alternative code is executed. Thus, for example, an app can check whether a camera is present. On an iPod touch, which has no camera, the user's photo library could be accessed as an alternative.

- To check whether a certain class exists, you can use the NSClassFromString() function. If the class is not found, the function returns nil.

- If a class exists, then its methods can also be queried. Every class derived from NSObject has the two methods instancesRespondToSelector and respondsToSelector, which return YES or NO depending on whether the queried method does or does not exist. Functions can be tested directly for NULL.

- Using UI_USER_INTERFACE_IDIOM(), you can query directly whether the app is running on an iPad. If it is, the function returns the value UIUserInterfaceIdiomPad.

Finally, using the preprocessor, you can branch the compiled code so that, with an Xcode project, different versions of an app can be built—for example, with the macro #if __IPHONE_OS_VERSION_MAX_ALLOWED > = 30200. The code that follows will be compiled only if Base SDK > = 3.2 is true. Base SDK can be set in the project settings.

You can also directly query the device type and iOS version number:

```
UIDevice * device = [UIDevice currentDevice];
NSLog(@"Model:%@", device.model);
NSLog(@"iOS Version:%@", device.systemVersion);
```

This returns something like the following:

```
2011-11-03 16:45:09.455 My Universal App[7772:207] Model: iPad Simulator
2011-11-03 16:45:09.462 My Universal App[7772:207] iOS Version: 3.2
```

Apple recommends, however, that you not base code branching solely on this information. If you do so anyway, you should typify classes whose existence you cannot assume dynamically with id instead of using the class name directly ("id myClass" instead of, for example, "CADisplayLink myClass"). Otherwise, you will get a compiler error, assuming that you have chosen the correct simulator under Deployment Target. If a class if typified with id, then unknown method calls on this instance are acknowledged with only a warning, but they should not be run on the device. To avoid execution, you must cause the code to branch at runtime based on the version number.

But how does one compare the various version numbers? This is quite simple: Since the iOS version number is of data type NSString, we can implement the NSString method compare:options: for a comparison:

```
NSString *deviceOS = [[UIDevice currentDevice] systemVersion];
if ([deviceOS compare: @"3.0" options: NSNumericSearch]

    = = NSOrderedAscending) {
    //iOS < 3.0
    } else {
    //iOS > = 3.0
}
```

With the optional specification NSNumericSearch, we stipulate that all numeric values within a string should be interpreted. The result of the comparison can return three possible values:

- NSOrderedAscending: the string to compare is *smaller* than the compare argument (ascending order).

- NSOrderedSame: the two strings are *equal.*

- NSOrderedDescending: the string to compare is *greater* than the compare argument (descending order).

If a new class is available from a particular iOS, you can specify, using an if-else branch, that its methods are to be used only for newer systems. We shall introduce another practical application in a later chapter, under the topic of game loops.

## 2.8.4 Example: Developing a Universal App

So much for theory. Let us look now at a framework that satisfies the given criteria for universal applications. Without this, our app would run only in the so-called iPad-compatibility mode; that is, it would make no use of the iPad-specific characteristics.

We would like to create a new framework for this example. Therefore, create a new project via FILE > NEW PROJECT. Again, we shall choose as our framework the "Empty Application." It is important now that, in the lower portion of the window, under "Device Family," you select the entry "Universal." The default is "iPhone"; alternatively, you can also choose just "iPad" if you want to exclude smaller resolutions. Next, you specify the file name of the new project. We shall choose the name "UniversalApp." You will find the project under this name in the examples for this book.

Then, in the emulator menu we choose, under HARDWARE > DEVICE, the iPad if it has not already been set. After the basic framework is complete, the project opens in the iPad simulator, where we see that the window takes up the entire domain of the simulator and there is no 2x enlargement button. All systems are "go," and our project is now running in the 1024 × 768 pixel resolution of the iPad.

### WHAT ARE XIB AND NIB FILES? WHY DO MANY CLASS NAMES BEGIN WITH NS?

The abbreviation NS stands for NeXTStep, the operating system developed in 1986 by NeXT Computer (first release, 1989). The company was founded by Steve Jobs and a number of other former Apple employees. In 1996, when Jobs returned to Apple and NeXT was purchased by Apple for $402 million, it was decided to use NeXTStep as the basis of a new operating system, namely Mac OS X. Today, the names of many classes hark back to these origins. The abbreviation NIB stands for NeXT Interface Builder and marks XML files that have been created with Interface Builder. To make it clear that NIB files use a pure XML text format, such files are stored with the file extension xib. Often, both names are used synonymously. In this book we shall avoid the use of Interface Builder and create the graphical user interface (GUI) elements that we need programmatically. Interface Builder is a WYSIWYG (what you see is what you get) editor for GUI elements; its construction is similar to that of, for instance, an HTML editor.

A look at the project structure reveals that Xcode has created iPad and iPhone folders, each of which has its own app delegate and an NIB file adapted to the appropriate window size. Moreover, the Plist is now located in the "Shared" folder; this is where the determination is made as to which app delegate with which window size will be executed after the app is launched.

The following new entries are found in the Plist table:

```
Main nib file base name: MainWindow_iPhone
Main nib file base name (iPad): MainWindow_iPad
```

And the following are found in XML view:

```
<key>NSMainNibFile</key>
<string>MainWindow_iPhone</string>
<key>NSMainNibFile~ipad</key>
<string>MainWindow_iPad</string>
```

This specifies the currently active main window.

The following are specifications regarding the supported screen orientations: "Supported interface orientations" contains the sole entry "Portrait (bottom home button)" and stipulates that for iPhone and iPod touch devices, the application should support only portrait mode (the home button is then at the bottom of the device).

Under "Supported interface orientations (iPad)" you will find, as expected, four entries:

- Portrait (bottom home button)

- Portrait (top home button)

- Landscape (left home button)

- Landscape (right home button)

In XML view, the Plist looks like this:

```
<key>UISupportedInterfaceOrientations</key>
<array>
    <string>UIInterfaceOrientationPortrait</string>
</array>
    <key>UISupportedInterfaceOrientations~ipad</key>
<array>
    <string>UIInterfaceOrientationPortrait</string>
    <string>UIInterfaceOrientationPortraitUpsideDown</string>
    <string>UIInterfaceOrientationLandscapeLeft</string>
    <string>UIInterfaceOrientationLandscapeRight</string>
</array>
```

To support the four possible orientations, you must use a `View-Controller`.

---

**TIP**

Ideally, you should avoid code duplication when you are developing a universal app. To make it possible to use a common code base, you should create a new folder, "Common," in Xcode by right-clicking to the left of the project view using ADD > NEW GROUP. Here is where you can place common code from which you branch using the appropriateapp delegate. In importing header files, you do not need to specify the folder name.

For our example project we first customize the Plist and add the four possible orientations for the iPhone entry "Supported interface orientations." Alternatively, for a universal app, you can explicitly overwrite the entry with the iPhone variant— that is, "Supported interface orientations (iPhone)."

For the newly created "Common" folder we use a right-click to choose ADD > NEW FILE and select the `UIViewController` subclass. As the name suggests, you can manage a number of views of your app with this class. For example, this class offers a listener for various screen orientations. You can ignore the check under the option "Targeted for iPad." We shall adapt the resulting code as follows. (Our focus is on the `shouldAutorotateToInterfaceOrientation:` method, which monitors the device's screen orientation.)

---

Listing 2.10 ViewController.h

```
#import <UIKit/UIKit.h>

@interface ViewController : UIViewController {
}

@end
```

Listing 2.11 ViewController.m

```objc
#import "ViewController.h"

@implementation ViewController

- (BOOL) shouldAutorotateToInterfaceOrientation:
  (UIInterfaceOrientation) interfaceOrientation {

    if (interfaceOrientation = = UIInterfaceOrientationPortrait) {
        NSLog(@"Orientation: UIInterfaceOrientationPortrait");
    }

    if (interfaceOrientation = =
       UIDeviceOrientationPortraitUpsideDown) {
        NSLog(@"Orientation: UIDeviceOrientationPortraitUpsideDown");
    }

    if (interfaceOrientation = = UIDeviceOrientationLandscapeRight) {
        NSLog(@"Orientation: UIDeviceOrientationLandscapeRight");
    }

    if (interfaceOrientation = = UIDeviceOrientationLandscapeLeft) {
        NSLog(@"Orientation: UIDeviceOrientationLandscapeLeft");
    }

    return YES;//all orientations are supported}
- (void) viewDidUnload {
    [super viewDidUnload];

}

- (void) dealloc {
    [super dealloc];

}

@end
```

Whenever you change the orientation (which is recognized by the device's motion sensor), the new orientation is sent to the method as an enum constant of type UIInterfaceOrientation. We need this value only to compare it with the current constant in order to determine the app's current orientation:

- UIInterfaceOrientationPortrait

- UIDeviceOrientationPortraitUpsideDown

- UIDeviceOrientationLandscapeRight

- UIDeviceOrientationLandscapeLeft

The four possible orientations correspond to the values in the Plist. We give YES as return value (shouldAutorotateToInterfaceOrientation: method), to make it clear that the app supports every orientation.

Now we have to include the view controller only in the app delegates associated with iPhone and iPad. The code is identical except for the _iPad/_iPhone suffixes.

Listing 2.12 AppDelegate_iPad.h

```
#import <UIKit/UIKit.h>

#import "ViewController.h"

@interface AppDelegate_iPad : NSObject <UIApplicationDelegate> {
    UIWindow *window;
    ViewController *viewController;
}
@end
```

Listing 2.13 AppDelegate_iPad.m

```
#import "AppDelegate_iPad.h"

@implementation AppDelegate_iPad

- (BOOL)application:(UIApplication *)application
    didFinishLaunchingWithOptions:(NSDictionary *)launchOptions {

    NSLog(@"App launched on iPad!");
    viewController = [[ViewController alloc] init];
    [window addSubview: [viewController view]];

    [window makeKeyAndVisible];
    return YES;
}

- (void)dealloc {
    [viewController release];
    [window release];
    [super dealloc];
}

@end
```

Using build settings, three different SDK settings can be made:

- ARCHITECTURES > BASE SDK: This should be the most current available (e.g., "Latest iOS 6.0").

- DEPLOYMENT > TARGETED DEVICE FAMILY: In the case of universal apps, "iPhone/iPad" must be selected. Otherwise, choose either "iPhone" or "iPad." This specification does not determine the SDK directly, but it has influence over the entries in the Plist table (the UIDeviceFamily is set dynamically by the build system).

- DEPLOYMENT > IPHONE OS DEPLOYMENT TARGET: Here you should choose the lowest possible setting. This also means, however, that the app will run only on devices from the given iOS forward; the app will not start on older iPhone operating systems.

The time has come to try out our universal app. The orientation of the simulator can be changed in the simulator app via

- Hardware > ROTATE LEFT

- Hardware > ROTATE RIGHT

Depending on the chosen simulator under Active SDK, you then obtain, for example, the following console output:

```
[Session started at 2011-11-02 17:34:58 +0200.]
2011-11-02 17:35:01.405 UniversalApp[3750:207] App launched on iPad!
2011-11-02 17:35:01.432 UniversalApp[3750:207] Orientation:
    UIInterfaceOrientationPortrait
2011-11-02 17:35:06.950 UniversalApp[3750:207] Orientation:
    UIDeviceOrientationLandscapeLeft
2011-11-02 17:35:09.061 UniversalApp[3750:207] Orientation:
    UIDeviceOrientationPortraitUpsideDown
2011-11-02 17:35:11.463 UniversalApp[3750:207] Orientation:
    UIDeviceOrientationLandscapeRight
2011-11-02 17:35:13.592 UniversalApp[3750:207] Orientation:
    UIInterfaceOrientationPortrait

[Session started at 2010-05-02 17:36:24 +0200.]
2011-11-02 17:36:25.149 UniversalApp[3800:207] App launched on iPhone!
2011-11-02 17:36:25.151 UniversalApp[3800:207] Orientation:
    UIInterfaceOrientationPortrait
2011-11-02 17:36:28.090 UniversalApp[3800:207] Orientation:
    UIDeviceOrientationLandscapeLeft
2011-11-02 17:36:30.183 UniversalApp[3800:207] Orientation:
    UIDeviceOrientationPortraitUpsideDown
2011-11-02 17:36:32.552 UniversalApp[3800:207] Orientation:
    UIDeviceOrientationLandscapeRight
2011-11-02 17:36:34.493 UniversalApp[3800:207] Orientation:
    UIInterfaceOrientationPortrait
```

As you can see, we have not hidden the status bar, and we can see at every change in orientation how the screen rotates; yet the status bar is positioned at the top (Figure 2.5). Furthermore, on the iPhone, the application fills the entire screen (minus the status bar).

If you want to allow only a specific orientation for your game, of course that is possible. For a game that is to be played only in landscape mode, without the screen being rotated automatically, you must customize the shouldAutorotateToInterface Orientation: method:

```
if (interfaceOrientation = = UIDeviceOrientationLandscapeRight) {
    return YES;
} else return NO;
```

**Figure 2.5** Regardless of the orientation of the device, text and status bar always appear at the top.

The return value will be YES only for the landscape-right orientation; all other orientations will be ignored. The method will continue to be called several times until the supported orientation has been found; otherwise, the default orientation will be chosen as a fallback. Therefore, you can force the game to start in the landscape orientation.

The current orientation of a device can be queried at any time via UIDevice:

```
if ([UIDevice currentDevice].orientation

    = = UIDeviceOrientationLandscapeLeft) {
    NSLog(@"Current orientation: UIDeviceOrientationLandscapeLeft");
}
```

The orientation property of the UIDevice instance always contains the current orientation (enum type: UIDeviceOrientation). There are seven different values. With other queries, you can determine whether the device is lying flat on the table with the display pointing down (for example, in order to make possible an automatic pause state).

### 2.8.5 Turning Off the Status Bar

For games, you probably want to make use of the screen in full-screen mode. The status bar can be deactivated directly in the applicationDidFinishLaunching: method by sending the following message to the UIApplication instance:

```
[application setStatusBarHidden:YES];
```

However, we know already that the applicationDidFinishLaunching: method is called relatively late—namely, after the app has already been initialized. During the start-up phase, the status bar would then be invisible. To deactivate the status bar directly after a click on the home button, you should place an appropriate instruction in the Plist file. Add a line and choose as key "Status bar is initially hidden." You can simply set a check as the value.

2. The Basics—How Does It All Work?

## 2.8.6  Adding Resources: App Icons and Splash Images

Before we deal further with orientation and show how the drawing area can be turned automatically, let us see how an app can add an icon that is displayed on the home screen. Up to now, there was only a white default image.

Apple recommends using 32-bit PNG files (8 bits each for red, green, and blue plus an 8-bit alpha channel for transparency).

- **Large app icon iPhone:** 57 × 57 pixels, 114 × 114 pixels (retina)

- **Large app icon iPad:** 72 × 72 pixels, 144 × 144 pixels (retina)

The size specifications come from Apple. For the iPhone, you simply need to include a file with the name "Icon.png." Optionally, for iPod Touch 4/5 and iPhone 4/4S/5, you can also add a retina icon of size 114 × 114 pixels and the suffix "@2x" in the file (iPad 3rd gen: 144 × 144 pixels). Since the image will be appropriately scaled automatically, you can include just *one* icon for all devices. We show here only the general approach to incorporating different icon sizes. The future will undoubtedly bring additional devices with different resolutions. Nevertheless, note the following: The PNG can have no transparent parts, it should have square corners, and it should have no gloss effect, since in order to give all apps the same look, these effects are created automatically by iOS. (Nevertheless, the icon's properties can still be configured in the Plist as required.)

We create two icons with a graphics program (such as Pixen or Photoshop):

- Icon.png

- Icon_72x72.png

But how do we add the image resources to our Xcode project? Simply copy the images into the project folder, via the finder outside Xcode, since Xcode uses its own file reference system (the so-called *Application Bundle*). Now we have to embed the files (they can also be videos, music files, or HTML files) via Xcode. Go by way of a right-click to GROUPS & FILES, to the left-hand sidebar, and create a new folder (NEW GROUP) called "Resources." Then add the image files with a right-click via ADD FILES TO…. Here you choose files that are already in the project folder.

To use custom icons for each size, we must also use the Plist. We delete there the entry "Icon File," replace it with "Icon files," and create the following key value pairs:

- Key Item 0: Icon.png

- Key Item 1: Icon_72x72.png

The name for the iPad icon can be whatever you wish, provided that it agrees with the entry in the Plist. The iPhone iOS then selects suitable icons from the Plist by checking their size.

For splash images, we can proceed similarly. A splash image is a graphic the size of the screen that is displayed during the start-up of the game. If you wish to load additional resources before the display of the first view, the splash image remains visible and thus serves as a sort of preloader screen.

We could again make things easy for ourselves and simply add a file named "Default.png." Just as with the icons, this image would automatically be displayed as a splash screen for all resolutions. For the iPad, however, we should specify the initial orientation—for example:

```
Initial interface orientation: Portrait (bottom home button)
```

The iPhone always starts in portrait mode in any case. But how do we proceed if we want the initial image that is displayed to depend on the orientation?

For a universal app, the appropriate start-up image should be displayed depending on the iPad orientation. The iOS selects a suitable image based on the size of the image and its name. From the motion sensor, the device knows how the iPad is being held. We have only to create images for landscape and portrait modes. Since we have not yet hidden the status bar, the height/width dimension is reduced from 1024 to 1004 pixels.

- **Splash iPhone/iPod:** Default.png (320 × 480 pixels), optional for retina: Default@2x.png (640 × 960 pixels), Default-568h@2x.png (640 × 1136 pixels)

- **Splash iPad 1:** Default-Portrait.png (768 × 1004 pixels)

- **Splash iPad 2:** Default-Landscape.png (1004 × 768 pixels)

If you now run the app in the simulator for iPad or iPhone, you will see the appropriate icon and the splash screen at the correct resolution. The iPhone always starts in portrait mode, while the iPad starts in the previously selected orientation. Try all four possible orientations and observe that the correct splash image is displayed. However, since we do not have many resources to load, the splash image is visible for only a short while. Apple therefore recommends that you display the app's next screen as the start image so that the transition does not occur too rapidly. In practice, however, there is enough to load that the splash image will stay long enough in view. For example, many firms display their company logo at this point (Figure 2.6).

## 2.8.7 Setting the App Name

As you may have noticed, the project name is displayed under the icon. This is not always desirable. The displayed name is hidden in the Plist under the entry

```
Bundle display name: ${PRODUCT_NAME}
```

To change the default string for ${PRODUCT_NAME}, choose in Xcode PROJECT > EDIT ACTIVE TARGET 'UNIVERSALAPP'. The build tab that opens contains the desired entry under "Packaging." For "Product Name" you might choose as value, for example, "My Universal App." Names that are too long will be shortened in the home-screen view by "…". The next time the app is started, the new name will appear under the icon.

| Key | Value |
|---|---|
| ▼ Information Property List | (17 items) |
| Status bar is initially hidden | ☐ |
| ▼ Icon files | (2 items) |
| Item 0 | Icon.png |
| Item 1 | Icon_72x72.png |
| Bundle versions string, short | |
| Localization native development re | English |
| Bundle display name | ${PRODUCT_NAME} |
| Executable file | ${EXECUTABLE_NAME} |
| Bundle identifier | com.yourcompany.${PRODUCT_NAME:rfc1034identifier} |
| InfoDictionary version | 6.0 |
| Bundle name | ${PRODUCT_NAME} |
| Bundle OS Type code | APPL |
| Bundle creator OS Type code | ???? |
| Bundle version | 1.0 |
| Application requires iPhone enviror | ☑ |
| Main nib file base name | MainWindow_iPhone |
| Main nib file base name (iPad) | MainWindow_iPad |
| ▼ Supported interface orientations | (4 items) |
| Item 0 | Portrait (bottom home button) |
| Item 1 | Portrait (top home button) |
| Item 2 | Landscape (left home button) |
| Item 3 | Landscape (right home button) |
| ▼ Supported interface orientations (iF | (4 items) |
| Item 0 | Portrait (bottom home button) |
| Item 1 | Portrait (top home button) |
| Item 2 | Landscape (left home button) |
| Item 3 | Landscape (right home button) |

**Figure 2.6** Entries in the Plist file.

## 2.8.8 Query Resolution and Text Output

To complete the basic framework, we add a main window in which later we are going to display our game. We orient ourselves on the Hello World2 example, in which a text is output to a view.

Since the view is to be used for both the iPad and the iPhone, we place the view in the Common folder in order to avoid code duplication.

**Listing 2.14** MainView.h

```
#import <UIKit/UIKit.h>

@interface MainView : UIView {
}

@end
```

**Listing 2.14.1** MainView.m

```
#import "MainView.h"

@implementation MainView

- (void) drawRect: (CGRect) rect {
```

```
        int w = rect.size.width;
        int h = rect.size.height;
        NSLog(@"MainView -> drawRect:%ix%i", w, h);

        CGContextRef gc = UIGraphicsGetCurrentContext();
        CGContextSetRGBFillColor(gc, 1, 1, 1, 1);
        NSString *str = @"Hello little bird!";
        UIFont *uif = [UIFont systemFontOfSize:40];
        [str drawAtPoint:CGPointMake(10, 10) withFont: uif];
    }

    @end
```

As you can see, we first output the currently available screen resolution via an `NSLog` call. The `drawRect:` method, as you have already seen in the Hello World2 example, is called with the parameter `CGRect`. This is the currently available rectangular screen area.

If we want to render our game, we can query the current resolution with

```
int w = rect.size.width;
int h = rect.size.height;
```

We can adjust the positions at which the game objects are to be drawn accordingly. To check whether the view is correctly oriented, we output the text "Hello little bird!"— regardless of the device's orientation in the upper left-hand corner—at x = 10, y = 10. In the next chapter we shall discuss in greater detail the coordinate system and text output. What is important for us at this point is simply to note that the coordinate system automatically adjusts itself when the orientation changes.

To display a new view, this time we use the view controller. This already contains a view, which we overwrite with our new view. We add the following method to the `ViewController.m` file:

```
- (void) viewDidLoad {
    mainView = [[MainView alloc] initWithFrame:

        [UIScreen mainScreen].applicationFrame];
    mainView.autoresizingMask =

        UIViewAutoresizingFlexibleWidth | UIViewAutoresizingFlexibleHeight;
    self.view = mainView;
    [super viewDidLoad];
}
```

The `viewDidLoad` method derives from the parent class `UIViewController` and is called as soon as the view controller is loaded. The `mainView` variable placed in the header is initialized as usual. The initialization method `initWithFrame: [UIScreen mainScreen].applicationFrame]` gives us via `UIScreen` as output value the current display size.

The specification in the next line is especially important, since we want to use the new dimensions for every change in orientation:

```
mainView.autoresizingMask =
    UIViewAutoresizingFlexibleWidth | UIViewAutoresizingFlexibleHeight;
```

Using a bit mask, the new view is informed that at each rendering operation, it should be flexibly adapted to the available resolution.

Finally, with `self.view = mainView;` we replace the view of the view controller with our own view. Alternatively, we could have used `[[self view] addSubview: mainView];` simply to overlay a new view on top, but in game programming, one generally does all right with one view.

Finally, in the `shouldAutorotateToInterfaceOrientation:` method we add the message

```
[mainView setNeedsDisplay];
```

This ensures that the view is redrawn at each change in orientation. The message `setNeedsDisplay` triggers the `drawRect:` method of `MainView`.

If we rotate the screen, we obtain, for example, the following messages:

```
2011-11-03 16:16:38.396 My Universal App[7594:207] MainView -> drawRect:
   1024x748
2011-11-03 16:16:39.974 My Universal App[7594:207] MainView -> drawRect:
   768x1004
```

Since the status bar is visible at the top of the screen, the resolution for landscape is limited to 1024 × 748 pixels, and for portrait it is 768 × 1004 pixels.

In practice, this means that the support of several resolutions can mean a significant increase in computational expense. In any case, it is not a good idea to change the orientation during a game. This is even truer with the iPhone, since here, in contrast to the iPad, there is no caps lock key (this can be done only in software).

If you decide to develop your game for a single orientation, you might at least consider whether you wish to allow a 180° rotation. Producers such as Gameloft offer this as a standard feature, and as we shall show, it is easy and cost free to implement. You have only to specify both landscape or both portrait orientations as supported in the `shouldAutorotateToInterfaceOrientation:` method—for example, `UIDeviceOrientationPortrait` and `UIDeviceOrientationPortrait UpsideDown` if the game is to be playable only in portrait mode. Since the screen rotates automatically, the resolution and origin of the coordinate system do not change.

Of course, you can also use the changing screen orientation creatively in game design. Examples of such a game principle include NOM (Living Mobile), a Java ME-One-Thumb-J'n'R, which has not as of yet been ported to iPhone & Co. The player moves along the bottom border of the screen. When the right-hand border is reached, the device has to be turned. For an iPhone implementation, one could specify this as a condition so that the figure's position *must* be unchanged at the bottom while the device is rotated.

# ▎ 2.9  Support for Retina Displays

With the iPhone 4/4S, iPad 3rd gen, and the iPod touch 4, the number of pixels has quadrupled, with iOS models with 320 × 480 pixels (163 pixels per inch—ppi) going to 640 × 960 pixels (326 ppi), and those with1024 × 768 pixels (132 ppi) to 2048 × 1536 pixels

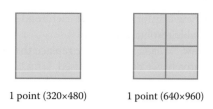

1 point (320×480)            1 point (640×960)

Figure 2.7 Retina displays can use four pixels for each image point.

(264 ppi).* However, since the display size of 89 millimeters (3.5 inches) has remained the same, Apple has advertised the new resolution as "retina resolution" (to give the impression that the resolution is equivalent to that of the human retina). In the new resolution, there are 4 pixels for each 1 pixel in the old resolution. Thus, graphics appear twice as sharp and can show more detail, provided that they are prepared for the new retina resolution (Figure 2.7).

Since the number of pixels in both the horizontal and vertical directions has doubled, the aspect ratio remains the same. Therefore, the 2x button on the iPad for iPhone games is omitted, and a game with resolution of 320 × 480 pixels looks the same on a retina device unless retina graphics are used, since the screen size remains the same. The iOS automatically takes care of scaling the graphic, which is brought pixel accurate to the doubled size without a blur effect. For this to work properly, the screen is considered not in terms of its actual pixel count, but instead in terms of image points.

A space ship at position (100, 100) is to be placed in a retina device at the same position. Even though the screen has four times as many pixels, the game still has only 320 × 480 image points, just as before.

There are two good reasons for adapting games explicitly for the retina resolution. First, you avoid wasting resources, since all nonretina graphics have to be scaled up by iOS. Second, your graphics could look somewhat better on a retina display to the extent that you have graphics of higher resolution. If you want to do without this advantage, you can simply scale up your graphics. Just make sure in your graphics program to choose the correct setting (in Photoshop, for example, "Nearest Neighbor") since, otherwise, the pixels will be blurred through interpolation (which sometimes makes photographs look better, but is not recommended for pixel graphics).

### 2.9.1  How Do I Support Retina Resolution?

Fortunately, there is not much to do. It suffices to provide each retina graphic name with the suffix @2x. For example, in addition to a graphics file "MySpaceShip.png" with dimensions of 32 × 32 pixels, you can include a second graphic—namely, "MySpaceShip@2x.png" with dimensions of 64 × 64 pixels.

We have added a folder named "retina" for each project in this book, in which all the graphics can be found with double resolution and with the appropriate suffix. Older devices will simply ignore this folder, while iOS retina devices will automatically look for

---

* Both iPhone 5 and iPod 5 support retina resolution as well, but have an extra space at the bottom. Instead of a 3.5-inch retina, the screen is now 4 inches with 640 × 1136 points (326 dpi), with an additional 176 points added to the bottom. To use this extra space in games, you will need to proceed as described for the iPad ratio and adapt the game play: A bigger screen will allow, for instance, more enemies, more obstacles, and so on.

an "@2x" graphic. It does not matter where your @2x variants are located. They simply have to be included somewhere, just like other resources.

As will be discussed more precisely in the following chapter, by default all images are loaded via

```
UIImage *pic = [UIImage imageNamed: picName];
```

Of course, as "picName" you give the old name—that is, "MySpaceShip.png." This ensures that the app runs the same way on both older and newer devices. And who knows? Perhaps there will soon be an "@4x" variant. What is important here is that the UIImage class always returns the dimensions of the graphic via the size property without the suffix. In fact, the game will be rendered, as before, with 320 × 480 image points, except that graphics can optionally have a higher resolution. This saves developers a great deal of effort in adapting the code to a variety of screen resolutions. The game logic continues to refer to the positions of the game elements, with retina devices simply profiting optically from the higher resolution. The only thing to watch out for is that there are a few peculiarities under OpenGL ES, and we will have more to say on that later.

## 2.9.2 Testing with the Retina Emulator

To test whether the higher resolution graphics are actually displayed, simply open any graphic with a graphics program like *Pixen* and select the graphic. Now choose the iPhone variant "iPhone (Retina)" in the emulator menu via HARDWARE > DEVICE and then the scaling factor under WINDOW > SIZE. If your screen is not large enough, scroll bars will appear on the side of the emulator. To see the graphic in its original size, you must, of course, set "100%"; otherwise, in the emulator you will see the graphic scaled.

# 3 Game Development From 0 to 60 in No Time Flat

## ◼ 3.1  How Do Games Work?

Now that we have done some preparation and know how Xcode projects and universal applications for iPhone/iPod touch and iPad are created, it is time to get down to the nitty-gritty of the main subject of this book. Games are graphics applications, and therefore they have very special requirements that distinguish them from traditional applications. For example, games cannot be created with Interface Builder or through the implementation of various UI components provided by the iOS SDK, unless we are talking about very simple games such as guessing games or quiz games.

### 3.1.1  All Right Then, but How Are Games Actually Made?

In a way, games are like movies. The illusion of a moving image is created by displaying a rapid sequence of individual pictures (frames). Every frame represents a particular state of the game—for example:

- **Frame 1**

  - Query: Where has the user touched the screen?

  - Move the player and the game pieces.

  - Move the opponent.

- Query: Have the opponent and player touched each other?

- Add up the points for the opponents that have been hit.

- …

- Draw the game elements at their current positions on the screen.

- **Frame 2**

  - Query: Where has the user touched the screen?

  - Move the player and the game pieces.

  - Move the opponent.

  - Query: Have the opponent and player touched each other?

  - Add up the points for the opponents that have been hit.

  - …

  - Draw the game elements at their current positions on the screen.

- **Frame 3**

  - Query: Where has the user touched the screen?

  - Move the player and the game pieces.

  - Move the opponent.

  - Query: Have the opponent and player touched each other?

  - Add up the points for the opponents that have been hit.

  - …

  - Draw the game elements at their current positions on the screen.

And so on. Before the game elements are rendered to the screen, the touch display is queried; after all, games are interactive applications and have to react to user input. In addition, the current game state is calculated and displayed on the screen. Since this process is repeated several times a second, one speaks in this context of a *game loop*.

There are various approaches to calculating the game elements between the frames. In practice, one often defines an offset that is assigned to a figure for each frame—its velocity, so to speak. Suppose that a Pong ball is supposed to fly across the screen from left to right, and its speed is 5 pixels per frame. Then we would calculate the x-position of the ball as follows:

```
x = x + 5
```

This would result in something like the following positions for the ball:

```
Frame 1: x = 0
Frame 2: x = 5
Frame 3: x = 10
...
```

So, suppose you have thus moved your first object across the screen. Now you have only to determine how an object is displayed on the screen and how to create a game loop. And there are additional questions that you have to answer, regardless of the platform for which you wish to develop your game.

## 3.1.2  What Do I Need to Know? Useful Questions

Before beginning the development process for a new platform, it is advisable to figure out exactly what you would like to know; otherwise, you can quickly get lost in the numerous sub-APIs—learning, say, how to set up an Internet connection or to send an SMS while losing sight of your true goal. Since games are graphics applications with moving images, we face the following questions:

- How are graphics, such as PNGs, for example, displayed on the screen?

- How can user input, such as touching the display, be recognized and processed?

- How can the display be periodically updated to create a game loop?

- How can the occurrence of collisions between various game elements be determined?

If you can answer these questions, then there is (almost) nothing between you and your first game. Of course, we shall be addressing additional topics, such as sound reproduction, the permanent storage of game states, and the creation of animated sprites.

# 3.2  The Two-Dimensional (2D) Coordinate System

All the parts of a game must be "drawn" on the screen. The extent of the screen thus represents, so to speak, the playground on which we can romp. This surface is also known as a canvas or viewport (the visible range), or simply a view.

As we saw in the section on universal apps, various orientations and resolutions can be supported, depending on the type of device. All iOS devices are compatible with the smallest resolution of 320 × 480 (width × height) pixels in portrait mode or held sideways like a traditional mobile game console at 480 × 320 pixels. The coordinate system in terms of which of the elements can be arranged on the screen has its origin at the upper left-hand corner of the screen. This corner therefore has coordinates $x = 0$ and $y = 0$.

Just as with the coordinate system from high-school mathematics, there is a horizontal x-axis and a vertical y-axis. The screen size limits the visible region of the two axes.

Using the procedure described in the section on universal apps, you can restrict the orientation of the viewport to portrait or landscape mode, or you can permit both orientations. The fact that the origin of the coordinate system does not change (it is always in the top left-hand corner, regardless of how the device is oriented) simplifies the support for differing resolutions. At runtime, you have only to determine the currently available boundaries: How wide is the screen and how high? The two values can be exchanged, depending on the orientation. You should never hard-code the width and height values; to do so would make later adaptation to other resolutions unnecessarily difficult.

We have already seen how to read out the width and height of the screen. Here, the dimensions of the status bar (time, battery state, etc.) are taken into account. One usually hides the status bar as part of the game design in order to obtain the greatest possible screen area (Figure 3.1).

Suppose you wish to draw a point at the center of the screen. The coordinates of this point in xy-coordinates can be obtained as follows, independently of the orientation and size of the screen:

```
int x = screenWidth/2;
int y = screenHeight/2;
```

And if you wanted to display a rectangle or a picture at the screen's center, you would use the following coordinates for its upper left-hand corner:

```
int x = screenWidth/2-rectWidth/2;
int y = screenHeight/2-rectHeight/2;
```

As you may already know, rectangles and other images are always rendered to the screen from their upper left-hand corner.

Of course, the coordinate system does not end at the edges of the screen. You could also place an object at position x = 9999, y = 9999; it just would not be visible. On the other hand, you can make objects "fly" onto the screen from top to bottom. But take heed: An object at position x = 600, y = 600 of size 50 × 50 pixels would not be visible on an iPhone,

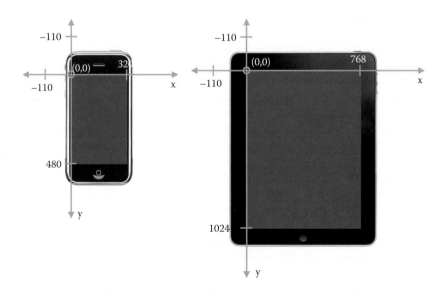

Figure 3.1 The iOS coordinate system. Left: iPhone 3GS; right: iPad.

though it would be visible on an iPad, but only if you create your app as a universal app or specifically for iPad resolution.

The iOS SDK is very frugal. If you develop your game only for the standard resolution of 320 × 480 pixels, the display will be optionally shown on other devices such as the iPad in enlarged format (the user can click on the 2x zoom button). This does not change the height and width of the screen. Instead, the graphics are simply scaled up by iOS, with the screen dimensions remaining the same. This is by no means obvious. On other mobile platforms one usually has to make adjustments. Apple, however, is (at least for now) ensuring downward compatibility and can guarantee that new products such as the iPad and iPhone 4/4S have access to the full app portfolio of the App Store. However, it is still the case that game projects developed exclusively for the iPad cannot be downloaded to the iPhone or iPod touch.

## ▎ 3.3   Setting Up an Example Project

Regardless of the particular game design, there are certain repetitive tasks that are the same for all games. Therefore, it is worthwhile setting up an example project that contains some of these elementary building blocks. Based on our current knowledge, these will include the following:

- An app delegate

- A view for drawing the game

- A screen query for the current screen dimensions

- A standard splash screen, which can be exchanged for something else later as desired

- An app icon for the home screen

We shall use and continually expand this template in the further course of this book. While in this chapter we shall be working with the UIKit, in later chapters we shall use OpenGL for graphics representation. It is only with OpenGL that you can achieve an acceptable frame rate for more complex games. Nevertheless, for getting started and learning the first steps of game development, the UIKit is useful due to its narrower capabilities.

Since we have already seen that the splash screen and the home screen icon can be implemented even on the iPad without any adjustment (and be scaled automatically by iOS), let us choose the 320 × 480 pixel portrait resolution, which can be used by all the devices of the iPhone family. With a universal app, you will see how to "upgrade" to other resolutions and orientations.

Using the model of the Hello World2 example, let us create a new project with an app delegate and a view (FILE > NEW > NEW PROJECT > IOS APPLICATION > EMPTY APPLICATION) and name the project "MyGame."

Core data, automatic reference counting, and unit tests remain deactivated, as well as a local Git repository, which you will not need for this example app.

Using ADD FILES TO "MYGAME", we also add in addition to the app delegate, which created a template for us, the MainView class. Then we adjust the delegate's code and that of the `MainView` class in such a way that they are identical to the Hello World2 example. We do not use such delegate methods as `applicationDidEnterBackground:` and `applicationWillEnterForeground:`, which have been available since iOS 4.0, since our game does not need the multitasking feature. Since users can update their devices' iOS at any time for free, it is not really necessary to develop your game to be compatible with the original iOS 2.0. On the other hand, you should not support the newest iOS exclusively. Even Apple recommends that you set the deployment target to an older version. And that is what we are going to do here. A good compromise is the iPhone iOS 3.2, which contains all the features that we need for our app.

Using the project settings, which can be accessed via the left-side window by clicking on the blue Xcode file symbol, we create the following project-specific settings in the corresponding "build settings" tabs under "TARGETS":

- ARCHITECTURES > BASE SDK: Latest iOS (iOS 6.0)

- DEPLOYMENT > TARGETED DEVICE FAMILY: iPhone

- DEPLOYMENT > IPHONE OS DEPLOYMENT TARGET: iPhone OS 3.2

- PACKAGING > PRODUCT NAME (e.g., "my first game")

We can complete the bundle identifier in the MyGame-Info.plist file: `com.yourcompany.${PRODUCT_NAME:rfc1034identifier}`. Just enter the name of your homepage here instead of `yourcompany`—for example, `com.qioo.${PRODUCT_NAME:rfc1034identifier}`. You have already set `PRODUCT_NAME` under "Product Name" in "Active Target Settings." Your project will be identified by iPhone iOS via "Bundle ID," and the product name will be displayed on the device under the app icon. This does not have to be the same as the project name.

Now turn off the status bar by adding the key "Status bar is initially hidden," checking the box under "Value" and choosing the option "Application does not run in background" since, as a rule, we do not need to support multitasking for game apps. Moreover, you have here the possibility of setting the specific category—for example, "Application Category: Games—Action Games."

We shall leave the remaining settings as they appear.

We now add an app icon and title picture. To do so, we need to copy two files into our project directory and add the following in Xcode via ADD FILES:

- **Icon.png:** 57 × 57 pixels

- **Default.png:** 320 × 480 pixels

- **Optional for Retina** displays:

  - Icon@2x.png: 114 × 114 pixels

  - Default@2x.png: 640 × 960 pixels

  - Default-568h@2x.png: 640 × 1136 pixels

If you omit the @2x variants, both PNGs will automatically be scaled up by iOS. Basically, every device that supports the retina resolution automatically looks for a file name with the suffix @2x. If such a file is not found, the standard resolution is used.

When you start the project, you should see the familiar screen from the Hello World2 example.

## 3.3.1 How Do I Create Global Variables?

Due to the variety of display dimensions, it is inadvisable to hard-code width and height in source code. Instead, you can set global variables. These must be created in Objective-C outside the implementation. We use the keyword `extern` for external access from other classes.

Listing 3.1 MainView.h

```
#import <UIKit/UIKit.h>

extern int W;
extern int H;

@interface MainView : UIView {}

@end
```

Listing 3.2 MainView.m

```
import "MainView.h"

int W = 320;//assign default values
int H = 480;

@implementation MainView

- (void) drawRect: (CGRect) rect {
    W = rect.size.width;//current dimensions of the screen
    H = rect.size.height;
    NSLog(@"W%i",W);
    ...
}

@end
```

We declare W and H outside the interface and implementation blocks, respectively, so that we can easily use the variables W and H from every class that `MainView.h` imports. Furthermore, we assign new values in the `drawRect:` method so that, in every call, we can take into account the actual current dimensions. Therefore, here W, H can be used globally, yet can be altered (even if we know already that the values will not change for our current project). To create constants, you can use `extern` together with the keyword `const`.

## ▌ 3.4  Drawing Class: Rendering Simple Forms

Let us begin with the programming of the drawing surface. Open Xcode, create a new project, and copy the MyGame project that you just created as a basis so that we have available the same classes.

Let us focus first on the `MainView` class, which provides us access to the iOS screen:

```
- (void) drawRect: (CGRect) rect {
   W = rect.size.width;
   H = rect.size.height;
}
```

So far, not much has happened: The view's `drawRect` method is called once, and it contains in the `rect` parameter the dimensions of the available drawing surface, WxH.

If we want actually to display something on the screen, we must first obtain the graphics context. It is through this that we have access to the video display and can output geometric forms, images, and text with the help of Core Graphics. Since Objective-C is built on C, a mixture with pure C code is a typical feature of iOS SDK. Even Core Graphics and Quartz 2D API are no exception; they contain many C functions, but no classes. Quartz is the name of the graphics engine on which Core Graphics is built, so both terms are often used synonymously. For reference, the "Quartz 2D Programming Guide" is recommended, which can be retrieved at *http://developer.apple.com/Mac/library/documentation/ GraphicsImaging/Conceptual/drawingwithquartz2d/Introduction/Introduction.html*.

The "Core Graphics Framework Reference" can be found at *http://developer.apple. com/iphone/library/documentation/CoreGraphics/Reference/CoreGraphics_Framework*.

We are not going to list all the possibilities of the library, but instead present exemplary applications by which you will be able to understand the API and realize your own first game ideas. We are interested in the graphics basics: lines, rectangles, circles, and the coloring of these elements.

### 3.4.1  How Do I Draw Lines?

First, a simple example: to draw a line from the top left to the bottom right using Core Graphics, you call the following code in the `drawRect:` method:

```
- (void) drawRect: (CGRect) rect {

   ...
   CGContextRef gc = UIGraphicsGetCurrentContext();
   CGContextSetRGBStrokeColor(gc, 1, 1, 1, 1);
   CGContextSetLineWidth(gc, 10.0);
   CGContextMoveToPoint(gc, 0, 0);
   CGContextAddLineToPoint(gc, W, H);
   CGContextStrokePath(gc);
}
```

Six whole lines of code, just to draw a line? That seems like a lot, but the underlying procedure is (almost) always the same:

1. Fetch the current graphics context.

2. Set the drawing color.

3. Set the line thickness.

4. Set a path.

5. Render the path to the screen with the given parameters.

First, we obtain, using the UIKit's parameterless `UIGraphicsGetCurrent` `Context()` function, a reference of type `CGContextRef`. But why do we need a reference to the current context? The answer is simple: There are several contexts that allow for drawing; for example, you could render onto an offline image that is available only in memory. (We shall see an application example later in the chapter on OpenGL ES.) At the moment, however, we want access to the display, so we fetch the currently valid screen reference. This will then be used for all subsequent operations on the relevant functions, such as, for example, the `CGContextSetRGBStrokeColor()` function, which also expects a context as its first parameter. Since the screen's default background color is black, we choose a white foreground. Core Graphics distinguishes between the fill color, which is used for filling in forms, and the stroke color:

```
CGContextSetRGBStrokeColor(CGContextRef context, CGFloat red,
    CGFloat green, CGFloat blue, CGFloat alpha)

CGContextSetRGBFillColor(CGContextRef context, CGFloat red,
    CGFloat green, CGFloat blue, CGFloat alpha)
```

For lines, of course, we use the stroke variant.

## 3.4.2  Specifying the Color and Transparency

Colors are specified using the RGB color scheme; the first parameter contains the amount of red, the second the amount of green, and the third the amount of blue. Each proportion ranges from 0.0 (0% color) to 1.0 (100% color):

```
CGContextSetRGBStrokeColor(gc, 1, 0, 0, 1);//red
CGContextSetRGBStrokeColor(gc, 0, 1, 0, 1);//green
CGContextSetRGBStrokeColor(gc, 0, 0, 1, 1);//blue
```

The last parameter behaves similarly, with a value from 0.0 (completely transparent) to 1.0 (opaque). This number is called the alpha value, and you can use it to set how transparent an object, such as a line, should be. A line with alpha value 0.5 will be semitransparent, and lines lying beneath such a line would show through where they intersect. You can imagine this parameter as the amount of paint used to draw a line: With alpha = 0.1, only a small amount of paint would be used, while alpha = 0.9 would indicate a large covering capacity, and drawings underneath such a line would be almost completely obscured.

## 3.4.3  Line Thickness

We now set the line thickness in pixels. We specify the width as being equal to 1.0 pixels with

```
CGContextSetLineWidth(gc, 1.0);
```

In our earlier example with a value of 10.0, we drew a rather thick line.

To be able to draw a line, both the initial and final points must be specified. From the point of view of Core Graphics, however, you set only the initial point and then give a command to draw a line to a subsequent point. Therefore, the call

```
CGContextMoveToPoint(gc, W/2, 0);
CGContextAddLineToPoint(gc, 0, H/2);
CGContextAddLineToPoint(gc, W, H/2);
CGContextAddLineToPoint(gc, W/2, 0);
```

draws a triangle on the screen. The drawing tool is not lifted, so to speak, and every end point becomes the next initial point.

Note, however, that so far, we have determined nothing more than a path. To fill this path with color, pixel for pixel, we need to make the following call:

```
CGContextStrokePath(gc);
```

That is, draw the path with the already specified parameters. Here, Core Graphics behaves like a finite-state machine: Each new function call changes the current state of the system. Once you set a color, this color is retained until it is overwritten by a new color.

### 3.4.4 Random Numbers and Abstract Art

With this knowledge and a `for` loop, we should already be in a position to draw a few random lines on the screen. Okay? Random numbers can be generated with the help of the function `arc4random()` from the standard library. In contrast to `random()`, this variant has the advantage that one does not have to set a starting value (seed). However, the function can return very large values, such as, for example, 1918726114. However, we can trim such numbers down to size using the modulo operator. A method that returns a random number between a lower bound (bottom) and an upper bound (top), including the bounds, can be written thusly:

```
- (int) getRndBetween: (int) bottom and: (int) top {
    int rnd = bottom + (arc4random() % (top+1-bottom));
    return rnd;
}
```

Add this method to the `MainView.m` implementation and declare it in the header:

```
@interface MainView : UIView {}

- (int) getRndBetween: (int) bottom and: (int) top;
@end
```

Now we can try it out; we call the random-number method as a test:

```
for (int i = 0; i<5; i++) {
    NSLog(@"%i", [self getRndBetween: -5 and: 5]);
}
```

The numbers returned might be something like the following:

```
2012-11-09 17:28:27.949 drawing class[1024:207] 5
2012-11-09 17:28:27.953 drawing class [1024:207] 0
```

```
2012-11-09 17:28:27.954 drawing class [1024:207] -3
2012-11-09 17:28:27.954 drawing class [1024:207] 2
2012-11-09 17:28:27.955 drawing class [1024:207] 2
```

We now need to choose a random value for every new point of the line within the visible region of the screen in order to complete our "masterpiece":

```
CGContextMoveToPoint(gc, W/2, H/2);
for (int i = 0; i<10; i++) {
    int x = [self getRndBetween: 0 and: W];
    int y = [self getRndBetween: 0 and: H];
    CGContextAddLineToPoint(gc, x, y);
}
```

Now just experiment a bit with various color and alpha values. It probably will not make you the next Picasso, but for your first venture into the world of iOS computer graphics, the results do not look all that bad.

## 3.4.5  How Do I Draw Rectangles?

In addition to lines, there are, of course, other basic forms that you can implement. In the source code, simply right-click (or Ctrl + click) on a CG... function and select "Jump to Definition." In the displayed CGContext.h you will find some available interfaces. Rectangles are declared as a design style in CGGeometry.h. These can also be displayed directly via GROUPS & FILES > FRAMEWORKS > COREGRAPHICS.FRAMEWORKS in the editor window. Rectangles are a form of structure (keyword struct) consisting of a point (origin, upper right) and a size specification (size, width × height):

```
struct CGRect {
  CGPoint origin;
  CGSize size;
};
typedef struct CGRect CGRect;
```

To render this structure to the screen, we need a special CG function:

```
void CGContextAddRect(CGContextRef c, CGRect rect);
```

By combining the two, we can render a rectangle to the screen:

```
CGRect rectangle = CGRectMake (100,100,50,50);
CGContextAddRect(gc, rectangle);
```

This draws a square of size 50 × 50 pixels at position x = 100, y = 100. As you may recall, the entire rectangle structure is passed to the drawRect: method. To color the display background, it suffices to make the following call:

```
CGContextSetRGBFillColor(gc, 1, 1, 1, 1);
CGContextAddRect(gc, rect);
CGContextDrawPath(gc, kCGPathFillStroke);
```

The function CGContextDrawPath() ensures that the fill color is accounted for by the constant kCGPathFillStroke along with the line thickness. You can therefore use this call as an alternative to `CGContextStrokePath()`. In this way, if you want to create any filled rectangles, all rectangles are drawn with the current stroke color and fill color.

Keep in mind that, in rendering with Core Graphics, every function call changes the current state. Thus, if you use the rectangle example along with the line example, a common picture will be generated from all paths. This can lead to interesting results. A call to `CGContextDrawPath(gc, kCGPathFillStroke)` is responsible, for example, for both overlapping lines and filled surfaces. You can avoid this by specifying a path through a direct call to `CGContextDrawPath(gc, kCGPathStroke)` (`kCGPathStroke` causes the lines to be drawn without the areas being filled in). It is advisable to outsource the respective drawing operations to independent methods. Moreover, you have available the functions `CGContextSaveGState()` and `CGContextRestoreGState()` for saving the current state and restoring it.

## 3.4.6 How Do I Draw Circles?

Circles and even ellipses are drawn by way of rectangles. "Now wait a moment!" you may be thinking. "How can that be?" Well, you specify a rectangle, and the function `CGContextAddEllipseInRect()` draws an ellipse that fits inside the rectangle in such a way that all four sides of the rectangle are touched. A circle is thus a special case that arises when the rectangle is a square. Since we usually want to construct a circle around its center point, we create a new method that creates a corresponding rectangle:

```
- (void) drawCircle: (int) x
                  y: (int) y
             radius: (int) radius
                 gc: (CGContextRef) gc {
   CGRect rect = CGRectMake (x-radius, y-radius, radius*2, radius*2);
   CGContextSetRGBFillColor(gc, 0,0,0,0);
   CGContextAddEllipseInRect(gc, rect);
}
```

We then call the method as follows:

```
[self drawCircle: 100 y:200 radius: 50 gc: gc];
```

We therefore pass the already retrieved graphics context `gc` as well as the radius and the xy-coordinates where the center of the circle is to be placed. It is of interest that we again specify the fill color with an alpha value of 0; we thereby overwrite the already set background color of the current state and ensure that the circle will be drawn unfilled. In subsequent graphics operations, we must then, of course, keep in mind that the fill color must be adjusted as needed in each case.*

---

* Core Graphics also offers numerous additional functions. For example, graphics can be output in a tiled fashion, an effect that is reminiscent of a tile map for game backgrounds. You can also create color gradients with alpha effects, and so on. You can obtain a good overview of all this in the example program "QuartzDemo" from Apple, available in the Apple Dev Center: *http://developer.apple.com/iphone/library/ samplecode/QuartzDemo/Introduction/Intro.html.*

### 3.4.7 Text Output (Fonts and Type Size)

For our Hello World example, we have seen how we can render texts to the screen:

```
CGContextSetRGBFillColor(gc, 1, 1, 1, 1);
NSString *str = @"Drawing Course";
UIFont *uif = [UIFont systemFontOfSize: 40];
[str drawAtPoint:CGPointMake(10, 10) withFont: uif];
```

The font color is not determined by the stroke color, but rather by the fill color. To render a string, we do not access the Core Graphics API, but instead use the UIFont class of the UIKit, which is easier to handle. As you can see in the example, the class also encapsulates access to a number of different fonts. In this case, we use only the system fonts together with a size specification. The render procedure is then taken over by the drawAtPoint:withFont: method of the NSString object.

To choose another font, call the class method fontWithName:size: of the UIFont class. For example:

```
UIFont *uif = [UIFont fontWithName:@"Verdana-Italic" size: 40];

//type style: Verdana, italic
```

The method expects predefined strings for the type style. An overview of available type styles can be found at *http://ajnaware.wordpress.com/2008/10/24/ list-of-fonts-available-on-the-iphone.*

Here are some additional available parameters:

```
@"Arial"
@"Arial-BoldMT"
@"Arial-ItalicMT"
@"Arial-BoldItalicMT"
@"Verdana"
@"Verdana-Bold"
@"Verdana-Italic"
@"Verdana-BoldItalic"
```

## ▌ 3.5 Integrating, Loading, and Displaying Images

Core Graphics also offers an interface for images and bitmap graphics. In practice, however, it is more usual to use—just as with fonts—the counterpart of the UIKit: UIImage.

Since with images we are dealing with external resources, we must first integrate them into our Xcode project. But first, where do we obtain suitable graphics for our game project?

If you do not happen to have a graphic designer for a friend, the creation of professional graphics can quickly become more expensive than the rest of the development. But you can make a virtue of necessity. The so-called scribble games have meanwhile obtained their own category in iTunes: games that look as though they were conceived during a boring class at school. A well-known example is *Doodle Jump.*

If you have more time and leisure, you can create your own pixel graphics using a drawing program such as Pixen, Gimp, or Photoshop. The iPhone supports alpha blending,

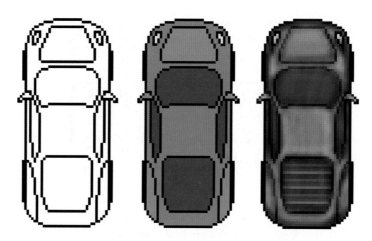

**Figure 3.2** Development of a car: first the outline, then the surface color, and finally the addition of a gradient.

so even with small graphics, clean straight lines can be created, with shadow effects on the edges. However, developers frequently eschew such effects in order to create a pixelated style reminiscent of the great classics from the Nintendo era.[*]

Typically, the development of a game graphic begins with the outline, as shown in Figure 3.2. The areas are filled in with a single color, using the filling tool and then finally given graded light effects to give the object more depth. Then there follows some fine-tuning as desired using feathering and wiping effects in your graphics program. Frequently, graphic artists also implement graphics pads.[†]

In order to avoid unnecessary cropping, you should create your graphics on a fully transparent background. The preferred format for iPhone game development is PNG with 24-bit color depth (RGB plus alpha).

Once the images are finished and ready for deployment, displaying them on the screen is as simple as rendering geometric forms; it is done directly in the view's `draw-Rect:` method. But first the graphics must be included in the Xcode project.

For the following example, we have created a new project based on the MyGame template. As always, it can be found in the download folder. It consists of the obligatory app delegate and a new class.

We recolor the car example given previously in Photoshop with the hue/saturation tool, obtaining three different color variants (`car_blue.png`, `car_green.png`, `car_red.png`) (Figure 3.3).

---

[*] Those interested in 8-bit style graphics can find inspiration in the book *Character Design for Mobile Devices*, by Lawrence Wright (NFGMan).

[†] Tip: True to the motto "there is an app for almost everything," you can turn your iPad into a graphics pad. The App Store is full of drawing programs, such as the free software Adobe Ideas, which is easy to use and lets you draw outlines for game graphics with your finger. The results can be exported later—for example, to Photoshop—for further refinement. Similar functions, but designed especially for working with pixels, are offered by such apps as DotEDITOR and C64 Paint XL. Apple recommends the following graphics tools: *http://itunes.apple.com/WebObjects/MZStore.woa/wa/viewRoom?fcId=363454307.*

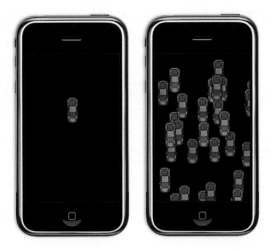

Figure 3.3 Left: car_blue.png in the iPhone simulator; right: randomly generated fleet of cars.

As you already know, resources and hence graphics must be included in the Xcode project. In order to store all the project's resources together with your project, it is advisable to copy the three PNGs into the project folder. In Xcode, you can now create an extra graphics folder or else include the images in the already existing "Resources" folder. To include the graphics as *already existing,* right-click on ADD FILES. The check under "Destination" should remain disabled.

Next, the graphics in the left-hand Groups & Files sidebar appear and are displayed in Xcode's own preview. Within Xcode, it does not matter in what folder you place the images. The iPhone OS looks for the images on its own within the resource bundle.

To bring the graphics to the display, we use the UIImage class of the UIKit. Add the following code to the drawRect: method:

```
- (void) drawRect: (CGRect) rect {
    @try {
        UIImage *carBlueImage = [UIImage imageNamed: @"car_blue.png"];
        [carBlueImage drawAtPoint: CGPointMake(140, 140)];
    }
    @catch (id theException) {
        NSLog(@"ERROR: image not found.");
    }
}
```

Now that was not so hard, was it? The UIImage class offers in imageNamed a class method that performs initialization based on the image name. As you can see, no path name is required. The display on the view takes place easily via the drawAt-Point: method, which expects a CGPoint structure as point. When you execute the code, the image is loaded via the imageNamed: method and displayed at position x = 140, y = 140.

To catch errors, you can add a try-catch statement to the code—just to be on the safe side.

### 3.5.1 One, Two, Three, Four: Can We Make a Lot More?

Now let us make a whole fleet of cars. Once you have created a UIImage instance, you can use that image as often as you like:

```
UIImage *carRedImage = [UIImage imageNamed: @"car_red.png"];
UIImage *carGreenImage = [UIImage imageNamed: @"car_green.png"];
for (int i = 0; i<10; i++) {
    int x, y;
    x = [self getRndBetween: 0 and: W];
    y = [self getRndBetween: 0 and: H];
    [carBlueImage drawAtPoint: CGPointMake(x, y)];
    x = [self getRndBetween: 0 and: W];
    y = [self getRndBetween: 0 and: H];
    [carRedImage drawAtPoint: CGPointMake(x, y)];
    x = [self getRndBetween: 0 and: W];
    y = [self getRndBetween: 0 and: H];
    [carGreenImage drawAtPoint: CGPointMake(x, y)];
}
```

After we have loaded two additional images, we use the getRndBetween:and: method from the previous chapter to generate random screen coordinates. In the for loop, we render the respective car instances via their drawAtPoint: method at a random position. As you can see, the method can be called as often as necessary, each time displaying a graphic in the view.

Furthermore, the UIImage class offers us the possibility of querying the dimensions of an already loaded image:

```
int picW = carBlueImage.size.width;
int picH = carBlueImage.size.height;
NSLog(@"dimsensions Pic:%ix%i", picW, picH);
```

The image will generally be rendered in its original size. However, using the drawIn-Rect: method, you can scale it, for example, by a factor of 2 (Figure 3.4):

```
//scale graphic
[carBlueImage drawInRect: CGRectMake(120, 250, picW*2, picH*2)];
```

Figure 3.4 A car enlarged and cars twice superimposed (upper left).

The graphic is thereby scaled so that it fills the given rectangle. (PNG graphics have a rectangular form as their basis, even if the transparent areas conceal this fact.)

Similarly, images can be transparently superimposed. There are variants of both the `drawAtPoint:` and `drawInRect:` methods for which an additional alpha value and constant for the blend effect can be given (here: `kCGBlendModeNormal`):

```
//display graphic transparently
[carBlueImage drawAtPoint: CGPointMake(40, 140)
              blendMode: kCGBlendModeNormal
                  alpha: 0.4];
[carBlueImage drawAtPoint: CGPointMake(25, 125)
              blendMode: kCGBlendModeNormal
                  alpha: 0.4];
```

Since the graphic is positioned with a slight offset, the image below can be seen through the upper one.

The `UIImage` class does not, unfortunately, offer direct support for rotations. However, with a few tricks, this can be accomplished.

First, we declare that we are going to outsource the code into its own method, which is done as follows:

```
- (void) rotateImage: (NSString*) picName
                  x: (int) x
                  y: (int) y
              angle: (int) a;
```

The method expects the name of an image, the xy-coordinates at which the upper left-hand corner is to be drawn, and the angle in degrees (0° to 360°) by which the graphic is to be rotated about its center.

Since angles for computer graphics are frequently given in radians, we provide two auxiliary methods for converting between degrees and radians:

```
- (float) getRad: (float) Deg {
    float rad = (M_PI/180) * deg;
    return rad;
}

- (float) getDeg: (float) rad {
    float deg = (180/M_PI) * rad;
    return deg;
}
```

We shall use the `getRad:` method. We have added its counterpart only for the sake of completeness. As you may remember from school, 180° corresponds to pi radians:

```
float pi = [self getRad: 180];
```

Converted to radians, 180° yields pi. As can be seen in the implementations of the methods, we have available through the BSD library (a C library that forms a part of Core OS) a pi constant in the form of `M_PI`, declared in `math.h` together with other mathematical functions, such as the sine `sin()`, cosine `cos()`, logarithm `log()`, and rounding down `floor()`.

We realize the rotation of an image in a roundabout way. Instead of rotating the figure, we rotate the entire coordinate system. For this we rely on Core Graphics. Since we have just seen that Core Graphics operates like a finite-state machine, we must be careful: Once the coordinate system has been rotated, all subsequent drawing operations will be influenced by this. Imagine a piece of paper on which you are drawing rectangles and now rotate the paper about the upper left-hand corner. If you now draw again on the paper, despite its oblique position, you will probably orient your drawing to the lower edge of the figure.

So that subsequent drawings remain unaffected by the rotation, we must restore the coordinate system to the original position and restore the previous state. Core Graphics offers the following functions for rotating the coordinate system and storing the state of the system:

```
- void CGContextSaveGState(CGContextRef c)
- void CGContextRestoreGState(CGContextRef c)
- void CGContextRotateCTM(CGContextRef c, CGFloat angle)
- void CGContextTranslateCTM(CGContextRef c, CGFloat tx, CGFloat ty)
```

Since rotations of the coordinate system take place about the origin (top left-hand corner of the display), we also need a translate function to center the object at this origin since, normally, our object is located somewhere on the screen and is not centered at the position x = 0, y = 0.

Both rotation and translation relate to the (*current transformation matrix: CTM*). The parameters tx and ty specify the number of pixels by which the origin should be translated.

With this knowledge, we can develop an algorithm that allows us to rotate any graphic that is to be drawn at the point x, y:

```
- (void) rotateImage: (NSString*) picName
                  x: (int) x
                  y: (int) y
              angle: (int) a {

    UIImage *pic = [UIImage imageNamed: picName];

    if (pic) {
        int w = pic.size.width;
        int h = pic.size.height;

        //1. save current graphics context
        CGContextRef ctx = UIGraphicsGetCurrentContext();
        CGContextSaveGState(ctx);

        //2. new coordinate origin: x+w/2, y+h/2
        CGContextTranslateCTM(ctx, x+w/2, y+h/2);

        //3. rotate coordinate system
        CGContextRotateCTM(ctx, [self getRad: a]);

        //4. render grahpic at position 0-w/2, 0-h/2
        [pic drawAtPoint: CGPointMake(0-w/2, 0-h/2)];

        //5. restore previous graphics context
        CGContextRestoreGState(ctx);
    }
}
```

The purpose of this method is to rotate the graphic about its center. Therefore, we first require the dimensions of the picture (w, h). We then store the current graphics context. This allows us to switch to any other coordinate system. We know that rotation takes place about the point 0, 0, and therefore we translate the origin using the translate method to the midpoint of the graphic (with respect to the old coordinate system). Now we can rotate to our heart's content and render the image. However, at the location of the new coordinate origin, the figure will be drawn with 0-w/2, 0-h/2 centered at the new origin, which also corresponds to the originally intended position on the display, though with other coordinates (see Translate). We have now only to restore the old graphics context and then the origin is again located in the upper left-hand corner. Thus, the coordinates of the rotated image again agree. We stuff the whole procedure inside an if statement:

```
if (pic) {
    ...
}
```

If the image name that is passed is not found, the UIImage image will be initialized with the value nil, and we can therefore check for true or false (nil corresponds to the Boolean truth value false).

To call the method, we place the following for loop in the drawRect: method of the view and use it to create 20 randomly rotated cars (Figure 3.5):

```
for (int i = 0; i<20; i++) {
    [self rotateImage: @"car_green.png"
                    x: [self getRndBetween: 0 and: W]
                    y: [self getRndBetween: 0 and: W]
                angle: [self getRndBetween: 0 and: 360]];
}
```

Since the rotation takes place via a detour of the coordinate system (the graphic itself is not rotated), you can rotate other elements using this same principle, such as text and geometric figures.

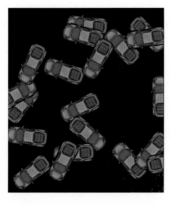

Figure 3.5 Randomly rotated cars.

## 3.6 The Game Loop and Frames—Bringing Pictures to Life

The game loop forms the heart and pacemaker of every game, seeing to it that the individual game objects (players, adversaries, objects, background, etc.) seem to be in motion. The principle is similar to that of a movie projector. We say that a film "runs," though it is actually the reel that is doing the running. The film itself consists of a series of still images. Motion arises from the fact that the individual frames are projected in rapid succession. To achieve the illusion of motion, the human eye requires a rate of 33 frames per second (FPS).

For the required 33 FPS to be achieved, certain concessions have to be made in the game design. Too many adversaries or complex animations can drag down the frame rate, and the game begins to stutter.

There are various techniques for implementing a stably running game loop. The most important task consists in displaying the frames as much as possible at regular intervals. In contrast to film, the motion of a game does not come out of a "can," but instead is generated frame by frame during the game. A frame corresponds to what is brought to the display in the `drawRect:` method of the current view. Time-based game loops calculate the time needed for the rendering process at each run through the loop and adjust the motions of the game figures accordingly. In this way, the distances between pixels remain the same, regardless of whether the game is played on a very fast or very slow system. However, the motion is not necessarily smooth; it depends on the execution speed. Such variations are unacceptable for fast action games. In practice, one therefore prefers a frame-based variant. If the game is running too slowly, the frame rate decreases; however, the mechanics of the game per frame remain the same and therefore the game is consistent from platform to platform. Porting to slow systems will in some cases require adjustments to the game design (fewer background graphics, no alpha shadows, etc.).

The iOS SDK offers two different timer classes that make possible the consistent calling of the `drawRect:` method:

- `NSTimer`: available with all iOS versions

- `CADisplayLink`: since iOS 3.1, a component of the QuartzCore framework

The use of the `CADisplayLink` class is recommended by Apple; it offers enhanced performance. However, it is unavailable in older iOS versions. Let us therefore begin by looking at the `NSTimer` variant. Based on the MyGame project, let us create a new project called "GameLoop."

We add the following method to the delegate class.

Listing 3.3 MyGameAppDelegate.m

```
- (void) startGameLoop {
    timer = [NSTimer scheduledTimerWithTimeInterval: 0.0303//33 FPS
                                            target: self
                                          selector: @selector(loop)
```

```
                                   userInfo: nil
                                   repeats: YES];
    }

    - (void) stopGameLoop {
        [timer invalidate];
        timer = nil;
    }
    - (void) loop {
        [mainView setNeedsDisplay];
    }

    - (void) applicationDidBecomeActive: (UIApplication *) application {
        [self startGameLoop];
    }

    - (void) applicationWillResignActive: (UIApplication *) application {
        [self stopGameLoop];
    }

    - (void) dealloc {
        [self stopGameLoop];
        [timer release];
        //...
    }
```

That does it. The game loop is now complete. We have declared the `timer` instance in the header with

```
id timer;
```

(instead of via `NSTimer *timer;` since later we shall initialize the `timer` instance depending on the iOS version based on another class). The second peculiarity is that with

```
mainView.backgroundColor = [UIColor grayColor];
```

we explicitly set a background color for the view. If you omit this statement, the view will not be completely redrawn on each new call so that moving graphics can form streaks. However, if the view has a background color, then the surface that the view occupies is colored from scratch on every rendering procedure, as if we were standing before a completely blank canvas on which we may draw our game (independently of the previous frame). In this case, we choose, however, the color gray instead of the color white, which can be specified directly with the `UIColor` class.

We now come to the actual game loop. As you already know, the game flow can be interrupted by a telephone call. To keep the game from running in the background, we implement the life-cycle methods to start and stop the game:

```
applicationDidBecomeActive:
applicationWillResignActive:
```

As you can see, to start, it suffices to initialize the timer object:

```
timer = [NSTimer scheduledTimerWithTimeInterval: 0.0303//33 FPS
                                        target: self
                                      selector: @selector(loop)
                                      userInfo: nil
                                       repeats: YES];
```

This "fires" a call to the class instance specified under `target`—in this case, the delegate class. The message is set via a selector directive; we specify here that the `loop:` method of the delegate class is to be called—and indeed interrupted—33 times per second. This value is specified as a `double` value (more precisely: `NSTimeInterval`) in seconds $1/33 = 0.0303$. We may ignore the parameter `userInfo`. Moreover, if you want to measure the actual time that is needed for the execution of the render procedure, you can do this using the system time, which is the time in milliseconds that has passed since the beginning of the computer age on January 1, 1970:

```
double startTime = [[NSDate date] timeIntervalSince1970];
//render
double endTime = [[NSDate date] timeIntervalSince1970];
```

If you now form the difference between `startTime` and `endTime`, you obtain the actual execution speed. For example, you could issue a warning if this value exceeds 33 FPS.

To stop the timer, we call the `invalidate` method and set the instance to `nil`. Done. The actual rendering takes place in the `loop:` method, which via the following informs our main view that this should be redrawn and that the `drawRect:` method should be called:

```
[mainView setNeedsDisplay];
```

To verify that the game loop works as expected, we specify in the `drawRect:` method how often it is called and let a car drive from top to bottom with a speed of three pixels per frame:

```
- (void) drawRect: (CGRect) rect {
    W = rect.size.width;
    H = rect.size.height;

    static int cnt = 0;
    cnt++;
    NSLog(@"Game Loop:%i", cnt);

    if (!carBlueImage) {
        carBlueImage = [UIImage imageNamed: @"car_blue.png"];
    }

    static int y = 0;
    y += 3;
    if (y > H) y = -100;
    [carBlueImage drawAtPoint: CGPointMake(W/2, y)];
}
```

This time, we have declared the graphic in the header using `UIImage *carBlueImage;`. If the variable `carBlueImage` has not yet been initialized, we load it

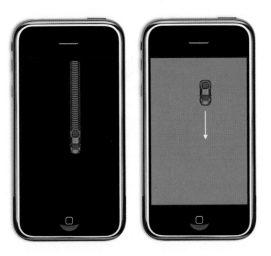

**Figure 3.6** Left: streaking, because the background color (`mainView.backgroundColor`) was not set; right: a clean drawing surface.

via the `imageNamed:` method and then render the graphic via `drawAtPoint:`. As you can see, we have increased the y-coordinate of the car by three. If y is greater than the height of the display, we reset the value, and the car again travels from top to bottom (Figure 3.6).

To avoid having to declare the y-variable in the header, we have implemented the `static` keyword with the `cnt` variable.

This means that we can declare the variable once within the method. When the method is called, the line is ignored (the variable has already been initialized as static), and we can use the variable like an instance variable. A practical solution!

With regard to the `cnt` variable, you can see in the debug console that the game loop is called several times a second.

All that remains is the implementation of the `CADisplayLink` variant, which provides additional performance stability. Since the class behaves similarly to the `NSTimer` variant, we have only to adapt the `startGameLoop:` method:

```
- (void) startGameLoop {
    NSString *deviceOS = [[UIDevice currentDevice] systemVersion];
    //33 frames per second -> time step between the frames = 1/33
    NSTimeInterval fpsDelta = 0.0303;

    if ([deviceOS compare: @"3.1"
                  options: NSNumericSearch] = = NSOrderedAscending) {
        timer = [NSTimer scheduledTimerWithTimeInterval: fpsDelta
                                                 target: self
                                               selector: @selector(loop)
                                               userInfo: nil
                                                repeats: YES];
    } else {
        int frameLink = 2;
        timer = [NSClassFromString(@"CADisplayLink")
            displayLinkWithTarget: self selector: @selector(loop)];
            [timer setFrameInterval: frameLink];
        [timer addToRunLoop: [NSRunLoop currentRunLoop]
```

```
                    forMode: NSDefaultRunLoopMode];
    }

    NSLog(@"Game Loop timer instance:%@", timer);
}
```

Depending on the iOS version number, we branch for older systems to the NSTimer variant. Starting with iOS 3.1, however, the CADisplayLink class is available and can be used. If you launch the code in the 3.0 simulator, you can see in the NSLog output that the NSTimer instance is being used. The compiler warnings that appear when the 3.0 simulator is used show that we have done everything correctly; the else part is not allowed to execute. Moreover, we have declared the timer variable to be of type id and thus can determine the class type dynamically. Had we declared the variable of type CADisplayLink, the compiler would have protested.

Since the CADisplayLink class is part of the QuartzCore framework, we must add it in the project settings and the build settings via "Link Binary With Libraries." If you want to verify the path, it is */Developer/Platforms/iPhoneOS.platform/Developer/SDKs/ iPhoneOSXX.sdk/System/Library/Frameworks/QuartzCore.framework*.

Here, XX stands for the SDK version—for example, 3.2 or 5.0. To use the framework, you just need to make this known in the header of the delegate class via

```
#import <QuartzCore/QuartzCore.h>
```

Since the framework is available here for all iOS versions, you should have nothing to worry about.

For reasons of compatibility, the initialization of the CADisplayLink class is done by the NSClassFromString() initializer. Then, as previously, we set the target class and the method to be called via the selector directive. We specify the interval directly and add the timer instance to the NSRunLoop pool. As before, the loop is stopped via an invalidate message.

The advantage of the CADisplayLink class is that it is better linked to the display and therefore represents for us a useful special case, since we want eventually to render the view. For non-display-related timer tasks, in contrast, we can continue to use the NSTimer class. However, this almost never arises in game programming, since the game and, with it, all the elements that are brought to the screen always move in time with the pacemaker (= game loop).

The implementation shown here can be used for all devices of the iPhone platform. Nevertheless, you should note that the dynamic assignment of the timer instance can result in performance differences (the NSTimer variant works somewhat more slowly for some iOS target devices). Therefore, you should be sure to test both versions. On the other hand, you could, of course, simply decide on a single variant. Then, NSTimer would be the universal solution to ensure that the game runs the same on all iOS devices. If you rely solely on the CADisplayLink class, you would force users with older devices to update their iPhone iOS.

Note also that the CADisplayLink variant is sensitive to NSLog calls and can react with a slight stutter. On the other hand, the NSTimer method is, as a rule, somewhat more immune. Since in this book we have a pedagogical agenda and will frequently make use of NSLog console output to trace program execution (we assume that you are executing the examples in debug mode with an attached USB cable), in most of the following examples we shall force the use of the NSTimer variant through the use of a *flag*:

```
bool forceTimerVariant = TRUE;
if (forceTimerVariant || [deviceOS compare: @"3.1"

    options: NSNumericSearch] = = NSOrderedAscending) {
//use NSTimer
} else {
     //use CADisplayLink
}
```

You have only to set the flag forceTimerVariante to FALSE in order to try out both variants according to the iOS.

## ■ 3.7 Clipping and Animation

We have seen how to move a graphic on the display. But what do we do when the graphic itself is to be animated—for example, a game character walking across the screen?

Imagine a flip book. Each page contains a different picture, with the sequence of motion divided into segments that are flipped before your eyes in sequence. This is precisely the principle that we wish to implement. In game programming, it has become common to place the individual images for an animation sequence in a single image file. As an example for this chapter, we have created a small walking zombie in bird's-eye view (Figure 3.7).

The animation consists of four frames. The left and right arms of the pixel zombie are alternately moved forward and backward together with the opposite foot, to represent a walking motion. Every frame is drawn from the upper left-hand corner. To awaken a zombie on the iPhone screen, we must accomplish two things:

1. **Clipping:** Each frame must be cut out in turn from the four-frame film strip. We can do this at runtime using clipping. We shall discuss this shortly.

2. **Find the appropriate frame number:** Why this? Well, the animation must be played in a loop in order to give the impression of continuous motion. The frames should *not* be displayed at the playback speed of 33 frames per second as clocked by the game loop. The resulting motion would be much too fast and scarcely visible. (It would be how Superman might run!) We must ensure that the frames

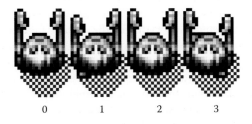

0    1    2    3

Figure 3.7 The graphic "zombie_4f.png" with four frames.

are played back in "slow motion." The aim would be, for example, the following variant:

```
Frame 0: Zombie-Frame 0
Frame 1: Zombie-Frame 0
Frame 2: Zombie-Frame 0
Frame 3: Zombie-Frame 1
Frame 4: Zombie-Frame 1
Frame 5: Zombie-Frame 1
etc.
```

Each frame is displayed for a longer period of time or, in other words, the passage from one zombie frame to the next takes place more slowly than the frame rate of the game loop. In the preceding example, the zombie frame is displayed three times before it is changed. Thus, the first frame remains visible for three frames of the game loop before the next segment of the motion is displayed.

A "frameStep" of five frames would look something like the following:

```
00000, 11111, 22222, 33333, 00000, 11111, 22222, etc.
```

Such a sequence of numbers can be obtained easily through a simple counter.

```
int cnt;       //internal counter
int frameNr;   //current frame
int frameCnt;  //number of frames in the film strip
int frameStep; //number of frames per iteration

- (int) updateFrame {
    if (frameStep ! = 0) {
        if (frameStep = = cnt) {
            cnt = 0;
            frameNr++;
            if (frameNr > frameCnt-1) {
                frameNr = 0;
                cycleCnt++;
            }
        }
        cnt++;
    }
    return frameNr;
}
```

This auxiliary method is called at each game-loop frame, and it returns the current frame number `frameNr`. The member variable `cnt` acts as a counter, which is increased until the last frame is reached: `frameCnt-1`. It is then reset to 0. With the `if` query, we check whether the internal counter has attained the value of `frameStep`, which specifies how often a graphic should be displayed without change. Finally, the method returns to us the current `frameNr`.

You can see that the desired number sequence is very easy to realize algorithmically: The speed at which a motion sequence runs is generally not accurate to the millisecond. Instead, it suffices to specify the frame step; the minimal value of 1 corresponds to the fastest possible sequence and is synchronized to the tempo of the game loop. For each frame of the game loop, one frame of the motion sequence is displayed. The larger the value of frameStep that is chosen, the more slowly the animation runs. It generally suffices to experiment with this value and simply choose the one that comes closest to the desired result. If you want to determine the time between the sequence steps more precisely, you can do this on the basis of the speed of the game loop: at 33 FPS and frameStep = 33, a new image of the film strip is displayed every second or represented by itself via clipping, with 66 frameSteps every 2 seconds, and so on.

But how does this technique called clipping work? As in so many cases, we achieve our desired result via a short detour. The goal here is to use clipping to "cut out" parts of the image in the form of a rectangle from a given image and to render them to the display. Core Graphics contains the CGContextClipToRect() function:

```
void CGContextClipToRect(CGContextRef c, CGRect rect)
```

This function expects a graphics context and a rectangle structure (x, y, width, height), by which the extent of the screen can be specified that should be reserved for subsequent drawing operations. The cutting out of a frame from our four-frame zombie film strip is done by means of a small trick:

```
UIImage *pic; //film strip with frames
CGPoint pos;  //current position

- (void) drawFrame {
    int picW = pic.size.width;
    int frameW = picW/frameCnt;
    int frameH = pic.size.height;

    frameNr = [self updateFrame];

    CGContextRef ctx = UIGraphicsGetCurrentContext();
    CGContextSaveGState(ctx);

    pos.x = rintf(pos.x);

    CGContextClipToRect(ctx, CGRectMake(pos.x, pos.y, frameW, frameH));
    [pic drawAtPoint: CGPointMake(pos.x-frameNr*frameW, pos.y)];

    CGContextRestoreGState(ctx);
}
```

The preceding code segment assumes the existence of a UIImage named pic. Later, we will introduce the associated class. Since the function CGContextClipToRect() clips a region from the current graphics context, we employ CG-ContextSaveGState(ctx) before the call to save the current state and then restore it on completion of the rendering process using CGContextRestoreGState(ctx). Of interest here are the rectangular section that is to be clipped and the position at which the frame is to be displayed. Let us examine the parameters.

The reserved screen area using clipping comprises the following:

- pos.x, pos.y is the current position of the zombie. Just as with a single image, this is with respect to the upper left-hand corner. Since we wish to give the clipping region to pixel accuracy, we round the x-position up or down to an integer in advance of using the function rintf(). In any case, the rendering position must consist of integer values, since there are no fractions of a pixel.

- `frameW` is the actual width of the zombie. Since we have arranged all the motion sequences of the zombie animation horizontally, as in a strip of film, we can determine the width of a zombie frame from the total number of frames—in our case, four.

- `frameH`, the height of the image section, is the height of the film strip, since we have arranged the sequence horizontally.

This means, then, that we will make only enough space on our drawing surface for a zombie. Now we have to position our film strip in such a way that, by clipping, the permitted screen area is congruent with the desired segment of the film strip:

- x-position of the film strip: `pos.x-frameNr*frameW`

- y-position of the film strip: `pos.y`

The y-position is the position of the zombie, which is logical since we have only frames that are arranged horizontally. We translate the x-position of the film strip to the left according to the exact number of frames that are located to the left of the desired segment (`frameNr*frameW`). If we wished to display the first zombie, we would have the following:

- x-position of the film strip: `pos.x-0*frameW = > pos.x`

For the last frame we would have:

- x-position of the film strip: `pos.x-3*frameW`

Thus, the position can be easily determined from the width of a frame and the frame number.

In order that subsequent drawing operations have the entire screen area available, we end by restoring the old state of the graphics context using `CGContextRestore GState(ctx)`.

The clipping function is very forgiving. If you draw outside the clipping region, the rendering process is ignored. One can imagine that the permitted screen area for drawing operations coincides with the clipping region: Everything drawn in this region is visible, but nothing else. Sections of the clipping region that lie outside the visible screen region or the viewport have no effect, but they are nonetheless permitted. The clipped region is always rectangular, and graphics lying outside it are "cut off" at the borders of the region. We have often made use of this effect in animation. In principle, you could use the clipping operation to reduce the size of the available screen region, with the difference that the region lying outside remains visible, of course, only if the clipping region is smaller than the screen region.

## 3.7.1 Clipping and Tiles

Especially on smaller displays, the space available for a game is often insufficient, and the background must be scrolled. If you have in mind the construction of particularly large game worlds, you can assemble the game's background from individual tiles. If the tiles are small—say, various background textures each of 24 × 24 pixels—then these can be arranged as in a film strip, and the relevant tile can be cut out using the clipping technique. For more complex textures—for example, a labyrinth with insurmountable walls—you can identify the game elements by referring to their tile number. To assemble such game worlds, one classically uses level editors, such as the well-known program Tile-Studio from GameBoy development, which identifies the tiles by means of a tile film strip.

Another advantage of tile-based level design is the savings in memory, since no large-area images have to be loaded. However, in developing for the iPhone and particularly for the iPad, there is generally enough working memory available, and the display also offers enough space that scrollable backgrounds are unnecessary. This means greater clarity and touch control that is easier to use. Just think about such successful titles as *Fieldrunners* (Subatomic Studios) and *Flight Control* (Firemint).

## 3.7.2  Creating Sprites

After these theoretical considerations, it is again time for another practical example. Beginning with our basic game loop framework, we shall create a new project and call it "Animation." As always, this can be found in the examples folder and can be downloaded from the website.

Since we have already seen that several variables are necessary for the animation of a game object (including the current frame number and the number of steps per frame), it makes sense to use a special class for this purpose. Moving and/or animated game objects such as our little pixel zombies are known as "sprites" in the game-programming world.

All right, then! Create one now by right-clicking on the classes folder and adding a new Objective-C class via ADD > NEW FILE. Give it the name "Sprite" and modify its header as follows.

Listing 3.4  Sprite.h

```
#import <UIKit/UIKit.h>

@interface Sprite : NSObject {
    UIImage *pic;     //film strip with frames
    CGPoint speed;    //pixel velocity per frame in the xy-direction
    CGPoint pos;      //current position
    int cnt;          //internal counter
    int frameNr;      //current frame
    int frameCnt;     //number of frames in the film strip
    int frameStep;    //number of frames per iteration
}

-(id) initWithPic: (NSString *) picName
        frameCnt: (int) fcnt
       frameStep: (int) fstp
           speed: (CGPoint) sxy
             pos: (CGPoint) pxy;
-(void) draw;
-(void) drawFrame;
-(int) updateFrame;

@end
```

Every sprite should have its own film strip, which we call simply "pic." Thus, each sprite has an xy-screen position, which we will maintain in a CGPoint structure and actualize at runtime. Similarly, we use the speed variable to specify how fast a sprite should move across the screen. We shall look at this more closely in a moment. The remaining members of the class should look familiar to you; they relate to the animation of the sprite.

Also, two of the four method signatures should be familiar.

- Our sprite must be initialized with individual values, and for this we set up the method initWithPic:frameCnt:frameStep:speed:pos: as a constructor taking five parameters whose properties determine a sprite: (1) the image to be used in the form of a film strip (picName), (2) the number of frames contained in a filmstrip (framCnt), (3) the speed of the animation frameStep, (4) the sprite's speed (speed), and (5) the current position with respect to the upper left-hand corner of a frame (pos).

- The draw method takes care of rendering the sprite; it calls the drawFrame method, which in turn retrieves the current frame number via the auxiliary method updateFrame.

Listing 3.5 Sprite.m

```
#import "Sprite.h"

@implementation Sprite

-(id) initWithPic: (NSString *) picName
        frameCnt: (int) fcnt
       frameStep: (int) fstp
           speed: (CGPoint) sxy
             pos: (CGPoint) pxy {

    if (self = [super init]) {
        pic = [UIImage imageNamed: picName];
        speed = sxy;
        pos = pxy;
        cnt = 0;
        frameNr = 0;
        frameCnt = fcnt;
        frameStep = fstp;
    }

    return self;
}

- (void) draw {
    pos.x+ = speed.x;
    pos.y+ = speed.y;
    [self drawFrame];
}

- (void) drawFrame {
    int picW = pic.size.width;
```

```
        int frameW = picW/frameCnt;
        int frameH = pic.size.height;

        frameNr = [self updateFrame];
        NSLog(@"frameNr:%i", frameNr);

        CGContextRef ctx = UIGraphicsGetCurrentContext();
        CGContextSaveGState(ctx);

        pos.x = rintf(pos.x);

        CGContextClipToRect(ctx, CGRectMake(pos.x, pos.y, frameW,
            frameH));
        [pic drawAtPoint: CGPointMake(pos.x-frameNr*frameW, pos.y)];

        CGContextRestoreGState(ctx);
}

- (int) updateFrame {
    if (frameStep = = cnt) {
        cnt = 0;
        frameNr++;
        if (frameNr > frameCnt-1) {
            frameNr = 0;
        }
    }
    cnt++;
    return frameNr;
}

-(void) dealloc {
    [pic release];
    [super dealloc];
}

@end
```

The implementation contains no surprises. We adopt drawFrame and update-Frame unchanged. The init method assigns the passed values to the members as expected and calls the init method of the parent class NSObject with

```
if (self = [super init]) {
    . . .
}
```

Since we have to allocate the sprite (just like any other object), we return an object instance with return self and, in fact, as you can see from the signature, as a generic object type id. This is a usual approach in Objective-C and makes possible a more dynamic manipulation of objects.

Finally, in the draw method, the object is positioned according to the speed structure:

```
        pos.x+ = speed.x;
        pos.y+ = speed.y;
```

- **speed.x** determines the pixel distance along the x-axis that is to be specified at each call. Positive values move the sprite to the right, while negative values move it to the left.

- **speed.y** gives the pixel speed with respect to the y-axis. Positive values move the sprite in the downward direction, while negative values let it move upward.

With `CGPointMake(0, -2)` we can create a point structure. Since the x-value is equal to 0 and we have y = –2, the object moves upward with a velocity of 2 pixels per frame if we call the `draw` method for every frame. A call to `CGPointMake(-3, -3)` would make the sprite walk diagonally up and to the left.

The function `CGPointMake()` conveniently expects parameters of type `CGFloat`. If your zombie is still too fast at 1 pixel per frame, you can slow him or her down with values between –1 and 0, for example, with `CGPointMake(0, -0.5)`.

You see, every `Sprite` object moves forward independently. Therefore, within the `draw` method you can also check for collisions with obstacles or with other sprites. While Core Animation for UI elements is a great help in setting up user interfaces, in game development a similarity to the real world carries more weight. Once created, you can let sprites loose in their game world and allow them to analyze their surroundings at each step with a certain degree of artificial intelligence. A player who encounters a gold coin can pick it up, a barricade forces a change in direction, an adversary will be automatically attacked, etc. Therefore, for the movement of sprites, it is advisable to encapsulate the movement algorithm within the object. As soon as the sprite is awakened and becomes alive, it looks after itself, so to speak. A very practical sort of parenting, do you not agree?

And now back to our `Sprite` class. Before we can use it, we have to integrate `zombie_4f.png` as a resource in Xcode via a right-click on ADD FILES:

```
- (void) drawRect: (CGRect) rect {
    W = rect.size.width;
    H = rect.size.height;

    if (!zombie) {
        zombie = [[Sprite alloc] initWithPic: @"zombie_4f.png"
                                    frameCnt: 4
                                   frameStep: 5
                                       speed: CGPointMake(0, -2)
                                         pos: CGPointMake(W/2, 400)];
    }

    [zombie draw];
}
```

To let our zombie loose on humanity, we place the preceding code in the `drawRect:` method of the `MainView` class. As you know, this is called, according to the tempo of the game loop, 33 times per second.

To audit the animation, let us output the sprite's current frame number at each game loop frame. This results in the following output to the console:

```
2012-11-24 12:58:51.337 Animation[4604:207] frameNr: 0
2012-11-24 12:58:51.365 Animation[4604:207] frameNr: 0
```

```
2012-11-24 12:58:51.397 Animation[4604:207] frameNr: 0
2012-11-24 12:58:51.431 Animation[4604:207] frameNr: 0
2012-11-24 12:58:51.464 Animation[4604:207] frameNr: 0
2012-11-24 12:58:51.497 Animation[4604:207] frameNr: 1
2012-11-24 12:58:51.530 Animation[4604:207] frameNr: 1
2012-11-24 12:58:51.563 Animation[4604:207] frameNr: 1
2012-11-24 12:58:51.596 Animation[4604:207] frameNr: 1
2012-11-24 12:58:51.629 Animation[4604:207] frameNr: 1
2012-11-24 12:58:51.661 Animation[4604:207] frameNr: 2
2012-11-24 12:58:51.695 Animation[4604:207] frameNr: 2
etc.
```

It worked! Every frame, beginning with the first frame = 0, is displayed, incremented, and then starts again at 0. The speed of a cycle is linked to the set FPS value and can be varied at each frame step. We therefore operate as we would with film: Frames are processed one after the other, and the projector (= game loop) determines how fast the film is run.

We have declared the zombies in the header with

```
Sprite *zombie;
```

If a zombie has not been initialized, we execute the if command and pass the desired parameters once. We specify the start position as x = W/2 and y = 400, which places the zombie halfway across the screen with enough room to escape to the top (Figure 3.8).

To release the zombie, simply give the following command:

```
[zombie draw];
```

As you can see, our zombie is of type Sprite. We can create as many instances of the class Sprite as we wish and thereby increase our zombie army. Of course, instead of the zombie film strip, you could use some other image and thereby create additional sprites with a variety of characteristics. If you wish to give your sprites individual abilities,

**Figure 3.8** Zombies walk the earth ...

then you create new classes derived from `Sprite`. Later, we will present a more complex example to illustrate this.

### 3.7.3 Organization Is Everything: Arrays

Suppose we want to create an army of 20 zombies. It would not be wise to create a separate member variable for each zombie; the code would become unnecessarily bloated. Instead, we can unite our sprites using arrays. For this purpose, Objective-C offers two classes of nonassociative arrays:

```
NSArray
NSMutableArray
```

`NSMutableArray` is derived from `NSArray` and gives support for a variable number of elements.

`NSArray`, in contrast, must be given a fixed size, and no new elements can then be added. The performance of `NSArray` is therefore a bit faster. Nonetheless, since in games we very often require a great deal of flexibility and we do not want to make our lives unnecessarily complicated, `NSMutableArray` is the better choice. Later, we shall consider the associative variant, which means that we can store key/value pairs:

```
NSDictionary
NSMutableDictionary
```

Here as well, `NSMutableDictionary` represents the variable variant of the parent class `NSDictionary`. Associative arrays are recommended whenever, for example, you need to look for a particular object in an array, such as the appropriate `UIImage` object (*value*) that was created on the basis of an `NSString` (*key*); you do not have to loop through the entire array to locate a particular element.

We shall fall back on the first variant (`NSMutableArray`) for our zombie army; we shall proceed *serially* and not give preference to any particular zombie. All zombies will be managed together in a loop and then rendered to the screen. Let us then let the undead proceed on their course, and let us declare an array in the header:

```
NSMutableArray *sprites;
```

The filling and the rendering of the zombies take place completely in the `drawRect:` method of the `MainView` class, to which we add the following code:

```
- (void) drawRect: (CGRect) rect {
    W = rect.size.width;
    H = rect.size.height;

    if (!sprites) {
        sprites = [[NSMutableArray alloc] initWithCapacity: 20];

        for (int i = 0; i<20; i++) {
            int fs = [self getRndBetween: 1 and: 10];
            int sy = [self getRndBetween: -3 and: -1];
            int px = [self getRndBetween: 0 and: W];
```

```
            int py = [self getRndBetween: H and: H+100];
            Sprite *sprite = [[Sprite alloc]

                initWithPic: @"zombie_4f.png"
                   frameCnt: 4
                  frameStep: fs
                      speed: CGPointMake(0, sy)
                        pos: CGPointMake(px, py)];
            [sprites addObject: sprite];
            [sprite release];
        }
    }

    for (Sprite *sprite in sprites){
        [sprite draw];
    }
}
```

To create zombie objects with various values, we again use the familiar getRndBetween:and: method.

If the sprites array was not initialized, we branch in the if command and create it with an expected size of 20 elements:

```
sprites = [[NSMutableArray alloc] initWithCapacity: 20];
```

This capacity specification provides for better memory management by Objective-C. We can add or delete elements later as required.

In the following for loop, the array is filled by creating a new Sprite object with random values 20 times. Adding to the array is done with the addObject: method:

```
    [sprites addObject: sprite];
    [sprite release];
```

Be sure that the Sprite objects are released immediately after their creation in order to avoid the creation of memory leaks. Objective-C's array classes increase their retain-Count for every added element. Therefore, we must immediately reduce this by one, since we will reference the object only through the array. Otherwise, the object could not later be cleared in the dealloc method:

```
-(void) dealloc {
    [sprites release];
    [super dealloc];
}
```

A call to [sprites release] has the effect of reducing retainCount of all objects stored in the array by one. Had we not previously reduced retainCount by one, the objects in the array would still have the value 1 and thus could not be released.

To remove objects from the array early, we have the removeObject: and remove-AllObjects: methods at our disposal:

```
[sprites removeObject: sprite];
[sprites removeAllObjects];
```

To render the zombies to the screen, it now suffices to iterate through the array and call the `draw:` method on all the zombies contained therein:

```
for (Sprite *sprite in sprites){
    [sprite draw];
}
```

This abbreviated version of a `for` loop gives us sequential access to all `Sprite` objects. The loop is exited automatically when the last element has been found. Take care not to add or remove any objects during the iteration, for otherwise you will receive the error message `Collection <NSCFArray: 0x3821c00> was mutated while being enumerated`. To manage objects dynamically, we have to employ a couple of tricks, which we shall introduce later in a more complicated example.

## ▌■ 3.8  Collision Control, Please!

What have we achieved so far? We have drawn cars of various colors on the display and set a small army of zombies on the march. Now let us join these two accomplishments and let the automobile industry compete against the zombie hordes. Can the diminutive pixel zombies withstand the onslaught of the onrushing autos?

To determine whether a zombie has been hit by a car, we need the next component of game development: collision control.

In almost every game, there are elements that can collide with other elements. Collision checks are made even in user interfaces; for example, to determine whether the mouse has clicked on some menu element, it must be checked whether the point on which the mouse has clicked is inside that element. In other words, you have to check whether the point has "collided" with the element. The simplest form of collision checking control is determining whether a point is located within a particular rectangle. Such a test is easy to implement:

```
//collision point <-> rectangle
- (bool) checkColPoint: (CGPoint) p
            withRect: (CGRect) rect {
    if ( p.x > rect.origin.x
      && p.x < (rect.origin.x+rect.size.width)
      && p.y > rect.origin.y
      && p.y < (rect.origin.y+rect.size.height)) {
        return true;
    }
    return false;
}
```

Since sprites are used in game programming and sprites have a rectangular form, collision checking for a pair of rectangles is very common. To do so, one compares the upper left-hand and lower right-hand corners of the first rectangle with the corresponding points of the second (see Figure 3.9).

To introduce this form of collision check and use it in a project, we shall use the animation example from the previous section as a template and create a new project in Xcode called "Collision."

Since we shall be working very often with the basic rectangular form of a sprite, we add a method to the `Sprite` class that returns the current rectangle. We have set

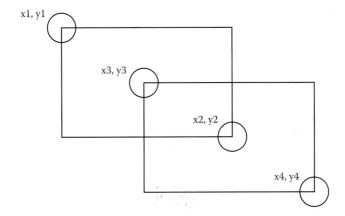

**Figure 3.9** Collision of two rectangles.

the dimensions of the sprite, `frameW` and `frameH`, in the class as members and initialized them in the `init` method with

```
int picW = pic.size.width;
frameW = picW/frameCnt;
frameH = pic.size.height;
```

With this, the implementation of the `getRect` method is easy:

```
- (CGRect) getRect {
    //rectangle at the current position of the sprite
    return CGRectMake(pos.x, pos.y, frameW, frameH);
}
```

Beginning with the rectangular structure, we can obtain the current vertices and execute the collision check:

```
//collision rectangle <-> rectangle
- (bool) checkColWithSprite: (Sprite *) sprite {
    CGRect rect1 = [self getRect];
    CGRect rect2 = [sprite getRect];

    //Rect 1
    int x1 = rect1.origin.x;//Rect1: upper left-hand vertex
    int y1 = rect1.origin.y;
    int w1 = rect1.size.width;
    int h1 = rect1.size.height;

    //Rect 2
    int x3 = rect2.origin.x;//Rect2: upper left-hand vertex
    int y3 = rect2.origin.y;
    int w2 = rect2.size.width;
    int h2 = rect2.size.height;

      int x2 = x1+w1, y2 = y1+h1;    //Rect1: lower right-hand vertex
      int x4 = x3+w2, y4 = y3+h2;    //Rect2: lower right-hand vertex

    if ( x2 > = x3
```

```
        && x4 > = x1
        && y2 > = y3
        && y4 > = y1) {
        return true;
    }
    return false;
}
```

We add the method to the Sprite class as well.

To signal that a collision has taken place between a car and a zombie, let us have the zombie utter a cry of anguish, which will be symbolized in a speech bubble:

This "individual" behavior of a zombie sprite is ideally realized in a subclasss derived from Sprite. For our collision test we shall therefore implement two different types of Sprite: a car sprite, on the one hand, and the zombie sprite, on the other. In order to be able to tell one sprite from another later on, we add to the Sprite class a type member of type int. We give it the default value of –1 in the init method.

We list the possible Sprite types in an enum list, which we declare outside the Sprite interface:

```
//sprite types
enum types {
    CAR,
    ZOMBIE
};


@interface Sprite : NSObject {...}
    ...
@end
```

To set an explicit Sprite type, we add to the class the following setter/getter:

```
- (void) setType: (int) spriteType {
    type = spriteType;
}


- (int) getType {
    return type;
}
```

As we shall see in the implementation of the Zombie subclass, the getter is used to carry out the collision check with the cars (alternatively, of course, you could use properties). But first consider the head of the Zombie class:

**Listing 3.6  Zombie.h**

```
#import "Sprite.h"

@interface Zombie : Sprite {
    UIImage *argghPic;
}

- (void) hitTest: (NSMutableArray *) sprites;

@end
```

The subclass includes only the ARGGH picture intended to illustrate the collision and a hitTest: method that performs the collision test based on the passed Sprite list.

**Listing 3.7  Zombie.m**

```
#import "Zombie.h"

@implementation Zombie

- (id) initWithPic: (NSString *) picName
          frameCnt: (int) fcnt
         frameStep: (int) fstp
             speed: (CGPoint) sxy
               pos: (CGPoint) pxy {

    argghPic = [UIImage imageNamed: @"arggh.png"];

    return [super initWithPic: picName
                     frameCnt: fcnt
                    frameStep: fstp
                        speed: sxy
                          pos: pxy];
}

- (void) hitTest: (NSMutableArray *) sprites {
    for (Sprite *sprite in sprites) {
        if ([sprite getType] = = CAR) {
            if ([self checkColWithSprite: sprite]){
                [argghPic drawAtPoint: CGPointMake(pos.x, pos.y -
                    argghPic.size.height)];
            }
        }
    }
}

@end
```

In the implementation of the Zombie class, we overwrite the initWithPic:frameCnt:frameStep:speed:pos: method so that the initialization of the zombies is not formally different from that of the other sprites. Within the method, we simply load the ARGGH image and call via super the overwritten version of the method to fill the Sprite object with the usual values.

Since the zombies are to perform the collision test independently, we add the new hitTest: method, in which we iterate through all the sprites and query via the getter as to the type. If it is a car, we call the collision check and render the ARGGH PNG if necessary.

Now we must take on the role of the automobile industry and create our fleet using the three car PNGs from the previous section. Zombies and cars will be initialized together in the drawRect: method of the MainView class, with cars driving from top to bottom, and zombies moving from bottom to top. To implement the new zombie class, we must, of course, import the header in the MainView class.

```
- (void) drawRect: (CGRect) rect {
    W = rect.size.width;
    H = rect.size.height;

    //initialize zombies and cars
    if (!sprites) {
        sprites = [[NSMutableArray alloc] initWithCapacity: 30];

        //zombies
        for (int i = 0; i<20; i++) {
            int fs = [self getRndBetween: 1 and: 10];
            int sy = [self getRndBetween: -3 and: -1];
            int px = [self getRndBetween: 0 and: W];
            int py = [self getRndBetween: H and: H+100];
            Zombie *zombie = [[Zombie alloc]

                initWithPic: @"zombie_4f.png"

                  frameCnt: 4

                 frameStep: fs

                     speed: CGPointMake(0, sy)

                       pos: CGPointMake(px, py)];
            [zombie setType: ZOMBIE];
            [sprites addObject: zombie];
            [zombie release];
        }

        //cars
        for (int i = 0; i<10; i++) {
                NSString *pic = @"car_blue.png";
                  if (i<3) pic = @"car_green.png";
            else if (i<6) pic = @"car_red.png";
            int sy = [self getRndBetween: 1 and: 3];
            int px = [self getRndBetween: 0 and: W];
            int py = [self getRndBetween: -100 and: 0];
            Sprite *car = [[Sprite alloc]

                initWithPic: pic

                  frameCnt: 1
```

```
                frameStep: 0
                    speed: CGPointMake(0, sy)
                      pos: CGPointMake(px, py)];
        [car setType: CAR];
        [sprites addObject: car];
        [car release];
    }
  }

  for (Sprite *sprite in sprites) {
      if ([sprite getType] = = ZOMBIE) {
          [(Zombie *) sprite hitTest: sprites];
      }
      [sprite draw];
  }
}
```

The zombies are created as in the animation example. This time, however, we use the
Zombie class and set the appropriate type via

```
[zombie setType: ZOMBIE];
```

We could also, of course, have set this in the overwritten init method. Here, however, we do it in a way similar to that used for the cars. Note that we give the value 1 for
frameCnt, since a car is not animated.

Since the Zombie class is derived from Sprite, we can handle the zombies like the
cars in a for loop; both of them ultimately use the draw method. To call the hitTest:
method, we must cast the Sprite element in the array via (Zombie *):

```
if ([sprite getType] = = ZOMBIE) {
    [(Zombie *) sprite hitTest: sprites];
}
```

This completes our first collision example. The hitTest: method runs over all
sprites and checks each Zombie object for a collision with a Sprite object if it is of type
CAR (Figure 3.10).

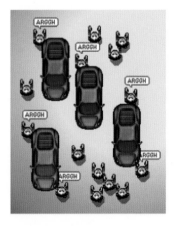

Figure 3.10 Open your mouth and say ... ARGGH!

If you execute the example, you will see that the zombies are "run over" by the cars, since these are drawn first. Thus, the car graphics are superimposed above the previously rendered zombie sprites. If you wanted to ensure that the speech bubble does not land under a car, you would have to render the bubble in an additional iteration after the rendering of the car.

As you can imagine, the rectangle collision method does not always yield results that correspond to the optics of the graphics. The transparent pixels on the edges are ignored, since only the surrounding rectangle—the so-called bounding box—is checked for a collision. You can increase the accuracy of the collision check by placing the bounding box more tightly around the graphic or using multiple bounding boxes for each object.

A further variant uses a bounding circle; that is, a collision occurs with respect to an imaginary circle in which the object resides. The center of the object should coincide with the center of the circle, and the radius should correspond to the extent of the graphic.

To show how a collision check is performed with circles, we refer to the famous theorem of Pythagoras, which you surely recall from your school days:

$$a^2 + b^2 = c^2$$

This theorem has an additional application beyond serving as the basis for collision calculations that can prove useful in game programming—namely, the calculation of the distance between two points.

### 3.8.1  Distance between Two Points

Suppose you want to know the distance between the two points, P1 (x1, y1) and P2 (x2, y2), in order to check whether there is even any point in carrying out a collision check on an object—that is, to check whether the object in question is anywhere nearby. For this, you have only to obtain the length between P1 and P2 as the longest side of a right triangle (i.e., the length of the hypotenuse) (Figure 3.11).

We can apply the Pythagorean theorem to determine the length of $c$. The third vertex of the triangle, P3, is derived from P1 and P2 (using the fact that it must be a right triangle) and has the coordinates P3 (x2, y1). This allows us to determine the lengths of $a$ and $b$:

$$a = x2 - x1$$

$$b = y2 - y1$$

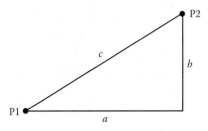

**Figure 3.11**  Right triangle with the segment joining points P1 and P2.

The Pythagorean theorem then yields

$$c^2 = (x2 - x1)^2 + (y2 - y1)^2.$$

Taking the square root of both sides give us

$$c = \sqrt{(x2-x1)^2 + (y2-y1)^2}.$$

Via `math.h`, Objective-C offers the methods that we need:

- **Squaring (the second value specifies the power)**

```
extern double pow(double, double);
extern float powf(float, float);
```

- **Extracting the square root**

```
extern double sqrt(double);
extern float sqrtf(float);
```

Instead of using the function `pow`, you could simply multiply directly:

$$(x2 - x1)^2 = (x2 - x1)(x2 - x1).$$

This brings with it a minimal boost in performance, which is worth mentioning. Even so, we can do without the greater precision of the `double` type, so we choose the `float` variant `sqrtf()`. We thus have the following method for determining the distance between two points:

```
- (int) getDistanceP1: (CGPoint) p1 andP2: (CGPoint) p2 {
    return sqrtf((p2.x - p1.x)*(p2.x - p1.x)
            + (p2.y - p1.y)*(p2.y - p1.y));
}
```

And now a few test calls:

```
int dist = [self getDistanceP1: CGPointMake(10, 0)
                          andP2: CGPointMake(8, 0)];
NSLog(@"distance:%i", dist);//= 2

dist = [self getDistanceP1: CGPointMake(7, 5)
                       andP2: CGPointMake(4, 16)];
NSLog(@"distance:%i", dist);//= 11
```

Incidentally, the formula can be just as easily applied in three-dimensional (3D) space. You have only to add in the z-coordinate:

**Distance d (in 3D space) between P1 (x1, y1, z1) and P2 (x2, y2, z2):**

$$d = \sqrt{(x2-x1)^2 + (y2-y1)^2 + (z2-z1)^2}.$$

## 3.8.2 Collision Checking with Circles

All right, then! What does the distance formula have to do with checking for collisions of circles? In fact, it has a lot to do with it. To paraphrase the famous soccer player and manager Sepp Herberger, "Circles are round." And that is the key to the formula we need, for every point of a circle is at the same distance—the radius—to the circle's center (Figure 3.12).

Thus, two circles collide precisely when the distance between their centers is less than the sum of their radii.

A circle is completely defined by its center and radius. Since the radius gives us the distance between the center and points on the circle, a circle can be described by the Pythagorean theorem.

For example, a circle with center at (0, 0) and radius = 3 is given in the 2D coordinate system by the equation

$$x^2 + y^2 = 3 * 3.$$

We can implement a collision check for circles using the following distance formula:

```
//collision circle <-> circle
- (bool) checkColWith: (CGPoint) p1
          radius1: (int) r1
            andP2: (CGPoint) p2
          radius2: (int) r2 {
    if ((p2.x - p1.x)*(p2.x - p1.x) + (p2.y - p1.y)*(p2.y - p1.y)
        < (r1 + r2)*(r1 + r2)) {
        return true;
    }
    return false;
}
```

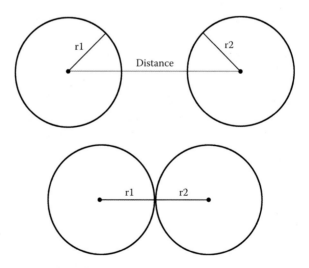

Figure 3.12 Bounding circles with distance and radii. In the lower picture, r1 + r2 = distance between the centers of circles that are just touching each other.

Since extracting square roots represents more work for the process than squaring and we have only to verify an inequality for the collision check, we could also square the sum of the radii and forget about the square roots. Thus, checking for a collision between circles is less work than calculating the distance between two points.

For three-dimensional space, we have to include the z-coordinate. A sphere is also completely described by the Pythagorean theorem:

**collision sphere <-> sphere:**

sphere 1: midpoint: MP1 (x1, y1, z1), radius: r1

sphere 2: midpoint: MP2 (x2, y2, z2), radius: r2.

A collision takes place whenever

$$(x2 - x1)^2 + (y2 - y1)^2 + (z2 - z1)^2 < (r1 + r2)^2.$$

Later on, we shall give an extensive example of the 3D versions of the collision check and distance calculation. For 2D games, bounding boxes work very well on account of the rectangular form of the graphics, so they are frequently used; for 3D games, sphere collision is faster and is therefore a very popular method.

# ▎ 3.9  User Input

We now know how to display moving images on the screen and to carry out collision calculations. There is one important component that needs to be considered before we can build our first game: Since games are interactive, we must see to it that—in contrast to movie-making—the user is able to influence the "plot." For example, the user could blow into the iPhone's microphone and thereby trigger a reaction or the input could be made via the touch display and/or the motion sensor. For lack of a traditional game pad controller, the iOS devices have established many new and creative input options. It was only with the advent of the iPhone that touch displays became very popular, although there had previously existed mobile phones that could be controlled by stylus or even with the touch of a finger.[*]

To introduce both the touch display and the motion sensor to control a game character, we shall create a new project called "UserInput" based on our collision project.

We can leave the source code initially unchanged. We just purge the `drawRect:` method of the `MainView` class by displaying only the background picture so that our player (and we) need no longer have to be content with a gray background:

```
- (void) drawRect: (CGRect) rect {
    W = rect.size.width;
    H = rect.size.height;

    if (!background) {
        background = [UIImage imageNamed: @"background.png"];
```

---

[*] Nor is the motion sensor an Apple invention. The game Marble Revolution (bit-side) won the 2005 German developer's prize in the category "most innovative technology" simply because it was one of the first games that made the motion control of Nokia's Symbian platform popular, long before Wii and EyeToy. In the first version, control was via the camera and then was later implemented for the motion sensor.

```
    }
    else {
        [background drawAtPoint: CGPointMake(0, 0)];
    }
}
```

The image "background.png" is 320 × 480 pixels in size and forms the foundation on which we are going to push around our figure. We created the background image with a round color gradient using the Quartz API and then stored it as a screen shot. (For performance reasons, you should avoid rendering gray scale or color gradients while the game is running.)

Every view is able to accept touch events. It all works very simply: To obtain the coordinates at which a finger has touched the display, it suffices to add the following method to the MainView implementation:

```
- (void) touchesBegan: (NSSet *) touches withEvent: (UIEvent *) event {
    //single tap
    UITouch *touch = [touches anyObject];
    CGPoint p = [touch locationInView:self];
    int xt = p.x;
    int yt = p.y;
    NSLog(@"Touch at%i,%i", xt, yt);
}
```

The method returns, for example, the following output:

```
2012-11-07 13:17:25.160 UserInput[16579:207] Touch at 161, 235
2012-11-07 13:17:26.736 UserInput[16579:207] Touch at 23, 47
2012-11-07 13:17:27.896 UserInput[16579:207] Touch at 298, 450
```

The iOS SDK offers support for a variety of gestures, such as pinch and swipe. The foundation for this is provided by the four UIResponder methods:

```
- (void)touchesBegan:(NSSet *)touches withEvent:(UIEvent *)event;
- (void)touchesMoved:(NSSet *)touches withEvent:(UIEvent *)event;
- (void)touchesEnded:(NSSet *)touches withEvent:(UIEvent *)event;
- (void)touchesCancelled:(NSSet *)touches withEvent:(UIEvent *)event;
```

In our implementation, we can, as required, override the desired method in a view and thereby respond to the display being touched. We shall not explore all the variants, since they are well described in the documentation and literature on iOS SDK. For most games, the preceding code will suffice. The touchesBegan:withEvent: method will then always be called when a finger touches the display. A single tap corresponds to a mouse click on the desktop (if more fingers are involved, one speaks of multitouch gestures). To respond to the touch, we need only the coordinates of the point at which the finger has touched the display. This is given by

```
UITouch *touch = [touches anyObject];

CGPoint p = [touch locationInView:self];
```

The NSSet instance contains the touch object, where we are interested only in the first element, since this represents a single tap (= the first finger that has touched the display). Then UITouch returns the desired point via the locationInView: method, which is called with our view as a parameter.

Before we consider what we are going to do with this point to influence the motion of our game character, we shall show how you can support multitouch events:

```
- (void) touchesBegan: (NSSet *) touches withEvent: (UIEvent *) event {

    [self setMultipleTouchEnabled: YES];

    NSSet *allTouches = [event allTouches];
    NSLog(@"Tap count:%i", [allTouches count]);

    //multitouch
    for (UITouch *touch in [allTouches allObjects]){
        CGPoint p = [touch locationInView:self];
        int x = p.x;
        int y = p.y;
        NSLog(@"multitouch at%i,%i", x, y);
    }
}
```

Here as well we overwrite the touchesBegan:withEvent: method. This time, however, we retrieve the UIEvent parameter, which gives us access via the allTouches: method to all touch events.

In order to retrieve multitouch events properly, we must "switch them on" via

```
[self setMultipleTouchEnabled: YES];
```

Otherwise, you would have to touch the display with all five fingers simultaneously (= the maximum number for touch events). Multitouch, in contrast, makes it possible for fingers to touch the display one after another. For each new finger, the method is called again. This allows you to determine the number of fingers that are currently touching the display (tap count) via

```
[allTouches count]
```

Then [allTouches allObjects] returns an NSArray, which you can iterate in a for loop to retrieve the coordinates:

```
2012-11-06 14:01:28.113 UserInput[896:207] Tap count: 5
2012-11-06 14:01:28.117 UserInput[896:207] multitouch at 82, 326
2012-11-06 14:01:28.122 UserInput[896:207] multitouch at 41, 164
2012-11-06 14:01:28.127 UserInput[896:207] multitouch at 118, 82
2012-11-06 14:01:28.131 UserInput[896:207] multitouch at 207, 431
2012-11-06 14:01:28.136 UserInput[896:207] multitouch at 231, 28
```

We can also access a particular item—for example, the touch event that occurs first:

```
UITouch *touch = [[allTouches allObjects] objectAtIndex: 0];
```

Unfortunately, the iPhone simulator provides no support for multitouch so that you can test your code only on an actual device. However, you can simulate a double tap by pressing the option key before the mouse click.

With a little creativity, you can think of various options for controlling a game figure with the fingers. For classical gamepad emulation, for example, you can add four virtual direction keys shown on screen to check for collisions with a tap event. Of much greater interest, however, is to find a control mechanism that cannot be implemented on a traditional gamepad. Suppose you want a figure to be able to move in all possible directions, and you simply tap a target point on the display. Now the figure moves toward this point. If you touch the screen above the figure, it runs upward; if you touch below it, it moves downward, etc. This is a bit reminiscent of a mouse tracker, and it can be implemented just as easily.

We again choose a zombie from the previous section as our player. Since we now want to control the player ourselves, we must further specialize the behavior of the Zombie class. To this end, we create a new Player class.

**Listing 3.8 Player.h**

```
#import "Zombie.h"

@interface Player : Zombie {
    CGPoint touchPoint;
}

- (void) setTouch: (CGPoint) touchPoint;

@end
```

**Listing 3.9 Player.m**

```
#import "Player.h"

@implementation Player

- (void) setTouch: (CGPoint) point {
    touchPoint = point;
    speed.x = (touchPoint.x - pos.x)/20;//deltaX
    speed.y = (touchPoint.y - pos.y)/20;//deltaY
}

@end
```

The Player class is used only to pass the touch point to the Player instance via a setter.*

Before we can run this example, we have to initialize and render the player. As previously, we do this, for the sake of simplicity, in the drawRect: method of the MainView class:

```
if (!player) {
    player = [[Player alloc] initWithPic: @"zombie_4f.png"
```

_____

* Of course, we can create a simplified setter through the properties, as we have seen already. But there is no harm in choosing the traditional way. This will make the code more easily portable to other systems.

```
                        frameCnt: 4
                        frameStep: 3
                           speed: CGPointMake(0, 0)
                             pos: CGPointMake(W/2, H/2)];

        [player setType: PLAYER];
}

[player draw];
```

Furthermore, we have extended the `Sprite` types to include the `Player` type, imported the `Player` header in the `MainView` header, and there also declared the `Player` instance via `Player *player`.

Before the zombies can start nibbling on our fingers, we have to pass the coordinates at which the finger has touched the display to the `setTouch:` method:

```
UITouch *touch = [touches anyObject];
CGPoint p = [touch locationInView: self];
[player setTouch: p];
```

We place the code, as expected, in the `touchesBegan:withEvent:` handler (Figure 3.13).

And now we can "let 'er rip." Wherever we touch the screen, the pixel image follows our finger by the most direct path, even diagonally if necessary—a clear advantage over the classical eight-way gamepad control. Moreover, the figure moves at varying speeds; thus, dynamically, longer distances are covered more quickly, and over short distances, our creation strolls leisurely. Let us look more closely at how we have accomplished this. The magic is concealed in the `setTouch:` method of the `Player` class:

```
speed.x = (touchPoint.x - pos.x)/20;//deltaX
speed.y = (touchPoint.y - pos.y)/20;//deltaY
```

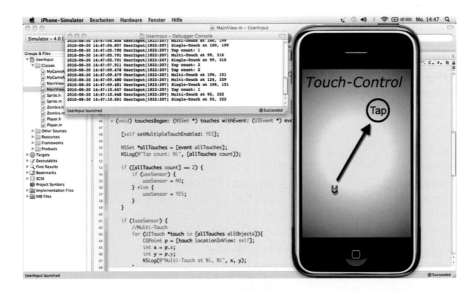

**Figure 3.13** The zombie always runs toward the finger (tap).

The sprite's `draw` method requires only the `speed` indication to move the sprite in the x- or y-direction in each frame. To change the figure's direction, we have only to adapt `speed.x` and `speed.y`. Behind the preceding code is concealed the two-point form of the equation $y = mx + n$.

A straight line is defined mathematically by two points (x1, y1) and (x2, y2), where the slope $m$ of the line is determine by differences between the point's x- and y-coordinates:

$$m = Delta\_Y/Delta\_X = (y2 - y1) - (x2 - x1).$$

Applied to a pixel zombie, the first point (x1, x2) marks the position of the sprite, and the second point indicates the position of the touch point. Since the zombie is supposed to move along a line from its current position to the touch point, we have only to add the slope of the line (*Delta_Y/Delta_X*) for the displacement of the figure in the x- and y-directions. We then divide the result by 20 so that the motion is not too rapid.

There is, however, one small flaw. We would expect the zombie to halt when it reaches the finger (after all, zombies are hungry). Instead, the fiend overshoots the mark and vanishes off the display. This problem is easy to solve. To stop the motion, we need to set the `speed` value to 0. To accomplish this, we overwrite the `draw` method of the `Player` class and check whether the current position of the sprite is behind the touch point:

```
- (void) draw {
    [super draw];

    //Stop movement
    if (speed.x > 0 && touchPoint.x < pos.x) speed.x = 0;
    if (speed.x < 0 && touchPoint.x > pos.x) speed.x = 0;
    if (speed.y > 0 && touchPoint.y < pos.y) speed.y = 0;
    if (speed.y < 0 && touchPoint.y > pos.y) speed.y = 0;
}
```

Now the figure can no longer leave the visible playing field, because it is impossible to trigger a touch event outside the display. As soon as the figure reaches the finger, it stops. However, the animation sequence continues to run. We can adapt this for all the sprites by checking in the `drawFrame` method of the `Sprite` class whether the `speed` variable is equal to 0 and, if it is, displaying a still image (`frameNr = 0`):

```
frameNr = [self updateFrame];
if (speed.x = = 0 && speed.y = = 0) {
    frameNr = 0;
}
```

We can still improve on the motion control. To move a zombie, the player has continually to remove a finger from the display and set it down somewhere else. It would be much more convenient if one could simply drag one's finger across the display and have the zombie react immediately to his victim's change in direction. This, too, can be fairly easily implemented: We have only to overwrite the `touchesMoved:withEvent:` method, which is to be called every time a finger changes its coordinates.

```
- (void) touchesMoved: (NSSet *) touches withEvent: (UIEvent *) event {
    UITouch *touch = [touches anyObject];
```

```
    CGPoint p = [touch locationInView:self];
    [player setTouch: p];
    int x = p.x;
    int y = p.y;
    NSLog(@"Touch moves at%i,%i", x, y);
}
```

If you keep your finger on the display, you can drag the zombie behind it and thereby keep it going indefinitely. But we have achieved even more. The code also shows a possible implementation of the swipe gesture. You can control the zombie not only by a single tap and continuous movement, but also by a *swipe*; if you tap the zombie and then quickly swipe your finger in another direction, the figure follows your finger until you release it.

For many games, you need a motion control that is active only while you are pressing a virtual forward button (as with classical gamepad emulation). A suitable implementation uses the `touchesEnded:WithEvent:` method, in which you can set the player's speed variable to 0 as soon as a finger is no longer touching the display:

```
- (void) touchesEnded: (NSSet *) touches withEvent: (UIEvent *) event {
    [player setSpeed: CGPointMake(0, 0)];//example
}
```

## 3.9.1  Querying the Motion Sensor

Touch-screen control for an iPhone game is not always a winning formula; for many games, motion control is a better alternative. Think of the *Labyrinth* game, for example, in which a marble must be maneuvered through a wooden maze by tilting the display. Control using a sensor is much easier to implement than you might think.

You can query the motion sensor in any class that implements the `UIAccelerometerDelegate` protocol. This protocol requires only the implementation of the `accelerometer:didAccelerate:` method, which is called by iPhone iOS at regular time intervals that we, as developers, can determine.

This method gives us access to the xyz-values that tell us the current position of the device.

To use the motion sensor, we must know whether the unit is tilted to the left or to the right and whether up or down. Moreover, we would also like to know by how much the device is tilted. You can see how a marble moving through a maze is an obvious application example. But we can use this control method for our zombies as well.

The implementation is in the `MainView` class. We include in the header the protocol specification `<UIAccelerometerDelegate>` and add a declaration of a `UIAccelerometer` instance through which we can initialize the motion sensor:

```
@interface MainView : UIView <UIAccelerometerDelegate> {
    UIAccelerometer *accelerometer;
    UIImage *background;
    Player *player;
}

- (void) accelerometer: (UIAccelerometer *) accelerometer
        didAccelerate: (UIAcceleration *) acceleration;
@end
```

We carry out the one-time initialization in the drawRect: method:

```
if (!accelerometer) {
    accelerometer = [UIAccelerometer sharedAccelerometer];
    accelerometer.delegate = self;
    accelerometer.updateInterval = 0.033;
}
```

The class method sharedAccelerometer gives us access to the sensor. As delegate we give our class (self). The method accelerometer:didAccelerate: agreed on via the protocol is thereby called by iOS as soon as the next update interval is complete, and we obtain new sensor data. The update interval is given in seconds. But be careful: A value that is too low would waste resources and quickly drain the battery. In practice, 0.033 gives accurate results, since the game loop is also running at 0.033 FPS.

To implement the sensor data immediately for controlling the sprite, we add another setter for the speed variable via

```
- (void) setSpeed: (CGPoint) sxy {
    speed = sxy;
}
```

So much for preparations. Now we can look at the accelerometer: didAccelerate: method, in which the actual interaction with the sensor takes place.

```
- (void) accelerometer: (UIAccelerometer *) sensor
        didAccelerate: (UIAcceleration *) acceleration {
    float x = acceleration.x;
    float y = acceleration.y;
    float z = acceleration.z;
    NSLog(@"Sensor: x:%f y:%f z:%f", x, y, z);

    int factor = 15;
    [player setSpeed: CGPointMake(x*factor, -y*factor)];
}
```

And that is about it. Via the UIAcceleration parameter, we can access the xyz-values directly, which lie in the range from –1 to 1 and are passed, amplified by the factor 15, directly to the players' setSpeed: method. For the y-value, we have only to change the sign, since the y-axis of the iOS coordinate system runs from top to bottom. The factor establishes, moreover, the maximal pixel speed and determines the sensitivity with which our pixel person responds to the sensor; the smaller the factor is, the more sluggish the figure is.

UIAcceleration provides the xyz-orientation as a UIAccelerationValue type, which is defined as a double. We need only float precision, and therefore we access the values accordingly. The meaning of the values xyz is as follows:

- **x:** –1 < 0 = tilted left, 0 < 1 = tilted right

- **y:** –1 < 0 = tilted down, 0 < 1 = tilted up

- **z:** –1 < 0 = display oriented up, 0 < 1 = display oriented down

To direct the movement of a game figure in any of the four directions, you need only look at the sign. The degree of tilt ranges from 0 (horizontal, 0°) to 1 and –1, each of which corresponds to an angle of 90°. If the display is tilted further, the display is no longer visible; it points downward, and the values wander from 1 or –1 back to 0. Therefore, in addition, you need the z-parameter, from which you can determine whether the tilt angle refers to a display that points upward.

For games, it is primarily the xy-values that are needed. In addition, you could use the z-parameter to pause the game if the user turns the device upside down. When the device is picked up again for further play, the expectation is that the display will be pointing upward (since most players do not hold the device over their heads the way Jimi Hendrix held a guitar, looking upward at the screen to play):

```
if (z < 0) NSLog(@"display correct.");
else NSLog(@"turn on sleep mode.");
```

Since the iPhone simulator offers no way to test the motion sensor, you will have to try out your program on the device itself. Furthermore, we should make sure that only one type of control is active: The default should be touch control. If the user taps with two fingers simultaneously on the display, the current control type is changed (*toggle*). To accomplish this, we will create a new Boolean variable as a flag:

```
bool useSensor;
```

We can then toggle the value in the `touchesBegan:withEvent:` method:

```
if ([allTouches count] = = 2) {//Doubletap
    if (useSensor) {
        useSensor = NO;
    } else {
        useSensor = YES;
    }
}
```

We now have only to query the flag in the relevant methods and set the corresponding code in an `if` block. Remember to switch the control type with a double tap when you try out the program on an actual device. If you are in motion-control mode and the figure has wandered off the screen, you will have to execute another double tap. The figure then rushes back to the visible screen area. The touch-control implementation automatically takes care of this.

You will find that both types of control have advantages and disadvantages. In the case of touch control, the finger often covers the figure on the screen or hinders the player's view of the game. Motion control, however, is very delicate and sometimes therefore too sensitive; it is difficult to keep the figure motionless at a single spot on the screen, since the sensor registers the least motion. At least here you can do something about this by defining an optional *threshold* below which there will be no movement of the game figure:

```
float threshold = 0.1;
if (x > threshold || x < -threshold) {
    [player setSpeed: CGPointMake(x*factor, ([player getSpeed]).y)];
}
if (y > threshold || y < -threshold) {
    [player setSpeed:

        CGPointMake(([player getSpeed]).x, -y*factor)];
}
```

You must, of course, make sure that you control the x- and y-speeds separately. Therefore, we pass a single value to the `setSpeed:` method and leave the other value unchanged by resetting the current value via a getter. The threshold should be adjusted as necessary. A value of 0.1 represents a good compromise between sensitivity and "shock resistance" (depending on how much your hand shakes).

# ▌ 3.10  All Together Now: GameManager and Sprite Management

We are now familiar with the components of an elementary game-development kit: Process user input, set up a game loop, and display graphics on the screen. This will enable you to implement many game ideas. But take note that, for games, many different types of data must be processed in real time and interactively. Thus, games are among the most demanding applications in computer science. It is not without reason that games are used as a benchmark for new hardware and that they drive the development of new CPUs and graphics cards.

In this section, therefore, we shall not stress the new features of the iOS SDK, but instead show by example how you can master the complexity of games with the means that are already in your hands. We shall only later use OpenGL ES to render graphics so that we can address the built-in graphics chips of iOS devices directly and thereby optimize performance.

Some important topics in game development have not yet been mentioned:

- Dynamic creation and management of sprites

- Unique animation effects—for example, for explosions

- Space-saving storage of resources and high-performance loading

- Preloader (load data in the background before the game begins)

- Simple user guidance with finite-state machines

- Organization of the source code for larger projects

All these different aspects of game development can be relatively straightforwardly managed by a central class, which we shall give the apt name "GameManager." Even for very simple games, it is important that you maintain an overview so that when you are programming, you can concentrate on what actually goes on during your game. In short, you must think about such things as how a number of sprites will be allowed to live and made to die in your game and how you can manage at a reasonable cost to organize all the various conditions under which they will find themselves in the course of a game (hero conquers adversary, hero dies, etc., or application-specific: game won, game lost, menu is displayed, etc.).

Since theory is dull and we can hardly wait to move our little pixel creatures once again on the small screen, let us unite the elements we have introduced thus far into a new game design.

Up to now, our little zombies have been unable to defend themselves when they were hit or run over by a car. The true expert on the life of zombies knows, of course, that a zombie actually could not care less. But now that we know how to frighten one of them by touching the screen with our finger, we can immediately make a little game out of this. Justice must be done, so let us see whether our zombie army might perhaps be able to emerge victorious against the overwhelming might of the automobile industry.

We establish the game design as follows: *You control a zombie army by finger, and you must ensure that they march toward the city as undisturbed by automobiles as possible. You win the game if you bring the required number of zombies across a green demarcation line.*

### 3.10.1  Game Elements

- **Background graphic:** this is a bird's-eye view of a street.

- **Master zombie (green):** this is the hero of the game, who can be moved across the screen by swipe control.

- **Reanimator:** this is an item that the master zombie can activate when he is standing on it. It creates a new zombie every five frames and is symbolized by a pixel skull surrounded by a red circle. Zombies thus created always travel from bottom to top.

- **Zombies:** they are brought to life by the master zombie. They march stoically at one pixel per frame up toward the demarcation line.

- **Demarcation line:** if a zombie reaches this line, it has reached its goal and can therefore reach the imaginary city unmolested.

- **Cars:** they always travel from top to bottom and try to prevent the zombies from invading the city. Cars cannot be destroyed. If a zombie or the player (represented by the master zombie) ends up under a car, it loses life points.

- **Health:** the player has 100 life points. Reanimated zombies each have 10 life points. While a zombie is in contact with a car, it loses one life point per frame (Figure 3.14).

### 3.10.2  Winning the Game

The game is won if the player brings at least 20 zombies across the demarcation line. To motivate the player, the number of lost zombies is displayed.

### 3.10.3  Defeat

The player loses if his or her life points are reduced to 0. If a zombie's life points shrink to 0, it is sent back to the underworld, indicated by an explosion animation (a gray cloud of smoke).

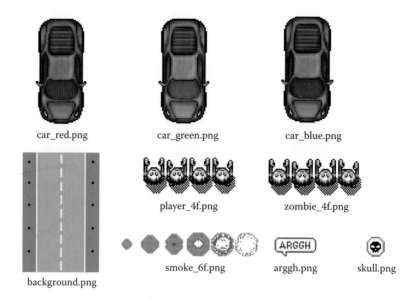

car_red.png     car_green.png     car_blue.png

player_4f.png     zombie_4f.png

smoke_6f.png     arggh.png     skull.png

background.png

**Figure 3.14** Overview of all the game graphics.

### 3.10.4  Control

You can move both the zombies and the green master zombie across the display by swipe control. The master zombie stops as soon as it reaches the end of the swipe gesture. The zombies, in contrast, continue to march upward after the end of the swipe by one pixel per frame. For a figure to be swipeable, the finger must touch the figure. Multitouch is not supported. However, by "traveling over" zombies with your finger, you can collect zombies and lead them along. The motion ends only when the finger is lifted.

### 3.10.5  HUD (Head-up Display)

The following information is displayed at the top of the screen:

- *HLT:* health of the master zombie (Health)

- *SVD:* number of zombies "saved" thus far (Saved)

- *LST:* number of "run over" zombies (Lost)

### 3.10.6  Menu Navigation

1. The splash screen is shown during the loading of game resources.

2. When all resources have been loaded, the game begins with a small greeting and introductory text. A tap begins the game.

3. Play!

4. If the hero dies, the game result is displayed. A new tap leads back to the welcome (step 2).

5. If the player wins, the result is also displayed. A new tap leads to the welcome (step 2).

The highlight of the game, which at the same time is the greatest difficulty, is to remain as long as possible on the reanimator, symbolized by the death's head, to avoid the cars and still protect the already created zombies from the cars and bring them as far forward as possible with a swipe. Since the cars are traveling downward at various speeds, gaps arise. But be careful: Without your intervention, the path to the safety of the green line is too long, and your knights of the living dead will have no chance against the might of the onrushing cars.

The speed of the cars and the zombies, the number of reanimators, the life points, and the number of zombies that have to be saved can all be varied, giving you the possibility of controlling the difficulty of the game and creating various levels of play.

Zombie games tend to be very popular in the App Store, such as, for example, the successful Fieldrunner clone *Plants vs. Zombies* (PopCap). Why not switch sides for once and give the poor defenseless fellows a hand? With touch control of iOS devices, there has arisen a relatively new game design that can be developed in a variety of ways (including with a different cast of characters). And yet the game is simple enough that it will not obscure the basics that have to be learned.

This section is best read while reading the source code of the example project in parallel. It is called simply "GameManager" and can found, as always, in the download folder of the book's website. We have based this project on the UserInput example of the previous section, using it as a template.

The already presented graphics can be found in the "Resources" folder and the source code under "Classes." As you can see, we have created in this folder, via a right-click, a new group, "GameElements," into which we have moved all the Sprite classes. You do not have to change the class's import commands. The group representation serves merely to provide a clearer view of the Xcode. The actual file structure remains unchanged.

For each of the five game elements, we have created a Sprite class, with Sprite as the common superclass.

- Sprite: defines the common properties of the sprites. Individual behaviors are implemented by new methods in the child classes or by overwriting the parent methods

- Zombie: our living dead, characterized by striving always to cross the green line

- Player: the master zombie, which has almost all the properties of a normal zombie (and also responds to touch), but does not always move upward

- Car: the cars; as soon as a car exits at the bottom of the screen, it reenters the screen from the top

- **Animation**: provides for animation effects, which in general are centered on a (rectangular) sprite

- **Reanimator**: a sinister device that is able, using a bit of OOP, to create armies of the living dead, digitally and without limit; *should not fall into the wrong hands*

With this overview, we leave the sprites for now and look at the remaining class structure, which contains only three classes: the familiar delegate, the MainView class, and the new GameManager.

The delegate provides as previously for the tempo of the game loop and calls the drawRect: method of the MainView class. This class is unchanged from the previous examples. The MainView class, on the other hand, has been simplified, since we want to move all the game-related properties to the new GameManager.

---

**Listing 3.10  MainView.h**

```
#import <UIKit/UIKit.h>
#import "GameManager.h"

@interface MainView : UIView {
    GameManager *gameManager;
}

@end
```

---

**Listing 3.11  MainView.m**

```
#import "MainView.h"

@implementation MainView

- (void) drawRect: (CGRect) rect {
    if (!gameManager) {
        gameManager = [GameManager getInstance];
    }

    [gameManager drawStatesWithFrame: rect];
}

- (void) touchesBegan: (NSSet *) touches withEvent: (UIEvent *) event {
    CGPoint p = [[touches anyObject] locationInView: self];
    [gameManager touchBegan: p];
}

- (void) touchesMoved: (NSSet *) touches withEvent: (UIEvent *) event {
    CGPoint p = [[touches anyObject] locationInView: self];
    [gameManager touchMoved: p];
}
```

```
-  (void)  touchesEnded:  (NSSet  *)  touches  withEvent:  (UIEvent  *)  event
      {
      [gameManager  touchEnded];
  }

-  (void)  touchesCancelled:  (NSSet  *)  touches  withEvent:  (UIEvent  *)
      event  {
      [gameManager  touchEnded];
  }

- (void)  dealloc  {
    [gameManager  release];
    [super  dealloc];
  }

@end
```

As you can see, the MainView class is now only a transit station that separates the characteristics of the iOS platform from the actual game logic.

The methods of touch control simply inform the manager as to the coordinates (CGPoint) of the current finger touch on the display and whether the finger has been removed (touchEnded).

You can recognize the central access point in the drawRect: method. In each frame, the manager's drawStatesWithFrame: method, which contains the current dimensions of the display in the form of a method of a CGRect structure, is called. Previously to this, the manager is initialized once:

```
if  (!gameManager)  {
    gameManager  =  [GameManager  getInstance];
}
```

Since we wish to implement the GameManager in all classes and since we know that there can be only one GameManager, we create this as a singleton. The class method getInstance therefore always returns the identical object instance. This method also ensures that only one manager instance can exist at runtime. A further advantage of the class method getInstance is that we obtain access to the manager in every class that imports the GameManager header. The implementation of the getInstance method in the GameManager class is based on the singleton pattern:

```
+  (GameManager*)  getInstance  {
    static  GameManager*  gameManager;
    if  (!gameManager)  {
        gameManager  =  [[GameManager  alloc]  init];
        NSLog(@"gameManager  created  as  a  singleton!");
        [gameManager  preloader];
    }
    return  gameManager;
}
```

The + sign specifies that the method is a class method. This means that no object instance is required to call the method; the class name suffices. Nevertheless, you obtain an instance that is created the first time the `getInstance` method is called. The `gameManager` is declared statically and therefore has a unique existence. The `if` command ensures that the instance is initially created. This is also a good place to load, via a preloader, the necessary resources for the game. As you can see, here we call the manager's `preloader` method, which loads global resources once. So that our game can begin without delay, the method ensures that the current game data are loaded into the `loadGame` method via

```
state = LOAD_GAME;
```

Since this takes place during the first call to the `drawRect:` method of the `MainView` class, the app's splash screen is displayed until the loading process has finished.

But let us not get ahead of ourselves. Let us look now at the structure of the `GameManager` class, which has to deal with a whole series of tasks and is correspondingly somewhat bigger. Here, with its pragma directives, Xcode offers an excellent way to structure the code.

### 3.10.7  Structuring Code

When you click in the source code window of the manager implementation on the function menu in the navigation bar, you see all the methods of the class in a single view (Figure 3.15).

Make sure that, in the Xcode preferences under "Code Sense," the check box next to "Sort list alphabetically" is not activated. The popup shows all the class's methods, and we jump directly to the desired method without a lot of scrolling. You can also see that

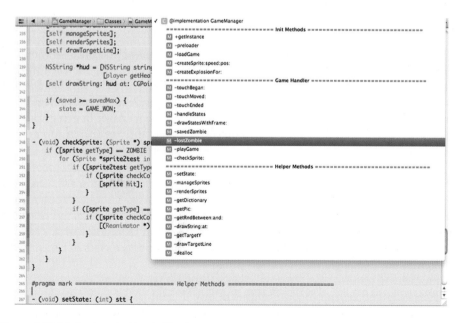

Figure 3.15  Method navigation in Xcode.

the `GameManager` class is divided into three regions. This comes from a pragma directive that was placed in the source code:

```
#pragma mark = = = = = = Game Handler = = = = = =
```

Of course, you can also see the overview of methods in the header. However, the function menu offers additionally the possibility of direct navigation to specific methods, a feature that avoids lengthy scrolling through large classes. For our example, we have the following subdivision:

- **Init methods:** Here are all the methods that are related to the creation of objects. In particular, this is where new sprites are created. The preloader is also here.

- **Game handler:** The game handler region manages the actual control of the game as it proceeds. Not only is user input handled here, but also the finite-state machine manages a clean separation of the game states. It is the `playGame` method in which the actual game takes place.

- **Helper methods:** No game can do without tools and auxiliary methods that carry out game-specific tasks or execute processes independently of the actual game design that are repeated over and over, such as the management of resources and sprites. This subdivision is therefore best suited to being bundled later into a separate class.

## 3.10.8  Resource Management

Let us take a look first at a task of the `GameManager` without which even the most unprepossessing game will never get off the ground: managing resources such as graphics, sounds, and level data. Indeed, for our game we have already created *nine* graphics—an impressive number! Each graphic occupies a place in working memory and requires a certain amount of time to load.* Up to now, in our first tentative steps at creating our first `Sprite`, we have not bothered with such questions. But now the time has come to look at things from a more professional viewpoint and dig more deeply into the `Sprite` class.

Why is this necessary?

Every `Sprite` has associated with it one or more PNGs, which are loaded with the help of the `UIImage` class from the file manager of the iPhone iOS:

```
UIImage *pic = [UIImage imageNamed: picName];
```

The variable `pic` (of type `UIImage`) represents here simply a pointer to the memory location in which the PNG was loaded. Although the PNG format allows for compressed and thereby space-saving storage of the image points, in working memory, it is stored uncompressed. Therefore, the street background `background.png` with a size of $320 \times 480$ pixels is only about 8 kB in size. Many areas of the image are monochrome

---

* It is not a good idea to create and destroy objects during runtime on many mobile gaming platforms; since short-term memory must be allocated and released for this process, there will be a brief stutter effect—although not so with the iPhone OS. Here, the platform reacts relatively robustly as long as we avoid the creation of graphics or other expensive operations during object allocation.

or only a few colors are used, etc. In memory, however, the image is represented pixel for pixel. Regardless of the subject, an image in memory occupies, at most, the following space:

*Memory use in bytes = width × height × 4.*

In other words, for each pixel, 4 bytes of color information are used (RGB plus alpha). Therefore, our background image already occupies 600 kB.

Moreover, no matter how often the identical PNG is loaded via the class image-Named, a *new* pointer to a *new* memory location is created every time. So if we need a 10 kB image for a sprite and we create this sprite 100 times, it will occupy almost 1 MB. You can see, then, that it makes sense to think about image resources.

So we now need to ensure that an image that has already been loaded can be *reused*. In this way, we also save the cost of additional loading of the image. Since we want to be able to create and destroy sprites during the course of the game, we need to avoid all the expensive routines from the initialization. The solution to this is a hash table that, in contrast to an array, offers direct access to a resource (key/value).

For this, we use the NSMutableDictionary of the Foundation framework. The dictionary (or hash table) must be able to be changed (mutable), since we may wish later to load other levels with other resources and must delete the currently loaded resources if the amount of RAM is insufficient. We have created the dictionary in the GameManager:

```
- (NSMutableDictionary *) getDictionary {
    if (!dictionary) {
        dictionary = [[NSMutableDictionary alloc] init];
        NSLog(@"dictionary created!");
    }
    return dictionary;
}
```

With the if statement, we make sure that the resource table is created only once. To store resources in it, we create an additional helper method for each resource type. Since we need a variety of graphics for our game, we settle on a getPic: method:

```
- (UIImage *) getPic: (NSString*) picName {
    @try {
        UIImage *pic = [[self getDictionary] objectForKey: picName];
        if (!pic) {
            pic = [UIImage imageNamed: picName];
            [[self getDictionary] setObject: pic forKey: picName];
            int memory = pic.size.width*pic.size.height*4;
            NSLog(@"%@ saved, Size:%i KB",
                picName, memory/1024);
            [pic release];
        }
        return pic;
    }
    @catch (id theException) {
        NSLog(@"ERROR:%@ not found!", picName);
    }
    return nil;
}
```

The NSDictionary methods objectForKey: and setObject:forKey: can be used to obtain existing records or create new ones. We use the image name as the parameter. If the image is not yet present in the dictionary, the objectForKey: method returns nil, and in the if part, we can create the image and store it in the table. Of course, as a key we again use the image name. In addition, let us output the amount of memory used. We have packaged the whole thing in a try-catch block to catch errors, for example, if the image name was written incorrectly. To avoid memory leaks, it is important to keep in mind that the NSDictionary increases the retainCount of the stored object by 1.

If the image is created, then retainCount = 1. If we add it to the table, then we have retainCount equal to 2. If the dictionary is now released, then the retainCount of all objects therein contained is reduced by 1. Our picture would then again have the value 1 and would not be deleted. As you know, the iOS SDK automatically deallocates all objects whose retain value is equal to 0. Therefore, we call the release method after adding an image, and in the manager's dealloc method, we use

```
[[self getDictionary] release];
```

to ensure that not only the dictionary is removed but also all the objects contained within it whose retain values were previously equal to 1. You can display the value at any time using

```
NSLog(@"%@ retain count:%i", picName, [pic retainCount]);
```

An additional advantage of the NSDictionary class is that, in using graphics, you do not have to worry any longer about release, since that is the task of the manager.

Instead of creating a new UIImage in the Sprite class, we call the getPic: method in the initializer:

```
pic = [[GameManager getInstance] getPic: picName];
```

The pointer pic of the Sprite instance always references the same memory location, regardless of how often the image is loaded by other classes. Furthermore, the getPic: method returns only the pointer to the current image if it has been loaded previously. This results in a not insignificant increase in performance.

## 3.10.9 Sprite Management

We now make some further demands on Sprite management: Up till now, we could display all the sprites simply by running through the array in which the Sprite objects were stored. Now, however, we would like to *create* or *delete* new sprites during the game.

The reanimator symbolizes this in our game design. But in fact, you will want to create new sprites on the fly in almost every game design: for example, new adversaries, objects to collect, movable obstacles, and so on. In addition, one-time events, such as explosions, are most simply implemented as sprites, which are created to allow the animation to take place and then are deleted from memory when the explosion sequence is over. Actually, this should be easily feasible using arrays. The catch is just that NSMutableArrays can add and delete elements dynamically, but this is not permitted to take place while you are iterating the array.*

However, if you try it, you will obtain the error message `Arrays cannot be mutated while being enumerated`. The reason is that, otherwise, the stored indices would change, and the array could no longer be properly iterated. We are saved here by a little trick. We create two additional arrays in which we store the new objects and those to be deleted:

```
//Active sprites that should be rendered
NSMutableArray *sprites;
//New sprites that should be added to the sprites list
NSMutableArray *newSprites;
//Inactive sprites that should be cleared
NSMutableArray *destroyableSprites;
```

We then create the arrays once in the preloader:

```
sprites = [[NSMutableArray alloc] initWithCapacity:20];
newSprites = [[NSMutableArray alloc] initWithCapacity:20];
destroyableSprites = [[NSMutableArray alloc] initWithCapacity:20];
```

And now what? Have a look at the `manageSprite` method, which we call at the start of every rendering process:

```
- (void) manageSprites {
    //Cleanup
    for (Sprite *destroyableSprite in destroyableSprites) {
        for (Sprite *sprite in sprites) {
            if (destroyableSprite = = sprite) {
                [sprites removeObject: sprite];
                break;
            }
        }
    }

    //Add new sprites
    for (Sprite *newSprite in newSprites){
        [sprites addObject: newSprite];
    }

    [destroyableSprites removeAllObjects];
    [newSprites removeAllObjects];
}
```

To render the sprites, we use, as we did earlier, the `sprites` array. In the `manageSprites` method, however, we iterate through the two new arrays for each frame iteration. First, we check whether there are any objects in `destroyableSprites` to be deleted. For each such object, we reenter the `sprites` array and delete the object using the `removeObject` method as soon as it is found.

---

* Immutable variants are available for both arrays and the dictionary without the addition of "Mutable" in the class name. These variants generally work faster than their mutable siblings, but not fast enough in practice to make up for the lost programming convenience.

The equality operator here is not comparing objects, but rather their pointers, and therefore it works very quickly. But beware: as soon as the object has been deleted, we must exit the inner for loop with a break command since, otherwise, we would catch the previously mentioned exception. We then continue in the outer for loop with the next destroyable object.

New sprites are added in a similar way to the sprites array. Here, however, since we are calling the addObject method on the sprites array, which is not currently being iterated, we can accomplish the task in a single step.

After we have added and deleted these sprites, we can optionally clear both auxiliary arrays with removeAllObjects, just in case some foreign objects may have crept in. (You never know how big a project will grow and what sort of mischief programmers might get into.)

To track the progress of the sprite manager, you can output the current content of the three arrays as follows:

```
NSLog(@"Sprites:%i destroyable:%i new:%i", [sprites count],
[destroyableSprites count], [newSprites count]);
```

Now, of course, we must ensure that the two auxiliary arrays are implemented. How, for example, do we add a Sprite to the destroyableSprites array? First, we note that in the playGame: method, the entire handling of a sprite is dealt with in two lines:

```
- (void) playGame {
    ...
    [self manageSprites];
    [self renderSprites];
    ...
}
```

After the manageSprite method has finished, we call the renderSprites method, which is expanded here only a bit beyond what we did in the previous examples:

```
- (void) renderSprites {
    for (Sprite *sprite in sprites) {
        if ([sprite isActive]) {
            [self checkSprite: sprite];
            [sprite draw];
        } else {
            [destroyableSprites addObject: sprite];
        }
    }
}
```

On the one hand, we iterate, as before, the sprites array and call the draw method of the Sprite class; on the other hand, we check each element to determine whether it is *active*.

The isActive method returns the current value of the active member of the Sprite class. We previously added this Boolean value to the Sprite class. Whenever we have determined that a Sprite is no longer needed, we set active = false.

The renderSprites method needs the rendering procedure only to launch the active sprites; inactive sprites are immediately banished to the destroyableSprites array and removed from memory.

Before the draw method is called on an active sprite, we inspect the sprite somewhat more closely; for this, we have added the checkSprite: method, in which we can carry out tasks on the sprite specifically related to the game. While the renderSprites method works independently of the particular game design and therefore belongs in the helper area, the checkSprite: method supports the active course of the game:

```
- (void) checkSprite: (Sprite *) sprite {
    if ([sprite getType] = = ZOMBIE || [sprite getType] = = PLAYER) {
        for (Sprite *sprite2test in sprites) {
            if ([sprite2test getType] = = CAR) {
                if ([sprite checkColWithSprite: sprite2test]) {
                    [sprite hit];
                }
            }
            if ([sprite getType] = = PLAYER
                && [sprite2test getType] = = REANIMATOR) {
                if ([sprite checkColWithSprite: sprite2test]) {
                    [(Reanimator *) sprite2test reanimate];
                }
            }
        }
    }
}
```

As you can see from the implementation, we carry out certain tasks for each sprite depending on its type:

- Zombies and the player are checked for collisions with cars sprites. When a collision has taken place, we call the new Sprite method hit. We have overwritten this in the Zombie and Player classes in order to define what is to happen when a Zombie or Player is hit.

- The player is additionally checked for a collision with the Reanimator item. If such is the case, we cast the sprite as Reanimator so that the reanimate method of the Reanimator class can be called. Later, we shall see more precisely what takes place in this sinister method.

We know how sprites can be deleted from memory on the fly. But how do we create them? Nothing could be simpler! We have already created a number of sprites. All we have to do now in using the GameManager is to provide a single interface:

```
- (void) createSprite: (int) type
                speed: (CGPoint) sxy
                  pos: (CGPoint) pxy;
```

Each Sprite in our game has a type, a speed, and an initial position. To define more individual characteristics, we branch inside the method according to each type. But be careful: We may not implement a switch-case statement. Objective-C forbids the creation of objects in a `case` statement, and therefore we branch here using `if` blocks. The process looks more or less the same for each type:

```
Zombie *zombie = [[Zombie alloc] initWithPic: @"zombie_4f.png"
                                     frameCnt: 4
                                    frameStep: 3
                                        speed: sxy
                                          pos: pxy];
[zombie setType: ZOMBIE];
[newSprites addObject: zombie];
[zombie release];
```

What is important here is that you add the new `Sprite` instance to the `newSprites` array. It will then be added to the actual `sprites` array in the `manageSprites` helper method as described previously.

Now in order to create a new `Sprite`, let us have a look at how the `Reanimator` operates. It has a single method and a counter that is increased at each frame and ensures that only one zombie is created every five frames:

```
- (void) reanimate {
    counter++;
    if (counter% 5 = = 0) {
        int px = [[GameManager getInstance] getRndBetween: 10 and: W-30];
        int py = [[GameManager getInstance] getRndBetween: H and: H+100];
        [[GameManager getInstance] createSprite: ZOMBIE
                                          speed: CGPointMake(0, -1)
                                            pos: CGPointMake(px, py)];
        [[GameManager getInstance] drawString: @"Re-Animate!"
                                           at: CGPointMake(pos.x-50,
                                               pos.y-30)];
    }
}
```

Easy as pie, right? Note that with `GameManager`, we call two additional helper methods: one to determine the random position of a new monster and the other to render a flickering "reanimate" activity indicator on the display using the `drawString:` method.

In our game, only new zombies will be created during runtime. The other objects (`Reanimator` items, `Player`, `Car`) are created only once, at the beginning of a new game, in the manager's `loadGame` method. There is one exception: If a zombie is run over, not only is it rendered inactive, but also an explosion animation is run to show that it has been returned from whence it came.* This one-time animation also involves a `Sprite`, which deletes itself after the animation sequence via `active = false`. But first things first.

## 3.10.10  One-Time Animation Sequences

Some animations are not looped endlessly. At times, one needs a one-time animation—for example, to animate the collection of an object or to explode an enemy spaceship.

---

* We can be forgiven such military action against these pixel creatures. After all, we know how we can bring them back to life later.

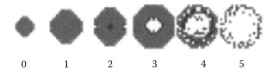

0       1       2       3       4       5

**Figure 3.16** smoke_6f.png.

For our game, we require a frame sequence that we can play whenever a zombie has run out of life force. Such explosion effects are used very often in games. By changing the alpha and color values in a system of particles, these can be rendered in real time. Sometimes, to enhance performance, prerendered animation phases are used, just as the movement sequence for our little zombie consists of individual frames. We now introduce these variants.

The foundation of the explosion animation is a sequence of six images (Figure 3.16). The principle of a one-time animation is always the same:

1. *Create a new animation object.*

2. *Play it at position xy.*

3. *Delete the animation object as soon as the animation is over.*

We have already worked out points 2 and 3 in our sprite management. (This is also why we are only now considering the topic of one shots.) To determine when the animation sequence has ended, we must make a small change to the Sprite class:

```
- (void) drawFrame {
    frameNr = [self updateFrame];
    ...
    [self renderSprite];
}

- (void) renderSprite {
    ...
}

- (int) updateFrame {
    if (frameStep = = cnt) {
        cnt = 0;
        frameNr++;
        if (frameNr > frameCnt-1) {
            frameNr = 0;
            cycleCnt++;
        }
    }
    cnt++;
    return frameNr;
}
```

First, we have split the drawFrame method into the two methods, renderSprite and updateFrame. This allows us to overwrite these methods as required. Furthermore, we have added, in the `updateFrame` method, the counter `cycleCnt`. This is increased by one whenever an animation cycle has run to completion. For our explosion animation, we need only a single iteration, since the smoke animation should appear only once. We therefore have only to overwrite the `drawFrame` method in the `Animation` class:

```
- (void) drawFrame {
    frameNr = [self updateFrame];
    if (cycleCnt = = 1) {
        active = false;
    }
    if (active) {
        [self renderSprite];
    }
}
```

Here, we simply check the value of `cycleCnt:`. If the smoke sequence has completed with the set number of `frameSteps`, we then set `active` to `false`, and the `GameManager` takes care of the rest for us.

However, we still have to consider where the animation is to be placed. In particular, explosion effects or even just our explosion smoke often have a different size from that of the game figures, yet they should be centered on top of them. Therefore, we have invested in an additional class method that, from this center, returns the upper left-hand corner, which is where the animation will ultimately be drawn:

```
+ (CGPoint) getOriginBasedOnCenterOf: (CGRect) rectMaster
                        andPic: (NSString *) picName
                   withFrameCnt: (int) fcnt {
    UIImage *picSlave = [[GameManager getInstance] getPic: picName];

    //Midpoint master
    int xmm = rectMaster.origin.x + rectMaster.size.width/2;
    int ymm = rectMaster.origin.y + rectMaster.size.height/2;

    //Origin of animation
    int xs = xmm-picSlave.size.width/2/fcnt;
    int ys = ymm-picSlave.size.height/2;
    return CGPointMake(xs, ys);
}
```

However, to keep the call to the animation as simple as possible, we hide the functionality in the `GameManager`:

```
- (void) createExplosionFor: (Sprite *) sprite {
    CGPoint p = [Animation getOriginBasedOnCenterOf: [sprite getRect]
                                    andPic: @"smoke_6f.png"
                               withFrameCnt: 6];
    [self createSprite: ANIMATION
                speed: CGPointMake(0, 0)
                  pos: p];
}
```

So, before we call the standardized creation mechanism for the sprites, we ask the class method `getOriginBasedOnCenterOf:` to return the exact position—based on the animation image and the `Sprite` rectangle—at which the animation is to be placed. Then the actual call to the smoke sequence takes a much simpler form:

```
[[GameManager getInstance] createExplosionFor: self];
```

Since the `createExplosionFor:` method expects a `Sprite` as a parameter, the call can be placed anywhere in a `Sprite` class. For our game, we place the call appropriately in the `hit` method of the `Zombie` class.

### 3.10.11   Finite-State Machines: Organization Made Easy

The Frameworks Core Graphics and OpenGL work with finite-state machines. But for a game as well, it makes sense to implement a simple finite-state automaton. As expected, we define this in the header of the `GameManager`:

```
enum states {
    LOAD_GAME,      //game data are loaded
    START_GAME,     //game can begin
    PLAY_GAME,      //game runs
    GAME_OVER,      //game is lost
    GAME_WON        //game is won
};
```

Of course, other states might be considered, but this example should suffice to demonstrate how one can set the program flow in a finite-state machine. The treatment of the states takes place in the central entry method `drawStatesWithFrame:`, which is called at each frame by the `MainView` class.

```
- (void) drawStatesWithFrame: (CGRect) frame {
    W = frame.size.width;
    H = frame.size.height;
    switch (state) {
        case LOAD_GAME:
            [self loadGame];
            state = START_GAME;
            break;
        case START_GAME:
            [background drawAtPoint: CGPointMake(0, 0)];
            [self drawString: @"Welcome!" at: CGPointMake(5, 5)];
            ...
            [self drawString: @"Tap screen to start!" at:
                CGPointMake(5, 145)];
            break;
        case PLAY_GAME:
            [self playGame];
            break;
        case GAME_OVER:
            [background drawAtPoint: CGPointMake(0, 0)];
            [self drawString: @"G A M E OVER" at: CGPointMake(5, 5)];
            ...
            [self drawString: @"Tap screen!" at: CGPointMake(5, 85)];
            break;
        case GAME_WON:
            [background drawAtPoint: CGPointMake(0, 0)];
```

```
            [self drawString: @"Y O U  M A D E  I T !" at:
                CGPointMake(5, 5)];
        ...
            [self drawString: @"Tap screen!" at: CGPointMake(5, 85)];
            break;
        default: NSLog(@"ERROR: Unknown game state:%i", state);
            break;
    }
}
```

We can now define what should happen for each state. After the state LOAD_GAME ends, the program automatically switches to the START_GAME state. For the PLAY_GAME state, the playGame method is called, and the START_GAME state simply waits for user input.

To force a state change, we can call the GameManager externally—for instance, in the Player class—when the player has lost his life points:

```
- (void) hit {
    [argghPic drawAtPoint:
        CGPointMake(pos.x, pos.y - argghPic.size.height)];
    health- ;
    if (health = = 0) {
        [[GameManager getInstance] setState: GAME_OVER];
    }
}
```

## 3.10.12  User Input

To determine when the user has interacted with the GameManager, we have declared three interfaces that, as described earlier, are fed input by the MainView class:

```
- (void) touchBegan: (CGPoint) p;
- (void) touchMoved: (CGPoint) p;
- (void) touchEnded;
```

As soon as the touchBegan: method is called, we know that the user has executed a tap to the display. We can use this information in our finite-state machine to change from the welcome screen to the game screen:

```
- (void) handleStates {
    if (state = = START_GAME) {
        state = PLAY_GAME;
    }
    else if (state = = GAME_OVER || state = = GAME_WON) {
        state = LOAD_GAME;
    }
}
```

For this, the handleStates method simply has to be called in the touchBegan: method. For example, if the game is in the state GAME_OVER, a single tap suffices for the handleStates method to switch to the LOAD_GAME state and then automatically to the START_GAME state.

But the three touch methods accomplish even more. For our game, not only the player, but also every zombie created, is controlled by a swipe gesture. Therefore, in these methods, we must iterate over all the sprites and forward the message to them:

```
- (void) touchBegan: (CGPoint) p {
    [self handleStates];
    if (state = = PLAY_GAME) {
        for (Sprite *sprite in sprites) {
            if ([sprite isActive]) {
                if ([sprite getType] = = ZOMBIE ||
                    [sprite getType] = = PLAYER) {
                    [(Zombie *) sprite setTouch: p];
                }
            }
        }
    }
}

- (void) touchMoved: (CGPoint) p {
    if (state = = PLAY_GAME) {
        [self touchBegan: p];
    }
}

- (void) touchEnded {
    if (state = = PLAY_GAME) {
        for (Sprite *sprite in sprites) {
            if ([sprite isActive]) {
                if ([sprite getType] = = ZOMBIE
                    || [sprite getType] = = PLAYER) {
                    [(Zombie *) sprite touchEnded];
                }
            }
        }
    }
}
```

Thus, the touch point is passed through all the way to the setTouch: method of the Zombie class:

```
- (void) setTouch: (CGPoint) point {
    if ([self checkColWithPoint: point]) {
        touchAction = true;
    }
    if (touchAction && !saved) {
        touchPoint = point;
        speed.x = (touchPoint.x - pos.x)/20;//deltaX
        speed.y = (touchPoint.y - pos.y)/20;//deltaY
    }
}

- (void) touchEnded {
    touchAction = false;
}
```

As you can see, we implemented the swipe in the same way as in our UserInput example, except that here we allow the swipe only for a particular type of Sprite.

Therefore, we have provided the `Sprite` class with a further collision method based on the previously introduced collision example:

```
if ([self checkColWithPoint: point]) {
    touchAction = true;
}
```

The flag `touchAction` is then set to `true` only when a finger collides with a sprite. Otherwise, we have added only a `saved` flag to the `Zombie` class, which is activated as soon as a sprite reaches the green demarcation line.

In order for a zombie to assume its original direction of motion after the end of the swipe gesture, the `draw` method is overwritten as follows:

```
- (void) draw {
    [super draw];

    //Stop movement
    if (speed.x > 0 && touchPoint.x < pos.x) speed.x = 0;
    if (speed.x < 0 && touchPoint.x > pos.x) speed.x = 0;
    if (speed.y > 0 && touchPoint.y < pos.y) speed.y = -1;
    if (speed.y < 0 && touchPoint.y > pos.y) speed.y = -1;

    if (pos.y < [[GameManager getInstance] getTargetY]) {
        saved = true;
        [self setSpeed: CGPointMake(0, -10)];
        if (pos.y < -30) {
            active = false;
            [[GameManager getInstance] savedZombie];
        }
    } else {
        saved = false;
    }
}
```

Here you can also see how the green line is handled: `getTargetY` returns the y-position. If the sprite is above this value, then the `saved` flag is set to `true`, and the sprite is accelerated so that it can begin the invasion as quickly as possible. We also use the `saved` flag in the `hit` method of the `Zombie` class, in order to exclude further injury of a zombie by a car. We have finally saved our zombies!

The swipe treatment for the `Player` is similar, with the difference that the `Player` is in a danger zone whether he is located above or below the green line and that he stands still after the swipe gesture. Therefore, we have again overwritten the `draw` method in the `Player` class. Furthermore, to prevent the player from leaving the screen borders in the heat of the action, we can optionally build the following check into the `draw` method:

```
if (pos.x > W-frameW) {pos.x = W-frameW; speed.x = 0;}
if (pos.x < 0) {pos.x = 0; speed.x = 0;}
if (pos.y > H-frameH) {pos.y = H-frameH; speed.y = 0;}
if (pos.y < 0) {pos.y = 0; speed.y = 0;}
```

This check has the effect that the player always remains fully visible, even on the edges. After all, a figure that was only half visible would be difficult to move and control.

### 3.10.13 HUD and Scoring

We have now described all the main tasks of the GameManager. Both the Sprite and finite-state machine have been deliberately treated very generally, in order to make them easily reusable in other games. We have again discussed special characteristics such as swipe control. With the finite-state machine we can also implement a simple menu. And, of course, every game needs to have a decent display of the score so that the player always knows how well or badly things are going. Let us conclude by looking once more at the final playGame method:

```
- (void) playGame {
    [background drawAtPoint: CGPointMake(0, 0)];
    [self manageSprites];
    [self renderSprites];
    [self drawTargetLine];

    NSString *hud = [NSString stringWithFormat:
        @"HLT:%i SVD:%i/%i LST:%i",
                    [player getHealth], saved, savedMax, lost];
    [self drawString: hud at: CGPointMake(5, 5)];

    if (saved > = savedMax) {
        state = GAME_WON;
    }
}
```

The entire game is expressed in under 10 lines. For displaying the HUD, we again use the auxiliary method drawString:. You are free to make the HUD more complex. If you are working with strings, you can use the stringWithFormat class method of the NSString class to integrate numeric values into the string, as is done with console output. We have integrated the point count into the Sprite classes, which in turn access the GameManager (Figure 3.17).

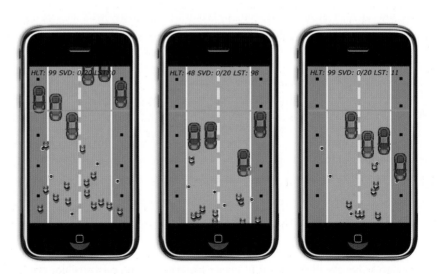

**Figure 3.17** Screen shots of the finished game.

3.  Game Development From 0 to 60 in No Time Flat

If you like, you can assign a bonus score based on the number of rescued zombies and give extra points for a low number of lost zombies. However you decide, at this point, you should be able to expand the game or use it as a basis for your own experimentation. For the coming larger projects, we shall build on the basic framework that we have constructed in this chapter.

# ▌ 3.11 Zappp, Brzzz, Booom, Pennng! Background Music and Sound Effects

Music and sound effects are very important for games. It was not so long ago that the most commonly used acoustic design mechanism in mobile games was the playing of time-inexpensive background MIDI files. Real-time sound effects were seldom found; the devices were too slow and the implementation of the interface was too poor and error prone. Those who remember the arcade classics from the 1980s know that a lot of atmosphere was lost. Even such illustrious home computers as the Commodore C64 gave a real edge to their games with their separate sound chip, such as the legendary SID chip.

For devices in the iOS family, there are fortunately several possibilities for providing games with exciting music and sounds. The most direct solution uses the so-called system sounds. These are also used by the iOS UI and can be incorporated via the AudioToolbox/AudioServices framework. After a sound has been created with its own ID, the sound can be played at any time via `AudioServicesPlaySystem Sound(soundID)`. The drawback is that polyphonic sounds cannot be thus implemented. That is, only one tone can be played at a time. In addition, the length of a sound is limited to 30 seconds. Better possibilities are offered by OpenAL, especially with regard to realistic 3D placement of sounds (above all when the playback is through headphones).

The most extensive facilities can be found in the Core Audio framework and Audio Queue Services. Here, even real-time access to the audio buffer is possible. Anyone wishing to develop music software with virtual synthesizers will find these a must. Since the framework sticks very closely to the hardware and therefore offers many low-level options, the code to produce even a simple sound is quite extensive. OpenAL is based directly on Core Audio so that one can develop high-end audio solutions with an acceptable amount of effort. Since OpenAL is closely related to OpenGL, we shall discuss this topic in a later chapter. For games with few sound effects, this overhead is unnecessary.

Therefore, the iOS SDK has offered, since version 2.2, the `AVAudioPlayer`, which is also part of the Core Audio Framework but abstracted from it; therefore, it can be used for game development with comparatively little effort.

## 3.11.1 Preparations: Integrating the Framework

To gain access to the audio interface, we must first integrate the `AVFoundation` framework. Let us begin a new project, called "Sound," based on the GameManager project from the previous section. We delete unused classes and resources (later, we shall introduce the relevant parts in greater detail). For playing sounds, as was the case for graphics, the `GameManager` class provides the central framework. You could, of course, include the following code in any other class you like.

The general procedure for integrating a framework is as follows:

- Via the left sidebar, switch to the project settings.

- Under "TARGETS," choose "Build Phases" and "Link Binary With Libraries."

- You should now see the available frameworks of the iOS SDK.

- Select the AVFoundation.framework.

- Import the framework in the header: #import <AVFoundation/ AVFoundation.h>

The absolute path to the framework is *Developer/Platforms/iPhoneOS.platform/ Developer/SDKs/iPhoneOSx.x.sdk/System/Library/Frameworks/AVFoundation.framework*. Now you can play your own sounds in every class that integrates the AVFoundation framework header:

```
NSString *path = [[NSBundle mainBundle] pathForResource: @"track1.wav"
                                                 ofType: nil];
AVAudioPlayer *sound = [[AVAudioPlayer alloc]
    initWithContentsOfURL: [NSURL fileURLWithPath: path] error: nil];
[sound play];
```

As you can see, the class is built less conveniently than, for example, UIImage; to fetch a sound from the resource folder, you must give the path to the file explicitly. The NSBundle and NSURL classes help you, however. You have only to take care that the sound file track1.wav is correctly integrated into the project via "Add -> Existing Files" (as was the case with images). Then, within Xcode, you can group the sound files in subfolders as you like. The type of specification is of no significance for the NSBundle class. The AVAudioPlayer reads the format information from the file header and throws an exception if an unsupported audio format is referenced.* We will show later how to trap errors.

## 3.11.2 How to Use the AVAudioPlayer

Once a player has been created, you have several methods at your disposal for further processing of your sounds:

- play: This plays the sound once (see the preceding example).

- prepareToPlay: This prepares the sound for playing; the sound is called implicitly in the call to play.

---

* Note: Instead of using the initWithContentsOfURL: method, you can feed the player with your own data. To do so, you can use the initWithData: method, which accepts an NSData object as the parameter. For example, you could load into this method an on-the-fly-generated WAV file that you have created in the program by software synthesis. The iPhone does not have a synthesizer chip like those of the famous personal computers of the 1980s or the GameBoy. But you can at least emulate such sounds with the initWithData: method, even if you cannot create them in real time. With the use of the AVAudioPlayer, the latencies would be too high. For real-time music applications, you should anyhow rely on the Low Level Core Audio framework and the Audio Queue Services.

- `pause`: Play is stopped; the sound remains ready for playing.

- `stop`: Play is stopped; the player is reset to its original state.

The `play` and `prepareToPlay` methods also return a Boolean value that shows whether the sound is playable. For each sound, you need precisely one `AVAudioPlayer` instance. You cannot prepare multiple sounds to be played with the same instance.

Before playing the sound, you can query and/or set a few useful properties:

- `sound.volume`: You can specify the playback volume as a `float` value in the range 0.0 (silent) to 1.0 (maximum volume). This can also be changed during playback—for example, to fade a sound in or out. Values greater than 1.0 distort the sound.

- `sound.numberOfLoops`: –1 means infinite repetition. Values greater than 0 give the number of repetitions. Clean-cut loops will be repeated seamlessly.

- `sound.duration`: This returns the length of the sound (`double` precision of type `NSTimeInterval`).

- `sound.currentTime`: Here you can determine when a sound should begin, also as a `double` value. If the value is greater than `sound.duration`, then, of course, you will not hear anything as it exceeds the length.

- `sound.playing`: This returns a Boolean value that tells whether the sound is currently playing.

The maximum length of a sound depends solely on the device's memory capacity. Of course, long sounds require more time to load.

## 3.11.3 Polyphony and Sound Formats

To play polyphonic sounds, you must create several instances of the `AVAudioPlayer`, each with its own sound. But be careful: The simultaneous playback of several distinct sounds requires an *uncompressed* sound format. The `AVAudioPlayer` supports at least the following sound formats:

- WAV, MP3, AIF, AAC, ALAC, CAF

These formats contain individual samples (amplitude of the waveform at each time interval) and various precisions and sampling rates. Therefore, the MIDI format is not supported by the player, since MIDI is not a true audio format, but rather contains control data for a sound database (thus, in principle, only the notes and not the actual waveform), while audio formats contain all the information to reproduce the sound wave. Thus, you can also reproduce natural sounds, such as the human voice, in contrast to the era of the Commodore C64. The SID chip is constructed like a synthesizer and provides oscillators, filters, and envelopes for sound generation, though it cannot reproduce stored sample data.

If you want to produce several sounds simultaneously on the iPhone, your best bet is the WAV format (8–24 bits, 8–44.1 Hz), since this stores the amplitudes in uncompressed form (linear PCM).

For compressed sounds such as AAC, MP3, or ALAC (Apple lossless), Core Audio implements a hardware-accelerated decoder; however, it can process only one sound at a time. This means that

- The simultaneous playback of WAV sounds is limited only by the power of the CPU and the amount of memory. The amplitude information can be passed directly to the speaker without having to be decoded.

- Only one MP3 sound can be played at a time (in addition to WAV sounds).

So why MP3? Longer music segments in WAV format with CD-compatible resolution can quickly grow to several megabytes in size. MP3 takes up much less space. However, since the iPhone iOS can process only one MP3 sound in the decoder, the MP3 format is suitable for longer segments of background music. Sound effects are generally not so long and can therefore be recorded in WAV format at a reasonable size. Of course, you are free to use WAV sounds exclusively. However, since MP3 sounds are converted in the hardware decoder into audible sounds, they require no additional computation time, so performance is unaffected and you use less memory space.*

### 3.11.4 Where Do I Find Suitable Sounds?

Now we know how sound is reproduced and which formats are suitable for which applications. On the web you can find numerous pages with open source samples that are freely available and indeed even complete tracks that can be used without a license. A collection of sound effects and noises can be found, for example, at *www. pacdv.com/sounds/index.html.* Just to be safe, always ask the sound provider whether the rights of use granted apply to your project. Alternatively, you can purchase sample CDs with preloaded loops and individually sampled instruments that you can use to piece together complete tracks. The audio material on such CDs is generally usable for your own projects at no additional charge, and the cost of such CDs is correspondingly high.

It is cheaper, of course, to produce your sounds yourself. The iPhone iOS has developed into a professional music production platform. Why not produce your own sounds with the tools provided?

A great-sounding monophonic synthesizer with an unfortunately somewhat cryptic operation is *Noise.io.* The program *Nanoloop,* on the other hand, derives from the GameBoy and provides the typical 1980s bleep sounds for the iPhone; the sequencer's operation is easy to learn. Somewhat more modern and electronic is the perfect TB-303/TR-909 emulation *TechnoBox* or, for something truly authentic, *Rebirth,* the PC classic from Propellerhead, newly reissued for the iPhone.

---

* Additional information on audio playback and supported formats can be found under "Audio Playback and Recording Formats" at *https://developer.apple.com/library/ios/#documentation/AudioVideo/Conceptual/MultimediaPG/UsingAudio/UsingAudio.html.*

**Figure 3.18** Korg iElectribe (iPad).

Typical game sounds are usually short and to the point. Therefore, specialized synthesizers for drum sounds work particularly well. For the iPad, Korg has put out the *iElectribe,* an emulation of the first hardware version of the famous virtual analog "Rhythm Synthesizer" of 1999. This program also has the advantage that created tracks can be exported directly as WAV files into iTunes. From there, of course, they can find their way directly into your Xcode project.

For the example project "Sound," we have created five sound effects and a drum loop with *iElectribe* and exported them without further processing into the project via "Bounce Pattern." We have set the speed of the sequencer for the sound effects in such a way that the decay of a sound coincides almost precisely with the length of a pattern. We thereby avoid postprocessing with audio editing software such as *WaveLab.* We have also exported the two-measure drum loop via "Bounce Pattern." The *iElectribe* automatically takes care that the WAV file is cut to beat accuracy (Figure 3.18).

The six sounds `track1.wav` and `sound1.wav` through `sound5.wav` can be found in the example project in the folder RESOURCES > SOUNDS.

### 3.11.5 Integrating Sounds into a Game

Okay, then, we have suitable sounds. But for trouble-free integration into our game projects, we still need a suitable playback engine. We have the following requirements:

- **Latency:** The sounds should be playable instantly at any time. We must therefore ensure that the sounds are already loaded.

- **Loops:** This is the repeated playback of a sound. If a loop that is already playing is instructed to play again, such a request should be ignored to avoid unpleasant overlap.

- **Polyphony:** Multiple sounds should be playable simultaneously.

- **End:** It should be possible to stop a sound at any time.

Polyphony is achieved through the use of WAV files. In addition to the required playSound method, the other requirements lead us to three additional methods, which we define in the header of the GameManager class as interfaces:

```
- (AVAudioPlayer *) getSound: (NSString *) soundName;
- (void) playSound: (NSString *) soundName;
- (void) loopSound: (NSString *) soundName;
- (void) stopSound: (NSString *) soundName;
```

The getSound: method works like the getPic: method, with a hash table in which the sounds are stored as AVAudioPlayer instances. The three methods for playing and ending a sound are then called by the getSound: method, so the getSound: method does not generally have to be called separately.

The following line plays back a sound once:

```
[[GameManager getInstance] playSound: @"sound1.wav"];
```

Repeated calls—for example, within a game loop—have the result that, at each call, the sound begins from the beginning: A genre-typical staccato effect arises, which can be desirable when shooting is taking place. However, it is better to use the playSound: method for event-related noises: when the player is wounded or a character jumps up, punches an adversary, etc. If you want to play the identical sound polyphonically, the WAV file must be integrated into multiple players.

For looped sounds and, therefore, ideally for background music, the following call suffices:

```
[[GameManager getInstance] loopSound: @"track1.wav"];
```

The sound will be repeated endlessly. If the end of the sound is reached, it is played again from the beginning. In contrast to the playSound: method, the loopSound: method behaves no differently inside the game loop; If the sound is already looped, a repeated request to play it is ignored.

To stop a sound, whether or not it is looped or even no longer playing, place the following code line (in every class that imports the GameManager header):

```
[[GameManager getInstance] stopSound: @"track1.wav"];
```

Before we introduce a practical example to test these methods, let us look once again at the implementation of the methods in GameManager:

```
- (AVAudioPlayer *) getSound: (NSString *) soundName {
    @try {
        AVAudioPlayer *sound = [[self getDictionary]
            objectForKey: soundName];
        if (!sound) {
            NSError *error;
            NSString *path = [[NSBundle mainBundle]
```

```
                    pathForResource: soundName ofType: nil];
            sound = [[AVAudioPlayer alloc]
                initWithContentsOfURL: [NSURL fileURLWithPath: path]
                error: &error];
            if (!sound) {
                NSLog(@"ERROR: Wrong sound format:%@. Description:%@",
                    soundName, [error localizedDescription]);
            } else {
                sound.volume = 0.7;
                int len = sound.duration;
                [[self getDictionary] setObject: sound forKey: soundName];
                NSLog(@"%@ loaded, duration:%i sec", soundName, len);
                [sound release];
            }
        }
        return sound;
    } @catch (id theException) {
        NSLog(@"ERROR:%@ not found!", soundName);
    }
    return nil;
}
```

As you can see, as with the getPic: method, we again use the
NSMutableDictionary. If the sound already exists, we return the Player instance
directly. It already contains the loaded sound, which can be played via the play method.
We may ignore the prepareToPlay method for brief sound effects for latency-free playback. Nonetheless, we should ensure that all sound instances are loaded before their first
use in the game. We accomplish this ideally in the preloader of the GameManager:

```
- (void) preloader {
    [self getSound: @"sound1.wav"];
    [self getSound: @"sound2.wav"];
    [self getSound: @"sound3.wav"];
    [self getSound: @"sound4.wav"];
    [self getSound: @"sound5.wav"];
    [self getSound: @"track1.wav"];
    ...
}
```

Only one Player is created for every WAV file. Therefore, we can play the individual
Players polyphonically, but simultaneous playback of the same file is possible only with
an additional Player.

But back to the getSound: implementation: We have placed the entire code in a try-
catch block, which gives us an error message if the sound file was not found in the file
system. If the sound exists in a format that the AVAudioPlayer does not support, the
initWithContentsOfURL of the AVAudioPlayer class returns a nil object. We use
an NSError object for error description, which returns via its localizedDescription
method the reason for the nil object. If all goes well, we set the default volume of the Player
from 1.0 to 0.7. For well controlled sounds, a volume of 0.3 might be fine, since the loudspeakers of the older iPhone generations sound quite loud and jarring. The user can, in any case,
regulate the volume with the external volume control on the iOS device. Furthermore, we
output the duration of the sound, rounded to seconds, over the console via

```
int len = sound.duration;
```

The actual precision of the `duration` field is of the type `double`, but we are not going to use that here.

The implementation of the three methods for precise playback of a sound is unspectacular:

```
- (void) playSound: (NSString *) soundName {
    AVAudioPlayer *sound = [self getSound: soundName];
      if (sound) {
        sound.currentTime = 0;
        if (!sound.playing) {
            sound.numberOfLoops = 0;
            [sound play];
        }
      }
}

- (void) loopSound: (NSString *) soundName {
    AVAudioPlayer *sound = [self getSound: soundName];
      if (sound) {
        if (!sound.playing) {
            sound.currentTime = 0;
            sound.numberOfLoops = -1;
            [sound play];
        }
      }
}

- (void) stopSound: (NSString *) soundName {
    AVAudioPlayer *sound = [self getSound: soundName];
      if (sound && sound.playing) {
        [sound stop];
      }
}
```

In the `playSound:` method, we check whether the sound has already been played and, if it has not been played, we play it. Independently of that, we always set the start position of the sound to zero via `currentTime`, to create the previously described stutter effect. We thereby ensure that every call to the method leads to an audible event. The `loopSound:` method, on the other hand, plays a sound only if it is not already being played and therefore queries the Boolean value `sound.playing`. Here, too, the start position of the sound is set to zero before each playback. With –1, we set the number of repetitions to infinity.

To conclude, let us consider a deployment scenario in which we want to loop one sound in the background and play the sound effects once per touch. Thus, we test the robustness of the sound playback on the iPhone; just as in a game, the sounds should be ready to play at any time. For this endurance test we can use a soundboard application, which plays back each sound following the pressing of a (virtual) key. The App Store offers a variety of soundboard applications. One variant of interest is the iPhone/iPad program *Bloom,* which was developed by the experimental musician Brian Eno together with Peter Chilvers (who worked on the hit game *Creatures*).

Every touch to the display plays back an audio file. The program keeps track of the temporal order of the touches and plays them in sequence, like a sequencer. However, the tones are altered algorithmically, so new sound sequences are produced in the spirit of generative music.

For our example, we are not going to go so far, but we shall at least keep to the following basic concept:

- Our five sound effects created with *iElectribe* should be played following a touch to the screen.

- The sounds will be distributed equally along the y-axis, corresponding to the pitch in the *Bloom* application.

- The game loop regulates the time course. The program should note the time at which a sound is triggered and play it in sequence.

- The loop encompasses 100 frames.

- Every press of the display creates a widening circle that slowly becomes more transparent and finally disappears entirely.

- If one presses the bottom left-hand part of the display, the looped background sound can be turned on or off.

- If one presses the bottom right-hand part of the display, all currently stored sound events will be cleared. The sequencer will be returned to its initial state.

That may sound a bit complicated, but with our previous knowledge, it is very easy to implement. All touch events that were registered along the time axis are stored in the sequencer and then played as soon as the next iteration places the corresponding time stamp. For this example program, we shall ignore the synchronization of the sound effects with the background loop since we want to use the frame number of the loop area merely for the implementation of the minisequencer.

Since the playback of a sound is linked to the rendering of a circle, we of course use the `Sprite` class for this. And since the sprite vanishes after the fadeout, we are dealing as well with an animation, with the difference that the fadeout of the alpha value does not depend on the frames of a film strip.

Listing 3.12 Sprite.h

```
#import "Sprite.h"

@interface Circle : Sprite {
    int radius;
    float alpha;
}

- (id) initWithRadius: (int) rds
                  pos: (CGPoint) pxy;

@end
```

## Listing 3.13 Sprite.m

```objc
#import "Circle.h"
#import "GameManager.h"

@implementation Circle

- (id) initWithRadius: (int) rds
                 pos: (CGPoint) pxy {

    if (self = [super init]) {
        radius = rds;
        pos = pxy;
        alpha = 1;
        active = true;

        NSString *sound = @"sound1.wav";
        int step = H/5;//5 sounds
        if (pos.y < step*1) {
            sound = @"sound1.wav";
        }
        else if (pos.y < step*2) {
            sound = @"sound2.wav";
        }
        else if (pos.y < step*3) {
            sound = @"sound3.wav";
        }
        else if (pos.y < step*4) {
            sound = @"sound4.wav";
        }
        else if (pos.y < step*5) {
            sound = @"sound5.wav";
        }
        [[GameManager getInstance] playSound: sound];
    }

    return self;
}

- (void) draw {
    alpha - = 0.03;
    radius + = 2;
    if (alpha < = 0) {
        active = false;
    }

    CGContextRef gc = UIGraphicsGetCurrentContext();
    CGContextSetRGBFillColor(gc, 0,1,0, alpha);
    CGRect rect =
        CGRectMake (pos.x-radius, pos.y-radius, radius*2, radius*2);
    CGContextAddEllipseInRect(gc, rect);
    CGContextDrawPath(gc, kCGPathFill);
}

@end
```

No PNG graphics are needed for the sound circle, and therefore we create a separate `init` method. The only parameters that we need for the circle are the initial radius and position at which the screen was touched; this position will be used in the `draw` method as the midpoint of the circle.

The sound that is produced depends only on the y-position, so we can select it and play it in the `initWithRadius:pos:` method as a function of the touch point. The y-axis is cut into uniform strips, depending on the screen height and the number of sounds (= `step`) so that we can adapt the program effortlessly to other iOS resolutions. Since we are ignoring the x-position, we have some scope to expand the app later—for example, to use the x-position to control the volume of the sound by adapting the sound methods in the `GameManager`.

Playing a sound takes place in the `init` constructor of the `Circle` class, so we need only to overwrite the `draw` method inherited from the `Sprite` to start the circle animation simultaneously: The radius will be increased by 2 pixels per frame and the alpha value reduced by 0.03. When the alpha value reaches 0 and the circle has become completely transparent and therefore no longer visible, we can then set the `active` flag to `false`, and the `Sprite` will be cleared from memory by the `GameManager` at the next iteration.

The creation of a new `Circle` object is done as it was previously in the `createSprite:speed:pos:` method of the `GameManager`. Since we are currently using only one `Sprite` for the sound app, the code is correspondingly simple:

```
- (void) createSprite: (int) type
              speed: (CGPoint) sxy
                pos: (CGPoint) pxy {
    if (type = = CIRCLE) {
        Circle *circle = [[Circle alloc] initWithRadius: 10
                                                    pos: pxy
                            ];
        [circle setType: CIRCLE];
        [newSprites addObject: circle];
        [circle release];
    } else {
        NSLog(@"ERROR: unknown Sprite type:%i", type);
    }
}
```

Before we call this method on a new touch, we have still to worry about the implementation of the sequencer, which has only to note the time and the touch position. We create a new class to store these data.

Listing 3.14 SoundEvent.h

```
@interface SoundEvent : NSObject {
    int frameTime;
    CGPoint pos;
}
```

```
-  (id)  initWithTime:  (int)  frt
                  pos:  (CGPoint)  pxy;

-  (int)  getTime;
-  (CGPoint)  getPos;

@end
```

Listing 3.15  SoundEvent.m

```
#import  "SoundEvent.h"

@implementation  SoundEvent

-  (id)  initWithTime:  (int)  frt
                  pos:  (CGPoint)  pxy  {

    if  (self  =  [super  init])  {
        frameTime  =  frt;
        pos  =  pxy;
    }
    return  self;
}

-  (int)  getTime  {
    return  frameTime;
}

-  (CGPoint)  getPos  {
    return  pos;
}

@end
```

There is no need to comment further on the structure of this class. Instead of an explicit formulation of a getter/setter pair, you can, of course, use the @property directive, which is typical of Objective-C. We create the sequencer according to the example of a sprite in the GameManager class as a variable array:

```
int  time;//frame  counter
NSMutableArray  *sequencer;
...
sequencer  =  [[NSMutableArray  alloc]  initWithCapacity:99];
```

The time variable represents a simple counter, which holds the number of iterations of the game loop. Since we have set up a loop area of 100 frames, the counter will be reset to 0 when it reaches 100. The complete implementation of the sequencer can thus take place in the playGame method of the GameManager:

```
-  (void)  playGame  {
    //frame  counter
```

```
    time ++;
    if (time > 100) {//loop area
        time = 0;
    }

    for (SoundEvent *event in sequencer) {
        if ([event getTime] = = time) {
            [self createSprite: CIRCLE
                        speed: CGPointMake(0, 0)
                          pos: [event getPos]];
        }
    }

    ...
}
```

For each frame, the `sequencer` array is iterated through all its elements, and it compares the stored frame with the current `time` frame. If the two are equal, a new `Circle` object is created, to which the stored position of the `SoundEvent` is passed, since this is applicable to the sound that is going to be played. We ignore the `speed` data, since the circle is not going to move.

To feed the new touch events into the sequencer, we have merely to adapt the `touch-Began:` method:

```
- (void) touchBegan: (CGPoint) p {
    [self handleStates];

    if (p.x < 130 && p.y > H-50) {
        static bool playMusic = true;
        if (playMusic) {
            [[GameManager getInstance] stopSound: @"track1.wav"];
            playMusic = false;
            NSLog(@"Loop off");
        } else {
            [[GameManager getInstance] loopSound: @"track1.wav"];
            playMusic = true;
            NSLog(@"Loop on");
        }
    } else if (p.x > W-60 && p.y > H-50) {
        NSLog(@"Clear sequencer");
        [sequencer removeAllObjects];
    } else {
        [self createSprite: CIRCLE
                    speed: CGPointMake(0, 0)
                      pos: p];

        SoundEvent *event = [[SoundEvent alloc] initWithTime: time pos: p];
        [sequencer addObject: event];
        [event release];
    }
}

- (void) touchMoved: (CGPoint) p {}
- (void) touchEnded {}
```

First, we provide here for the treatment of the two buttons that toggle the loop sound and clear the sequencer array. We determine whether a button has been pressed by

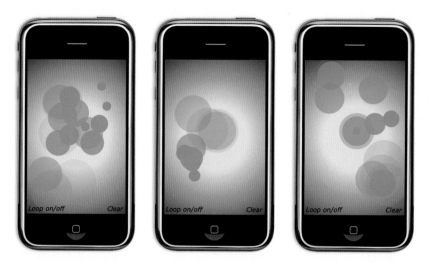

Figure 3.19 The Sound app in action.

the touch position. You can, of course, create your own buttons to beautify the program; for this you can either use the predefined UI components of the UIKit or implement the button as an immovable sprite.

If the touch point is not over one of the two buttons, we play the sound via the `createSprite:speed:pos:` method and store the current position together with the `time` variable in a `SoundEvent` object (Figure 3.19). Done!

If you like, you can enhance the application with your own sounds or modify the restriction on the loop area. You will see that even the original iPhone can play quite a few sound events simultaneously. But sooner or later you will have to call it quits: Too many events eventually bring even the most powerful processor to its knees. To be sure, the newer devices of the iPhone family such as the iPad 2 and iPhone 4S will bear a greater computational burden than the first generations. But as a rule, for games, you do not need more than two simultaneous sound effects and one background soundtrack. If you require a greater level of polyphony, you should use the OpenAL library, which will be introduced in an upcoming chapter. There we shall introduce the same interfaces as in the present project so that the performance differences can be easily compared. Of course, we must also consider that the use of the UIKit and Core Graphics to render the sound circle requires more computational power than an optimized access to the graphics chip using OpenGL. But with the resulting app, you can nevertheless already test which sound effects and tracks go together and which do not. And perhaps you will create an innovative music game beyond the umpteenth remake of *Senso* (Ralph H. Baer, Milton Bradley).

# ▌▌ 3.12  Storing Data

Mobile games are often played by people on the move and therefore must support being interrupted during a running game—for example, when a long-delayed flight is finally called. In short, you must ensure that you can store the current state of the game and restore it when the game is restarted. And perhaps, in addition, you would like to store the high scores achieved or the current game level.

How does it work? Well, first we need to know when things should be stored. Whenever the user presses the home button, the `applicationWillResignActive:` method of the delegate is executed, and here you can trigger the memory-storing process. But how are the data to be stored and in what format?

We have seen a number of times that iPhone iOS offers several options:

- **Via the app's file system:** Each app has its own memory region, which you can access via the `NSFileManager`.

- **Using the `NSUserDefaults` class:** This is also the first choice for managing options via the iOS settings menu (*Settings Bundle*).

- For **database applications,** the SQLite database is available.

- The API **Core Data** offers system-level access. Core Data is also used by the SQLite database.

- Finally, you have the possibility of storing data via the `UIWebView` and an **HTML page** embedded within it. This is given by the integrated WebKit browser, which supports the HTML5 standard and thereby also the long-term storage of data, including via a `localStorage` object (JavaScript).

For saving high scores or game states, there is the `NSUserDefaults` class. In addition to support for simple data types such as `NSInteger`, `float`, and `BOOL`, this class also allows for the storing of objects. You can therefore, if you wish, *freeze* the current state of a game at any time.

To give an example, let us create a new project, "DataStorage," which can be found in the download folder. As a template, we shall use the GameManager project.

Two methods suffice for reading and storing objects, which we add to the GameManager class:

```
- (void) saveObject: (id) object key: (NSString *) key {
    NSUserDefaults *storage = [NSUserDefaults standardUserDefaults];
    [storage setObject: object forKey: key];
}

- (id) readObjectForKey: (NSString *) key {
    NSUserDefaults *storage = [NSUserDefaults standardUserDefaults];
    return [storage objectForKey: key];
}
```

Access to an `NSUserDefaults` instance can occur at any time via the class method `standardUserDefaults`. Since we wish to store objects of various types, we choose the generic type `id`. For every stored item, we must assign a key in the form of an `NSString`. This makes it possible to read out the stored value at a later time.

Of course, a stored item can be deleted:

```
[storage removeObjectForKey: key];
```

You can store and read a primitive data type such as `int` as follows:

```
//store
[storage setInteger: 22 forKey: @"an integer"];
//read
int val = [storage integerForKey: @"an integer"];//val = 22
```

The key to identify the item is, in this case, the string @"an integer." In practice, however, you will likely not be storing isolated integer values or other simple data types. Instead of initiating a number of separate memory operations, it is more efficient to store your data in an object and then place that object in the device's long-term memory with a single write instruction.

For the following example, we shall store a quotation from Samuel Taylor Coleridge's famous poem "Kubla Khan" from the year 1797. Since strings are objects, we use the previously implemented methods `saveObject` and `readObjectForKey`:

```
//store
NSString *ColeridgeQuote =
    @" But oh! that deep romantic chasm which slanted down the green
        hill athwart a cedarn cover!";
NSString *KublaKey = @"KublaKey";
[self saveObject: ColeridgeQuote key: KublaKey];

//read
NSString *result = [self readObjectForKey: KublaKey];
if (result) {
    NSLog(@"Storage output:%@", result);
}
```

We place the code in the `loadGame` method of the `GameManager`. Since we know that `KublaKey` returns an `NSString` object, we can assign this result directly to the `result` instance.

### 3.12.1  Example: High Scores

To store multiple data at one go, we again turn to the `NSMutableDictionary` class. For each new high score, a congratulatory message should be output to the console, while all high scores are stored permanently in the `NSMutableDictionary` instance. With each new high score, the number of entries increases by one. As a key for a new high-score entry, we use the current date and time. Since games on mobile devices are generally played by only one player, it does not make a lot of sense to associate the high-score list with user names; instead, we give the time at which the high score was obtained. We shall determine the high score for our example using the previously implemented random-number generator. The implementation takes place entirely within the `loadGame` method of the `GameManager`, so when the app is launched, the old high scores and possibly new high score are output.

How do we implement such a high-score list? First of all, we need to get the current date via the `NSDate` class:

```
NSDate* date = [NSDate date];
NSDateFormatter *dateFormatter = [[NSDateFormatter alloc] init];
[dateFormatter setDateStyle: NSDateFormatterShortStyle];
[dateFormatter setTimeStyle: NSDateFormatterLongStyle];
NSString *dateString = [dateFormatter stringFromDate: date];
```

To put the date in a readable format, we use the `NSDateFormatter`. This converts the date to a country-specific format depending on the language setting of the device (accessed via the settings menu). We can also specify a style for both the date and the time by using the `NSDateFormatterLongStyle`. The "LongStyle" returns the current time in seconds. This is useful, since we wish to identify the high score by the date and time, and a game can last less than a minute.

The one-time creation and output of the high-score table via an `NSMutableDictionary` instance presents no challenges:

```
//create high-score table
NSString *highscoresKey = @"highscoresKey";
NSMutableDictionary *highscores =
    [self readObjectForKey: highscoresKey];
if (!highscores) {
    highscores = [[NSMutableDictionary alloc] initWithCapacity: 10];
}

//read scores
NSArray *keys =
    [highscores keysSortedByValueUsingSelector: @selector(compare:)];
NSNumber *score = [NSNumber numberWithInt: 0];
for (id key in keys) {
    score = [highscores objectForKey: key];
    NSLog(@"Date:%@, Score:%@", key, score);
}
```

In reading out the high scores, we would like to *sort* the values alphanumerically. This is handled by the iOS-supplied `compare:` method, since we simply want to sort `NSInteger` values. To use our own sorting method, we must overwrite this method. The `NSDictionary` class offers the practical `keysSortedByValueUsingSelector` method, to which we can pass the `compare:` method via an `@selector` directive. As result, we obtain the date keys sorted according to high-score entries. We have now only to output all the entries in a `for` loop. The result might look something like this:

```
2012-11-25 14:55:41.139 Storage[14632:207] Date: 25.11.12 14:53:04 MESZ,
    Score: 333
2012-11-25 14:55:41.140 Storage[14632:207] Date: 25.11.12 14:55:41 MESZ,
    Score: 337
2012-11-25 14:55:41.141 Storage[14632:207] Date: 25.11.12 14:53:24 MESZ,
    Score: 429
2012-11-25 14:55:41.141 Storage[14632:207] Date: 25.11.12 14:53:20 MESZ,
    Score: 536
2012-11-25 14:55:41.142 Storage[14632:207] Date: 25.11.12 14:53:29 MESZ,
    Score: 672
```

Saving a new high score is now just a formality:

```
//store a score
int newScore = [self getRndBetween: 1 and: 9999];
if (newScore > [score intValue]) {
    NSLog(@"NEW HIGHSCORE:%i!", newScore);
    NSNumber *scoreObj = [NSNumber numberWithInt: newScore];
    [highscores setObject: scoreObj forKey: dateString];
```

```
        [self saveObject: highscores key: highscoresKey];
    } else {
        NSLog(@"Score:%i. Sorry, no new high score.", newScore);
    }
```

If the random new high score is larger than the previously output high score in the stored list, we add a new entry and output a congratulatory message over the console. You can see that we have first wrapped the simple int value in an NSNumber object so that this can be stored in the dictionary as an object (numberWithInt:). Conversely, we change this back into an int value in order to be able to compare the previously stored high score with the current high score (intValue). It is practical here that the list expanded by the new high score can be completely retained as an object via the NSUserDefaults instance.

# 4 Making Connections: Multiplayer Games with Game Kit and Game Center

## ▌ 4.1  Introduction

iPhone, iPod touch, and the iPad are networked devices and were therefore destined to host multiplayer games. Because apps are downloaded by most users over Wi-Fi, you can assume that your users have access to a wireless local area network (WLAN) for playing multiplayer games. This is necessary if latency times are to be kept to a minimum, especially for fast action games. In addition to Internet connections, iOS devices can communicate with each other via Bluetooth. Such ad hoc networks assume that the players are at the same location and therefore do not need an Internet connection or an intermediate server, since the players are directly connected to each other (peer to peer [P2P]).

Regardless of the quality of the connection, you can create connections to the Internet via the WebKit framework. In this case, the players are not directly connected to each other, but rather communicate over an intermediate server that receives game-packet data and forwards them to the respective players.

That setting up such a server involves additional computational cost becomes clear when several thousand users attempt to access the system at the same time. Thus, if you have in mind extending a game to include multiplayer functionality, it makes sense to look for a third party to undertake this task. Popular APIs (application programming indexes) are provided by, among others, OpenFeint, ngmoco ("Plus+"), and Chillingo ("Crystal").

Even Apple has offered similar functionality since iOS 4.1 (since iOS 4.2 for the iPad as well) with the Game Center App (here you can open an account directly on the device and begin multiplayer games) and the associated Game Kit API and considers itself a social gaming network. The framework covers the most common tasks of a multiplayer service:

- Account management (Apple ID and player pseudonym, profile photo)

- Friends (invitations, status updates)

- Online high scores, achievements (depending on progress in the game)

- Matchmaking (anonymous or with friends)

- Sending and receiving of packet data

- Voice chat

- Support for asynchronous (real-time) or synchronous (turn-based, players wait online/offline for the opponent's move) games

- Support of variable networks via Bluetooth, WLAN, or over the air (network–operator dependent)

Despite its name, this API offers no special support for game development but serves merely to manage connections in general and the connection to the Game Center App in particular.

The API is well documented and contains many code examples. You will find the framework reference at *http://developer.apple.com/library/ios/#documentation/GameKit/Reference/GameKit_Collection/_index.html*. You can download an extensive Game Kit Programming Guide as a PDF document from *http://developer.apple.com/library/ios/documentation/NetworkingInternet/Conceptual/GameKit_Guide/GameKit_Guide.pdf*.

While OpenFeint, according to its homepage, supported more than 6,900 games (iOS/Android) in late 2011, the number for GameKit games may be significantly more than that. Already 3,000 iOS developers have tried the GKTapper example app right after its first launch in December 2011. This can be seen in the number of players in the high-score lists (where it is possible that the list has been reset since the example was uploaded).

The integration of GameKit into your own game apps can be accomplished with only a few steps, and you should therefore not shy away from extending your game at least to an online high-score list. Such a leaderboard contains, in addition to the list of high scores, the pseudonyms (and optional photos) of all the players who have ever uploaded a high score for your game. As a bonus, you will obtain useful user data, such as the number of registered users of your app.

Apple's Game Center Service is divided into three parts:

- **Game Center App (preinstalled since iOS 4.1/4.2):** This is the central interface for all games supported by the Game Center API. Once you equip your game with at least one leaderboard, your app appears in a player's Game Center App and can

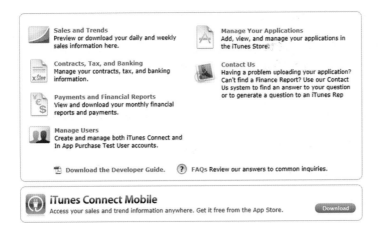

**Figure 4.1** iTunes Connect homepage.

optionally be launched directly from there. In addition, through the app, users can manage their own login data and lists of friends.

- **iTunes Connect:** Before you can use the GameKit API, the game has to be "registered" through iTunes (Figure 4.1).

- **GameKit API:** Through the API, developers have free access to all of its services. This includes the hosting of high-score lists on Apple's servers as well as P2P connections over a central remote server. We shall discuss the possibilities of the GameKit in more detail later.

Of course, you can use the GameKit for other apps as well, and they do not even have to be games. With P2P data exchange, you could, for instance, develop a friend-finder app, and with integrated VoiceChat, you could provide the telephone companies with some competition.

Among the most important tasks of the GameKit is hosting leaderboards (aka high scores). We have already shown how to store a leaderboard on an iOS device. Much more interesting, of course, is the possibility of players being able to send their scores to a central server so that they can compare their accomplishments with those of others. With the GameKit and iTunes Connect, you can manage as many such lists as you like for each of your games. Not only hosting is taken care of, but also the display of the list view on the device, such as the roulette-table optics of the Game Center App; you could even design your own graphics.

# ◼ 4.2 Setting Up iTunes Connect

Before you can get going with the GameKit, you have to activate the Game Center Service for your game over iTunes. You can get to its website via the Apple Dev Center or directly at *https://itunesconnect.apple.com/WebObjects/iTunesConnect.woa*.

Even if you have no intention of ever publishing your game in the App Store, you must still create your project through the menu item MANAGE YOUR APPLICATIONS > ADD NEW APP (Figure 4.2 and Figure 4.3). This also means that you upload a trial

**Manage Your Applications**
**Add, view, and manage your applications in the iTunes Store.**

Figure 4.2  Entry point: "Manage Your Applications."

App Information

Enter the following in **English**.

App Name    My New Game

SKU Number  com.domain.MyNewGame

Bundle ID   Select
            You can register a new Bundle ID here.

Does your app have specific device requirements? Learn more

Cancel                                          Continue

Figure 4.3  Creating a new app.

512 × 512 icon and at least one screen shot. But do not worry; you are preparing your app over the website for only a hypothetical publication. All your data remain confidential. Moreover, you need neither a private nor a public certificate for testing your app.

Apple provides a "mirror" version of your server data so that the app can be tested with all the Game Center services in a "sandbox." You do not, however, have to give this another thought. Once your app goes live, your data end up on the public servers, which behave in exactly the same way and simply access a different database.

This also means, however, that you will need an Internet connection for testing a Game Center app, since all data such as high scores end up on an Apple server and cannot be stored locally through the API. But we still have a way to go first. As with any new app, you must create a bundle ID (Figure 4.4), which can also be entered directly online. Here you can simply give the product name from the Plist—for example, "com.qioo.MyNewGame." For our example, we shall choose the name "GameKitBasics."

Then you must return to "App Information" and complete the process. In the metadata, give an app name, such as "My New Game" or "GK Basics." It is under this name that your app will be displayed within the Game Center.

You can also activate the Game Center Service for your game via the *Enable* button. Moreover, here you will find buttons to create new leaderboards or achievements (Figure 4.5).

After completing the information for your app, on the "App Information" page you will find a button labeled "Manage Game Center," which allows you to edit the entries that you made earlier.

Under "App Information," you can manage your leaderboards and achievements at any time. Moreover, you can delete all uploaded data through the button "Delete Test Data" (Figure 4.6).

| Description | | Apple Push Notification service | In App Purchase | Game Center | iCloud | Action |
|---|---|---|---|---|---|---|
| 5SW4543B49.qioo.com.GameK...<br>GameKitBasics | ⊘ Configurable for Development<br>⊘ Configurable for Production | ● Enabled | ● Enabled | ⊘ Configurable | Configure |

Figure 4.4 Setting the bundle ID.

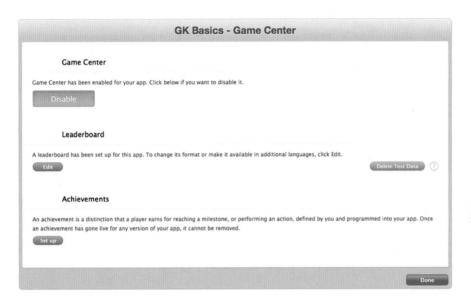

Figure 4.5 Activating the Game Center.

Let us now create a new high-score list for our project. Begin by choosing a "Leaderboard ID." For the example in this book, we have chosen the ID "com.qioo. GameKitBasics.Highscores." You will find the complete app in the download folder under "GameKitBasics." Moreover, you must set at least one language as the "Default," which in most cases is English (Figure 4.7).

- **LeaderBoard Reference Name:** Here the name of the high-score list is set as it will later be displayed in your game. You can also create a variety of lists, such as for the level or degree of difficulty.

- **Leaderboard ID:** This must be a unique name within Apple. Thus, it makes sense to use the reverse domain name server (DNS) naming convention—namely, your homepage is part of the ID, with the URL given backward. It is under this ID that the high-score list will later be identified from within the app—for example, to download the latest scores.

- **Score Format Type:** Not every game has a point score. You could also track time or money, for example. For points, you choose the value integer.

- **Sort Order:** Via "low to high" or "high to low," you determine the order in which points are to be sorted. For a high-score list, one typically chooses "high to low," since higher scores are better and therefore should lead the rankings.

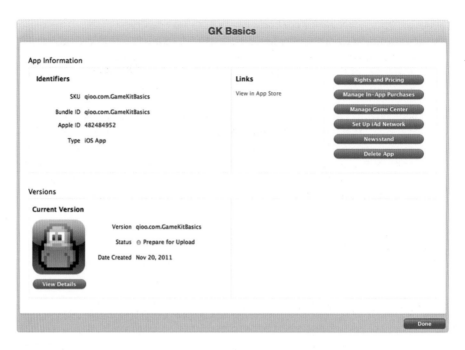

Figure 4.6  App information.

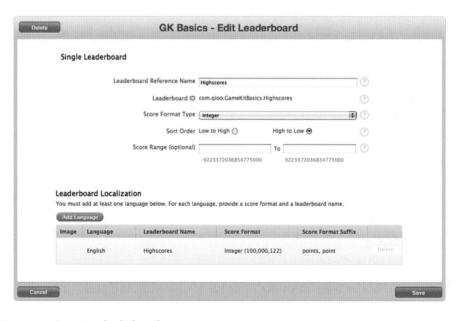

Figure 4.7  Creating a leaderboard.

- **Score Range:** In principle, leaderboards can support the complete 64-bit integer range, though you can optionally restrict this range. Moreover, leaderboards allow all possible score values, no matter how high. Thus, not only the highest scores end up in the list. However, only the highest value for a given player is allowed, and lower values are ignored.

- **Localization:** Here you can customize the point table for one of the currently supported languages. At least one language is required (default), which is then also displayed if the device's current language setting is not (yet) supported by iTunes. In "Score Format" you set the period versus comma convention. You can also specify a localized unit (singular and plural). For high scores, simply choose "point" and "points." If there should be a space between a number and a suffix, just add a space before the suffix.

You proceed similarly to create achievement lists. We now have a high-score list that is hosted by Apple's servers. We have only to provide it with data from an app.

# ▌ 4.3 The Road to the Game Center Test App

Let us create a new, empty template in Xcode and begin by adding "GameKit.framework" via LINK BINARIES. We want the app's involvement with the Game Center to be as easy as possible, so we ideally bundle all the functionality into one class. The following interfaces are the minimum requirement:

- Login (register a user at the Game Center)

- Score upload (any score will be uploaded over iTunes Connect to the just created list)

- Display the high-score list (including downloading the latest scores of other users)

It is a good idea to have the high-score list displayed via the GameKit. Optionally, you could display the data of the high-score list in its own view. Since both achievements and leaderboards (and later player matching) will be managed over a ViewController, we derive the Game Center interface from a `UIViewController`.

Listing 4.1 GCHelper.h

```
#import <UIKit/UIKit.h>
#import <GameKit/GameKit.h>

extern NSString *highscoreListName;

@interface GCHelper: UIViewController
                 <GKLeaderboardViewControllerDelegate>

+ (GCHelper *) getInstance;
- (void) showMessage: (NSString*) message;
- (BOOL) login;
```

```
- (void) reportScore: (int) score;
- (void) showHighscores;

@end
```

You can recognize the functionalities that we have been talking about by the method signatures of the GCHelper class. Moreover, we must, of course, integrate the GameKit via #import <GameKit/GameKit.h>. Since the high-score list is placed over our current Game View, we also need the GKLeaderboardViewControllerDelegate protocol, through which we announce that the GCHelper class implements the required interface method(s). In this case, the high-score list has a *Done* button that, when pressed, calls the delegate's leaderboardViewControllerDidFinish: method. Through this we can then later take the necessary steps to exit the view.

In addition, we have defined an external variable named highscoreListName for the ID created in iTunes Connect. Finally, the class definition is completed with a getInstance method and a showMessage: method. The first takes care of simple access from every class that integrates the GCHelper header, while the latter serves to display a UIAlertView with any desired message. The GameKit API uses alerts—for example, for the login mask or error messages. It is thus a good idea to display your own informational messages as alerts.

**Listing 4.2** GCHelper.m

```
#import "GCHelper.h"

//This name must correspond to the name in iTunes Connect.
NSString *highscoreListName = @"com.qioo.GameKitBasics.Highscores";

@implementation GCHelper

static GCHelper *gcHelper;

+ (GCHelper *) getInstance {
    if (gcHelper = = nil) {
        gcHelper = [[GCHelper alloc] init];
        NSLog(@"Warning:
            GCHelper should be created via an AppDelegate.");
    }
    return gcHelper;
}

- (id) initWithNibName: (NSString *) nibNameOrNil
              bundle: (NSBundle *) nibBundleOrNil {
    gcHelper = [super initWithNibName: nibNameOrNil bundle:
                                    nibBundleOrNil];
    return gcHelper;
}

- (void) showMessage: (NSString *) message {
    UIAlertView *alert = [[[UIAlertView alloc]
```

```
            initWithTitle: @"GC Helper Message"
                  message: message
                 delegate: NULL
            cancelButtonTitle: @"OK"
            otherButtonTitles: NULL] autorelease];
        [alert show];
}

- (BOOL) login {
    //...
}

- (void) reportScore: (int) score {
    //...
}

- (void) showHighscores {
    //...
}

- (void) leaderboardViewControllerDidFinish:
    (GKLeaderboardViewController *) viewController {
    //...
}

@end
```

The main task of the GCHelper is to manage a high-score list. First, we define the highscoreListName string as we did in iTunes Connect. Because of the DNS convention, it is certain that this name will be unique worldwide. Since the class represents a ViewController, we implement the standard initWithNibName:bundle: method and return a static gcHelper instance, which we obtain via the getInstance method. Since there is only one Game Center Service per game, it makes sense to make the class available as a singleton instance. The showMessage: method encapsulates the creation of the UIAlertView. When you display several alerts in sequence, the currently displayed one is automatically closed; otherwise, the user will have to close the dialog with the *OK* button. We shall use the alerts for debugging and for the login.

### 4.3.1 Game Center Login

Before you can communicate with the Game Center Service, the player must have successfully logged into the system. As you can see in the following implementation, there are four possible alerts:

```
- (BOOL) login {
    //4.1 for iPhone/iPod Touch, 4.2 for iPad
    NSString *iOSVersion = [[UIDevice currentDevice] systemVersion];
    BOOL isSupported =
        ([iOSVersion compare: @"4.2"
                     options: NSNumericSearch] ! = NSOrderedAscending);

    if (NSClassFromString(@"GKLocalPlayer") && isSupported) {
        if([[GKLocalPlayer localPlayer].authenticated = = NO) {
```

```
[[GKLocalPlayer localPlayer]
    authenticateWithCompletionHandler: ^(NSError *error) {
        if (error ! = NULL) {
            [self showMessage: @"Error: registration failed."];
        } else {
            [self showMessage: @"Registration successful."];
            return YES;
        }
    }];
} else {
    [self showMessage: @"Already registered."];
    return YES;
}
} else {
[self showMessage:
    @"Please update iOS. Game Center Service not supported."];
}
return NO;
}
```

First, it is checked whether the Game Center API is available. Since we want to include the iPad, we permit service only for at least iOS 4.2. Moreover, we check whether the required GKLocalPlayer class is available on the device. If the login is unsuccessful, you should not call the subsequent Game Center Service methods (Figure 4.8).

Alternatively, you can activate the Game Center Key option in the Plist so that the app is installed only on devices that have access to the GameKit API.

## 4.3.2 Blocks as Callback Handler

Through the GKLocalPlayer class you can check at any time whether a player is currently logged in. If such is not the case, we implement the authenticateWith CompletionHandler: method, which displays for us an announcement in the form of

Figure 4.8 Login procedure for Game Center Services.

a `UIAlertView`. As you can see from the test app in the emulator, the sandbox message is shown under all the dialogs to emphasize that the data are not going to a live server. An exception is the registration of an Apple ID, which will then actually exist outside the sandbox, even if it was created through a sandbox dialog.

Since the registration of a player takes place over the Internet, it can take a certain amount of time. The transmission of data and the evaluation of the server response are completely encapsulated in GameKit. You will simply be informed when the response has arrived and whether an error has occurred. To facilitate the handling of an asynchronous event, programmers like to implement callbacks, which are methods that one can pass as a parameter to other methods. Now the invoked method can decide when the callback method should be invoked.

For implementing callback methods in Objective-C, one uses ^blocks. These derive from the C language and are indicated by a prefixed caret (^). You might define a block method thusly:

```
int (^substractOne)(int);

substractOne = ^(int number) {
    return number--;
};
```

You would call the method as follows:

```
int result = substractOne(8);//result = 7
```

As you can see, the method `substractOne` expects an integer parameter and returns an integer. Since the method was defined as a block, you can now use this method as a parameter and pass it to other methods.

This is useful in the `authenticateWithCompletionHandler:` method. Instead of the name of the block method, we pass the block's parameter list directly. This is what is called an anonymous method: The method body is implemented directly as a part of the method signature and is used only here.

Thus "`^(NSError *error)`" means that we are dealing with a callback that expects an `NSError` object as parameter and is called when the method `authenticateWith-CompletionHandler:` determines the appropriate time. If we are interested in the text of the error message, we can have it output via `[error localizedDescription]`. For the login procedure, we would like to know whether an error is present (`error` object is not NULL) or not (`error` object is NULL).

The login takes place effectively via a single method. Indeed, it could not be simpler. Usually, you would execute the login method automatically in the background when the app is launched so that you could process a score upload at any time later.

### 4.3.3 High-Score Upload

It is also useful to use a callback for uploading scores. The `reportScore:` method expects only the currently achieved score. The GameKit API then takes care of the rest in the background. But you should provide for a backup in case of an error, since there is nothing more aggravating for a player than not to be able to report a hard earned high score that is lost the next time the app is launched. We have already shown in the chapter on data storage how to save a high-score list locally on the device. You could

---

also alert the player that a connection problem has occurred so that he or she could try again later:

```
- (void) reportScore: (int) score {
    GKScore *scoreUploader =
        [[[GKScore alloc] initWithCategory: highscoreListName] autorelease];
    scoreUploader.value = (int64_t) score;
    [scoreUploader reportScoreWithCompletionHandler: ^(NSError *error) {
        if (error ! = NULL) {
            [self showMessage: @"Error: Uploading of score failed."];
        } else {
            [self showMessage: @"High score successfully uploaded."];
        }
    }];
}
```

The actual upload of the score takes place in a GKScore instance, which at initialization we inform as to the name of the desired iTunes high-score list. The attained score is assigned to the value member and sent in the background via reportScore-WithCompletionHandler: to the Apple server.

## 4.3.4 High-Score List

To display the attained score in the high-scores list, we must download the current score from the Internet. For this, the GameKit provides the GKLeaderboardView Controller class:

```
- (void) showHighscores {
    //Show Highscore view
    GKLeaderboardViewController *leaderboardController =
        [[GKLeaderboardViewController alloc] init];
    if (leaderboardController ! = NULL) {
        leaderboardController.category = highscoreListName;
        leaderboardController.leaderboardDelegate = self;
        [self presentViewController: leaderboardController
                        animated: YES completion: nil];
    }

    //Load Highscores data
    GKLeaderBoard* leaderBoard = [[[GKLeaderboard alloc] init] autorelease];
    leaderBoard.category = highscoreListName;
    [leaderBoard
        loadScoresWithCompletionHandler: ^(NSArray *scores, NSError *error) {
            if(error ! = nil) {
                [self showMessage: [NSString stringWithFormat:
                    @"Error:%@", [error localizedDescription]]];
            }
        }];
}

- (void) leaderboardViewControllerDidFinish:
        (GKLeaderboardViewController *) viewController {
    //Close Highscore view
    [self dismissModalViewControllerAnimated: YES];
    [viewController release];
}
```

Figure 4.9 High-score list.

Since the download data are downloaded in the background, we can display the high-score list without a delay. As soon as the data arrive, the GameKit ensures that the list is updated. The desired iTunes high-score list must also be passed to the `GKLeaderboardViewController` instance via the `category` member. Furthermore, we set the `GCHelper` class as delegate so that, by the agreed-upon protocol, the `leaderboardViewControllerDidFinish:` method is called as soon as the user chooses to exit the high-score list (Figure 4.9).

As is usual for a `UIViewController`, the current view is overlaid by a new view as soon as the `presentViewController:animated:completion:` method is called.

Now that the list has been displayed, we can worry about the data in the list, which can be queried via the `GKLeaderboard` class. Here as well, the desired ID of the high-score list must be announced via the `category` member. Then the data can be queried via the `loadScoresWithCompletionHandler:` method. You can see from the parameter list for the callback that, in addition to an `NSError` object, an array is also returned with the scores. With this, you could, say, process the score data yourself to implement your own list representation.

Both `GKLeaderboardViewController` and `GKLeaderboard` can be customized with other parameters according to your own wishes and ideas. For example, you could determine the date on which a score was transferred, filter the list on particular players, or set a default time scope; each leaderboard would offer three variants: "today," "past week," and "all." For example, you could determine that the all-time high-score list should always be preselected with

```
timeScope = GKLeaderboardTimeScopeAllTime;
```

## 4.3.5  Integrating the GCHelper into Your Own App

Since we previously rendered the playing field directly to a `UIView`, we must now consider how we can combine this with the `GCHelper`. In fact, with the `GCHelper` class, this

Figure 4.10 The high-score list can also be opened via the preinstalled Game Center app.

involves a `UIViewController` so that we can directly assign the `MainView` as a `view` member.

To test the GameKit, we create a `MainView` class in the usual way so that it has a `drawRect:` method that is periodically called by the `AppDelegate`.

After we have initialized the `MainView` on which our game is to be rendered as usual in the `AppDelegate`, we assign it directly to the `view` member of the `GCHelper`:

```
gcHelper = [[GCHelper alloc] init];
gcHelper.view = mainView;
self.window.rootViewController = gcHelper;
```

Then we make the `gcHelper` instance the `RootViewController`, since this is how the `MainView` will be displayed, as well as the high-score list (Figure 4.10).

In the `MainView` we increase a counter at each frame that represents our test score. We also define three buttons:

- **Login:** calls the login method of the `GCHelper`. The call takes place in `MainView` via `[[GCHelper getInstance] login];`.

- **Submit:** uploads the currently displayed value of the counter into the high-score list. The call takes place via `[[GCHelper getInstance] reportScore: score];`.

- **Show:** displays the high-score list. The call takes place via `[[GCHelper getInstance] showHighscores];`.

Based on our test app, you can see that the GameKit reacts with an alert when, for example, the *Submit* button is pressed even though the login was not complete. The implementation of the GameKit is almost foolproof.

Without our intervention, the high-score list uses the 512 × 512 icon that we had to set initially via iTunes Connect. Furthermore, we can see the name of the app and the (localized) name of the high-score list. The same holds for the achievement list, which you create along the same lines. That is, you first create it in iTunes Connect and then you can integrate the list via GCHelper. The display takes place analogously via GKAchievementViewController and also uses the appropriate CompletionHandler to load the data (GKAchievement loadAchievementsWithCompletionHandler:).

# ∎ 4.4  Multiplayer Games

The real excitement comes when you pit human players against each other. Since Apple provides the complete infrastructure free of cost, this greatly reduces your effort. Nevertheless, there is still much work to do. Plan on your test phase taking a considerable amount of time. For example, some networks cannot be properly simulated in the emulator—not to mention that you can open only one emulator instance at a time. In any case, it is difficult to simulate the actual behavior of a human opponent.

Basically, you have first to decide whether you want to implement a turn-based game (such as chess and Monopoly) or whether the players should do battle against each other in real time. The former of these is supported via the framework's GKTurnBased classes, beginning with iOS 5.

For a real-time game, you will need to have available a sufficiently fast Internet connection. By default, the connectionTypesMask value of the GKPeerPicker is set to the value GKPeerPickerConnectionTypeNearby, so you have a fast Bluetooth connection. Alternatively, you can set the GKPeerPickerConnectionTypeOnline constant so that the exchange of game data takes place over WLAN or an over-the-air network. Here, an intermediate Apple remote server takes over data transmission from device to device. This cannot be done in a local Bluetooth network, which is usually faster, since the round trip to the server is unnecessary. For this, the physical presence of the player is necessary and the maximum number of players is limited to four, since the Bluetooth stack of iOS devices currently cannot process a larger number of connections. For online games, 16 players, at most, can take part simultaneously.

## 4.4.1  Matchmaking and Sessions

To start a multiplayer game, you need players. For this, Apple provides the GKPeerPickerController class. Every player is uniquely identified within the game via a peer ID of type NSString. Once the game has started, data transfer takes place via the GKSession instance. For this, a delegate is defined that is called whenever data from other players arrive (Figure 4.11).

```
//Set the delegate for game session
[self.gameSession setDataReceiveHandler: self withContext: NULL];
```

When data arrive, the delegate method receiveData:fromPeer:inSession:context: is called:

```
- (void) receiveData: (NSData *) data
         fromPeer: (NSString *) peer
```

Figure 4.11 Apple's example application GKTank.

```
        inSession: (GKSession *)session
           context: (void *) context {
//Parse data packet (example)
unsigned char *incomingPacket = (unsigned char *)[data bytes];
int *pIntData = (int *) &incomingPacket[0];
int packetType = pIntData[0];
//...
}
```

You can analyze the data sent by a player or peer using the NSData object. Conversely, you can call the sendDataToAllPeers:withDataMode:error: method to send data to all the players.

```
//Data packet to be sent
int packetSize = 2 * sizeof(int);
unsigned char networkPacket[packetSize];
int *pIntData = (int *) &networkPacket[0];
pIntData[0] = packetType;//for example, 22 = score
pIntData[1] = packetData;//the score

NSData *packet = [NSData dataWithBytes: networkPacket length: packetSize];
[session sendDataToAllPeers: packet
             withDataMode: GKSendDataReliable
                    error: nil];
```

Alternatively, you have available as well the sendData:toPeers:withDataMode:error: method to inform select players about an update of a local player.

Since in a multiplayer game it is always possible that a player will leave a game in progress (either willingly or unwillingly—for example, by entering a dead zone), the GKSession class informs you about such occurrences via the session:peer:didChangeState: delegate:

```
//Connection state has changed
- (void) session: (GKSession *) session
```

```
            peer: (NSString *) peerID
  didChangeState: (GKPeerConnectionState) state {
     if (state = = GKPeerStateDisconnected) {
        //...
     }
  }
}
```

From the `peerID` you also know which player is no longer able to participate actively in the game. A complete example with two tanks that fight to the death is given by Apple through the Dev Center. The source code of the app GKTank is available at *https://developer.apple.com/library/prerelease/ios/#samplecode/GKTank/Introduction/ Intro.html#//apple_ref/doc/uid/DTS40008918* (see the screen shots).

# 5 OpenGL ES: Turbocharged!

## 5.1 Why OpenGL ES?

Fasten your seat belts! OpenGL ES provides for the highest speeds through its closeness to the graphics hardware on iOS devices. This additional bump in performance cannot be achieved with Core Graphics. Furthermore, the interface provides, particularly in the three-dimensional (3D) domain, for native rendering and realistic graphics effects.

You will not have to throw everything you have learned so far out the window. From sprite management to touch control to the programming of sound effects, these building blocks stay the same, because OpenGL ES (= Open Graphics Library for Embedded Systems) is a pure programming interface for the development of 2D and 3D graphics-based apps. (Advanced libraries such as GLU/GLUT are not available on the iPhone, and the audio extension OpenAL represents too much overhead for games in most cases.)

With the UIKit, we have been able to realize our ideas very quickly, but with an increasing number of sprites to represent simultaneously, sooner or later things will start to slow down. Additionally, UIKit and Core Graphics offer no support for 3D graphics. And, in any case, some of the UI animation effects of the iOS SDK were implemented internally by way of OpenGL ES.

Interestingly, OpenGL and the variant OpenGL ES tailored to mobile devices have existed for a number of years, entirely independently of Apple's iPhone & Co. OpenGL ES was successfully used not only in game consoles such as the Playstation 3, but also in many mobile platforms such as Google's Android and the Symbian operating system.

Even the new Linux-based Maemo/MeeGo platform with devices such as the Nokia N900 and Nokia N9 supports OpenGL ES.

Do you remember late summer of 2008? The iPhone SDK had been available only a few months in beta; nevertheless, there was already a large and growing number of carefully crafted 3D games in the App Store. Many developers were already familiar with the OpenGL interface from other systems and could therefore adapt their code relatively easily to the new iPhone platform.

In fact, OpenGL ES is based on the C language and, since the iOS SDK also supports C/C++, contact with Objective-C can be reduced to a minimum, even if that is not particularly to be recommended because, in the end, the iOS SDK and hence the operating system of the iOS devices are based on Objective-C.

On the other hand, OpenGL ES is not the only place where C appears inside the SDK: Core Graphics is a C application programming interface. And like Core Graphics, OpenGL ES operates like a finite-state machine; there are numerous "switches," such as "light on," that, when activated, remain valid until the "light out" command is issued. In OpenGL ES, the corresponding instructions are as follows:

```
glEnable(GL_LIGHTING);
...
glDisable(GL_LIGHTING);
```

But more on that later—we do not want to get ahead of ourselves (even if we cannot wait to get going).

## ▌ 5.2  What Is OpenGL ES, and How Is It Constructed?

The specifications for OpenGL and OpenGL ES are managed by a nonprofit consortium that goes under the somewhat sinister sounding name of Khronos Group, Inc., in which almost all the major companies of the mobile industry participate, such as Nokia, Sony Computer Entertainment, Samsung Electronics, Motorola, Google, and, of course, Apple Inc., to name a few.

No wonder, then, that OpenGL ES has the ambition of providing a platform-independent API. Whether you are developing for Symbian, Android, or the iPhone, your interaction with the interface will be almost identical on all platforms.

OpenGL ES offers very direct access to the graphics hardware. For the API to be usable on different systems, an additional abstract interface that encapsulates the individual types of access is necessary: *EGL*. Although EGL is optional, a variant is offered for practically all operating systems. For the iOS SDK, this interface is the EAGL-API; among other things, this is responsible for providing access to the screen and to link the UIView with a CAEAGLLayer (instead of the CALayer) to make rendering to the display possible. In simplified form, one can imagine it as seen in Figure 5.1.

While the desktop version of OpenGL offers advanced libraries such as GLU (OpenGL Utility Library) and GLUT (OpenGL Utility Toolkit), which take care of basic system-wide functionalities such as window access, input handling, and positioning of the camera in virtual space, OpenGL ES is limited to the bare essentials. This means de facto that we have to look after all that stuff ourselves. But do not worry (be happy). Most of these tasks have to be accomplished only once, so we are not compelled to go too deeply into all this.

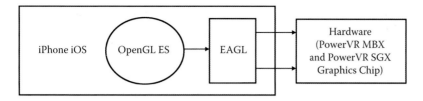

Figure 5.1 Interaction between OpenGL ES, EAGL, and the graphics hardware.

Likewise, for the following examples we shall not introduce the entire API, but will concentrate instead on what is most significant for us as game developers.

First, we note that there are currently two different versions of OpenGL ES:

- **OpenGL ES 1.0/1.1** is supported by all devices of the iPhone family. Version 1.0 is upwardly compatible to 1.1.

- **OpenGL ES 2.0** supports iPhone 3GS and above. There is simplified access to iOS 5 via the GLKit.

OpenGL ES 2.0 was specified as early as 2007, but has been supported only since the release of the iPhone 3GS (2009). This means that the majority of devices available at the time are *not* compatible with version 2.0. Nevertheless, all 2.0 devices also support version 1.1. OpenGL 2.0 runs only on graphics chips whose hardware can be programmed via so-called shader programming. This allows you to influence the rendering pipeline and to stipulate attributes for every vertex and every fragment. However, this flexibility has its price and has a longer learning curve.

Many functions that were available under OpenGL ES 1.1 must be replaced in OpenGL ES 2.0 through your own programming. However, you have the possibility to test at runtime whether 2.0 is available and, if not, to switch to 1.1. So now comes the question:

## 5.2.1 Which Version of OpenGL ES Should I Choose?

We could turn this question around and ask why you should support 2.0. Well, you will find scarcely a program that is written solely for version 2.0 (with the exception of some titles written exclusively for iPad). The advantages of OpenGL ES 2.0 become noticeable in high-end games and are hardly visible to the layperson. Version 2.0 is distinguished more by the architecture of the API than by superior visual possibilities. One might say that OpenGL ES 2.0 is not necessarily the most current API but rather offers an alternative approach. Both API variants are well under 100 kB, so that OpenGL ES 1.1 should be available in parallel on all future devices. Conversely, there is at present not a single device that supports 2.0 exclusively. And keep in mind that because of the lower market penetration, a game should support at least 1.1. If you have the time and inclination, you can upgrade later to 2.0 features.

Therefore, our focus in this book will be on OpenGL ES 1.1. Once you understand the basics of 1.1, it should not be difficult later to understand the structure of OpenGL ES 2.0 (provided that you are motivated to make the effort). With the GLKit available since iOS 5,

Apple also provides a new library that not only simplifies development under ES 1.1, but also reduces the differences between ES 1.1 and 2.0. For example, with the GLKit, one can eliminate cumbersome ES2 shader programming with a few lines of code. In a later chapter, we will discuss how to work with the new GLKit.

# ▮ 5.3 OpenGL ES: Basic Questions

Instead of presenting the entire API in gruesome detail, we shall briefly look at the aspects that are of relevance to us as game developers. However, to give ourselves an overview, it makes sense to use the navigation options inside Xcode; at any place in the source code, you can view the allowable parameters and method signatures by right-clicking on > JUMP TO DEFINITION or FIND TEXT IN DOCUMENTATION.

The official documentation of OpenGL ES 1.1 can be found at *http://www.khronos.org/opengles/sdk/1.1/docs/man*.

For questions and problems around OpenGL ES, you might want to visit the official Khronos help forum (*http://www.khronos.org/message_boards*). But even Apple itself has set up a tutorial with its "OpenGL ES Programming Guide": *http://developer.apple.com/iphone/library/documentation/3DDrawing/Conceptual/OpenGLES_ProgrammingGuide/Introduction/Introduction.html*.

Unfortunately, the examples (and instructions) are not necessarily limited to the essentials and show rather the general possibilities. And the literature on OpenGL ES 1.1, particularly with respect to game development, is as good as nonexistent. Let us begin, therefore, with the simplest and most basic questions:

- How do I draw a line, a triangle, or a rectangle?

- How are textures implemented?

- How can I animate a sprite?

- How does collision detection work?

- How do I scroll the display?

- Where do I get 3D models, and how do I integrate them?

On this basis, we shall later introduce a somewhat more complex game architecture.* Basically, however, you can simply read the following introduction and then experiment on your own. But first let us set up an OpenGL ES project; the process is the same for both 2D and 3D projects. Differences lie only in the choice of perspective (2D or 3D) and the use of a depth buffer (3D).

---

* The following examples were tested on the original iPhone, the slowest device of the iPhone family. To this extent, the OpenGL ES examples represent functioning (and, hopefully, readable) code, which still has the potential for optimization. Thus, for example, we have done without the introduction of PVRTC textures (a special compression format for PNGs) and vertex buffer objects (VBOs). It is a matter of debate whether VBOs are in fact faster to render on the iPhone; it often depends on the model data and the texture coordinates.

## ■ 5.4  Properly Integrating OpenGL ES

We recall that we previously have rendered our games using the `drawRect:` method of a `UIView`. For OpenGL ES, it is no different. We therefore begin with a similar basic structure, which consists of a delegate, a view, and the `GameManager`. The final structure can be found in the project folder of this book under "OGL_Basics." It consists of three (familiar) classes:

1. `MyGameAppDelegate` initializes the `MainView` and begins the game loop.

2. `MainView` initializes OpenGL, initializes the `GameManager`, periodically calls the `drawStatesWithFrame:` method of the `GameManager`, and forwards the touch input to the `GameManager`.

3. `GameManager` determines the OGL perspective, takes responsibility via the `drawStatesWithFrame:` method for rendering the game, processes the touch input, and manages the game's resources.

The use of classes is no different from that in our previous examples.

To make the OpenGL ES library available, we must integrate the `OpenGlES.framework` via Xcode. Using "Build Phases" in the project settings and "Link Binary With Libraries," select `OpenGlES.framework` (Figure 5.2).

If you open the OpenGL ES folder, you will see that both the ES1 and ES2 headers are already integrated. You could thus use the OpenGL ES 2.0 functions in the simulator without further ado (which we shall not do). See also the definition of

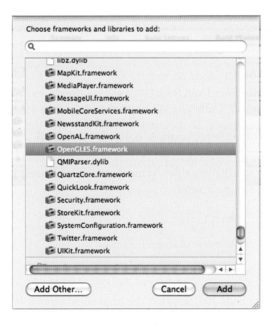

**Figure 5.2**  Integrating the OpenGL ES framework via Xcode.

the EAGL interface, which we shall be needing soon to make the `MainView` usable in OpenGL ES.

To make the framework usable, you have to import the headers; in the `MainView` header, we therefore add the following import statements:

```
#import <OpenGLES/EAGL.h>
#import <OpenGLES/ES1/gl.h>
#import <OpenGLES/ES1/glext.h>
#import <QuartzCore/QuartzCore.h>
```

The QuartzCore framework is needed for the `CAEAGLLayer`. Otherwise, you have only to integrate `ES1/gl.h` in every class that needs to access OpenGL functions. Therefore, add the following line to the `GameManager` header:

```
#import <OpenGLES/ES1/gl.h>
```

The `drawStatesWithFrame:` method of the manager should, as previously, also be called by the `MainView` class, where the tempo of the game loop is defined by the delegate class. The `MyGameAppDelegate` class differs only slightly from the previous examples and takes care of calling the `setupOGL` method in addition to initializing the `MainView` class:

```
mainView = [[MainView alloc] initWithFrame:
    [UIScreen mainScreen].applicationFrame];
mainView.backgroundColor = [UIColor grayColor];
[mainView setupOGL];
```

Otherwise, as usual, the class begins the game loop and periodically calls the `loop` method:

```
- (void) loop {
    [mainView drawRect:[UIScreen mainScreen].applicationFrame];
}
```

The `MainView` class is derived from `UIView`, but thanks to EAGL, it creates a direct connection to the graphics hardware: We must ensure that the view is redrawn and that the previous content is cleared. To maintain consistency with the previous examples, we call the `drawRect:` method manually in the loop and pass the current screen dimensions via `applicationFrame`. As a result, this means for the `MainView` class that the `drawRect:` method is called once per frame as usual and passes the W,H dimensions to the manager via the `rect` parameter:

```
- (void) drawRect: (CGRect) rect {
    ...
    [gameManager drawStatesWithFrame: rect];
    ...
}
```

The ellipses in the code indicate that the implementation is not yet complete—but one thing at a time! To integrate OpenGL, you need to do the main work in an instance derived from `UIView`—in our case, the `MainView` class.

Listing 5.1  MainView.h

```
#import <UIKit/UIKit.h>
#import "GameManager.h"
#import <OpenGLES/EAGL.h>
#import <OpenGLES/ES1/gl.h>
#import <OpenGLES/ES1/glext.h>
#import <QuartzCore/QuartzCore.h>

@interface MainView : UIView {
    GameManager *gameManager;

    EAGLContext *eaglContext;
    GLuint renderbuffer;
    GLuint framebuffer;
    GLuint depthbuffer;
    GLint viewportWidth;
    GLint viewportHeight;
}
- (void) setupOGL;

@end
```

Let us look first at the header declaration. There is only one method: the already mentioned setupOGL method. As a member, we require, in addition to the GameManager, the EAGLContxt through which we obtain access to the OpenGL graphics context (more precisely: the render pipeline) and three variables for the buffer, as well as the screen dimensions viewportWidth and viewportHeight.

As you can see, OpenGL defines its own data types in order to ensure platform independence. Of course, instead of GLint you could also simply use int, but that would be bad style and should be avoided, especially since later we are going to have to declare the appropriate OpenGL data type explicitly. Right-click on "Jump to Definition" to see which data types are declared for OpenGL ES; they include GLbyte, GLfloat, and GLshort. We will not need all the data types.

### 5.4.1  What Is Up with the Three Buffers?

A buffer here is a reserved memory location for OpenGL ES into which our app can read and write data. Since OpenGL manages the buffer, the placement and formatting of data will be optimized internally.

All drawing operations are initially written to the *render buffer*, which holds the 2D color information of a scene or of a frame. For 3D apps, the z-index is also used to store depth information for each pixel in the *depth buffer*. Both then end up in the *frame buffer,* which, as the terminal point of the graphics pipeline, provides for a perspectively correct representation (Figure 5.3).

That sounds more complicated than it really is, but in any case, we fortunately do not have to concern ourselves too much about it. The MainView class takes care of creating all three buffers as well as the graphics context, and that is about it. Once we have overcome this hurdle, we can begin with the actual rendering tasks, which have been appropriately outsourced to the GameManager along with the determination of the OGL perspective

---

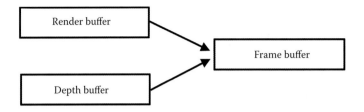

Figure 5.3 Three buffers: render buffer, depth buffer, and frame buffer.

(2D or 3D). Nevertheless, it would not hurt to take a closer look at the implementation of the MainView class.

Listing 5.2 MainView.m

```objectivec
#import "MainView.h"

@implementation MainView

+ (Class) layerClass {
    return [CAEAGLLayer class];
}

- (void) setupOGL {
    ...
}

- (void) drawRect: (CGRect) rect {
    ...
}

- (void) touchesBegan: (NSSet *) touches withEvent: (UIEvent *)
    event {
    CGPoint p = [[touches anyObject] locationInView: self];
    [gameManager touchBegan: p];
}

- (void) touchesMoved: (NSSet *) touches withEvent: (UIEvent *)
    event {
    CGPoint p = [[touches anyObject] locationInView: self];
    [gameManager touchMoved: p];
}

- (void) touchesEnded: (NSSet *) touches withEvent: (UIEvent *)
    event {
    [gameManager touchEnded];
}

- (void) touchesCancelled: (NSSet *) touches withEvent: (UIEvent *)
    event {
    [gameManager touchEnded];
}
```

```
-(void) dealloc {
    [gameManager release];
    [super dealloc];
}

@end
```

We have initially omitted the setupOGL and drawRect: methods to give a better overview of the MainView class. As you can see, there is nothing much new here. We receive the touch input through the four familiar methods and forward it to the GameManager. To make an "OGL view" from our view, we simply overwrite the layerClass class method:

```
+ (Class) layerClass {
    return [CAEAGLLayer class];
}
```

In place of the CALayer (= Core-Animation Layer), which would identify our view as a conventional UIView, we now return the CAEAGLLayer class and identify ourselves even before the initialization as an OpenGL view.

Let us now look at the implementation of the setupOGL method:

```
- (void) setupOGL {
    CAEAGLLayer *eaglLayer = (CAEAGLLayer *) self.layer;
    eaglLayer.opaque = YES;

    eaglContext = [[EAGLContext alloc] initWithAPI:
        kEAGLRenderingAPIOpenGLES1];
    if (!eaglContext || ![EAGLContext setCurrentContext: eaglContext]) {
        [self release];
    } else {
        //render buffer
        glGenRenderbuffersOES(1, &renderbuffer);
        glBindRenderbufferOES(GL_RENDERBUFFER_OES, renderbuffer);

        //frame buffer
        glGenFramebuffersOES(1, &framebuffer);
        glBindFramebufferOES(GL_FRAMEBUFFER_OES, framebuffer);
        glFramebufferRenderbufferOES(GL_FRAMEBUFFER_OES,
            GL_COLOR_ATTACHMENT0_OES,
            GL_RENDERBUFFER_OES,
            renderbuffer);

        //graphics context
        [eaglContext renderbufferStorage: GL_RENDERBUFFER_OES fromDrawable:
            eaglLayer];
        glGetRenderbufferParameterivOES(GL_RENDERBUFFER_OES,
            GL_RENDERBUFFER_WIDTH_OES, &viewportWidth);
        glGetRenderbufferParameterivOES(GL_RENDERBUFFER_OES,
            GL_RENDERBUFFER_HEIGHT_OES, &viewportHeight);

        //depth buffer (3D only)
        glGenRenderbuffersOES(1, &depthbuffer);
        glBindRenderbufferOES(GL_RENDERBUFFER_OES, depthbuffer);
        glRenderbufferStorageOES(GL_RENDERBUFFER_OES,
```

```
        GL_DEPTH_COMPONENT16_OES, viewportWidth, viewportHeight);
    glFramebufferRenderbufferOES(GL_FRAMEBUFFER_OES,
        GL_DEPTH_ATTACHMENT_OES, GL_RENDERBUFFER_OES, depthbuffer);
    glBindRenderbufferOES(GL_RENDERBUFFER_OES, renderbuffer);//rebind

    if (!gameManager) {
        gameManager = [GameManager getInstance];
    }
    }
}
```

Aside from the fact that at the end of the method we initialize the GameManager, the opaque parameter is set to YES via the CAEAGLLayer instance. Apple recommends this for enhanced performance: An opaque layer needs less computing time.

Then we initialize the OGL graphics context:

```
eaglContext = [[EAGLContext alloc] initWithAPI: kEAGLRenderingAPIOpenGLES1];
```

As you can see, we are dealing here with OpenGL ES version 1.1. For OpenGL ES 2.0, you would instead have to pass the constant kEAGLRenderingAPIOpenGLES2.

If the context assignment was successful, we initialize the three buffers; the corresponding functions are specified by Apple as an _OES extension. Once the variables for the color-rendering buffer and frame buffer have been set and both buffers created, we can let the EAGL graphics context know about the buffers and integrate the variables for the viewport dimensions.

Finally, we create the depth buffer so that we will not have to make any later adaptations to the MainView class for 3D games. Make sure to link the render buffer again after the creation of the depth buffer. We will deactivate the depth buffer later when we set the OGL perspective for our first 2D attempts.

The parameters used to create the buffers are suitable for all the examples in this book; again, we will not have to make any adjustments later.

Finally, you should clear the created buffers and the EAGL layer in the dealloc method:

```
if (eaglContext) {
    glDeleteRenderbuffersOES(1, &depthbuffer);
    glDeleteFramebuffersOES(1, &framebuffer);
    glDeleteRenderbuffersOES(1, &renderbuffer);
    [eaglContext release];
}
```

Thus, we may now turn to the implementation of the drawRect: method and show how the buffers will be addressed there:

```
- (void) drawRect: (CGRect) rect {
    glViewport(0, 0, viewportWidth, viewportHeight);
    glClearColor(0.5, 0.5, 0.5, 1.0);
    glClear(GL_COLOR_BUFFER_BIT | GL_DEPTH_BUFFER_BIT);

    [gameManager drawStatesWithFrame: rect];

    [eaglContext presentRenderbuffer: GL_RENDERBUFFER_OES];
}
```

First, we determine the viewport view, the `glViewport()` function. The default values apply to a full screen, but with this method, you can resize the viewport as well.

To give ourselves a clear canvas at each frame, we explicitly delete the visible screen area:

```
glClearColor(0.5, 0.5, 0.5, 1.0);
glClear(GL_COLOR_BUFFER_BIT | GL_DEPTH_BUFFER_BIT);
```

With `glClearColor()` we specify the color with which we are going to overpaint the viewport (here it is gray), and then we delete the current color information from the render and depth buffers. For 2D games, it suffices simply to pass the GL_COLOR_BUFFER_BIT flag to the `glClear()` function, since the z-value is always zero.

Once the render buffer has been thus decontaminated, a new rendering process can begin:

```
[gameManager drawStatesWithFrame: rect];
[eaglContext presentRenderbuffer: GL_RENDERBUFFER_OES];
```

We have placed the actual rendering process in the previously mentioned `GameManager` method `drawStatesWithFrame:`. To render a scene, the render buffer must finally be perspectively rendered via the EAGL context and the frame buffer. This is done by the `presentRenderbuffer:` method based on the previously determined perspective.

---

*Note: To ensure that we select the appropriate graphics context at each frame, we can optionally reset the EAGL context at every frame via the* `setCurrentContext:` *method and again link the buffers being used. Since we are using only a single context and buffer, this is unnecessary for our example. You can find out via the* `UIView` *method of the* `layoutSubview` *whether the layer properties have changed, in which case you will have to re-create the EAGL graphics context and again link the render buffer. In its OpenGL ES Application-Template, which you can launch via Xcode, Apple shows how this can be done. Of course, the implementation of the view will thereby be somewhat more extensive.*[*]

---

## 5.5 The OpenGL Coordinate System

OpenGL supports both 2D and 3D programming, which differ with respect to the chosen perspective, which can be set with the following two functions:

Two-dimensional perspective:

```
glOrthof (GLfloat left, GLfloat right, GLfloat bottom, GLfloat top, GLfloat zNear, GLfloat zFar);
```

---

[*] There is also the possibility of combining a classic UIView (CALayer) with an OGL view (CAEAGLLayer)—for example, to render NSStrings to the OGL view. However, Apple does not recommend this for performance reasons. If you do not want to render your menu screens with OpenGL ES, you could, of course, easily switch between a UIView and an OGL view. The UIKit is designed to support several UIViews (keyword: UIViewController).

Three-dimensional perspective:

```
glFrustumf (GLfloat left, GLfloat right, GLfloat bottom, GLfloat top,
GLfloat zNear, GLfloat zFar);
```

We will look at 3D perspective later. For the following examples, we shall limit ourselves to 2D scenery and show the use of the glOrthof() function. Determining the perspective is the last new building block that we need to set up a basic OpenGL ES structure.

The implementation of the perspective takes place in the GameManager class, whose structure is familiar to us. We have seen earlier that the MainView class still calls the central drawStatesWithFrame: method of the GameManager. In this, we branch to the PLAY_GAME state and there call the playGame method. The playGame method thereby represents our playground for the next examples, in which we shall take our first tentative steps into the realm of OpenGL ES.

You may recall that the GameManager class is initialized statically and then calls the preloader method. In this, we can set once via

```
[self setOGLProjection];
```

the desired perspective

```
- (void) setOGLProjection {
    //set view
    glMatrixMode(GL_PROJECTION);
    glLoadIdentity();
    glOrthof(0, W, H, 0, 0, 1);//2D perspective

    //enable Modelview: switch to rendering of vertex arrays
    glMatrixMode(GL_MODELVIEW);
    glEnableClientState(GL_VERTEX_ARRAY);
    glDisable(GL_DEPTH_TEST);//2D only
}
```

This call uses the glOrthof() function to ensure that the coordinate origin is at the upper left-hand corner of the screen. The positive x-axis points to the right, and the positive y-axis points downward.

Although the glOrthof() function, in contrast to its 3D counterpart glFrustumf(), ignores the z-coordinate in the calculation of the frame buffer, we should nevertheless explicitly turn off the depth buffer via glDisable(GL_DEPTH_TEST) (Figure 5.4).

The parameters zNear and zFar for 2D perspective can be ignored and are set to the default values of 0 and 1. With left/top (0/0) and right/bottom (W/H), we set the upper left-hand and lower right-hand corners of the viewport. A call to

```
glOrthof(0, W, H, 0, 0, 1);
```

thus creates a classical 2D coordinate system, as is usual in computer graphics, with the y-axis pointing downward. You can, however, change the parameters of the glOrthof() function so that you obtain the familiar coordinate axes from your schooldays, with the origin at the center of the screen and the y-axis pointing upward. An example of this is given later.

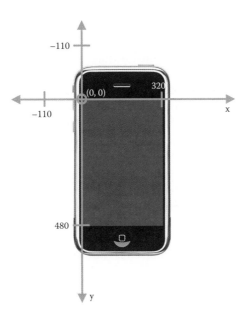

**Figure 5.4** Two-dimensional coordinate system under OpenGL ES.

Perspective is figured mathematically by a matrix calculation. OpenGL ES uses two types of matrix calculations that are of relevance to us; they can be activated via the `glMatrixMode()` function. Only one mode can be used at a time:

- GL_PROJECTION: To determine the perspective, we must activate the GL_PROJECTION mode. Then the current matrix should be replaced by the identity matrix. This is accomplished by a call to `glLoadIdentity()`. Now we can use `glOrthof()` and `glFrustumf()` to specify the type of perspective and projection of the scene on the 2D display.

- GL_MODELVIEW: Once we have determined the perspective, only models are displayed for the following rendering operations. Therefore, we can permanently switch to GL_MODELVIEW mode, and then all further matrix operations will pertain only to the model view.

But wait! What do we mean actually by *modeling?* For 2D and 3D games under OpenGL ES, we cannot simply specify that we wish to display a picture at position xyz. We must first determine precisely where the individual image points are to be located. That is, we need a model that consists of individual vertices.

## 5.5.1  Triangulation

As you may know, in computer games, *polygons* are rendered that are composed of numerous small triangles. There is a simple reason for this: To describe a surface (in 2D or 3D) mathematically, one needs at least three points. The surface that is determined by three points is a triangle.

Regardless of whether we wish to display a 2D or 3D triangle on the screen, we must specify the triangle's vertices. Later, you can specify an image that is to be displayed on top of this triangular surface, a so-called texture. But first, every graphical object that we can render to the screen consists simply of a pair of vertices: the model. Therefore, we permanently activate the GL_MODELVIEW-Matrix mode, since we know that from now on, only models in the form of vertices will be rendered. This model is usually passed as an array; therefore, we have additionally set the next OpenGL ES state:

```
glEnableClientState(GL_VERTEX_ARRAY);
```

There are other client states that we can activate in parallel, but we shall be using the GL_VERTEX_ARRAY state repeatedly. All that we can render for OpenGL ES is arrays consisting of individual vertices; the world consists only of vertices. For this reason, we have at the outset no drawImage: method; even text is not so easy to output. The API concentrates on direct hardware access, and we must implement methods such as drawImage: and drawString: ourselves. But do not worry because it is not very difficult.

## ▋ 5.6 Simple Drawing Operations

Although the OpenGL ES framework shows only a gray screen so far, we have already conquered the biggest hurdle. And the good news is that we no longer have to deal with buffers, matrices, or perspective. We can leave all this behind us (for now) and consider the playGame method, through which we would like, finally, to output our first few graphics.

The *Hello World* of OpenGL programming consists in outputting the simplest surface form: a white triangle (Figure 5.5):

```
- (void) playGame {
    [self drawOGLTriangle];
}

- (void) drawOGLTriangle {
    GLshort vertices[] = {
          0,  250, //lower left
        250, 250, //lower right
          0,   0, //upper left
    };

    glVertexPointer(2, GL_SHORT, 0, vertices);
    glDrawArrays(GL_TRIANGLES, 0, 3);
}
```

We have outsourced the code for displaying the triangle to a separate method and placed the vertices of the triangle in an array of type GLshort. There are three vertices, consisting of two xy-coordinates each, making six array elements in all.

The sequence of points is given in counterclockwise order beginning with the lower left-hand corner (x = 0, y = 250).

Did we say that everything consists of triangles? Well, not quite. In addition to triangles there are also points and lines, but that is it. All other 2D and 3D forms must be derived from these primitives. The basis is always a vertex, which may consist of two (*2D, xy*), three (*3D, xyz*), or even four (*4D, homogeneous coordinates*) components.

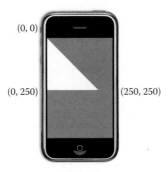

(0, 0)

(0, 250)  (250, 250)

**Figure 5.5** Hurrah, our first triangle!

For our 2D perspective, we have arranged the coordinate system in such a way that the coordinate units can be given in pixels. Thus, the point x = 10, y = 20 is located 10 pixels from the left-hand border of the screen and 20 pixels from the top. For a 3D coordinate system, in contrast, one speaks only of units, since there is no fixed reference point: The point x = 10, y = 20, z = –100 could be anywhere on the display, depending on the perspective with which one looks at the scene.

But back to our triangles in 2D space. All right, then, we have specified three vertices. What happens now? How does a white surface materialize from three points? Okay, we did not specify a color, so OpenGL simply renders everything in white. To specify a different color, we have only to call the function `glColor4f()` before drawing. Since OpenGL functions as a finite-state machine, this color specification remains in effect until some other color is set. The parameters are *R-G-B plus alpha*, with each value falling in the range 0 to 1.

To color the triangle green, you would just add the following code:

```
glColor4f(0, 1, 0, 1);
```

But what about our surface? Just as the Eskimos have many ways of saying "snow," OpenGL ES has many ways of making vertices *visible*—that is, to render them. Indeed, OpenGL ES features the following primitives:

```
GL_POINTS
GL_LINES
GL_LINE_STRIP
GL_LINE_LOOP
GL_TRIANGLES
GL_TRIANGLE_STRIP
GL_TRIANGLE_FAN
```

You can see in Figure 5.6 how the individual points must be placed in the array to get a given result.

The desired parameter is then passed to the `glDrawArrays()` function. To create graphical output from an array of arbitrary elements, the following three steps must be followed:

1. Create an array with the desired vertices.

2. Feed the array into the OpenGL ES rendering pipeline. An array variable is simply a pointer to its first element. OpenGL ES provides the function

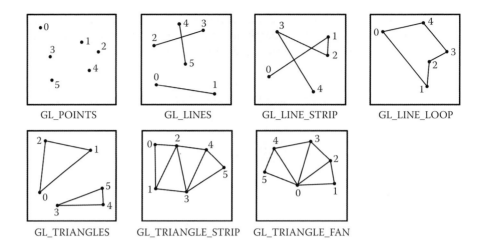

Figure 5.6 Overview of available primitives.

glVertexPointer (GLint size, GLenum type, GLsizei stride, const GLvoid *pointer). The first parameter specifies how many components a vertex possesses. (This is not at once clear from the array, so we need to specify it explicitly.) Possible values are 2, 3, and 4. Then you give the data type of the elements. OpenGL supplies a suitable constant for each data type. Since we have declared the array as GLshort, we choose the constant GL_SHORT. You probably know that a data type determines how much space an element occupies in memory. So that OpenGL can iterate through all the elements of an array, we must specify how many bytes an element occupies in memory. Using the stride parameter, you can, however, specify an offset between the elements. For us, this value is simply 0. Finally, we specify an array pointer: glVertexPointer(2, GL_SHORT, 0, vertices).

3. Now that OpenGL knows where the array with the vertices is located, we have only to trigger the rendering process. We give three additional parameters to the glDrawArrays() function in order to determine how the vertices are to be visualized: glDrawArrays (GLenum mode, GLint first, GLsizei count). We have already introduced the mode parameter earlier. To draw the triangle without filling it in, we would simply pass the parameter GL_LINE_LOOP instead of GL_TRIANGLES, and to display just the vertices, we would pass GL_POINTS. The next two parameters, first and count, are used to set additional properties of the vertices:

- first: This is the index of the first array element that is to be rendered. To render the entire array, we begin with 0. However, you can skip over elements so that only part of the array is rendered.

- count: OpenGL does not yet know how long our array is. Instead of our simply specifying the length of the array, however, OpenGL expects here the number of vertices that we wish to render. So, we have two coordinates (xy) per vertex and wish to render three vertices beginning with the first element— that is, element 0 (our array has length 2*3 elements): `glDrawArrays(GL_TRIANGLES, 0, 3)`.

Let us consider a further example: To define a line between two given points, we could write the following method:

```
- (void) drawOGLLineFrom: (CGPoint) p1 to: (CGPoint) p2 {
    GLshort vertices[] = {
        p1.x, p1.y,
        p2.x, p2.y
    };
    glVertexPointer(2, GL_SHORT, 0, vertices);
    glColor4f(1, 0, 0, 1);
    glDrawArrays(GL_LINES, 0, 2);
}
```

A horizontal red line is then defined by a call to

```
[self drawOGLLineFrom: CGPointMake(0, H/2) to: CGPointMake(W, H/2)];
```

However, this example has one small catch: We pass the vertices of the line as parameters to the method. So, using this, we could move the line across the screen and change the coordinates at runtime. But how would that work for a complex 3D model consisting of thousands of vertices? To move it across the screen, we would have to move each point manually and render the altered array. OpenGL offers a much more elegant solution that allows us to *scale, rotate,* or *translate* all the vertices in our scene that are currently in memory. We do not have to know how these matrix operations function mathematically, since OpenGL ES offers the following functions:

```
//translate
glTranslatef (GLfloat x, GLfloat y, GLfloat z);
//rotate
glRotatef (GLfloat angle, GLfloat x, GLfloat y, GLfloat z);
//scale
glScalef (GLfloat x, GLfloat y, GLfloat z);
```

We will look at the bottom two functions later. To be able to move the model safely—without having to worry about any effects on other models—OpenGL ES offers a mechanism that might be familiar to you: To carry out a rotation with Core Graphics, we stored the old state of the graphics context, then carried out the rotation, and finally restored the original state.

There exists an original state for OpenGL ES that we can create at any time by calling the `glLoadIdentity()` function and thereby replacing all the current matrix operations by the identity matrix; however, we would thereby also reset any changes we had made. Therefore, OpenGL stores changes to the matrix in a stack; up to 16 matrices can lie on the stack in `GL_MODELVIEW` mode. We do not need that many, however. We have only to ensure that we retain a copy of the current matrix (with all the previously executed transformations). We can then make the desired changes on this and render it. Then we delete the current matrix from the stack, and the system finds itself back in the original state. For this purpose, OpenGL ES offers the following two functions:

```
glPushMatrix();
//... transform the matrix
//... render
glPopMatrix();
```

Through the transformation, the entire coordinate system is changed. To translate a model consisting of individual vertices, we actually do not translate the model, but rather the coordinate system. After the model has been rendered, we can translate the coordinate system to its old position or else create the previously stored coordinate system; the function `glPushMatrix()` pushes a duplicate of the current matrix onto the stack. We can thereby make the desired changes—for example, translate, rotate, or scale our model—and then feed it to the render buffer. Then the `glPopMatrix()` function sees to it that the top element is popped from the stack so that the previous element is now on top (and thereby replaces the current matrix): The current matrix is now in the exact same state as it was previously. Of course, we can carry out this process with any number of additional models. For every model, the same starting position holds; that is, all models operate with the same matrix.

So much for theory. In practice, this all works very simply, as we shall soon see. We would now like to implement a new method for drawing a rectangle:

```
- (void) drawOGLRect: (CGRect) rect {
    GLshort vertices[] = {
        0,                  rect.size.height,//lower left
        rect.size.width,    rect.size.height,//lower right
        0,                  0,//upper left
        rect.size.width,    0 //upper right
    };
    glVertexPointer(2, GL_SHORT, 0, vertices);
    glColor4f(1, 1, 0, 1);
    glPushMatrix();
    glTranslatef(rect.origin.x, rect.origin.y, 0);
    glDrawArrays(GL_TRIANGLE_STRIP, 0, 4);
    glPopMatrix();
}
```

Instead of placing the vertices directly into the array, we now position the rectangle at the origin (0, 0) and simply change its size (`width/height`).

To render the rectangle to the desired xy-position, we call the function `glTranslatef()`, and since the method always expects a z-value as well, we set it to 0. To keep the function from continually translating the coordinate system, we bracket the call with a `glPushMatrix()`/`glPopMatrix()` pair and thus can call the method repeatedly. The translation thereby has an effect only on the current matrix (Figure 5.7).

In fact, we always render the rectangle at position (0, 0), temporarily moving the coordinate system by multiplying the current matrix by the translation matrix (this is done for us by the `glTranslatef()` function). Since the old matrix is then restored, subsequent operations encounter an unchanged coordinate system; our rectangle is nonetheless located at the desired position, since we had already moved it to the render buffer.

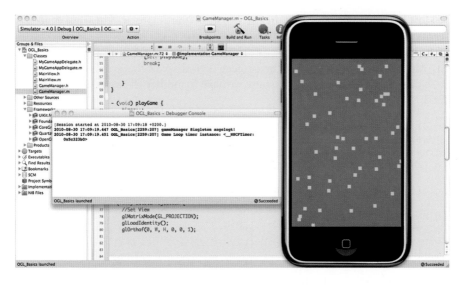

Figure 5.7  Randomly generated yellow rectangles (10 × 10 pixels) and a red line.

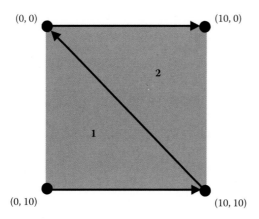

Figure 5.8  Every rectangle consists of two triangles.

As you may have noticed, a rectangle consists of four vertices (Figure 5.8). This is because we have chosen the array mode GL_TRIANGLE_STRIP, since a rectangle actually consists of *two* triangles that share two vertices. We can therefore reduce the array from six vertices to four. Each new point now automatically forms a new triangle with the two previous points.

# ▌ 5.7  Digression: Math Plotter

If you find it unpleasant that our coordinate system has its origin at the upper left-hand corner—perhaps because you are used to something different from your schooldays— do not let it bother you. As already mentioned, you can change the parameters of the `glOrthof()` function to obtain the classical coordinate system from high-school mathematics.

We have created an example project based on our framework that we call "OGL_MathPlotter." The goal of the project is to display the graph of a given function. To construct the coordinate system, we have to modify the `setOGLProjection` method:

```
- (void) setOGLProjection {
    //set view
    glMatrixMode(GL_PROJECTION);
    glLoadIdentity();

    glOrthof(-W/2, W/2, -H/2, H/2, 0, 1);

    glMatrixMode(GL_MODELVIEW);
    glEnableClientState(GL_VERTEX_ARRAY);
    glDisable(GL_DEPTH_TEST);//2D only
}
```

As you can see, the only change is in the parameters of the function `glOrthof()`:

- `Left/top` refers to the point (`-W/2`, `H/2`).

- `Right/bottom` refers to the point (`W/2`, `-H/2`).

Thus, the origin is located right in the middle of the display, and each of the (visible) axes has a total length that corresponds to the dimensions of the display. The sign indicates that the positive x-axis points to the right and the positive y-axis points upward (Figure 5.9).

After this preliminary work, it is easy to display the graph of any mathematical function:

```
- (void) draw2DGraphPlotter {
    //x-axis
    [self drawOGLLineFrom: CGPointMake(W/2, 0) to: CGPointMake(-W/2, 0)];
    //y-axis
    [self drawOGLLineFrom: CGPointMake(0, H/2) to: CGPointMake(0, -H/2)];

    for (float x = -W/2; x < W/2; x + = 0.01) {//range of values of x
        //the function
        float y = 0.01 * x*x;//compressed quadratic function
        GLfloat point[] = {
            x, y
        };
        glVertexPointer(2, GL_FLOAT, 0, point);
        glDrawArrays(GL_POINTS, 0, 1);
    }
}
```

After having used the `drawOGLLineFrom` to draw the two axes, we can use a `for` loop to iterate through the range of values of a mathematical function:

$$y = 0.01^{*}x^2$$

**Figure 5.9** The graph plotter with a third-degree polynomial.

We render the results of the equation as a point array of type `GL_POINTS`. A point is rendered for each x-value.

To render a third-degree polynomial of the form

$$y = a^*x^3$$

we simply replace our quadratic function:

```
float y = 0.0001 * x*x*x;
```

As a result, we obtain the graph shown in the screen shot. Since the axes, with dimensions ±160 and ± 240 pixels, are considerably longer than what you are used to from school, we have chosen a to be as small as possible to compress the graph.

Alternatively, you could enlarge the graph view by, for example, shrinking the parameters of the `glOrthof()` function proportionally, which increases the display area, or you could scale the coordinate system using the `glScalef()` function. We will see the use of this function in a later example.

## 5.8  And Pictures? What Is All the Talk about Textures?

As game developers, there is no way that we are going to be satisfied with surfaces of a single color. However, it is not so easy to display pictures—for example, in PNG format—in this way for 2D and 3D games. It can be done only with so-called textures. As a platform-independent API, OpenGL ES does not concern itself with special picture formats. To create a texture, one has to prepare the individual pixels of the image. So we are faced with the problem of creating a usable picture. We shall solve this problem with the help of Core Graphics.

A texture is basically nothing but a normal picture: The pixel data are written to a section of memory reserved by OpenGL ES, and from there they can be used to create a picture. The dimensions of the initial picture play no role; the texture will be mapped onto a specific area determined by the vertices and thereby scaled and cropped, or even wrapped. There are several ways of creating textures. Normally, in creating a 3D model, a graphic designer also determines a suitable wrap. The texture should be understood

5.8  And Pictures? What Is All the Talk about Textures?

179

as an unrolled carpet that then later will be rendered to the vertices based on the texture coordinates. To each vertex there corresponds precisely one texture coordinate.

For 2D games, the process is simplified, since now both the texture and our area have two dimensions, with a rectangular shape.

*Note: For the graphics hardware to work efficiently with the textures of the model, the dimensions of the texture must be a power of 2. Otherwise, instead of the texture, a white surface will be displayed. However, the height and width do not have to be the same. The maximal width and height of a texture for a device of the iPhone family is 2048 pixels. Some permissible values are 32 \* 64, 128 \* 128, 512 \* 32, and 1024 \* 2048.*

Transparent surfaces are allowed. That is, the alpha channel is fully supported.

Let us begin to render our first texture to the display. The goal is generally to render arbitrary PNGs by a simple method, such as the following (Figure 5.10):

```
[self drawOGLImg: @"player.png" at: CGPointMake(x, y)];
```

We would now like to address the implementation of such a method. Let us create a new project based on our framework called "OGL_Texture." The complete project can be found under this name in the download page for this book.

We choose as a graphic to display a $64 \times 64$ pixel spaceship. Like all our graphics, this one is based on a rectangle (in fact, a square). We have already seen how to define a rectangular 2D shape in OpenGL ES:

```
GLshort imageVertices[] = {
    0,      height, //lower left
    width,  height, //lower right
    0,      0,      //upper left
    width,  0       //upper right
};
```

So far, so good. But how does it work with textures? We can replace width/height in the array with 64, and then our area is exactly that of the PNG. Since a texture coordinate is associated with each vertex, we need an additional array with precisely four texture coordinates (Figure 5.11):

```
GLshort textureCoords[] = {
    0, 1,//lower left
    1, 1,//lower right
    0, 0,//upper left
    1, 0 //upper right
};
```

Not so difficult at all—but watch out! Texture coordinates can be stretched or compressed at will, and therefore it makes no sense to give the actual coordinates. Thus, the domain of values for a 2D texture is by definition *always* between 0 and 1.

To make it clear that the texture coordinates are not to be confused with normal coordinates, we will call them *st*-coordinates (sometimes called *uv*-coordinates), where *s* corresponds to the x-value, and *t* to the y-value. Since the dimensions of all texture templates as well as that of the player.png graphic must be a power of 2 and therefore divisible

**Figure 5.10** player.png.

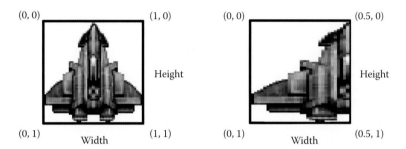

**Figure 5.11** The texture is mapped to the vertices. Left: 1 to 1; right: stretched.

by 2, it is easy to divide up a texture: If, for example, we want to map the left side of our spaceship onto a surface, we would use the texture coordinates from 0 to 0.5:

```
GLfloat textureCoords[] = {
    0,   1,//lower left
    0.5, 1,//lower right
    0,   0,//upper left
    0.5, 0 //upper right
};
```

---

*Note: We must, of course, choose* GLfloat *as the data type. Since our vertex surface still has the dimensions* width * height, *the texture will be stretched in the direction of its width along the surface. On the other hand, if you wish to preserve the proportions and represent the left part of the spaceship without distortion, you must halve the vertex array as well.*

---

You can see that for the texture coordinates it is completely irrelevant what the actual dimensions of the original graphic are. The dimensions of the texture are always 1 × 1.

But for now, let us forget about dividing up a texture. To display a graphic, we require only the graphic's four vertices (depending on width, height) and the four vertices of the texture (always 1, 1).

Once you have created a texture in OpenGL ES, it is stored in memory as an integer ID and can be used repeatedly. Since the code for creating a texture is rather extensive, we place it in a new class called Tex. First, the good news: There is no difference between creating a texture for 2D games and creating one for 3D games, so we can use the class again later.

---

**Listing 5.3** Tex.h

```objc
#import <OpenGLES/ES1/gl.h>

@interface Tex : NSObject {
    GLuint textureID;
    int width;
    int height;
}

//initializer
- (void) createTexFromImage: (NSString *) picName;

//create the texture - helper
- (GLubyte *) generatePixelDataFromImage: (UIImage *) pic;
- (void) generateTexture: (GLubyte *) pixelData;

//render the texture
- (void) drawAt: (CGPoint) p;

//getter
- (GLuint) getTextureID;
- (int) getWidth;
- (int) getHeight;

@end
```

As you can see, the `Tex` class merely stored the texture ID and the dimensions of the texture template as a member. In addition to a couple of getters, we have the following four methods:

- **(void) createTexFromImage: (NSString *) picName;**

  - To create a new texture, the name of the image file should suffice. This method calls internally the two helpers `generatePixelDataFromImage:` and `generateTexture:` for the actual creation of the texture.

- **(void) drawAt: (CGPoint) p;**

  - At this point, we should be able to draw the texture at any point.

- **(GLubyte *) generatePixelDataFromImage: (UIImage *) pic;**

  - To create the texture, we must first access the raw pixel information. For any `UIImage`, this method returns its bytes as an array.

- **(void) generateTexture: (GLubyte *) pixelData;**

  - We can pass the byte representation to this method, which uses the pixel data to make an OpenGL texture. Since textures are located within a reserved area of memory, the method does not return anything. Instead, it stores the new texture ID in the member variable `textureID`. As a rule, texture IDs begin with 1 and are increased by 1 for each new texture.

Before we go into the implementation of these methods, let us look at the basic structure of the `Tex` class.

---

**Listing 5.4  Tex.m**

```
#import "Tex.h"

@implementation Tex

- (void) createTexFromImage: (NSString *) picName {
    ...
}

- (GLubyte *) generatePixelDataFromImage: (UIImage *) pic {
    ...
}

- (void) generateTexture: (GLubyte *) pixelData {
    ...
}

- (void) drawAt: (CGPoint) p {
    ...
}

- (GLuint) getTextureID {
    return textureID;
}

- (int) getWidth {
    return width;
}

- (int) getHeight {
    return height;
}

- (void) dealloc {
    NSLog(@"Delete texture, ID:%i", textureID);
    glDeleteTextures(1, &textureID);
    [super dealloc];
}

@end
```

In the `dealloc` method we have already implemented the function `glDelete-Textures()`. With this, a texture can be deleted at any time from the OpenGL memory area. Since several textures can be deleted, the first parameter is 1: We want to delete only *one* texture with ID `textureID`.

---

The implementation of createTexFromImage: is not particularly difficult:

```objc
- (void) createTexFromImage: (NSString *) picName {
    UIImage *pic = [UIImage imageNamed: picName];

    int scaleFactor = 1;

    float iOSVersion = [[[UIDevice currentDevice] systemVersion]
                        floatValue];
    if (iOSVersion > = 4.0) {
        if (pic.scale > = 2) {
            scaleFactor = pic.scale;
        }
    }

    if (pic) {
        //set the texture's dimensions
        width = pic.size.width * scaleFactor;
        height = pic.size.height * scaleFactor;
        if ((width & (width-1)) ! = 0 || (height & (height-1)) ! = 0
            || width > 2048 || height > 2048) {
            NSLog(@"ERROR:%@ width and/or height is not a power of 2
                    or is > 2048!", picName);
        }

        //create pixel data
        GLubyte *pixelData = [self generatePixelDataFromImage: pic];

        //create the texture from the pixel data and store as ID
        [self generateTexture: pixelData];

        //clean-up
        int memory = width*height*4;
        NSLog(@"%@-Pic-Textur erzeugt, Size:%i KB, ID:%i", picName,
                memory/1024, textureID);
        free(pixelData);
        [pic release];

        width/= scaleFactor;
        height/= scaleFactor;
    } else {
        NSLog(@"ERROR:%@ not found, texture not created.", picName);
    }
}
```

Using the string that is passed, we create a completely normal UIImage. In addition, we check whether the texture has valid dimensions. The if query checks, using the & bit operator, whether they are powers of 2. The actual creation of the texture then takes place through the following calls:

```objc
GLubyte *pixelData = [self generatePixelDataFromImage: pic];
[self generateTexture: pixelData];
```

We then clean up the memory a bit and output the texture's maximum memory consumption. Since we are not using PVRTC textures, 4 bytes are needed for each pixel. Thus, the largest possible texture occupies

$$2048 \times 2048 \ast 4 = 16{,}384 \text{ MB}$$

of memory. Our $64 \times 64$ texture, on the other hand, consumes only 16 kB.

To read retina graphics from iOS 4.0 and up in the correct dimensions, we must employ a scale factor, since UIImage returns the image size in image points instead of in pixels.

Let us now look at how we can read out the bytes of a UIImage. As already mentioned, this is not the responsibility of OpenGL ES, so we fall back on Core Graphics:

```
- (GLubyte *) generatePixelDataFromImage: (UIImage *) pic {
    GLubyte *pixelData = (GLubyte *) calloc(width*height*4, sizeof(GLubyte));
    CGColorSpaceRef imageCS = CGImageGetColorSpace(pic.CGImage);
    CGContextRef gc = CGBitmapContextCreate(pixelData,
                                            width, height, 8, width*4,
                                            imageCS,
                                            kCGImageAlphaPremultipliedLast);
    CGContextDrawImage(gc, CGRectMake(0, 0, width, height), pic.CGImage);//
render pic to gc
    CGContextRelease(gc);
    return pixelData;
}
```

Like any good graphic API, Core Graphics also offers the possibility to render an image off-line. So we use a little trick: We get ourselves a new graphics context and render our image onto this. Then everything that we have drawn to this context lands automatically in the memory location reserved for it, which we then have only to return.

But let us not get ahead of ourselves: First, we reserve memory via the calloc function, corresponding exactly to the previously mentioned formula: *w*h*4*.

We can now create a new bitmap context. For this, Core Graphics offers the function

```
CGContextRef CGBitmapContextCreate(
    void *data,
    size_t width,
    size_t height,
    size_t bitsPerComponent,
    size_t bytesPerRow,
    CGColorSpaceRef space,
    CGBitmapInfo bitmapInfo);
```

Everything that is rendered to this context ends up in the memory location pointed to by the pointer data. Furthermore, we also give the dimensions, specifying 8 bits per component; with the constant kCGImageAlphaPremultipliedLast, we specify standard RGBA behavior (we are rendering only one image), and, finally, we pass the color space of the image to the function. We have gotten this from the function CGImageGetColorSpace(), to which we give the Core Graphics representation of the UIImage.

Once the new graphics context exists, we can render to it; in our case, a call to CGContextDrawImage() does the trick. The image will be drawn at (0, 0), of course, since the context corresponds to the size of the image.

Then we have only to release some memory (for the graphics context, though not, however, for the color space) and can return the pixel data. And why should the color space not be released? Here we mention the "golden rule" of the Core Foundation: Functions with a "get" in their name take care of their own release, while those with a "create" do not

5.8 And Pictures? What Is All the Talk about Textures?

185

(= owned by caller). Therefore, `CGBitmapContextCreate()` requires a release call to avoid leaks, unless you implement ARC (= automatic reference counting, since iOS 5).

The preceding procedure allows us to create textures out of other elements, such as strings. You know that OpenGL ES by nature does not support text output (but more on that later).

To make an implementable texture from pixel data, we must turn again to OpenGL ES:

```
- (void) generateTexture: (GLubyte *) pixelData {
    glGenTextures(1, &textureID);
    glBindTexture(GL_TEXTURE_2D, textureID);
    glTexParameteri(GL_TEXTURE_2D, GL_TEXTURE_MIN_FILTER, GL_LINEAR);
    glTexImage2D(GL_TEXTURE_2D, 0, GL_RGBA, width, height, 0, GL_RGBA,
        GL_UNSIGNED_BYTE, pixelData);

    //globally activate texture-related states
    glEnable(GL_BLEND);
    glBlendFunc(GL_ONE, GL_ONE_MINUS_SRC_ALPHA);
    glEnableClientState(GL_TEXTURE_COORD_ARRAY);
    glTexParameterf(GL_TEXTURE_2D, GL_TEXTURE_WRAP_S, GL_CLAMP_TO_EDGE);
    glTexParameterf(GL_TEXTURE_2D, GL_TEXTURE_WRAP_T, GL_CLAMP_TO_EDGE);
}
```

Before we create the texture, we first anchor and bind the `textureID`, set suitable parameters that control the wrapping behavior, and finally create the texture with the `glTExImage2D()` function, to which we pass the pixel data, together with other parameters such as the dimensions and the color model including the alpha channel. You can specify with the texture parameters that the texture should be wrapped in the *s* or *t* direction (`GL_TEXTURE_WRAP_S`, `GL_TEXTURE_WRAP_T`). Here, we set the parameter `GL_CLAMP_TO_EDGE` so that the texture coordinates 1:1 can be mapped to the vertices. Of course, OpenGL ES offers additional options for controlling the behavior of the texture; with the default setting shown, however, you should be able to deal with the most common applications.

Finally, we activate the appropriate blend function, which determines how we should treat transparent surfaces. The constant `GL_ONE_MINUS_SRC_ALPHA` causes transparent surfaces to be cross-faded with other transparent surfaces according to their alpha values. Furthermore, we use the constant `GL_TEXTURE_COORD_ARRAY` to activate permanently the use of the texture coordinate array during the rendering process. We do not yet thereby establish that all surfaces are to be textured from now on, but simply make possible the use of such an array.

After completion of the `generateTexture:` method, if everything has gone smoothly, the `textureID` should point to a new texture, which we can then use during the rendering process:

```
- (void) drawAt: (CGPoint) p {
    GLshort imageVertices[] = {
        0,      height,  //lower left
        width,  height,  //lower right
        0,      0,       //upper left
        width,  0        //upper right
    };
```

```
GLshort textureCoords[] = {
    0, 1,//lower left
    1, 1,//lower right
    0, 0,//upper left
    1, 0 //upper right
};

p.x = (int) p.x;
p.y = (int) p.y;

glEnable(GL_TEXTURE_2D);//all surfaces are now textured

glColor4f(1, 1, 1, 1);
glBindTexture(GL_TEXTURE_2D, textureID);
glVertexPointer(2, GL_SHORT, 0, imageVertices);
glTexCoordPointer(2, GL_SHORT, 0, textureCoords);

glPushMatrix();
glTranslatef(p.x, p.y, 0);
glDrawArrays(GL_TRIANGLE_STRIP, 0, 4);
glPopMatrix();

glDisable(GL_TEXTURE_2D);
}
```

In the two arrays, imageVertices and textureCoords, we store, as already shown, the dimensions of the original rectangle aligned at the origin (0, 0) and the texture coordinates (valid for all images). So that OpenGL can render the texture precisely, we cast p as an integer value.

Then, the texture flag is turned on via glEnable(GL_TEXTURE_2D). As long as we do not shut it off (at the end of the method), all surfaces will be covered with the current texture, which we activate via

```
glBindTexture(GL_TEXTURE_2D, textureID);
```

Of course, it is possible to use different texture coordinates for each texture, so in the next step, we refer to the two previously created arrays (imageVertices and textureCoords).

Then, we can enter the rendering process as usual and render the texture at the desired point, which is always given as the upper left-hand corner of the image.

Voilà! That does it. Using the following, we can display our first texture on the screen at position (100, 100)*:

```
Tex *tex = [[Tex alloc] init];
[tex createTexFromImage: @"player.png"];
[tex drawAt: CGPointMake(100, 100)];
```

As promised, we are now going to show how to create a texture from an NSString so that you can output text. But note that this process is not suitable for particularly long

---

* Instead of passing the vertices and texture coordinates as an array, we can use an OES extension that allows for the direct rendering of 2D textures; glDrawTexiOES (GLint x, GLint y, GLint z, GLint width, GLint height) is the integer variant given here as an example. The function operates on texels and therefore offers less flexibility vis-à-vis matrix operations.

texts or the score display since, for each string, a *new* texture is created, and if you do not delete the new texture, memory will be quickly depleted. But for simple announcements such as "game over," this technique works perfectly well. You could also, of course, use this method to create a bitmap font so that you can reuse the textures. For example, to display the score, you would need only 10 textures, and then the score could be assembled from the digits 0 to 9.

In order to expand the Tex class to support strings, we need to add two new methods:

```
- (void) createTexFromString: (NSString *) text;
- (GLubyte *) generatePixelDataFromString: (NSString *) text;
```

The first method is similar to the previously shown UIImage counterpart, except that it sets the texture dimensions by itself based on the text length. We support only a single line of text. Because of the restrictions on texture size, our texture will have to be bigger than the displayed text:

```
- (void) createTexFromString: (NSString *) text {
    //set texture dimensions
    int len = [text length]*20;
    if (len < 64) width = 64;
    else if (len < 128) width = 128;
    else if (len < 256) width = 256;
    else width = 512;//max width text
    height = 32;

    //create pixel data
    GLubyte *pixelData = [self generatePixelDataFromString: text];

    //create the texture from the pixel data and store the ID
    [self generateTexture: pixelData];

    //clean-up
    int memory = width*height*4;
    NSLog(@"%@-text-texture created, Size:%i KB, ID:%i", text, memory/1024,
        textureID);
    free(pixelData);
}
```

As you can see, the maximum length is 512 pixels. In addition, we set the texture's height at 32 pixels; that is, we do not support variable font size. Nevertheless, with your current knowledge, you should be able to implement such functionality yourself. Depending on the font size, you may have to settle for wasting space in some circumstances due to the "power-of-2" requirement.

We render the string, as we did the UIImage previously, to a bitmap context:

```
- (GLubyte *) generatePixelDataFromString: (NSString *) text {
    const char *cText = [text cStringUsingEncoding: NSASCIIStringEncoding];
    GLubyte *pixelData =
        (GLubyte *) calloc(width*height*4, sizeof(GLubyte));
    CGColorSpaceRef rgbCS = CGColorSpaceCreateDeviceRGB();
    CGContextRef gc = CGBitmapContextCreate(
                        pixelData,
                        width, height, 8, width*4,
                        rgbCS,
                        kCGImageAlphaPremultipliedLast);
```

```
int size = 22;//font size, smaller than height
CGContextSetRGBFillColor(gc, 0,1,0,1);//font color
CGContextSelectFont(gc, "Verdana", size, kCGEncodingMacRoman);
int ys = height-size;//swapped y-axis
//render text to gc:
CGContextShowTextAtPoint(gc, 0, ys, cText, strlen(cText));
CGContextRelease(gc);
return pixelData;
}
```

Since Core Graphics offers no direct support for NSString objects, we first create a char string, which we then can render with the function CGContextShowTextAtPoint(). As you can see, for the sake of simplicity, we specify the font size (*22*) and the font (*Verdana*), as well as the font color (*0,1,0,1 = green*). But here as well, it should be no problem to adapt the method with respect to these parameters. Take care in positioning the graphic that the y-axis of the graphics context points upward (we are not in the OpenGL coordinate system).

If you want to output a Hello World you can do so as follows:

```
Tex *tex = [[Tex alloc] init];
[tex createTexFromString: @"Hello, World!"];
[tex drawAt: CGPointMake(100, 100)];
```

However, you may have rightly noticed that we are not yet quite done; the handling of textures is not yet quite optimal. Usually, we want to output a text or image in a game loop, and it would be a pity if we had to re-create the texture at each iteration. We should therefore end by setting up a clean resource management.

Conveniently, we can fall back on our existing hash-table solution. Expand the GameManager class with an NSMutableDictionary, in which we store the textures:

```
- (NSMutableDictionary *) getDictionary {
       if (!dictionary) {//hash table
             dictionary = [[NSMutableDictionary alloc] init];
             NSLog(@"Dictionary created!");
       }
       return dictionary;
}

- (void) removeFromDictionary: (NSString*) name {
     [[self getDictionary] removeObjectForKey: name];
}
```

To create the textures, we use an additional helper method that uses the supplementary parameter imgFlag to decide whether a text or an image should be used as the template for the texture:

```
- (Tex *) getTex: (NSString*) name isImage: (bool) imgFlag {
     Tex *tex = [[self getDictionary] objectForKey: name];
     if (!tex) {
           tex = [[Tex alloc] init];
           if (imgFlag) {
                [tex createTexFromImage: name];
           } else {
                [tex createTexFromString: name];
           }
```

5.8  And Pictures? What Is All the Talk about Textures?

189

```
            [[self getDictionary] setObject: tex forKey: name];
            NSLog(@"%@ stored in dictionary as a tex.", name);
            [tex release];
        }
        return tex;
}
```

We now have only to implement two suitable render methods:

```
- (void) drawOGLImg: (NSString*) picName at: (CGPoint) p {
    Tex *tex = [self getTex: picName isImage: YES];
    if (tex) {
        [tex drawAt: p];
    }
}

- (void) drawOGLString: (NSString*) text at: (CGPoint) p {
    Tex *tex = [self getTex: text isImage: NO];
    if (tex) {
        [tex drawAt: p];
    }
}
```

To render an image, we need only call

```
[self drawOGLImg: @"player.png" at: CGPointMake(100, 100)];
```

The drawOGLImg method queries the hash table as to whether a texture class with the name of the image exists so that we can use the method in a game loop without danger.

In some situations, we also need the dimensions of the image, which we can accomplish with the following convenient method:

```
- (CGSize) getOGLImgDimension: (NSString*) picName {
    Tex *tex = [self getTex: picName isImage: YES];
    if (tex) {
        return CGSizeMake([tex getWidth], [tex getHeight]);
    }
    return CGSizeMake(0, 0);
}
```

Let us look at a practical example of our newly created method:

```
- (void) playGame {
    CGSize textureSize = [self getOGLImgDimension: @"player.png"];
    int w = textureSize.width;
    int h = textureSize.height;

    static int yStep = 0;
    yStep - = 1;

    for (int x = 0; x < W; x + = w) {
        for (int y = 0; y < H; y + = h) {
            [self drawOGLImg: @"player.png" at: CGPointMake(x, y + yStep)];
        }
    }

    [self drawOGLString: @"OpenGL ES rules!" at: CGPointMake(60, 100)];
}
```

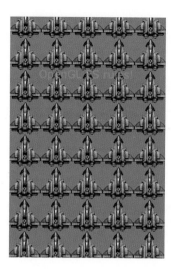

Figure 5.12 Forty fighter textures and a text texture.

By means of two nested `for` loops, we output the `player.png` texture to the screen 40 times. The spaceships fly slowly upward, and over them we render a text as proof that this aspect functions correctly (Figure 5.12).

Now, that was not so very difficult, was it? We should now be able to put together a game with any collection of 2D graphics using OpenGL ES. At the end of this section, we reduced the texture creation and display of a texture to a single method so that, in the future, we will not have to fuss with the details of texturing.

# 5.9 Onward to the Matrix: The Transformation Functions

Before we create animated textures in the next section using clipping (over the texture coordinates), we return to the subject of movement and transformation of (textured) objects. Do not worry; this is a very easy section and is nothing to be concerned about.

We have already met the necessary functions for transforming an object and seen the function `glTranslatef()` in action. The method can also be used for textures:

```
- (void) translate {
    static int x = 160-32;
    static int y = 480-32;
    y - = 1;

    glPushMatrix();                                          //1.
    glTranslatef(x, y, 0);                                   //2.
    [self drawOGLImg: @"player.png" at: CGPointMake(0, 0)];//3.
    glPopMatrix();                                           //4.
}
```

You will find this code segment as usual in the example project for this chapter: "OGL_Movement." The basic principle for the transformation of objects—translation, rotation, and distortion—is always the same:

1. Fetch a copy of the current matrix stack.

2. Iterate the operation on the copy of the current matrix stack.

3. Render.

4. Reactivate the old matrix.

We have already discussed these steps extensively. You can see that this works as well in combination with the new drawOGLImg method. Note that for this example, we are rendering the image at position (0, 0). As a result, the spaceship is moved upward (y - = 1). Rotations can be accomplished just as easily:

```
- (void) rotate {
    static int a = 0;
    a - = 10;
    glPushMatrix();
    glTranslatef(160, 240, 0);//centrally located
    glRotatef(a, 0, 0, 1);
    [self drawOGLImg: @"player.png" at: CGPointMake(0, 0)];
    glPopMatrix();
}
```

The first parameter specifies the angle of rotation in degrees; since we are increasing it continuously, the result is a circular motion around the coordinate origin. We have moved the coordinate system to the middle of the screen (160, 240), using glTranslatef(), so that the object rotates about the center of the screen.

If we wanted the object to rotate about its center, we would have to center it at the origin. We shall demonstrate this in the next section.

After the rotation angle, we specify about which axis (x-y-z) the object is to be rotated; for a 2D system, only the z-axis makes sense (0-0-1), which points vertically away from the viewer. For 3D systems, you can rotate about more than one axis at a time. You would rotate about all three axes as follows:

```
glRotatef(a, 1, 1, 1);
```

But beware: The order of the transformations has a great influence on the matrix calculations. Whether you first rotate a model and then translate or first translate and then rotate leads to different results. As a rule of thumb, one can say that the last transformation should be executed first, and then the others, before the array is finally moved to the render buffer. This means that in the preceding example, we actually first rotate the object about (0, 0) and only then translate. In the source code, you must, of course, maintain the reverse sequence.

The third and last transformation function allows for the scaling of an object:

```
- (void) scale {
    static float s = 1;
```

```
static int sf = 1;//sign
s - = 0.01 * sf;
if (s < 0 || s > 1) {
    sf * = -1;
}

glPushMatrix();
glTranslatef(160, 240, 0);
glScalef(s, s, 1);
[self drawOGLImg: @"player.png" at: CGPointMake(0, 0)];
glPopMatrix();
}
```

The degree of scaling s is specified for each axis (x-y-z):

- **s = 1 means** no scaling (original size)

- **0 < s < 1 means** shrink

- **s > 1 means** enlarge

In order to scale the image proportionally in the in x- and y-directions, the first two parameters have to be equal. A scaling in the direction of the z-axis makes no sense for a 2D game. In the code shown previously, the s-value oscillates between 0 and 1. Since the graphic is always positioned at the center of the screen, with a size of 0, the object lies right at the center of the screen. To scale a graphic with a size > 0 at the center of the screen, the graphic would first have to be translated. For 3D games, scaling seldom gives useful results, since the optical effect is similar to a translation in the direction of the z-axis; for 2D games, scaling can lead to interesting effects and give the illusion of spatial depth to the game (Figure 5.13).

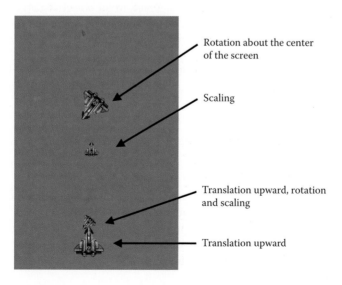

Rotation about the center of the screen

Scaling

Translation upward, rotation and scaling

Translation upward

**Figure 5.13** Types of motion.

Of course, you can implement all three transformation functions together. Here is an example:

```
- (void) allTogether {
    static int x = 160;
    static int y = 480;
    static int a = 0;
    static float s = 1;
    static int sf = 1;//sign
    y - = 1;
    a - = 10;
    s - = 0.01 * sf;
    if (s < 0 || s > 1) {
        sf * = -1;
    }

    glPushMatrix();
    glTranslatef(x, y, 0);
    glRotatef(a, 0, 0, 1);
    glScalef(s, s, 1);
    [self drawOGLImg: @"player.png" at: CGPointMake(0, 0)];
    glPopMatrix();
}
```

Pay close attention to the order of translation and rotation since, otherwise, you will end up with unexpected results. In the future, we shall apply translation and rotation within the Tex class and so again approach the already familiar game mechanisms that we learned about in the first chapters of this book. The positioning of the textures at the origin (0, 0) was used in this chapter simply for better illustration of the examples.

## ▌ 5.10  Animations with Texture Clipping

Both scaling and rotation are usually implemented in an object-centered way so that a realistic effect results. As an example of rotation, we will now build this into the Tex class. Furthermore, we shall show in a later game project how to move a Sprite object in circles; this generally takes place outside the Tex class.

Since we want not only to rotate sprites, but also to introduce the principle of texture clipping, we create a new method in the Tex class (the completed project is called "OGL_Animation"):

```
- (void) drawFrame: (int) frameNr
        frameWidth: (int) fw
             angle: (int) degrees
                at: (CGPoint) p;
```

As a basis for the animation, we again use the film strip PNG, in which the various phases of the animation are ordered in sequence (Figure 5.14).

The method takes the current frame number of the film strip (with eight frames, the first frame has the number 0 and the last frame has the number 7). Furthermore, we pass the frame width in pixels. For a PNG with a width of 128 pixels and two frames, the frame width is equal to 64 pixels.

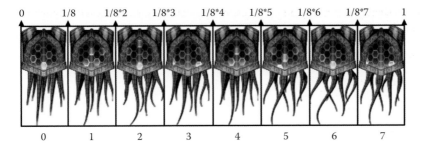

| 0 | 1/8 | 1/8*2 | 1/8*3 | 1/8*4 | 1/8*5 | 1/8*6 | 1/8*7 | 1 |

| 0 | 1 | 2 | 3 | 4 | 5 | 6 | 7 |

**Figure 5.14** octo_8f.png with frame numbers and s-texture coordinates.

In addition, we pass the desired rotation angle in degrees. In the case of 0°, the texture would be rendered *unrotated*. For 90°, it would point to the right, and so on. Finally, we specify the point at which the upper left-hand corner of the frame is to be drawn.

In contrast to the previous Core Graphics examples, the texture coordinates perform the clipping for us; we need no dedicated function for this. Texture clipping is based on the fact that you subdivide the film strip horizontally into equal segments. Since all frames have the same height, we need to adapt only the *s*-coordinates for each frame (along the x-axis). The actual width of the film strip plays no role here.

Our film strip consists of eight frames. The texture frame width is therefore 1/8. From this we obtain the following:

**Frame 0:** from ×1 = 0 to ×2 = 1/8

**Frame 1:** from ×1 = 1/8*1 to ×2 = 1/8*2

**Frame 2:** from ×1 = 1/8*2 to ×2 = 1/8*3

**Frame 3:** from ×1 = 1/8*3 to ×2 = 1/8*4

etc.

We can, of course, easily pack all of this into a formula:

```
GLfloat txW = 1.0/(width/fw);//texture width
GLfloat x1 = frameNr*txW;
GLfloat x2 = x2 = x1 + txW;//or: x2 = (frameNr+1)*txW;
```

Thus, the texture coordinates of the current frame are as follows:

```
GLfloat textureCoords[] = {
    x1, 1,//lower left
    x2, 1,//lower right
    x1, 0,//upper left
    x2, 0 //upper right
};
```

From the texture coordinates, we can easily determine directly which part of the film strip is to be mapped to the rectangular base. With this knowledge, we can now implement the method:

```
- (void) drawFrame: (int) frameNr
        frameWidth: (int) fw
             angle: (int) degrees
                at: (CGPoint) p {

    p.x = (int) p.x;
    p.y = (int) p.y;

    GLshort imageVertices[] = {
        0,    height, //lower left
        fw,   height, //lower right
        0,    0,      //upper left
        fw,   0       //upper right
    };

    GLfloat txW = 1.0/(width/fw);
    GLfloat x1 = frameNr*txW;
    GLfloat x2 = x2 = x1 + txW;//or: x2 = (frameNr+1)*txW;
    GLfloat textureCoords[] = {
        x1, 1,//lower left
        x2, 1,//lower right
        x1, 0,//upper left
        x2, 0 //upper right
    };

    glEnable(GL_TEXTURE_2D);

    glColor4f(1, 1, 1, 1);
    glBindTexture(GL_TEXTURE_2D, textureID);
    glVertexPointer(2, GL_SHORT, 0, imageVertices);
    glTexCoordPointer(2, GL_FLOAT, 0, textureCoords);

    glPushMatrix();
    glTranslatef(p.x+fw/2, p.y+height/2, 0);
    glRotatef(degrees, 0, 0, 1);
    glTranslatef(0-fw/2, 0-height/2, 0);
    glDrawArrays(GL_TRIANGLE_STRIP, 0, 4);
    glPopMatrix();

    glDisable(GL_TEXTURE_2D);
}
```

Other than in the altered texture coordinates, the implementation of the method differs from the drawAt: method only with respect to the rotation:

```
glTranslatef(p.x+fw/2, p.y+height/2, 0);
glRotatef(degrees, 0, 0, 1);//angle = 0 = no rotation
glTranslatef(0-fw/2, 0-height/2, 0);
```

As mentioned earlier, the graphic is to be rotated about its own center. This is at the point

```
(p.x+fw/2, p.y+height/2, 0)
```

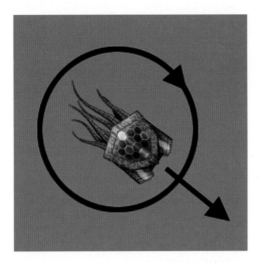

Figure 5.15 Rotation about its own axis and diagonal translation downward.

To carry out the rotation as desired, we must translate the system twice. Recall the reverse order in the execution of the matrix calculations (Figure 5.15):

1. Translate to the center of the graphic:

```
glTranslatef(0-fw/2, 0-height/2, 0);
```

2. The rotation now takes place about the origin. The graphic is rotated about itself, since the origin and center of the graphic are identical:

```
glRotatef(degrees, 0, 0, 1);
```

3. The object is moved to the target position, the first translation is reversed, and the graphic is again aligned at the upper left-hand corner:

```
glTranslatef(p.x+fw/2, p.y+height/2, 0);
```

Now, to show our new method in action, we must, of course, ensure that the frame numbers are passed at appropriate intervals to the method. Later, we shall move this operation to the Sprite class. To test the procedure at this stage, we create a new Tex member variable in the GameManager, which we initialize in the preloader method:

```
Tex *octoTexture;
...
octoTexture = [self getTex: @"octo_8f.png" isImage: YES];
```

We determine the frame number in the familiar way via an if statement and a modulo operation, which takes care of the spacing:

```
- (void) playGame {
    timer++;
```

```
static int frameNr = 0;
static int frameW = 64;
static int angle = 0;
static int x = 0;
static int y = 0;

if (timer% 3 = = 0) {
    frameNr ++;
    if (frameNr > 7) {
        frameNr = 0;
    }
}

angle++;
x++;
y++;

[octoTexture drawFrame: frameNr
            frameWidth: frameW
                angle: angle
                   at: CGPointMake(x, y)];
}
```

The timer variable gives the current number of passes through the game loop. As you can see, additional variables are needed, so we are compelled to put all this in its own class. In Section 5.12, we shall demonstrate this with a concrete game project.

# ▌ 5.11   The Final Frontier: Scrolling and Parallax Scrolling

The level of a game can be composed of individual background images (called tiles) and/or consist of several planes that are layered on top of one another and can be shifted depending on the motion of the player to give the impression of depth ("parallax scrolling").

The mechanism of scrolling can be explained in terms of a bird's-eye view: The game character is seemingly stuck in the center of the game, but since the background is moving, one gets the impression that the figure is moving forward. The trick is that the character is *indeed* moving forward, while the entire game is moved depending on how the figure moves so that the figure is always centered.

Before we can demonstrate this principle, we need a background on which the figure can move. As a game figure we shall use the spaceship from the previous sections.

The background for our spacecraft will consist of two superimposed textures, which are parallax scrolled against each other. The clouds graphic clouds.png is semitransparent, so the background.png underneath is visible (Figure 5.16). For the game area to be tiled with both graphics, the graphic must be able to be connected to itself on the top, bottom, left, and right. You can create tiles from any template—for example, with Photoshop's pattern generator.

Before we come to the actual scrolling, let us first look at how the background can be moved relative to the game figure's positions (the entire project can be found, as always, in the download folder; its name is "OGL_Parallax").

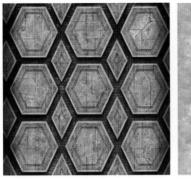

Figure 5.16  background.png, clouds.png.

Our goal is first of all to bring an arbitrary background graphic to the display and then move it. Since we can stack as many parallax layers as we like on top of each other, it makes sense to create a new class (even though our example uses only two background layers):

Listing 5.5  ParallaxLayer.h

```
#import "Tex.h"

@interface ParallaxLayer : NSObject {
    //layer texture
    Tex *tex;

    //dimensions of the layers
    int layerW;
    int layerH;

    //reference point of the parallax layer relative to the player's
    position
    float refX;
    float refY;

    //previous player's position
    float oldPx;
    float oldPy;
}

- (id) initWithPic: (NSString *) picName;
- (void) drawWithFactor: (float) factor
            relativeTo: (CGPoint) pos
              atOrigin: (CGPoint) o;

@end
```

Since the background image is rendered as a texture, we must, of course, also import our Tex class. Before coming to the members, let us first look at the method signatures.

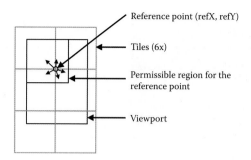

**Figure 5.17** Parallax scrolling.

The `initWithPic:` method should be clear: Here we create a new layer instance. Then the parallax layer is displayed via the method (Figure 5.17):

```
- (void) drawWithFactor: (float) factor
            relativeTo: (CGPoint) pos
              atOrigin: (CGPoint) o;
```

The parameters are

- `(float) factor`: The factor determines how quickly the plane is to move in relationship to the player. A factor of 1 would move the plane at the same rate as the player, but in the opposite direction (after all, the movement of the plane is meant to depict the player's forward motion). A factor of 2, on the other hand, would move the plane at half the player's rate; the larger the factor is, the more slowly the plane moves. Since the player moves, rather than the ground under his feet, the parallax layer never moves faster than the player.

- `(CGPoint) pos`: This informs the method of the player's current position.

- `(CGPoint) o`: As long as we are not scrolling the game world, we can pass the origin (0, 0). This will change later when we add the scrolling mechanism. We shall show later why this is the case.

So much for now on the structure of the class. We now introduce a few theoretical considerations as to how we can bring the method to life.

The best way to fill the display with tiles is to choose a reference point starting from which we can render the surrounding tiles, continuing the process until the screen is completely covered. We then need to move only a single point to move all the planes relative to the player; since the tiles are joined seamlessly, this point is moved inside a region that corresponds exactly to the size of a tile.

The coordinates of this reference point (`refX`, `refY`) result from the player's motion in the xy-direction. We can obtain this by comparing the current position (`pos.x`, `pos.y`) with the previous one (`oldPx`, `oldPy`).

Now we have only to consider the region within which the reference point is moved; when the point reaches an edge, it is moved to the opposite edge. In this way, we obtain a seamlessly flowing motion, since the admissible region corresponds precisely to the size of a tile. Let us check this with regard to the implementation:

5. OpenGL ES: Turbocharged!

Listing 5.6 ParallaxLayer.m

```objc
#import "ParallaxLayer.h"
#import "GameManager.h"

@implementation ParallaxLayer

- (id) initWithPic: (NSString *) picName {
    self = [super init];

    tex = [[GameManager getInstance] getTex: picName isImage: YES];
    layerW = [tex getWidth];
    layerH = [tex getHeight];

    refX = 0;
    refY = 0;
    oldPx = 0;
    oldPy = 0;

    return self;
}

- (void) drawWithFactor: (float) factor
             relativeTo: (CGPoint) pos
               atOrigin: (CGPoint) o {
    //return player's change in position
    //with respect to the previous frame
    float px = pos.x;
    float py = pos.y;
    float diffX = px - oldPx;
    float diffY = py - oldPy;
    oldPx = px;
    oldPy = py;
    //move the parallax layer relative to the player
    //factor = 1 -> speed = actor
    //factor = 2 -> speed = actor/2 (half as fast)
    //etc.
    refX - = diffX/factor;
    refY - = diffY/factor;

    //the reference point is moved within these boundaries
    if (refX > layerW)  refX = 0;
    if (refX < 0)       refX = layerW;
    if (refY > layerH)  refY = 0;
    if (refY < 0)       refY = layerH;

    //completely tile the viewport with Layer, beginning at the
    //reference point
    for (float x = o.x + refX-layerW; x < o.x + W; x+ = layerW) {
        for (float y = o.y + refY-layerH; y < o.y + H; y+ = layerH) {
            [tex drawAt: CGPointMake(x, y)];
        }
    }
}

@end
```

In the `initWithPic:` method we create the texture and initialize the member. The implementation of the `drawWithFactor:relativeTo:atOrigin:` proceeds according to the process described earlier. In two nested `for` loops, we then finally tile the display with the texture. As you can see, the xy-coordinates at which the texture is rendered refer to the reference point and the origin. The tiling ends when the screen width or screen height is reached.

To show the class in action, we create a new player texture and the two parallax layers in the `GameManager`:

```
//player
Tex *playerTexture;
int playerX;
int playerY;

//parallax layer
ParallaxLayer *back;
ParallaxLayer *clouds;
...

//player texture
playerTexture = [self getTex: @"player.png" isImage: YES];
int playerW = [playerTexture getWidth];
int playerH = [playerTexture getHeight];

//center the player
playerX = W/2 - playerW/2;
playerY = H/2 - playerH/2;

//parallax layer
back = [[ParallaxLayer alloc] initWithPic: @"background.png"];
clouds = [[ParallaxLayer alloc] initWithPic: @"clouds.png"];
```

The player texture is initially placed at the center of the screen. In the game loop (`playGame`) of the manager, we move the player upward and render the background:

```
//move the player upward
playerX + = 0;
playerY - = 1;

//render the background
[back drawWithFactor: playerY
        relativeTo: CGPointMake(playerX, playerY)
          atOrigin: CGPointMake(0, 0)];

//render the player
[playerTexture drawAt: CGPointMake(playerX, playerY)];
```

What will happen? That is right! The spaceship/player moves upward at a constant rate of 1 pixel per frame; the background tile, however, does not move at all because as a factor we have passed the current y-coordinate `playerY` of the player.

Another example is that to move the background together with the player, we must pass the factor –1, since the player also moves at this rate.

And now to a realistic application case (Figure 5.18):

```
//move player upward
playerX + = 0;
playerY - = 1;
```

```
//render parallax layers
[back drawWithFactor: 2
           relativeTo: CGPointMake(playerX, playerY)
             atOrigin: CGPointMake(0, 0)];

[clouds drawWithFactor: 1
            relativeTo: CGPointMake(playerX, playerY)
              atOrigin: CGPointMake(0, 0)];
```

The player is again moved upward at a constant rate. The two parallax layers `back` and `clouds` are moved in the opposite direction:

- `back` moves downward at half the player's rate (factor = 2) and gives the effect of somewhat greater depth.

- `clouds` is moved downward at the player's rate (factor = 1), with the result that the layer seems to lie above the `back` layer, but lower than the player.

You can test the correct behavior experimentally with other values of `playerX` and `player`, varying the scroll speed and the player's direction (opposite) and speed.

That the player moves upward while the two layers move downward corresponds to reality; yet, as player you would like to know where you are going. In short, we must see to it that the player is located in the middle of the screen.

And, finally, we implement the scrolling technique (Figure 5.19). Imagine that a virtual camera is filming the player from above. We then see the camera's image on the

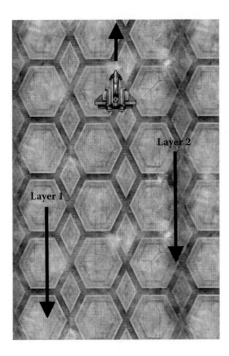

Figure 5.18 The two parallax layers are moved downward while the player flies upward.

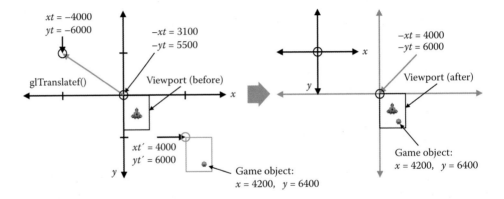

**Figure 5.19** Scrolling.

display, and the ground that the player and the camera cover can be recognized by the landscape passing by (our two parallax layers).

In fact, this technique is considerably easier to implement. We do not need a virtual camera or the like; instead, we have only—yet again—to move the coordinate system.

The movement now takes place permanently, so we store the current translations in both members xt and yt:

```
float xt;
float yt;
```

Furthermore, we add a getter that always tells us the screen origin:

```
- (CGPoint) getViewportOrigin {
    return CGPointMake(-xt, -yt);
}
```

Since the entire game world is moved to position (xt, yt), the upper left-hand point on the display has the opposite coordinates (-xt, -yt). We must now pass this changing origin as a reference point to the parallax layers.

That is it. The scrolling carries out the new scrollWorld method for us. We call it inside the game loop before the rest of the rendering process takes place (Figure 5.20):

```
- (void) playGame {
    [self scrollWorld];

    //move player upward
    playerX + = 0;
    playerY - = 1;

    //render parallax layers
    [back drawWithFactor: 2
            relativeTo: CGPointMake(playerX, playerY)
              atOrigin: [self getViewportOrigin]];

    [clouds drawWithFactor: 1
              relativeTo: CGPointMake(playerX, playerY)
                atOrigin: [self getViewportOrigin]];
```

```
    //render the player
    [playerTexture drawAt: CGPointMake(playerX, playerY)];
}

- (void) scrollWorld {
    int playerW = [playerTexture getWidth];
    int playerH = [playerTexture getHeight];
    xt = W/2 - playerW/2 - playerX;
    yt = H/2 - playerH/2 - playerY;
    glLoadIdentity();
    glTranslatef(xt, yt, 0);
}
```

As you can see, the result is that everything functions according to plan. The player's coordinates change continually. Starting from the player's (centered) position, the game world is moved, and the player/spaceship remains in the middle of the screen while the parallax layers indicate the direction of flight.

Since the scrollWorld method is supposed to affect the entire game world, we load the identity matrix via glLoadIdentity() so that, for every new frame, the world finds itself in its original state and the origin (0, 0) is again located in the upper left-hand corner of the screen. After the identity matrix is loaded, we move the system as a function of the current player position.

This translation is then preserved for the subsequent rendering processes so that an additional game object at position (4200, 6400) is also in fact rendered in this position.

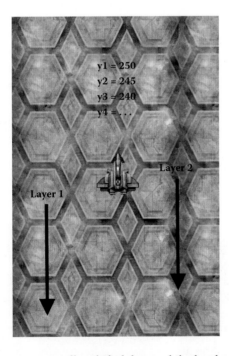

**Figure 5.20** The two layers move parallax-shifted down, while the player remains in the middle of the screen. The player's y-coordinates illustrate the forward motion (from the player's point of view).

If the player is by chance nearby, then this game object can be seen on the screen; otherwise, it is not.

You can also see from the `scrollWorld` method how the current per-frame translation is derived from the player's coordinates:

```
xt = W/2 - playerW/2 - playerX;
yt = H/2 - playerH/2 - playerY;
```

The current position of the player is subtracted from the coordinates of the center of the display; here, this refers to the unscrolled position at which the player has to be rendered to appear centered on the screen.

The actual scrolling mechanism is a mere six lines of code and has the additional advantage of maintaining the original coordinates of all game objects. This, of course, makes game development easier for us, since in creating animation paths for our sprites, we do not have to worry about whether or how the game field is scrolled.

## 5.12 Going Out with a Bang: An OpenGL ES Shooter

We have by now filled up our OpenGL ES kit with powerful ingredients. Now let us begin with a new game project and combine what we have already learned with the previously developed basic techniques of game development (sprite management, input handling, collision control, etc.).

We have already seen how a sprite can be rotated about itself, so let us combine this with the scrolling mechanism. The player/spaceship from the previous section should be able to turn in every direction while remaining in the middle of the screen and, while flying forward, can explore the entire 360° world.

For the mechanics of this game, we have several famous models to examine (Figure 5.21). The first game of this sort may have been the arcade game *Bosconian* (Namco, 1981), followed by *Time Pilot* (Konami, 1982) and its excellent successor *Time Pilot '84* (Konami, 1984). Also worth mentioning are *Sinistar* (Williams, 1982) and *Vanguard II* (SNK, 1984). The little known arcade game *Cerberus* (Cinematronics, 1985) adapted the control principle in an unusual way and is more in the direction of *Asteroids* (Atari, 1979) and *Spacewar!* (MIT, 1961).

Of course, in the 1980s, the usual control mechanism was the eight-way joystick, so we are compelled to adapt the concept of control to the new millennium using the touch control of the iPhone.

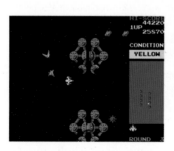 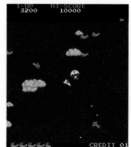 

**Figure 5.21** Bosconian (Namco), Time Pilot (Konami), and Time Pilot '84 (Konami).

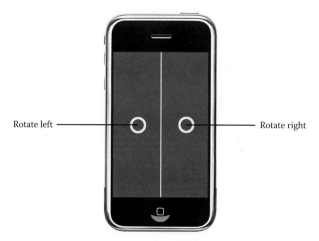

Rotate left ——————  ——————— Rotate right

**Figure 5.22** The steering concept.

To this end, we divide the screen into two halves: If the player touches the left half, the spacecraft turns to the left, while if she touches the right half, the spaceship turns to the right. If the player stops touching the screen, the spaceship moves forward in a straight line at the most recently set angle (from the viewpoint of the pilot) (Figure 5.22).

The game plan is typical for the genre: *As the pilot, you attempt to remain alive as long as possible. Your spaceship is under constant attack. Any hit by the enemy is fatal. You can steer to the left and to the right and attempt to eliminate as many adversaries as possible.*

The following adversaries populate the game world:

- **Mines:** immovable, indestructible, rotating about themselves

- **Fighters:** traveling individually or in swarms, they can move, like the player, through 360°

- **Octo:** mechanical octopus, a sort of drone also called the grabber, whose deadly tentacles must be avoided

The complete game project can be found in the download folder under the name "OGL_Shooter." While we assemble the game as an example, it would not hurt to look at the final source code in parallel and look at the individual components in context. We have attempted to make the structure of the game as simple and straightforward as possible (Figure 5.23).

## 5.12.1   Complete Framework

We select as our basis the project "OGL_Parallax" from the previous section so that our game already boasts the following classes:

- `MyGameAppDelegate`: initializes `MainView`; triggers the game loop.

- `MainView`: initializes the `GameManager`; passes the touch input to the `GameManager`; initializes OpenGL ES; periodically calls the `GameManager`.

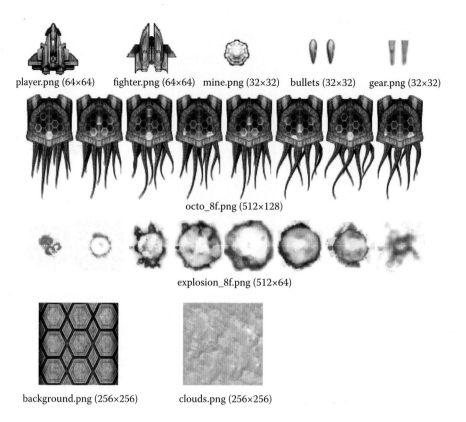

player.png (64×64)    fighter.png (64×64)    mine.png (32×32)    bullets (32×32)    gear.png (32×32)

octo_8f.png (512×128)

explosion_8f.png (512×64)

background.png (256×256)          clouds.png (256×256)

**Figure 5.23** The game graphics at a glance.

- `GameManager`: manages resources; controls and renders the game.

- `Tex`: creates and renders textures.

- `ParallaxLayer`: parallax-translated game backgrounds.

Up through the `GameManager`, we do not need to make any changes in the classes. To complete the game, we create eight new classes in the folder "GameElements," for which the sprite class is the parent class and the seven other classes are derived directly or indirectly from it:

- `Sprite`: parent class of all sprites

- `Player`: the player, derived from `Sprite`

- `Octo`: animated basic adversary, derived from `Sprite`

- `Mine`: a mine, derived from `Sprite`

- `Fighter`: adversary, derived from `Octo`

- Bullet: the player's ammunition, derived from Sprite

- Gear: player's propulsion graphic, derived from Bullet

- Animation: animation class, used to represent an explosion sequence, derived from Sprite

You can see that the inheritance relations are quite clear. The animation class is identical to that in the zombie game, except that here textures are used instead of UIImages. However, before we go more deeply into the implementation of the Sprite classes, we must complete the basic framework of the GameManager class.

For resource management, we again implement our Sprite array in addition to the NSDictionary. We also establish the Player as a member in GameManager.h:

```
Player *player;
NSMutableArray *sprites;//active sprites
NSMutableArray *newSprites;//new sprites
NSMutableArray *destroyableSprites;//inactive sprites
NSMutableDictionary* dictionary;//resources hash table
```

In addition, we specify the following game states in the header:

```
enum states {
    LOAD_GAME,
    START_GAME,
    PLAY_GAME,
    GAME_OVER
};
```

In the preloader method, we can create the resource container once and for all:

```
- (void) preloader {
    sprites = [[NSMutableArray alloc] initWithCapacity:20];
    newSprites = [[NSMutableArray alloc] initWithCapacity:20];
    destroyableSprites = [[NSMutableArray alloc] initWithCapacity:20];

    //preload OGL textures
    [self getTex: @"fighter.png" isImage: YES];
    [self getTex: @"octo_8f.png" isImage: YES];
    [self getTex: @"explosion_8f.png" isImage: YES];
    [self getTex: @"player.png" isImage: YES];
    [self getTex: @"mine.png" isImage: YES];
    [self getTex: @"bullets.png" isImage: YES];
    [self getTex: @"gear.png" isImage: YES];

    //parallax layer
    back = [[ParallaxLayer alloc] initWithPic: @"background.png"];
    clouds = [[ParallaxLayer alloc] initWithPic: @"clouds.png"];

    [self setOGLProjection];

    state = LOAD_GAME;
}
```

Since the textures are managed independently of the sprites, we can create all the required textures in advance in order to avoid delays later.

Textual components can also be optionally loaded now—for example:

```
[self getTex: @"abc" isImage: NO];
```

Due to the small number of textures, we can do without this in our case.

We continue with the `loadGame` method, which is called before every game and creates a fresh start state:

```
- (void) loadGame {
    [sprites removeAllObjects];
    [newSprites removeAllObjects];
    [destroyableSprites removeAllObjects];

    //player
    [self createSprite: PLAYER
                 speed: CGPointMake(0, 0)
                   pos: CGPointMake(0, 0)];
}
```

In this method you can also optionally load textures for an additional level and delete textures that are no longer needed—for example:

```
[self removeFromDictionary: @"myTex1.png"];
```

Since we have implemented only one level, the game begins again after "game over"—unchanged, with the same textures—so that we do not need to load any new textures or delete any that are already there.

The generation of a new sprite follows the pattern of the zombie game and should contain no surprises:

```
- (id) createSprite: (int) type
              speed: (CGPoint) sxy
                pos: (CGPoint) pxy {
    if (type = = PLAYER) {
        player = [[Player alloc] initWithPic: @"player.png"
                                    frameCnt: 1
                                   frameStep: 0
                                       speed: sxy
                                         pos: pxy];
        [player setType: PLAYER];
        [newSprites addObject: player];
        [player release];
        return player;
    } else if (type = = BULLET) {
        Bullet *bullet = [[Bullet alloc] initWithPic: @"bullets.png"
                                            frameCnt: 1
                                           frameStep: 0
                                               speed: sxy
                                                 pos: pxy];
        [bullet setType: BULLET];
        [newSprites addObject: bullet];
        [bullet release];
        return bullet;
    } else if (type = = GEAR) {
        Gear *gear = [[Gear alloc] initWithPic: @"gear.png"
                                      frameCnt: 1
```

```
                                       frameStep: 0
                                          speed: sxy
                                            pos: pxy];
        [gear setType: GEAR];
        [newSprites addObject: gear];
        [gear release];
        return gear;
    } else if (type = = OCTO) {
        Octo *octo = [[Octo alloc] initWithPic: @"octo_8f.png"
                                      frameCnt: 8
                                     frameStep: 3
                                         speed: sxy
                                           pos: pxy];
        [octo setType: OCTO];
        [newSprites addObject: octo];
        [octo release];
        return octo;
    } else if (type = = MINE) {
        Mine *mine = [[Mine alloc] initWithPic: @"mine.png"
                                      frameCnt: 1
                                     frameStep: 0
                                         speed: sxy
                                           pos: pxy];
        [mine setType: MINE];
        [newSprites addObject: mine];
        [mine release];
        return mine;
    } else if (type = = FIGHTER) {
        Fighter *fighter = [[Fighter alloc] initWithPic: @"fighter.png"
                                               frameCnt: 1
                                              frameStep: 0
                                                  speed: sxy
                                                    pos: pxy];
        [fighter setType: FIGHTER];
        [newSprites addObject: fighter];
        [fighter release];
        return fighter;
    } else if (type = = ANIMATION) {
        Animation *ani = [[Animation alloc] initWithPic: @"explosion_8f.png"
                                               frameCnt: 8
                                              frameStep: 3
                                                  speed: sxy
                                                    pos: pxy];
        [ani setType: ANIMATION];
        [newSprites addObject: ani];
        [ani release];
        return ani;
    } else {
        NSLog(@"ERROR: unknown sprite type:%i", type);
        return nil;
    }
}
```

Every sprite has a type (type), a velocity (speed), and a start position (pos). The different forms of motion of the various sprites are controlled in the different subclasses. You can also see that every sprite has a single initialization method initWithPic:frameCnt: frameStep:speed:pos:, which we call with the appropriate values. The parameters derive from the graphics (name of the graphic, number of frames in the film strip). Sprites that are not animated have only one frame and therefore the `frameStep` is equal to 0.

We shall review the implementation of the sprites in a moment. But first we would like to add the method for displaying a one-time explosion; this also corresponds to the implementation in the zombie game and thus requires no further comment:

```
- (void) createExplosionFor: (Sprite *) sprite {
    CGPoint p = [Animation getOriginBasedOnCenterOf: [sprite getRect]
                                        andPic: @"explosion_8f.png"
                                   withFrameCnt: 8];
    [self createSprite: ANIMATION
             speed: CGPointMake(0, 0)
               pos: p];
}
```

Let us look at the handling of touch events in the `GameManager`:

```
- (void) touchBegan: (CGPoint) p {
    [self handleStates];
    if (state = = PLAY_GAME && player) {
        [player setTouch: p];
    }
}

- (void) touchMoved: (CGPoint) p {
    if (state = = PLAY_GAME) {
        [self touchBegan: p];
    }
}

- (void) touchEnded {
    if (state = = PLAY_GAME && player) {
        [player touchEnded];
    }
}

- (void) handleStates {
    if (state = = START_GAME) {
        state = PLAY_GAME;
    }
    else if (state = = GAME_OVER) {
        state = LOAD_GAME;
    }
}
```

Following the established pattern, we pass the touch point on the display directly to the `Player` instance, provided that the game is in the `PLAY_GAME` state. Otherwise, we control the switch between the start and game-over screens via `handleStates`. Both screens also serve to present some help texts, as you can see in the implementation of `drawStatesWithFrame`:

```
- (void) drawStatesWithFrame: (CGRect) frame {
    W = frame.size.width;
    H = frame.size.height;
    CGPoint o = [self getViewportOrigin];
    switch (state) {
```

```
        case LOAD_GAME:
            [self loadGame];
            state = START_GAME;
            break;
        case START_GAME:
            [self drawOGLString: @"Tap screen to start!" at:
                CGPointMake(o.x, o.y)];
            [self drawOGLString: @"How to control the ship:" at:
                CGPointMake(o.x, o.y + 50)];
            [self drawOGLString: @"Tap left - turn left." at:
                CGPointMake(o.x, o.y + 75)];
            [self drawOGLString: @"Tap right - turn right." at:
                CGPointMake(o.x, o.y + 100)];
            break;
        case PLAY_GAME:
            [self playGame];
            break;
        case GAME_OVER:
            [self playGame];
            [self drawOGLString: @"G A M E   O V E R" at:
                CGPointMake(o.x, o.y)];
            break;
        default: NSLog(@"ERROR: unknown game state: %i", state);
            break;
    }
}
```

Since our game can find itself in a scrolled state, we must align the texts at the upper left-hand corner of the display. This does not always have to be (0, 0), as we have seen. We see as well from the drawStatesWithFrame: method that the actual game takes place in the playGame method, which, however, holds no great surprises for us:

```
- (void) playGame {
    timer++;
    [self scrollWorld];

    //parallax layers
    [back drawWithFactor: 2
            relativeTo: [player getPos]
             atOrigin: [self getViewportOrigin]];
    [clouds drawWithFactor: 1
              relativeTo: [player getPos]
               atOrigin: [self getViewportOrigin]];

    [self generateNewEnemies];
    [self manageSprites];
    [self renderSprites];
}
```

Do you not agree that it is all quite straightforward? The well-known sprite-manager methods take care, as they did in the zombie game, that the sprites can be integrated without modification.

The manageSprites method is used to create and delete sprites and is no different from the earlier implementation in the zombie game—likewise for the renderSprites method, which iterates over all active sprites and calls their draw method. It is only the player's draw method that we call separately at the end of the method so that the spaceship cannot be covered by other sprites. Since the method is otherwise the same, we do not print it again here.

## 5.12.2 Game Play

However, we have added a new method to the `playGame` method. The `generate-NewEnemies` method ensures that our player is continually confronted with new adversaries. They must appear at specific time intervals and in specific places; time, location, and number of adversaries also define the level of difficulty of the game and therefore also define the game play of the shooter.

How do we determine, however, where the adversaries are to appear? What we would like to avoid if possible is for the adversaries to appear just anywhere—either too far from the player, so that the player has no chance to shoot them, or too close, so that the adversaries appear suddenly on the screen and thereby create unfair game situations.

One possible approach to a solution is to define an area outside the viewport in which the adversaries can be created and positioned (Figure 5.24).

We dimension this region in terms of the screen width and height by creating a buffer zone that corresponds to the maximal dimensions of the largest sprite, which in our case is the mechanical octopus with 128 pixels:

```
- (CGPoint) getRndStartPos {
    int px, py;//positioning outside the screen
    int f = 128;//buffer zone (frameW and frameH)
    int flag = [self getRndBetween: 0 and: 3];
    switch (flag) {
        case 0: //top
            px = [self getRndBetween: -f-W and: f+W*2];
            py = [self getRndBetween: -f-H and: -f];
            break;
        case 1: //left
            px = [self getRndBetween: -f-W and: -f];
            py = [self getRndBetween: -f-H and: f+H*2];
            break;
        case 2: //right
            px = [self getRndBetween: f+W and: f+W*2];
            py = [self getRndBetween: -f-H and: f+H*2];
            break;
        case 3: //bottom
            px = [self getRndBetween: -f-W and: f+W*2];
            py = [self getRndBetween: f+H and: f+H*2];
            break;
    }
    CGPoint o = [self getViewportOrigin];
    return CGPointMake(o.x + px, o.y + py);
}
```

The `getRndStartPos` method returns a random position within the designated region outside the viewport. Since the viewport changes in relation to the player, we use the current origin.[*]

---

[*] This type of positioning assumes continuous movement. If the player remains for a long time in the same place (or makes loops), then the number of adversaries outside the viewport continues to grow. The best strategy for mastering the game is therefore to fly through as wide an area as possible.

5. OpenGL ES: Turbocharged!

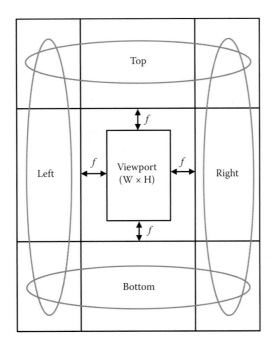

**Figure 5.24** The adversaries are generated in four zones—TOP, LEFT, RIGHT, and BOTTOM—that remain outside the viewport.

To generate a new adversary, we now need only the type and speed in the xy-direction so that we can implement a new auxiliary method:

```
- (void) generateEnemy: (int) type
             speedX: (int) sx
             speedY: (int) sy {
    CGPoint startPos = [self getRndStartPos];
    [self createSprite: type
              speed: CGPointMake(sx, sy)
                pos: startPos];
}
```

Then we can also create the straightforward method `generateNewEnemies` for controlling the game play:

```
- (void) generateNewEnemies {
    //octos
    if (timer% 12 = = 0) {
        int sx = [self getRndBetween: -3 and: 3];
        int sy = [self getRndBetween: -7 and: -1];
        [self generateEnemy: OCTO speedX: sx speedY: sy];
    }

    //mines
    if (timer% 5 = = 0) {
        [self generateEnemy: MINE speedX: 0 speedY: 0];
    }

    //fighters
```

```
    if (timer% 18 = = 0) {
        [self generateEnemy: FIGHTER speedX: 7 speedY: 7];
    }
}
```

The time interval and thereby the number of adversaries are determined by a modulo operator. The random speed of the octos leads to some moments of surprise. The mines, in contrast, do not move and hence provide orientation points within the scrolling environment. The speed and direction of motion of a fighter is to be considered a set of initial values; we will adjust the path of motion later inside the class.

Our playing field is now populated with adversaries, and to control the game we are going to need collision detection. As you might have guessed, the Sprite class (see following section) has a checkColWithSprite: method that checks for a collision between two arbitrary sprites and a hit method that is called in case of a collision.

With this knowledge, we can now implement the complete checkSprite: method:

```
- (void) checkSprite: (Sprite *) sprite {
    if ([sprite getType] = =PLAYER || [sprite getType] = =BULLET) {
        for (Sprite *sprite2test in sprites) {
            if ([sprite2test getType] = =OCTO
                || [sprite2test getType] = =FIGHTER) {
                if ([sprite checkColWithSprite: sprite2test]
                    && state ! = GAME_OVER) {
                    [sprite hit];
                    [sprite2test hit];
                }
            }
            if ([sprite getType] = =BULLET && [sprite2test getType] = =MINE) {
                if ([sprite checkColWithSprite: sprite2test]) {
                    //mines cannot be destroyed
                    [sprite hit];
                    [[GameManager getInstance] createExplosionFor: sprite];
                }
            }
            if ([sprite getType] = =PLAYER && [sprite2test getType] = =MINE) {
                if ([sprite checkColWithSprite: sprite2test]) {
                    [sprite hit];
                }
            }
        }
    }
}
```

We have to consider the following Sprite types: PLAYER, BULLET, OCTO, FIGHTER, and MINE. As you can see in the if statement, the entire Sprite array is iterated for the Player and every Bullet instance and checked for a collision between the Player and a Bullet. Octos and Fighters can be handled in the same way. Since Mine objects are indestructible and represent an insurmountable barrier, they are treated separately for the Player and each Bullet. Every Bullet that hits a Mine should trigger an explosion. Likewise, the player should explode if it hits a Mine object, while the Mine itself does not explode.*

---

* You can, of course, change the behavior of a mine. However, we have decided that as indestructible unexploded ordnance, the mines provide a more interesting game.

## 5.12.3 The Sprite Class

Once we have completed the basic structure of the game within the `GameManager` class, we can focus on the game elements that are derived directly or indirectly from the `Sprite` class.

The `Sprite` is based strongly on the earlier implementation of the zombie game. Due to some peculiarities that result from the game design and, of course, through the use of OpenGL ES, we would nonetheless like to print the entire class here.

**Listing 5.7** Sprite.h

```objc
#import <UIKit/UIKit.h>
#import <OpenGLES/ES1/gl.h>
#import "Tex.h"

//sprite types
enum types {
    PLAYER,
    BULLET,
    GEAR,
    OCTO,
    MINE,
    FIGHTER,
    ANIMATION
};

@interface Sprite : NSObject {
    Tex *tex;            //texture film strip
    CGPoint speed;       //pixel speed per frame in the x-, y-directions
    CGPoint pos;         //current position
    int cnt;             //internal counter
    int frameNr;         //current frame
    int frameCnt;        //number of frames in the film strip
    int frameStep;       //number of frames per iteration
    int frameW;          //width of a frame
    int frameH;          //height of a frame
    int angle;           //angle in degrees through which a sprite is
                         //turned
    int type;            //sprite type
    int tolBB;           //bounding box- tolerance
    int cycleCnt;        //number of repetitions of the film strip
    bool forceIdleness;  //no animation when sprite is not moving
    bool active;         //inactive sprites are deleted by GameManager
    bool autoDestroy;    //tolerance region -> active = false
}

-(id) initWithPic: (NSString *) name
        frameCnt: (int) fcnt
       frameStep: (int) fstp
           speed: (CGPoint) sxy
             pos: (CGPoint) pxy;
- (void) additionalSetup;
- (void) draw;
- (void) drawFrame;
- (void) renderSprite;
```

```
- (int) updateFrame;
- (CGRect) getRect;
- (bool) checkColWithPoint: (CGPoint) p;
- (bool) checkColWithRect: (CGRect) rect;
- (bool) checkColWithSprite: (Sprite *) sprite;
- (void) hit;
- (float) getRad: (float) grad;
- (void) setType: (int) spriteType;
- (int) getType;
- (void) setSpeed: (CGPoint) sxy;
- (CGPoint) getSpeed;
- (CGPoint) getPos;
- (bool) isActive;

@end
```

### Listing 5.8  Sprite.m

```
#import "Sprite.h"
#import "GameManager.h"

@implementation Sprite

-(id) initWithPic: (NSString *) picName
        frameCnt: (int) fcnt
       frameStep: (int) fstp
           speed: (CGPoint) sxy
             pos: (CGPoint) pxy {

    if (self = [super init]) {
        tex = [[GameManager getInstance] getTex: picName isImage: YES];
        speed = sxy;
        pos = pxy;
        cnt = 0;
        frameNr = 0;
        frameCnt = fcnt;
        frameStep = fstp;
        //warning: number of frames * frameW must equal graphic width
        frameW = [tex getWidth]/frameCnt;
        frameH = [tex getHeight];
        angle = 0;
        type = -1;
        tolBB = 10;//make bounding box smaller
        forceIdleness = false;
        active = true;
        autoDestroy = false;
        [self additionalSetup];
    }

    return self;
}

- (void) additionalSetup {
    //override for individual setup
}
```

```objc
- (void) setType: (int) spriteType {
    type = spriteType;
}

- (int) getType {
    return type;
}

- (CGRect) getRect {
    return CGRectMake(pos.x, pos.y, frameW, frameH);
}

- (void) setSpeed: (CGPoint) sxy {
    speed = sxy;
}

- (CGPoint) getSpeed {
    return speed;
}

- (CGPoint) getPos {
    return pos;
}

- (bool) isActive {
    return active;
}

- (void) draw {
    if (active) {
        pos.x+ = speed.x;
        pos.y+ = speed.y;
        [self drawFrame];
    }
}

- (void) drawFrame {
    frameNr = [self updateFrame];
    if (forceIdleness && speed.x = = 0 && speed.y = = 0) {
        frameNr = 0;
    }
    [self renderSprite];
}

- (void) renderSprite {
    int tolBBBkp = tolBB;
    tolBB = 0;

    CGPoint o = [[GameManager getInstance] getViewportOrigin];
    if ([self checkColWithRect: CGRectMake(o.x, o.y, W, H)]) {
        [tex drawFrame: frameNr
            frameWidth: frameW
                 angle: angle
                    at: CGPointMake(pos.x, pos.y)];
    } else if (autoDestroy) {
        int dist = H*3;
        if (![self checkColWithRect:
```

```
                  CGRectMake(o.x-dist, o.y-dist, W+dist*2, H+dist*2)]) {
            active = false;
        }
    }

    tolBB = tolBBBkp;
}

//180 Deg = PI Rad -> [self getRad: 180] = PI
- (float) getRad: (float) deg {
    float rad = (M_PI/180) * deg;
    return rad;
}

- (int) updateFrame {
    if (frameStep = = cnt) {
        cnt = 0;
        frameNr++;
        if (frameNr > frameCnt-1) {
            frameNr = 0;
            cycleCnt++;
        }
    }
    cnt++;
    return frameNr;
}

- (void) hit {
    //override for individual collision handling
}

//collision point <-> rectangle
- (bool) checkColWithPoint: (CGPoint) p {
    CGRect rect = [self getRect];
    if ( p.x > rect.origin.x
        && p.x < (rect.origin.x+rect.size.width)
            && p.y > rect.origin.y
        && p.y < (rect.origin.y+rect.size.height)) {
        return true;
    }
    return false;
}

//collision rectangle <-> rectangle
- (bool) checkColWithRect: (CGRect) rect {
    CGRect rect1 = [self getRect];
    CGRect rect2 = rect;

    //Rect 1
    int x1 = rect1.origin.x+tolBB;//Rect1: point upper left
    int y1 = rect1.origin.y+tolBB;
    int w1 = rect1.size.width-tolBB*2;
    int h1 = rect1.size.height-tolBB*2;

    //Rect 2
    int x3 = rect2.origin.x;//Rect2: point upper left
    int y3 = rect2.origin.y;
```

```
        int w2 = rect2.size.width;
        int h2 = rect2.size.height;

        int x2 = x1+w1, y2 = y1+h1; //Rect1: point lower right
        int x4 = x3+w2, y4 = y3+h2; //Rect2: point lower right

        if ( x2 > = x3
            && x4 > = x1
            && y2 > = y3
            && y4 > = y1) {
            return true;
        }
        return false;
}

- (bool) checkColWithSprite: (Sprite *) sprite {
    return [self checkColWithRect: [sprite getRect]];
}

- (void) dealloc {
    [super dealloc];
}

@end
```

Let us look briefly at some particular features:

- Instead of a `UIImage` instance, every `Sprite` has a `Tex` instance. This is initialized together with the other members in the `initWithPic:frameCnt:frameStep:speed:pos:` method.

- The determination of the width of a frame (`frameW`) assumes that the texture template's width is fully utilized. This works only if the frame width is a power of 2. To allow other widths, you must adapt the code accordingly, though you will consequently waste some space in the film strip.

- To use the `sin()` and `cos()` functions, we have to convert the degree measure of an angle to radians (rad). The conversion uses the fact that 180° corresponds to pi = 3.14159... radians. Our conversion method is called `getRad:`.

- For the collision calculation (rectangle <-> rectangle), we pass a `CGRect` structure as bounding box. Using the parameter `tolBB`, we shrink the bounding box to give the sprites more leeway. Not all sprites fit into the ideal rectangular shape. You can alter the parameters individually for each sprite or optionally use several smaller bounding boxes that approximate the contours of the sprite as accurately as possible. However, we have not done any of this to keep things as simple as possible.

In the `renderSprite` method we carry out two additional collision checks:

```
- (void) renderSprite {
    int tolBBBkp = tolBB;
    tolBB = 0;
```

```
CGPoint o = [[GameManager getInstance] getViewportOrigin];
if ([self checkColWithRect: CGRectMake(o.x, o.y, W, H)]) {
            [tex drawFrame: frameNr
                 frameWidth: frameW
                      angle: angle
                         at: CGPointMake(pos.x, pos.y)];
} else if (autoDestroy) {
    int dist = H*3;
    if (![self checkColWithRect:
        CGRectMake(o.x-dist, o.y-dist, W+dist*2, H+dist*2)]) {
        active = false;
    }
}

tolBB = tolBBBkp;
}
```

A `Sprite` is rendered only if it is visible in the current viewport. This is the case whenever it collides with the viewport rectangle (o.x, o.y, W, H). If a collision is detected, the texture is rendered; otherwise, it is not, so as to relieve the graphics processor. If no collision has occurred, the sprite is deactivated after leaving a tolerance zone equal to three times the screen height (`dist = H*3`) and thereby deleted from memory by the sprite manager. To manage this, a second collision check is made with the rectangle of the tolerance zone (o.x-dist, o.y-dist, W+dist*2, H+dist*2). This check is made only if the flag `autoDestroy` of the given sprite was set to `true`.

Since both collision checks are to consider the actual frame width and height, rather than the more narrowly drawn bounding box, we have to increase the `tolBB` parameter to 0 for the duration of the check.

### 5.12.4  The Game Elements

Now that our `Sprite` class exists, we can begin working on the game elements. Let us have a look first at the `Player` class.

---

**Listing 5.9**  Player.h

```
#import "Sprite.h"

@interface Player : Sprite {
    CGPoint touchPoint;
    bool touchAction;
    bool moveLeft;
    int speedScalar;
    bool dead;
}

- (void) setTouch: (CGPoint) touchPoint;
- (void) touchEnded;
- (void) fire;

@end
```

Listing 5.10  Player.m

```objc
#import "Player.h"
#import "GameManager.h"

@implementation Player

- (void) additionalSetup {
    touchAction = false;

    //center the player
    pos.x = W/2 - frameW/2;
    pos.y = H/2 - frameH/2;

    dead = false;
    angle = 0;
    speedScalar = 5;
    speed.y = -speedScalar; //constant "forward" motion
}

- (void) draw {
    static int angleStep = 3;
    if (touchAction) {
        if (moveLeft) {
            angle- = angleStep;
        } else {
            angle+ = angleStep;
        }
        angleStep++;
        if (angleStep > 10) {
            angleStep = 10;
        }
        speed.x = sin([self getRad: angle])*speedScalar;
        speed.y = -cos([self getRad: angle])*speedScalar;
    } else {
        angleStep = 3;
    }

    pos.x + = speed.x;
    pos.y + = speed.y;

    if (!dead) {
        [self fire];
        [self drawFrame];
    }
}

- (void) fire {
    int sX = pos.x + frameW/2 - 16;
    int sY = pos.y + frameH/2 - 16;
    if (cnt% 5 = = 0) {
        Bullet *bullet =
            [[GameManager getInstance]
                createSprite: BULLET
                    speed: CGPointMake(speed.x*3, speed.y*3)
```

```
                            pos: CGPointMake(sX, sY)];
            [bullet setAngle: angle];
}
    if (cnt% 1 = = 0) {
        Gear *gear =
        [[GameManager getInstance]
            createSprite: GEAR
                speed: CGPointMake(-speed.x, -speed.y)
                pos: CGPointMake(sX, sY)];
        [gear setAngle: angle];
    }
}

- (void) setTouch: (CGPoint) point {
    touchAction = true;
    if (point.x < W/2) {
        //steer to the left
        moveLeft = YES;
    } else {
        //steer to the right
        moveLeft = NO;
    }
}

- (void) touchEnded {
    touchAction = false;
}

- (void) hit {
    if (!dead) {
        dead = YES;
        speed.x = 0; speed.y = 0;
        touchAction = false;
        [[GameManager getInstance] setState: GAME_OVER];
        [[GameManager getInstance] createExplosionFor: self];
    }
}

@end
```

In addition to the task of triggering the GAME_OVER state when the player is hit (see the hit method), the class has essentially three things to manage:

1. Steering and movement of the player

2. Continuous fire

3. Rendering the gear graphics

Let us go through these points one at a time. With the setTouch: method, we obtain the current touch point on the display. In accordance with our steering concept, the left half of the screen should lead to a turn to the left, and the right half to a turn to the right. This is managed for us by a simple if statement. To keep the rotation active while the finger is touching the display, we store the current direction in the moveLeft variable, which is of type bool.

The actual rotation of the spacecraft then takes place in the draw method. Using the member variable angle of the Sprite parent class, we can specify the sprite's rotation angle. Since we also want to move the sprite itself along a circular path, we need to adjust the velocity and direction of motion, both of which are determined by the variable speed.

You might recall from your high-school days how the unit circle is defined in terms of the sine and cosine functions (Figure 5.25).

We know already that the speed variable enables independent motion in the x- and y-directions. On the other hand, the spaceship's rotation angle should also reflect the direction of travel. We therefore must decompose the angle into its x- and y-components corresponding to the direction of the spaceship.

Now, it is precisely this that takes care of the unit circle for us: The hypotenuse always has length 1 (point O to point P). If our spaceship is located at point O, it can move in any direction (360°). If we imagine an arrow at the end of the hypotenuse at point P, then the hypotenuse can point in every possible direction. In addition, the right triangle determined by the hypotenuse gives us the distances that must be traveled in the x- and y-directions to get from point O to point P. These other two sides of the triangle define the sine and cosine, which is very convenient for us.

We can thereby calculate the change in direction directly from the rotation angle:

```
speed.x = sin([self getRad: angle]);
speed.y = -cos([self getRad: angle]);
```

Since sine and cosine oscillate between –1 and 1 and we would like to move the spaceship somewhat faster, we have to multiply these values by some fixed quantity. Since the speed variables together constitute a mathematical vector, we call this scaling factor a scalar (speedScalar).

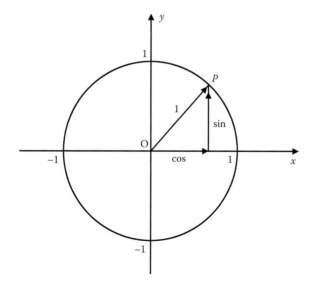

**Figure 5.25** Unit circle with sine and cosine.

Depending on the truth value of moveLeft, we can increase or decrease the rotation angle angle. To make the turning motion more sensitive, we increase the rotation angle as a function of the duration of touch contact. The rotation begins somewhat more slowly (angleStep = 3) and then is later somewhat faster (maximal value: angleStep = 10). Both values can be adjusted to taste.

Now let us discuss the sustained firing. The goal is to generate a new Bullet at regular intervals, with the direction of the Bullet corresponding to the current direction of the Player.

The control takes place entirely within the fire method. The timing of the Bullets is again solved with a modulo operator (cnt% 5). Here, of course, you can experiment with other values. Instead of firing automatically, you could alternatively put an additional button on the display, and then the player's fire method would be called only when this button was pushed.

Before we can call the createSprite method of the GameManagers, we have to position the shot so that it is centered on the player.

Since the createSprite method does not allow the rotation angle to be passed, we instead call a getter on the returned instance:

```
[bullet setAngle: angle];
```

Thus, we ensure that the newly created instance is turned in the same direction as the player. The direction of the shot can be given directly via the speed direction vector.

As you might have guessed, we have solved the gear animation using the same principle, though in the reverse direction. The gear.png graphic represents translucent white smoke that is to be expelled from the spaceship's two engine nozzles. With cnt% 2 you create a flickering animation of the engine. To display this constantly, simply set the value cnt% 1. As you may have noticed, we have not simply "glued" the engine to the spaceship corresponding to the current direction of the spaceship, but instead created a tail-like effect: The engine smoke changes according to the player's change in direction with a slight delay, thus giving a more realistic simulation.

We have accomplished this with a small trick. If they do not hit any obstacle, the Bullets are automatically deleted from memory in the renderSprite method when they reach the tolerance region (just as with every other sprite). In principle, this holds as well for the engine smoke since we have placed this, like the Bullets, centered on the player, but for some reason it does not work like that. We shall see shortly why this is *not* the case.

First, we present the Bullet, which contains no particular secrets.

Listing 5.11 Bullet.h

```
#import "Sprite.h"

@interface Bullet : Sprite {
}

- (void) setAngle: (int) degree;

@end
```

5. OpenGL ES: Turbocharged!

**Listing 5.12 Bullet.m**

```objc
#import "Bullet.h"
#import "GameManager.h"

@implementation Bullet

- (void) setAngle: (int) degree {
    angle = degree;
    autoDestroy = true;
}

- (void) hit {
    active = false;
}

@end
```

We have derived the `Gear` class, which is responsible for the engine smoke, from
`Bullet`:

**Listing 5.13 Gear.h**

```objc
#import "Bullet.h"

@interface Gear : Bullet {
}

@end
```

**Listing 5.14 Gear.m**

```objc
#import "Gear.h"

@implementation Gear

- (void) draw {
    if (active) {
        pos.x+ = speed.x;
        pos.y+ = speed.y;
        [self drawFrame];
        if (cnt > 3) {
            active = false;
        }
    }
}

@end
```

As you can see, here we have overwritten the `draw` method in order to use the internal `cnt` variable, which is constantly increased, to deactivate the sprite. This is the trick that we mentioned before. The `Gear` sprite is continually regenerated, but after more than three iterations of the game loop, it deactivates itself (`cnt > 3`). Indeed, the `Gear` texture is rendered to the screen not once, but several times. We can see only the last piece, since the others are hidden by the player sprite. Since the `Gear` sprites are generated with a time delay, the direction appears to be slightly time delayed with respect to the current game direction.

If you increase the `cnt` limit (for example, `cnt > 40`), you will see how the smoke snakes behind the player (Figure 5.26).

Let us briefly carry out another test. Our player is moving, thanks to the sine and cosine, through the game, but we can see this only indirectly by way of the scrolled parallax backgrounds.

As a test, comment out the `scrollWorld` method in the `playGame` method of the `GameManager`. Since the game area no longer scrolls, you can more easily identify the player's circular path, but move quickly enough that your spaceship does not disappear from the scene (Figure 5.27).

We shall use the same type of locomotion for the `Fighter` adversaries. First, however, let us take a look at the other two types of adversaries.

---

**Listing 5.15** Octo.h

```
#import "Sprite.h"

@interface Octo : Sprite {
}

@end
```

Figure 5.26 Left: normal engine animation; right: with cnt > 40.

5. OpenGL ES: Turbocharged!

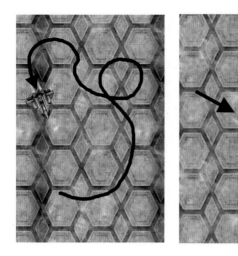

Figure 5.27 Left: scrolling is deactivated; right: with scrolling.

```objc
#import "Octo.h"
#import "GameManager.h"

@implementation Octo

- (void) additionalSetup {
    autoDestroy = true;
}

- (void) hit {
    active = false;
    [[GameManager getInstance] createExplosionFor: self];
}

@end
```

It is easy to see from this example that the Sprite class keeps much of the logic out of the implementation of the individual sprites. For the mechanical octopus, we have only to ensure that it is automatically deleted when the autoDestroy flag is activated. Moreover, in the hit method we take care of the explosion. The Tex class supports the already animated textures, which are called via the Sprite class, so we do not have to worry about the animation of the sprite in the Octo class. Even the explosion is based on an animated frame sequence, which, however, runs only once. We saw how that works when we studied the zombie game; in the Octo class, we have only to pass its own instance so that the GameManager class can center the sequence on the octopus.

## Listing 5.17 Mine.h

```
#import "Octo.h"

@interface Mine : Sprite {
    int sign;
}

@end
```

## Listing 5.18 Mine.m

```
#import "Mine.h"
#import "GameManager.h"

@implementation Mine

- (void) additionalSetup {
    autoDestroy = true;
    sign = [[GameManager getInstance] getRndBetween: -1 and: 1];
    if (sign = = 0) {
        sign = 1;
    }
}

- (void) renderSprite {
    angle+ = (sign*5);
    [super renderSprite];
}

@end
```

The class Mine is also derived directly from Sprite and has as its sole special feature a randomly set sign (sign), which sets the direction of rotation of the Mine.

We now come to the most interesting adversary, which, like the player, can move in a circle.

## Listing 5.19 Fighter.h

```
#import "Octo.h"

@interface Fighter : Octo {
    int angleOffset;
    int pathCnt;
    int speedScalarX;
    int speedScalarY;
}

@end
```

**Listing 5.20** Fighter.m

```
#import "Fighter.h"

@implementation Fighter

- (void) additionalSetup {
    angle = 0;
    angleOffset = 3;
    pathCnt = 0;
    speedScalarX = speed.x;
    speedScalarY = speed.y;
    autoDestroy = true;
}

- (void) draw {
    int animationPath[] = {-5, -5, -5, 5, 5, 5, -5, 5, 3, 3, 5, 5, -5};
    if (cnt% 10 = = 0) {
        angleOffset = animationPath[pathCnt];
        pathCnt ++;
        if (pathCnt > sizeof(animationPath)/sizeof(int)-1) {
            pathCnt = 0;
        }
    }

    angle + = angleOffset;
    speed.x = sin([self getRad: angle])*speedScalarX;
    speed.y = -cos([self getRad: angle])*speedScalarY;

    pos.x + = speed.x;
    pos.y + = speed.y;

    [self drawFrame];
}

@end
```

Movement works here just as it does with the player. With the sine and cosine functions we determine the directional vector speed from the current rotation angle. But where do we get the current rotation angle? There is no user input as in the player class.

As always, the solution is simple. We simply specify the angle. To do so, we have created the array animationPath, which contains the previously determined changes in direction. Of course, you could also make changes randomly at discrete time intervals, but such a predefined animation path has an unpleasant side effect, which we shall look at now.

This animation path is repeated indefinitely, and you can easily tell that we have again determined the time intervals for the change in direction with a modulo operator (Figure 5.28).

Experiment with different animation paths; each element of the array contains an angle that prescribes the current direction of the sprite. Of course, the array can be as long as you like. With sizeof(animationPath)/sizeof(int), we can determine the length of the C-array. (There is no advantage here to implementing an NSArray.)

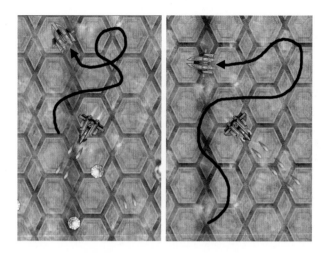

**Figure 5.28** The fighters move, like the player, along a curved path.

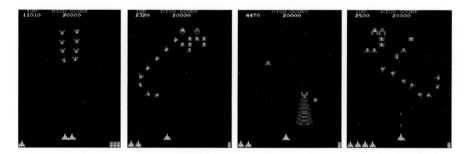

**Figure 5.29** Enemy attack patterns in Galaga (Namco).

Perhaps you recall the impressive motion of the enemies in the game classic `Galaga` (Namco, 1981; Figure 5.29)?

And perhaps you have wondered how this was done?

Well, the insect-like adversaries appear in various formations that are repeated several times during the game. The interesting effect is achieved by the row formation of the swarms of adversaries, which are arranged one behind the other like compartments in a train. On closer inspection, it turns out that all the adversaries traverse the same path, only with a time delay. Does this remind you of anything?

That is right! We have already implemented this behavior. To allow the `Fighters` to fly about as in Galaga, we have merely to create time-delayed `Fighters`—indeed, always in the same initial position.

Another timer must ensure that the number of `Fighters` created is limited. The sequence is as follows:

1. *Is it time to create new* `Fighters`*?*

2. *If yes, then create new* `Fighters` *at position xy.*

3. *Continue to create new* Fighters *until the maximal number is reached.*

4. *End.*

Pretty simple, is it not? To allow a Galaga swarm of Fighters to arise, we build the algorithm described before in the generateNewEnemies method of the GameManager:

```
static int fighterCnt = 15;//number of fighters per row
static CGPoint startP;
if (fighterCnt = = 15 && timer% 20 = = 0) {//create a new row?
    fighterCnt = 0;
    startP = [self getRndStartPos];
}
if (timer% 9 = = 0 && fighterCnt < 15) {//timer determines the offset
    fighterCnt++;
    [self createSprite: FIGHTER
                 speed: CGPointMake(7, 7)
                   pos: startP];
}
```

As our timer we use the internal counter of the GameManager together with a modulo operator. The number of Fighters per row is limited to 15 (fighterCnt). During the Fighter creation phase, we increment this value. At the same time, this value serves as a touchstone to decide whether new Fighter rows should be generated. (There should always be only one row created.) Finally, the smooth process of formation is taken care of by the animation path, which we have already created in the Fighter class (Figure 5.30).

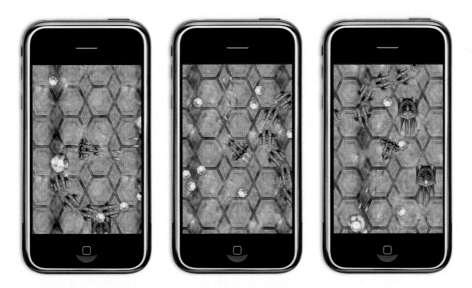

Figure 5.30 Screen shots of the complete game.

# ▍ 5.13  Support for Retina Displays under OpenGL ES

Under OpenGL ES, adaptation to the higher resolution of a retina display takes place automatically, as described in Section 2.9 in Chapter 2. It suffices to include a "@2x" variant of the graphics in the project. This is recommended for improved performance since, otherwise, the graphics will be scaled internally by iOS.

## 5.13.1  Accurate Pixel Rendering

A fractional position such as (100.25752, 200.73472) instead of (100, 200) leads to OpenGL ES mapping the texture to the nearest vertex, resulting in a distorted (100, 201). When a graphic is rotated, a blurred or interpolated transition can also arise between pixels, since the stepped transitions are not easily preserved under rotation. For 3D games, this effect is even more pronounced, due to the additional z-coordinate. In the 2D Tex class, we have already addressed this problem by casting the image points at which the texture is to be rendered as integers. Moreover, in creating the texture, we considered the scaling factor of the UIImage instance. For retina displays, the scale property has a factor of 2, while the size property gives the size of the image in image points. The actual size of the image that is loaded is therefore

```
widthOriginal = pic.size.width * pic.scale;
heightOriginal = pic.size.height * pic.scale;
```

This holds, of course, only for retina displays, since scale otherwise contains the value 0. Since iOS has been based on image points since version 4.0, the global constants for W and H do not have to be changed. Nevertheless, with the scaling factor in the Tex class, we make sure that the textures are created in the original resolution and therefore can be represented on a retina display unscaled if you have included "@2x" graphics. In addition, you can influence how OpenGL ES interpolates graphics. In the Tex class we have chosen the setting GL_LINEAR, so that rotated graphics do not look too pixelated. Alternatively, you can choose the setting GL_NEAREST.

## 5.13.2  Should I Utilize Full Resolution?

Basically, as game developers, we are dependent on the 320 × 480 image points. Nevertheless, the question arises whether we could create a game not in image points, but rather in the full resolution, so that a sprite at position (400, 700) could be rendered to the display at that actual position. Normally, an object at that position would no longer be visible, since the retina display is divided into image points of which there are only 320 × 480 pixels. However, with OpenGL ES we have direct access to the rendering interface, so we can in fact force a pixel-for-pixel resolution.

Let us consider this in a purely theoretical digression. First, in the Tex class, the values of width and height returned by the UIImage class must be multiplied by a factor of 2 in such a way that the properties of the texture are also congruent with the doubled dimensions; width and height always return the same values, since we want to render in pixels and not in image points. In this way, all textures obtain the original resolution of the retina graphics. Moreover, the global W and H values must be set for the display size to the retina resolution (that is, W = 480, H = 960). In this way, the perspective also changes, and enlarged textures appear pixel accurate and sharp on the screen. Finally, the touch points on the larger display have to be converted and again multiplied by a factor of 2; that is, p.x = p.x * 2 and p.y = p.y *2. The game now has the full 640 × 960 pixels at its disposal and must be adjusted accordingly.

Of course, this works only for retina devices. To determine whether you have the retina resolution available, it suffices to look at the drawRect: method, which sets the current resolution via the glViewport() function. The values of viewportWidth and viewportHeight were previously assigned via the glGetRenderbufferParame-terivOES() method, and they correspond to 480 and 960 pixels under retina resolution and to 320 × 480 pixels otherwise. Therefore, a sprite on a retina device would vanish only on reaching position x = 960 (landscape mode), while on older devices, this would occur at x = 480 (landscape). The practical benefit of this is likely to be small, but you can see that it is in fact possible to use the higher resolution. If you want to support a different resolution—for example, the 4-inch retina resolution of the iPhone 5 and the iPod 5—you just have to use 640 × 1136 instead of 640 × 960 pixels.

## 5.13.3  Info: Pay Attention to Performance

Since the graphics chip has to render four times the number of pixels under retina, depending on the complexity of the game, this can lead to a drop in performance. Even on slower Macs, a performance difference can be observed in the emulator. Therefore, starting with iOS 4.0, you have an additional adjustment option for the resolution. Using contentScaleFactor, you can set the desired scaling for a UIView interface, and with the contentsScale property, this can be set explicitly for a CAEAGLLayer. For the examples in this book, the scale factor is automatically 2, since we have overwritten the drawRect: method of the view by which rendering is implicitly done at the higher resolution. To increase performance, you can dispense with retina graphics and set the scale factor to 1 in the setupOGL method of the MainView:

```
eaglLayer.contentsScale = 1;
```

But beware: you will have to define your own drawRect: method (for example, drawRect2:); otherwise, the scale factor with be adjusted automatically by iOS to the current display size. After this change, OpenGL ES will have only one viewport with 320 × 480 image points, and the graphics chip will have correspondingly less work to do. If you have included "@2x" graphics in the project, these will be automatically adapted to the new resolution.

The examples in this book run fast enough on retina devices that this adaptation is unnecessary. Apple recommends that, for every app, one check whether it runs fast enough on a retina display under OpenGL ES. You can obtain further information in the section "Supporting High-Resolution Displays Using OpenGL ES" in the "OpenGL ES Programming Guide for iOS" at *http://developer.apple.com/library/ ios/#documentation/3DDrawing/Conceptual/OpenGLES_ProgrammingGuide/ WorkingwithEAGLContexts/WorkingwithEAGLContexts.html*.

# 6 The Third Dimension 3D Games

## 6.1  How Are 3D Games Constructed?

The leap into the third dimension is only a small step for mankind once we have implemented OpenGL ES for 2D games: We have seen that the transformation function expects three coordinates (x-y-z) by default, and for 2D games we could simply set the z-coordinate to 0. Moreover, the `MainView` class, which handles the creation of the OpenGL ES graphics context and initializes the three requisite buffers (render buffer, frame buffer, and depth buffer), also already supports the 3D representation of models. Therefore, for our leap into the third dimension, we require only three adjustments:

1. Set the perspective (via `setOGLProjection`).

2. Activate the depth buffer (z-axis).

3. Ensure that models have three coordinates (vertex arrays).

That does not sound too complicated and in fact, it is not. There is a different reason why 3D games are considered technically challenging: Imagine a typical representative of the genre, such as a first-person shooter, an automobile race, or a third-person action adventure. How are these games *put together*?

The player is in a landscape that can be freely explored and can be examined from a variety of viewpoints. Within this landscape are to be found 3D models of cars, people, monsters, and so on that have to look good from all sides. Because of the spatial extent of the objects, not only must various textures be developed, but their forms have to be modeled with the help of highly complex external editors. Even the creation of the simplest 3D scenes can easily exceed the time and budget of the hobby developer.

In addition to the creation of scenes and models, there are, of course, other hurdles to overcome: Spatial representation allows for more realism, so the physical movements of the models should be as realistic as possible. And perhaps you also want to consider additional light sources and properties of materials (Figure 6.1).

Before planning a 3D game, you should think long and hard about all that goes into it and whether you can really go it alone. You do not have all of eternity, after all. Two years spent working by yourself on a 3D game is probably not a good idea, given the fast pace of the App Store. Do not underestimate the risk that your game design will have become obsolete or be overshadowed by the latest technology coming out of the big game studios.

Nevertheless, the subject is far too exciting to ignore. And as you will see, the basics can be developed rather easily.

We already know that for OpenGL ES, *everything* consists of vertices. Whether you want to represent a mountainous landscape, a dungeon, or a car model, 3D games are composed of individual models that in turn consist of numerous vertices. Regardless of the game design, you will have to accomplish the following key tasks:

- Creating models (using external modeling software or building on basic geometric forms)

- Positioning these models in space

- Animating the models

- Checking for collisions among the models

- Positioning a camera

How, then, with these building blocks, is a 3D game created? Here are two suggestions:

- **Example 1:** For a simple car-racing game, you need at least a two-dimensional plane on which to represent the road using textures. If you exclude the third axis (ups and downs of the road) for practical reasons, you can check for collision with the road with a 2D tile map. The racing cars, as well as such obstacles as houses by the side of the road, are 3D models that are placed in the plane and (in the case of the cars) can move along the track.

Figure 6.1 Shadow Guardian (Gameloft), Supersonic HD (Kuuasema), and Reckless Getaway (Polarbit).

- **Example 2:** For a doom-shooter or labyrinth game, again you create a two-dimensional playing surface; the walls are made of a number of 3D blocks that you place on the basis of a 2D tile map. Raised levels or stages are excluded. Your game figure moves on the 2D tile map, and collisions occur as well via the tile map, which determines where the walls are erected. As you can see, here as well you do not have to check for collisions between the player and the vertical walls but simply transfer the ideas from 2D game development. You can also compare the position on the ground (2D collision) for movable objects such as the player, monsters, or projectiles, though under some circumstances, it can be simpler to check the models for collision directly against each other.

You see, then, that although many 3D games seem very impressive at first glance, they are based on some simple basic concepts. Even game developers put on their trousers one leg at a time.

So let us begin by finding suitable solutions to the core tasks outlined here. Then, with that in hand, we shall develop a 3D space-shooter game.

# 6.2 The Basic Framework

To create our first 3D project, we use as a basis the framework from the 2D chapter, which, you will recall, consists of three classes:

- `MyGameAppDelegate`

- `MainView`

- `GameManager`

You will find the complete project in the download folder under the name "OGL3D_Basics."

In order to set up the 3D perspective and activate the depth buffer, which was already created in the `MainView` class, we have only to adapt the `setOGLProjection` method of the `GameManager`:

```
- (void) setOGLProjection {
    glLoadIdentity();

    //set view
    glMatrixMode(GL_PROJECTION);
    zNear = 0.1;
    zFar = 2500;
    fieldOfViewAngle = 45;
    float top = zNear * tan(M_PI * fieldOfViewAngle/W);
    float bottom = -top;
    float left = bottom * W/H;//side ratio: W/H
    float right = top * W/H;
    glFrustumf(left, right, bottom, top, zNear, zFar);//3D perspective

    //Enable Modelview: change to rendering by vertex arrays
    glMatrixMode(GL_MODELVIEW);
    glEnableClientState(GL_VERTEX_ARRAY);
    glEnable(GL_DEPTH_TEST);
    glDepthFunc(GL_LESS);
}
```

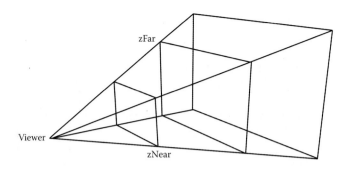

Figure 6.2 Frustum of a pyramid with parallel planes zNear and zFar.

Just as we saw in setting up a 2D perspective, we must first shift OpenGL ES into matrix mode GL_PROJECTION. Instead of the glOrthof() function, we now use the glFrustumf() function, which expects the same parameters.

Using this method, we establish the perspective on the game, but *not* the camera position. We shall worry about that later. However, this function also ensures that one camera exists—namely, the viewer looking at the scene, who is located directly over the coordinate origin and looks down along the negative z-axis. The field-of-view angle is 45° (fieldofViewAngle, corresponding to the camera lens). Since the viewer should perceive what goes on in three-dimensional space, we require depth information: zFar. All objects located beyond this boundary are invisible, as are objects located in front of zNear. Thus, these two parameters are known as *clipping panes*.

Using these parameters, we can calculate the dimensions left/right/bottom/top as shown in the implementation (Figure 6.2).

When we add a camera later, we will see that zNear and zFar change relatively to the camera position. That is, the viewer will never be able to see objects farther than 2,500 units (= zFar). The parameters for zNear and zFar must, by definition, both be greater than 0. It is common practice to choose zNear as small as possible so as to keep the blind spot between the viewer and zNear as small as possible, and to choose zFar as large as possible, but not too large; otherwise, performance could break down if too many objects have to be rendered.

Finally, in the setOGLProjection method, we activate the depth buffer (GL_DEPTH_TEST), set the standard alpha function (GL_LESS), and permanently enable the passing of vertex arrays via the client state GL_VERTEX_ARRAY. You know all about this from Chapter 5.

## ▮ 6.3 The 3D Coordinate System

With the project settings shown, we thus have the following coordinate system (Figure 6.3):

- The origin is at the center of the screen.

- The positive x-axis points to the right.

- The positive y-axis points upward.

- The positive z-axis points toward the viewer, while the negative z-axis points into the screen.

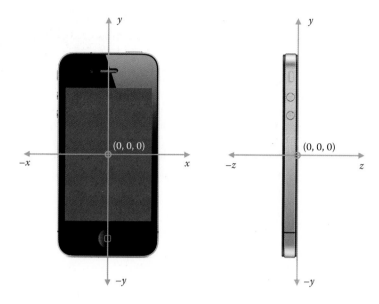

Figure 6.3 Three-dimensional coordinate system under OpenGL ES.

We are thus dealing with a right-handed Cartesian coordinate system (if you hold your right hand so that the fingers curl from the x-axis to the y-axis, the thumb points upward). This is in contrast to DirectX, for which the positive x-axis points into the screen.

In contrast to the 2D case, here there are no fixed units for the coordinates. The point P (10, 30, −20) therefore does not refer to pixel data; instead, one speaks simply of units. The point P is therefore located as follows:

- Units from the origin parallel to the x-axis: 10

- Units from the origin parallel to the y-axis: 30

- Units from the origin parallel to the z-axis: −20

The reason for the units is simple: Because of the perspective and camera position, the actual pixel position on the screen is determined only after the projection calculation of the vertices in the frame buffer. A line located near the viewer thus seems longer than one of the same length that is farther away.

# ■ 6.4 Drawing Simple Shapes

With the figure of this coordinate system in mind, we can already imagine where objects must be located in order for them to be visible. Since we have not yet set up a camera, we are looking directly at the origin along the negative z-axis. Here are a few examples:

- The point P1 (0, 0, −6) is located in front of the viewer. The distance is -zNear-6 units. Therefore, the point lies within the visible domain.

- The point P2 (0, 0, –60) is located in front of the viewer. The distance is -zNear-60 units. Therefore, the point lies within the visible range, but is farther away than the point P1.

- The point P3 (0, 0, 6) lies behind the viewer and is not visible.

As already described for 2D programming, we have several constants available to render a (spatial) area from vertices. We use the same functions as before and can access the same constants (GL_POINTS, GL_LINES, GL_TRIANGLES, etc.).

The difference with 2D is that we can now give three coordinates per vertex, though we do not have to. Let us first consider an example of how we can render a line in space consisting of only xy-coordinates:

```
- (void) drawLine {
    GLbyte vertices[] = {
        0, 0,//vertex 1
        1, 0 //vertex 2
    };
    glPushMatrix();
    glColor4f(1, 1, 0, 1);//set drawing color
    glVertexPointer(2, GL_BYTE, 0, vertices);//2 values per vertex
    glTranslatef(0, 0, -zNear-0.0001);
    glDrawArrays(GL_LINES, 0, 2);//2 = number of vertices
    glPopMatrix();
}
```

Since we have set the spatial perspective, the z-coordinate is automatically added, with the value 0 (Figure 6.4).

The first point on the line is located at (0, 0); that is, at the origin. The second point, (1, 0), is one unit to the right along the x-axis.

Since the z-value for both points is 0, we can see the line only when we temporarily move the coordinate system backward; as before, we use the pair glPushMatrix()/glPopMatrix() for this.

**Figure 6.4** A yellow line and that is it!

The translation of the z-axis is `-zNear-0.0001`. That is, we have moved the line 0.0001 units *in front of* the `zNear` clipping pane, so we can just see the line. The line runs well beyond the display to the right: The distance up to the right of the screen depends on the perspective, the screen resolution, and the z-position and is about 0.0315 units.* But beware that, if you want to render a line of this length, you must, of course, choose the correct data type in the `drawLine` method—that is, `Glfloat/GL_FLOAT` instead of `GLbyte/GL_BYTE`. When we work later with 3D models, we will generally use the `GLfloat` data type.

Next on the agenda is the OpenGL ES "Hello World" (again a triangle). This time, we give the z-coordinate explicitly:

```
- (void) drawTriangle {
    GLbyte vertices[] = {
        -1,  1,  0, //vertex 1
         1, -1,  0, //vertex 2
         1,  1,  0  //vertex 3
    };
    glPushMatrix();
    glColor4f(0, 1, 0, 1);
    glVertexPointer(3, GL_BYTE, 0, vertices);//3 values per vertex
    glTranslatef(0, 0, -6);//move somewhat farther backward
    glDrawArrays(GL_TRIANGLE_STRIP, 0, 3);//3 = number of vertices
    glPopMatrix();
}
```

We have just seen that directly in front of the `zNear` clipping pane, the distance from the origin to the lateral edge is just under 0.0315 (in relationship to the current environment). To see the triangle, we move the model six units to the rear. Note as well that we now have to prescribe three values per vertex with `VertexPointer`.

The triangle is still parallel to the xy-plane, so it could just as well be handled by 2D graphics. But as a test, change the z-coordinate(s) and observe the change in perspective.

We can make the 3D perspective even clearer by rotating a surface (Figure 6.5):

```
- (void) drawRectangle {
    //rectangle composed of two triangles
    GLbyte vertices[] = {
        -1,  1,  0, //upper left
         1,  1,  0, //upper right
        -1, -1,  0, //lower left
         1, -1,  0  //lower right
    };
    glPushMatrix();
    glColor4f(0, 0, 1, 1);
    glVertexPointer(3, GL_BYTE, 0, vertices);//3 values per vertex
    glTranslatef(0, 0, -6);
    static int angle = 0; angle + = 2;
    glRotatef(angle, 1, 0, 0);//to allow the x-axis to rotate
    glDrawArrays(GL_TRIANGLE_STRIP, 0, 4);//4 = number of vertices
    glPopMatrix();
}
```

---

* You can calculate the value or determine it by trial and error by converting the screen coordinates to 3D world coordinates—that is, the reverse way of putting data into the frame buffer. A discussion of this can be found, for example, in Fournier and Fussell (1988).

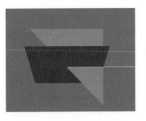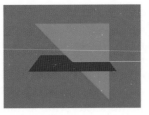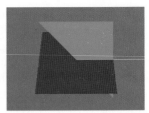

**Figure 6.5** Rotation of a rectangular surface.

The rectangle—consisting of two triangles—has four vertices that span a rectangular area centered at the origin. The rotation is about the x-axis. Such a rectangle could also be made using a texture, thereby instantly turning any 2D game into a 3D version. Of course, the surfaces rendered in the example have no volume; we shall consider models with spatial extension later. The basic principle is unchanged: The shape of an object is specified by its vertices.

# ▌ 6.5  Texturing Surfaces

For performance reasons, it makes sense not to construct a 3D game completely with 3D models. You may recall the strangely flat trees along the side of the road in some 3D car-racing games, which somehow look realistic, yet look the same from every angle. The reason for this is that rectangular textured surfaces are used—that is, surfaces with no z-extension that are always turned to face the viewer. Such sprites are sometimes called *billboards,* and we are going to implement billboards together with 3D models a bit later when we make use of a camera. Textured surfaces can also be used to good effect when their faces are not always turned toward the viewer.

Imagine one of the 2D fighters from the previous game that is able to turn pirouettes in 3D space. To accomplish this, we have merely to cover the rectangular surface of the fighter with the fighter texture. With the settings used already in the basic design, the texture is automatically visible from both sides of the surface (front and back).

As a basis, we choose the project from the previous chapter and add to it the Tex class that we have already created. The completed project goes under the name "OGL3D_Texture."

Since we want to make the rendering process for 3D models more flexible, we remove the draw method from the Tex class so that the methods for texture creation remain unchanged in the class.

Furthermore, we again add to the GameManager the familiar resource management from the 2D part.

This produces the following code for the rotating 2D fighter, which we add to the GameManager class and call repeatedly in the playGame method:

```
- (void) drawTexture {
    Tex *tex = [[GameManager getInstance] getTex: @"fighter.png"
                                        isImage: YES];
    GLuint textureID = [tex getTextureID];

    //maintain aspect ratio at a height of 1
    int w = [tex getWidth]/[tex getHeight];
    int h = 1;
```

```
GLfloat vertices[] = {//center on the origin
    -w,   h,   0, //upper left
     w,   h,   0, //upper right
    -w,  -h,   0, //lower left
     w,  -h,   0  //lower right
};

GLfloat textureCoords[] = {
    1, 0, //lower right -> mapped to the last vertex (w, -h, 0)
    0, 0, //lower left
    1, 1, //upper right
    0, 1  //upper left-> mapped to the first vertex (-w, h, 0)
};

int verticesLength = sizeof(vertices)/sizeof(GLfloat);

//render obj model
glEnable(GL_TEXTURE_2D);//all surfaces are now textured
glVertexPointer(3, GL_FLOAT, 0, vertices);
glBindTexture(GL_TEXTURE_2D, textureID);
glTexCoordPointer(2, GL_FLOAT, 0, textureCoords);
glColor4f(1, 1, 1, 1);//no extra color

//matrix operations
glPushMatrix();

//fly upward, z-depth = -16 units
static float y = -8;
y + = 0.2;
if (y > 8) y = -8;
glTranslatef(0, y, -16);

//turn a pirouette
static int angle = 0;
angle + = 10;
glRotatef(angle, 0, 1, 0);

glDrawArrays(GL_TRIANGLE_STRIP, 0, verticesLength/3);
glPopMatrix();

//clean-up
glDisable(GL_TEXTURE_2D);
}
```

First, following the familiar pattern, we get ourselves the texture ID for the fighter graphic. So that we can choose the vertices to be proportional to the actual graphic, we derive the width from the aspect ratio of the original graphic. You know that in the 3D world there are no pixel units. However, the later positioning of the object will be made easier if we center it on the origin (and thereby no longer begin from the upper left-hand corner, which would certainly lead to confusion in the case of 3D objects). Moreover, we can carry out the rotation directly without having first to translate the object.

For the texture coordinates we choose the same parameters as before; we are always dealing with a surface with w = 1 and h = 1, but we need to reverse the order of coordinates, since the y-axis in our 3D coordinate system now points downward instead of upward.

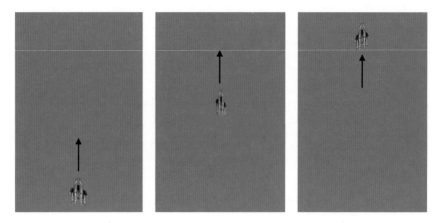

**Figure 6.6** A 2D fighter spins upward.

The remainder of the code should look familiar, with no differences from the texturing of the previously discussed 2D graphics.

The vertex pointer points to our rectangle's vertices, each of which consists of xyz-coordinates onto which the 2D texture is to be mapped. We choose the color RGBA = 1, 1, 1, 1, which means that the texture will *not* be colored in and is represented unchanged (the color of the texture pixels will be multiplied by the color white); any previously set color will be thereby overwritten (Figure 6.6).

To have the fighter fly upward, we call the glTranslate() method. The fighter's z-depth has been set to –16 units; at this depth, the vertex points of the surface correspond, in relation to the perspective, most closely to the original size of the graphic. As a test, we can, of course, make this value smaller, sending the fighter farther into the depths of the spatial volume.

Since the surface is already centered on the xy-origin, we can allow the model to be rotated directly about the y-axis; the y-axis of the model already corresponds to the y-axis of the coordinate system.

## ▌▉ 6.6  Texturing 3D Objects

Of course, we do not want to work only with textured 2D surfaces in our 3D games. To create three-dimensional objects, one usually uses a 3D editor for creating and modeling the necessary vertices. To make the principle understandable, let us first create an object programmatically. The simplest 3D object is a cube, and we already have experience with rectangular surfaces (Figure 6.7).

We choose the edge length of the cube to be two units, so when the cube is centered at the origin, the coordinates run from –1 to 1. The cube has six faces (front, back, top, bottom, left, and right) and requires one texture for each face.

As texture we choose the background graphic from our 2D shooter. Since the texture coordinates for each face of the cube are to be mapped to the identical square surface, we have to duplicate the coordinates in the array six times.

The cube has six faces—each with four vertices—for a total of 24 vertices, each consisting of three coordinates (xyz), so that the array has 72 elements.

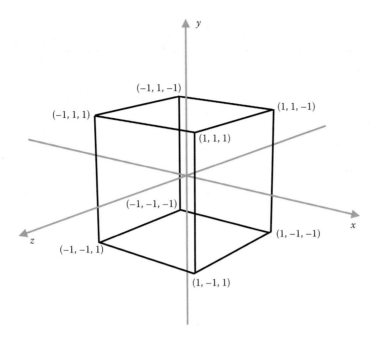

Figure 6.7 A cube with edge length 2 centered at the origin.

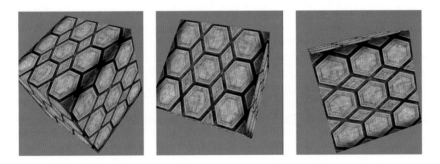

Figure 6.8 Rotating textured cube.

The array of texture coordinates, in contrast, has 72 vertices—to each vertex there is associated a texture coordinate—but has only 48 elements altogether, since the z-value for the texture coordinates is unnecessary.

To render a textured cube, we can implement the following method (Figure 6.8):

```
- (void) drawCube {
    GLfloat vertices[] = {
        -1, -1,  1, //front
         1, -1,  1,
        -1,  1,  1,
         1,  1,  1,

        -1, -1, -1, //back
        -1,  1, -1,
```

```
        1,  -1,  -1,
        1,   1,  -1,

       -1,   1,   1, //top
        1,   1,   1,
       -1,   1,  -1,
        1,   1,  -1,

       -1,  -1,   1, //bottom
       -1,  -1,  -1,
        1,  -1,   1,
        1,  -1,  -1,

       -1,  -1,   1, //left
       -1,   1,   1,
       -1,  -1,  -1,
       -1,   1,  -1,

        1,  -1,  -1, //right
        1,   1,  -1,
        1,  -1,   1,
        1,   1,   1
};

GLfloat textureCoords[] = {//6 faces = 6 textures
    1, 0, //lower right
    0, 0, //lower left
    1, 1, //upper right
    0, 1, //upper left

    1, 0, //lower right
    0, 0, //lower left
    1, 1, //upper right
    0, 1, //upper left

    1, 0, //lower right
    0, 0, //lower left
    1, 1, //upper right
    0, 1, //upper left

    1, 0, //lower right
    0, 0, //lower left
    1, 1, //upper right
    0, 1, //upper left

    1, 0, //lower right
    0, 0, //lower left
    1, 1, //upper right
    0, 1, //upper left

    1, 0, //lower right
    0, 0, //lower left
    1, 1, //upper right
    0, 1 //upper left
};

Tex *tex = [[GameManager getInstance] getTex: @"textur.png"
                                    isImage: YES];
```

```
GLuint textureID = [tex getTextureID];

int verticesLength = sizeof(vertices)/sizeof(GLfloat);

//render obj model
glEnable(GL_CULL_FACE); //ignore invisible surfaces
glCullFace(GL_BACK);

glEnable(GL_TEXTURE_2D); //all surfaces are now textured
glVertexPointer(3, GL_FLOAT, 0, vertices);
glBindTexture(GL_TEXTURE_2D, textureID);
glTexCoordPointer(2, GL_FLOAT, 0, textureCoords);
glColor4f(1, 1, 1, 1);//no extra color

//matrix operations
glPushMatrix();
glTranslatef(0, 0, -5);
static int angle = 0; angle + = 2;
glRotatef(angle, 1, 1, 1);
glDrawArrays(GL_TRIANGLE_STRIP, 0, verticesLength/3);
glPopMatrix();

//clean-up
glDisable(GL_TEXTURE_2D);
glDisable(GL_CULL_FACE);
}
```

This time, we let the model rotate simultaneously about all three axes, but we still need to ensure that the rear sides of the model are not rendered, since we do not want to waste any computation time. This technique is known as *backface culling* and we can apply it very easily:

```
glEnable(GL_CULL_FACE);
glCullFace(GL_BACK);
```

The first step is to activate culling; in the second step, we determine the rear side that is not to be rendered. GL_BACK refers here to the rear side of the cube; it is determined automatically by the perspective. Alternatively, you could also "cull" the front side, though that makes sense only in a few, rare cases. Moreover, GL_BACK is set already by default.

However, backface culling can be undesirable: Recall the rotating fighter from the previous section. In that case, we wanted to show both the front and the back. Therefore, we deactivate the GL_CULL_FACE switch at the end of the drawCube method in order to give other rendering methods a clean state.

Our cube boasts an impressive 72 vertices, though they can be determined relatively easily with a bit of thought. The situation with other basic shapes is different: We could probably make ourselves a pyramid without too much trouble—but a sphere? To be sure, a sphere can be defined mathematically, but there is no mathematically perfect sphere in the 3D world; after all, as you know, all 3D models have to be constructed of polygonal basic forms. Thus, it is possible only to construct an approximation to the round shape of a sphere. The technique of decomposing shapes into polygons is called tessellation, and the polygons thus obtained must then be further decomposed into triangles through the process of triangulation. If you search the Internet for the word "tessellation," you will find a number of algorithms to create such shapes programmatically.

The idea is always to construct a formula that returns the vertices of the shape. Even from the cube, which we have already created, we can form any number of 3D objects through deformation. We obtain a sort of crazed effect by minimally changing the vertices at each call to the drawCube method:

```
for (int i = 0; i < verticesLength; i++) {
    vertices[i] += ([self getRndBetween: -1 and: 1] * 0.02);
}
```

The result is that the box shakes violently back and forth, as though a devil were inside trying to get out.*

## ▍ 6.7  Let There Be Light

It has perhaps occurred to you that our cube is lighted equally from all sides. That we none-theless recognize the cubic form is due entirely to the texture. If we were to remove the texture, we would see on the display a uniform white spot with changing contours.

In order to be able to recognize the cubic form without textures, we have to illuminate the cube; then, from the cube's shadows, we will be able to recognize its shape.

Of course, light is also helpful for textured models, since chiaroscuro effects provide for greater realism. In addition to light, you can also specify various materials that determine how the light is to be reflected. For our examples, however, the use of a standard material property will suffice, which we can permanently activate via the flag GL_COLOR_MATERIAL.

OpenGL ES supports a variety of light types (GL_AMBIENT, GL_DIFFUSE, and GL_SPECULAR, among others) and up to eight light sources (GL_LIGHT0 to GL_LIGHT7). For each light source you can also specify a color with which that source illuminates the scene. For example, you could shine a yellow light on a white cube. Moreover, you can specify the location of the light source using a directional vector.

For our example, we will be content with the standard lighting:

```
- (void) setLight {
    glEnable(GL_LIGHTING); //enable light
    glEnable(GL_COLOR_MATERIAL); //standard material reflection

    glEnable(GL_LIGHT0); //turn on light source 0 (8 sources maximal)
    GLfloat color0[] = {1, 1, 1, 1}; //color of light
    glLightfv(GL_LIGHT0, GL_DIFFUSE, color0); //type of light = "diffuse"
    GLfloat light_position0[] = {0, 1, 0, 0}; //light comes from above
    //position light source
    glLightfv(GL_LIGHT0, GL_POSITION, light_position0);
}
```

We call the method once, at the end of the setOGLProjection method, so that the 3D scene will be permanently lit. In the directional vector light_position0, we have

---

* Perhaps you have heard something of skin deformation. It is in principle the same thing, except that the model is deformed according to particular mathematical processes. Otherwise, 3D game figures would look rather faceted. Skin deformation causes, for example, a realistic change in an arm mesh without the arm hav-ing to be assembled out of rigid basic forms.

set x = 0, y = 1, and z = 0 so that the light shines downward along the y-axis. Our models will thus be lit from above. The light color is white so that we do not distort the original color of the model.

Before we can illuminate textured or untextured 3D models, there is one additional problem to be solved. The light does not yet work as one would expect, and the reason for this is that our 3D model is not yet complete. What is missing?

In order to illuminate a plane surface, OpenGL ES needs to know in what direction this surface is pointing. More precisely, for every plane, we must specify a vector that points in a direction perpendicular to the plane. Only then can the light falling on our scene be determined realistically. Such a perpendicular vector is also called a normal to the plane. If the vector additionally has length 1, then the normal is said to be normalized.

As you know, three points determine a plane, so it would be no problem for OpenGL ES to compute the normal given the vertices. However, that would degrade performance considerably, so we are better off specifying the normal vectors ourselves, and we shall do so in the form of an array.

Because our cube is such a simple shape, we can easily determine the normals for each face:

```
 0,   0,   1, //front
 0,   0,  -1, //back
 0,   1,   0, //top
 0,  -1,   0, //bottom
-1,   0,   0, //left
 1,   0,   0, //right
```

As you can see, the normal of the front face points one unit along the z-axis (0, 0, 1), and so on. For more complex models, it becomes more difficult to compute the normals. Fortunately, all 3D modeling programs support the exportation of normals, so we are not going to have to concern ourselves with this issue later.

To integrate the normals into the rendering procedure, we have to specify the normal for each vertex, similarly to what we did for texture coordinates. That is, we create a normal array with 24 vectors, each of which consists of xyz-values—that is, 72 elements in all.

To activate the normal array, we must, of course, throw a switch and then assign a pointer to the current normal array:

```
glEnableClientState(GL_NORMAL_ARRAY);
glEnable(GL_NORMALIZE);
. . .
glNormalPointer(GL_FLOAT, 0, normals);
```

With the constant GL_NORMALIZE, we also specify that all normals are to be automatically normalized—that is, given length 1 if that is not already the case. Once it is certain that the normals have been normalized, this specification can be omitted for improved performance. However, the improvement is not great, so we can flip the switch in our examples without worrying.

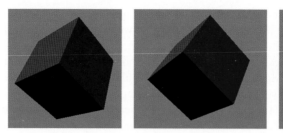

Figure 6.9  Rotating blue cube without texture and illuminated from above.

To render an untextured cube with normals and a blue color, we implement the following method (Figure 6.9):

```
- (void) drawCube_noTexture {
    GLfloat vertices[] = {
        -1, -1,  1, //front
         1, -1,  1,
        -1,  1,  1,
         1,  1,  1,

        -1, -1, -1, //back
        -1,  1, -1,
         1, -1, -1,
         1,  1, -1,

        -1, 1,   1, //top
         1, 1,   1,
        -1, 1,  -1,
         1, 1,  -1,

        -1, -1,  1, //bottom
        -1, -1, -1,
         1, -1,  1,
         1, -1, -1,

        -1, -1,  1, //left
        -1,  1,  1,
        -1, -1, -1,
        -1,  1, -1,

         1, -1, -1,//right
         1,  1, -1,
         1, -1,  1,
         1,  1,  1
    };

    GLfloat normals[] = {
        0,  0,  1, //front
        0,  0,  1,
        0,  0,  1,
        0,  0,  1,

        0,  0, -1, //back
        0,  0, -1,
```

```
      0,   0,  -1,
      0,   0,  -1,

      0,   1,   0, //top
      0,   1,   0,
      0,   1,   0,
      0,   1,   0,

      0,  -1,   0, //bottom
      0,  -1,   0,
      0,  -1,   0,
      0,  -1,   0,

     -1,   0,   0, //left
     -1,   0,   0,
     -1,   0,   0,
     -1,   0,   0,

      1,   0,   0, //right
      1,   0,   0,
      1,   0,   0,
      1,   0,   0
    };

    //number of array elements
    int verticesLength = sizeof(vertices)/sizeof(GLfloat);

    //render obj model
    glEnableClientState(GL_NORMAL_ARRAY);//activate normal arrays
    glEnable(GL_NORMALIZE);

    glEnable(GL_CULL_FACE);//ignore invisible surfaces
    glCullFace(GL_BACK);

    glVertexPointer(3, GL_FLOAT, 0, vertices);
    glNormalPointer(GL_FLOAT, 0, normals);

    glColor4f(0, 0, 1, 1);//color

    //matrix operations
    glPushMatrix();
    glTranslatef(0, 0, -7);
    static int angle = 0; angle + = 2;
    glRotatef(angle, 1, 1, 0);
    glDrawArrays(GL_TRIANGLE_STRIP, 0, verticesLength/3);
    glPopMatrix();

    //clean-up
    glDisableClientState(GL_NORMAL_ARRAY);
    glDisable(GL_NORMALIZE);
    glDisable(GL_CULL_FACE);
}
```

As you can see, except for the fact that we are now leaving off the texture and have activated a normals array, the code remains the same. To illuminate textured models, of course, you also have to specify the normal at each vertex of the model. From now on, we shall supply all our models with normals—the lights remain on.

---

# ■ 6.8 Creating, Loading, and Integrating 3D Models

You would have great difficulty in developing your own 3D games without the use of 3D modeling software. Of course, you could alternatively implement your own basic forms such as cubes, pyramids, and spheres, but even these basic forms are much easier to create and export using an external software application.

Since OpenGL ES functions as a pure graphics interface, it does not possess functionality for importing 3D models. Moreover, having such functionality would limit the platform independence, since certain formats would be given precedence over others—not to mention the fact that the accurate and flexible importation of model data would represent an additional burden on the API. So why not transfer the task to the developer?

Therefore, this is how things stand. We must pose the following questions:

- *What software should I use for creating the models?*

- *In what format should I export the models?*

- *How can I import and use the format?*

Let us begin with the second question. This is a *very critical* question, since today's 3D programs are extremely complex and able to generate realistic models, so parsing a proprietary format can take a large amount of time. A better alternative might be to choose a freely available and open format that is not too complex and is supported by a large number of 3D programs. Indeed, such a format exists that is based on ASCII: the Obj format. Originally developed by Wavefront Technologies, Obj supports a number of advanced features, not all of which we should feel obliged to use. Instead, we proceed pragmatically and concentrate on what we have already learned: vertex arrays, texture coordinates, and normal arrays.

With this, the first question would be answered as well. You can create your models with just about any modeling tool, from the free software Blender all the way up to Maya or 3ds Max; each of these programs supports *.obj files as export. Alternatively, you can avoid the use of modeling software entirely and search out freely available Obj models on the Internet. Professional game studios frequently purchase such models on a fee basis.

## 6.8.1 Faces

There is still something else to consider. Before we can use the Obj format, we have to clarify what is meant by *faces*. Faces are not a peculiarity of Obj, but rather play a role in other formats as well. In principle, they represent a way to store data in a space-saving form. Therefore, we are fortunate that OpenGL ES supports faces directly.

For our cube, we defined 24 vertices. However, the cube actually contains only eight distinct vertices, the number 24 arising from the fact that the same vertex is referenced more than once per face. The idea behind faces is to store only these eight vertices in the vertex array. In order for OpenGL ES to know from which points a particular triangle is to be generated, a second array is used that contains indices to the vertex array—namely, for each vertex of a triangle, one index that refers to the vertex in the vertex array.

In practice, one cannot always demonstrate that the use of faces improves performance. That depends on the model itself, among other things, but at least the use of memory decreases, in particular with models with thousands of vertices.[*]

To integrate faces into the rendering process, proceed as before; that is, pass the vertex array as a pointer. However, to render the faces, instead of calling

```
glDrawArrays(GL_TRIANGLE_STRIP, 0, verticesLength/3);
```

you now call

```
glDrawElements(GL_TRIANGLES, facesLength, GL_UNSIGNED_SHORT, faces);
```

The `faces` array contains the indices of the triangles, and with the constant GL_TRIANGLES we specify that the array contains three vertices (= triangle) per face. The `glDrawElements()` function accepts in addition only the length specification of the array (`facesLength`) and the data type. Warning: Since the array contains only indices, only the two data-type constants GL_UNSIGNED_BYTE and GL_UNSIGNED_SHORT are permitted.

From now on, we shall work only with models that we create with an external tool. To render the models, we need the following arrays:

- **Model without texture**

  - Vertex array

  - Normal array

  - Faces array

- **Model with texture**

  - Vertex array

  - Normal array

  - Texture-coordinate array

  - Faces array

## 6.8.2 Construction of an Obj File

Our goal now is to obtain this array information. Once we have it, we can render the model as shown previously, independently of whether it is a car, a mountain, or a Tetris block.[†]

---

[*] Compare *http://www.khronos.org/message_boards/viewtopic.php?f=4&t=187&p=2135&hilit=drawelements#p2135*.

[†] If you already have experience with some other format, you can, of course, use that. You should know, however, how to access the necessary arrays.

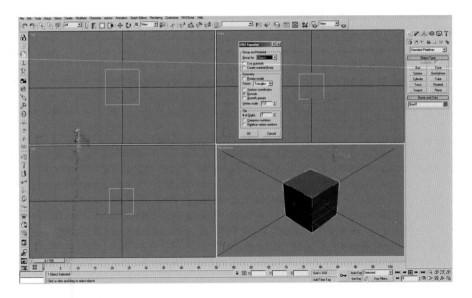

Figure 6.10  3ds Max with cube and OBJ exporter.

Before we can analyze the structure of an Obj file, we must first create a simple model with a 3D tool. To this end, we use 3ds Max from Autodesk, since this program is used most frequently for games and many free programs are modeled on it. In any case, we are not going more deeply into the operation of the program. You can create simple basic forms without much prior knowledge using CREATE > STANDARD PRIMITIVES.

To produce a first Obj file, choose "Cube" as the basic form. You can accomplish this with a few mouse clicks. Make sure that you position the cube as close to the center of the coordinate system as possible (Figure 6.10).

Then choose FILE > EXPORT and, for file type, choose "Wavefront Object (*.OBJ)." You will now see a small window: the OBJ exporter. Under "Faces," select "Triangles," since we want to render all the faces as triangles. Also check "Normals." For the number of decimal places, a precision of one place will suffice ("# of Digits: 1"). You can see that you can generate texture coordinates for every 3D model automatically; however, the precise wrapping of the object with the texture is something that you should undertake yourself with the modeling software. Here, however, we are not going to do that.

The result is a text file called "cube.obj," which you can find under RESOURCES > GFX in the example project for this section (name: "OGL3D_obj_Models").

Listing 6.1  cube.obj

```
# Max2Obj Version 4.0 Mar 10th, 2001
#
# object Box01 to come...
#
v -7.5 -7.2 -7.8
```

```
v 7.3 -7.2 -7.8
v -7.5 7.6 -7.8
v 7.3 7.6 -7.8
v -7.5 -7.2 7.0
v 7.3 -7.2 7.0
v -7.5 7.6 7.0
v 7.3 7.6 7.0
# 8 vertices

vn 0.0 0.0 -1.6
vn 0.0 0.0 -1.6
vn 0.0 0.0 -1.6
vn 0.0 0.0 -1.6
vn 0.0 0.0 1.6
vn 0.0 0.0 1.6
vn 0.0 0.0 1.6
vn 0.0 0.0 1.6
# 8 vertex normals

g Box01
f 1//1 3//3 4//4
f 4//4 2//2 1//1
f 5//5 6//6 8//8
f 8//8 7//7 5//5
f 1//1 2//2 6//6
f 6//6 5//5 1//1
f 2//2 4//4 8//8
f 8//8 6//6 2//2
f 4//4 3//3 7//7
f 7//7 8//8 4//4
f 3//3 1//1 5//5
f 5//5 7//7 3//3
# 12 faces

g
```

The structure of the Obj file is easy to understand: In front of every vertex you see an abbreviation that describes what the vertex represents. We use the following abbreviations:

- **v** (vertex)

- **vt** (texture coordinate)

- **vn** (normal)

- **f** (face)

Texture coordinates can also be specified with three elements per coordinate, where the last value is 0, as a rule. In processing texture coordinates, we must, of course, consider this in setting the pointer (three components, instead of two, per coordinate).

Moreover, the faces are again divided into *vertex face/texture face/normal face*.

If one of these values is absent (for example, because you did not export any texture coordinates), the value is simply omitted—that is, *vertex face//normal face*.

Since a face consists of three vertices, three indices must be given for each face. In our Obj file, the first triangle therefore consists of indices 1, 3, and 4 (f 1//1 3//3 4//4). The cube has 12 faces, since each of the six square faces is composed of two triangles (6 * 2 = 12).

We are interested only in the vertex index; if the other face indices (texture and normal) are unequal to those in the vertex array, we can no longer use the glDrawElements() function. This is because all face elements (vertices, texture coordinates, and normals) are arranged in the array in the same order. If that is not the case, you will have to do without faces and use the glDrawArrays() function, which means also that you first have to reassemble the arrays using the indices. Take great care in exporting that the indices always have the same value.

### OBJ

The Obj format begins counting indices at 1 instead of 0. If we later want to use the data of the Obj file, we must take care to reduce the index by 1.

In order to be able to insert the arrays obtained in Obj format more easily into the source code, we have made a simple formatter available on the Internet at the URL *http://www.qioo.de/objformatter*. You may also use your own formatter or read in and parse the Obj format directly as a file via the iOS SDK (Figure 6.11).

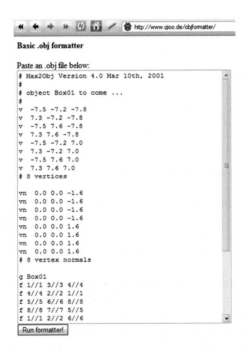

**Figure 6.11** The online formatter with the Obj data of the exported cube.

The use of the script is self-explanatory; simply paste the ASCII text of the Obj file into the input field and press "Run formatter!" You then obtain the following output on the website:

```
The.obj-file has been formatted: 27.07.10 - 17:52:12

Formatted.obj:

# Max2Obj Version 4.0 Mar 10th, 2001
#
# object Box01 to come...
#

Vertices:
-7.5, -7.2, -7.8, 7.3, -7.2, -7.8, -7.5, 7.6, -7.8, 7.3, 7.6, -7.8, -7.5,
    -7.2, 7.0, 7.3, -7.2, 7.0, -7.5, 7.6, 7.0, 7.3, 7.6, 7.0,
# 8 vertices

Vertex normals:
0.0, 0.0, -1.6, 0.0, 0.0, -1.6, 0.0, 0.0, -1.6, 0.0, 0.0, -1.6, 0.0, 0.0,
    1.6, 0.0, 0.0, 1.6, 0.0, 0.0, 1.6, 0.0, 0.0, 1.6,
# 8 vertex normals

g Box01

Faces (index starts with 0):
0, 2, 3, 3, 1, 0, 4, 5, 7, 7, 6, 4, 0, 1, 5, 5, 4, 0, 1, 3, 7, 7, 5, 1, 3,
    2, 6, 6, 7, 3, 2, 0, 4, 4, 6, 2,
# 12 faces

Vertex x-Range from: -7.5 to: 7.3
Vertex y-Range from: -7.2 to: 7.6
Vertex z-Range from: -7.8 to: 7.0
Suggested radius for bounding sphere: 7.6333333333333
Warning: Supplied faces might be too complex. Supported format example:
    22/22/22 7/7/7 10/10/10
```

You can see that vertices, normals, and faces are arranged in such a way that we can use them in our source code by copying and pasting without any further adaptation. Moreover, the script ensures that the faces begin with 0. (Obviously, we output only the vertex index of the face; nothing else is supported by OpenGL ES, and the use of the glDrawArrays() function as a fallback is something that we hope to avoid; see previous discussion.)

The warning given earlier also relates to this situation: Since the texture coordinate is absent during the exportation, the faces format does not correspond to the expected format, in which all three indices (vertex, texture, and normal) must be equal. The script checks only for equality; if a component is missing, the indicated warning is output. But a quick look into the Obj file suffices, and we find that, indeed, the vertex and normal always point to the same index, so everything is all right.

Additionally, the script returns useful information for the creation of bounding boxes and bounding spheres. Using the vertex data, the maximum distance between the vertices in the x-, y-, and z-directions is specified. Along the x-axis, the extent in the preceding example is from –7.5 to 7.3, which represents a distance of 14.8 units. From the decimals, you can see that we positioned the cube manually in the editor, and it is therefore not positioned exactly in the center; this small inexactitude is acceptable, since the object in any case will be freely movable later. From the maximum value, we can determine the average value and thus suggest a radius for a bounding sphere: 7.6333333333333. Of course, in practice, not all models are constructed so uniformly as our cube, so the radius will be only an approximate value that does not always provide for the object being completely surrounded.

For more complex 3D models, however, it can be useful to create several bounding boxes/spheres around an object (for example, head, left arm, right arm, torso, legs). For most elements of a game, however, you should be fine with a single bounding box or bounding sphere.

But back to our Obj file. Let us see whether we have done everything correctly and transfer the vertices and indices into our source code:

```
- (void) drawCube {
    //data come from an obj file,
    //converted with www.qioo.de/objformatter/
    GLfloat vertices[] = {//8 vertices
        -7.5, -7.2, -7.8, 7.3, -7.2, -7.8, -7.5, 7.6, -7.8, 7.3, 7.6, -7.8,
        -7.5, -7.2, 7.0, 7.3, -7.2, 7.0, -7.5, 7.6, 7.0, 7.3, 7.6, 7.0
    };

    GLfloat normals[] = {//8 normals
        0.0, 0.0, -1.6, 0.0, 0.0, -1.6, 0.0, 0.0, -1.6, 0.0, 0.0, -1.6, 0.0,
        0.0, 1.6, 0.0, 0.0, 1.6, 0.0, 0.0, 1.6, 0.0, 0.0, 1.6
    };

    GLushort faces[] = {//12 faces = 6 cube faces at 2 triangles each
        0, 2, 3, 3, 1, 0, 4, 5, 7, 7, 6, 4, 0, 1, 5, 5, 4, 0, 1, 3, 7, 7, 5,
        1, 3, 2, 6, 6, 7, 3, 2, 0, 4, 4, 6, 2
    };

    //number of array elements
    //int verticesLength = sizeof(vertices)/sizeof(GLfloat);
    int facesLength = sizeof(faces)/sizeof(GLushort);

    //render obj model
    glEnableClientState(GL_NORMAL_ARRAY);//activate normal arrays
    glEnable(GL_NORMALIZE);

    glEnable(GL_CULL_FACE);//ignore invisible faces
    glCullFace(GL_BACK);

    glVertexPointer(3, GL_FLOAT, 0, vertices);
    glNormalPointer(GL_FLOAT, 0, normals);

    glColor4f(0, 1, 0, 1);//color

    //matrix operations
    glPushMatrix();
    glTranslatef(0, 0, -50);
    static int angle = 0; angle + = 2;
    glRotatef(angle, 1, 1, 0);
    glDrawElements(GL_TRIANGLES, facesLength, GL_UNSIGNED_SHORT, faces);
    glPopMatrix();

    //clean-up
    glDisable(GL_NORMALIZE);
    glDisable(GL_CULL_FACE);
}
```

6. The Third Dimension 3D Games

As you can see, the preceding code differs from previous examples only in the use of the `glDrawElements()` function, which accesses the faces (instead of `glDrawArrays()`), which in turn refer to the vertices. Since we give the `faces` array directly in the `glDrawElements()` function as a pointer, we do not need to call an extra pointer function for the faces, as we still always have to do for the vertices and normals.

With this we have created, loaded, and displayed our first 3D model with an editor. Let us venture to try a more complex model; the standard example in this area is probably the famous 3D teakettle, which you may include if you wish. But 3ds Max offers a whole host of other interesting shapes that you can create with two or three mouse clicks. We shall choose the "torus knot," which you can find under "Create -> Extended Primitives" (Figure 6.12).

The corresponding Obj file can also be found in the example project under "gfx." The model consists of 1,440 vertices, 1,440 normals, and 2,880 faces (Figure 6.13):

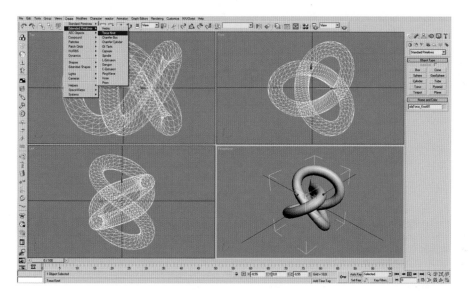

**Figure 6.12** 3ds Max with torus knot.

**Figure 6.13** Cube und torus knot rotating in the iPhone simulator.

```
- (void) drawTorusKnot {
    //data come from the obj file
    //converted with www.qioo.de/objformatter/
    GLfloat vertices[] = {
        20.4, 10.9, -0.5, 21.1, 12.4, 1.0, 20.7, 14.3, 2.1, 19.5, 16.1, 2.5,
        17.7, 17.4, 2.1,...
    };

    GLfloat normals[] = {
        0.7, -0.7, -0.0, 0.9, -0.3, 0.4, 0.8, 0.1, 0.6, 0.5, 0.5, 0.7, 0.1,
        0.8, 0.6, -0.4,...
    };

    GLushort faces[] = {
        0, 12, 13, 0, 13, 1, 1, 13, 14, 1, 14, 2, 2, 14, 15, 2, 15, 3, 3,
        15, 16, 3, 16, 4, 4,...
    };

    //number of array elements
    //int verticesLength = sizeof(vertices)/sizeof(GLfloat);
    int facesLength = sizeof(faces)/sizeof(GLushort);

    //render obj model
    glEnableClientState(GL_NORMAL_ARRAY);//activate normal arrays
    glEnable(GL_NORMALIZE);

    glEnable(GL_CULL_FACE);//ignore invisible faces
    glCullFace(GL_BACK);

    glVertexPointer(3, GL_FLOAT, 0, vertices);
    glNormalPointer(GL_FLOAT, 0, normals);

    glColor4f(0, 1, 1, 1);//color

    //matrix operations
    glPushMatrix();
    glTranslatef(0, 0, -110);
    static int angle = 0; angle + = 2;
    glRotatef(angle, 1, 1, 1);
    glDrawElements(GL_TRIANGLES, facesLength, GL_UNSIGNED_SHORT, faces);
    glPopMatrix();

    //clean-up
    glDisable(GL_NORMALIZE);
    glDisable(GL_CULL_FACE);
}
```

## ▮ 6.9 Additional 3D Models with Texture

With reference to our first 3D game project, we create two additional 3D models for which, this time, we also export the texture coordinates (Figure 6.14).

The first object is an asteroid, and the second is a reconnaissance unit of an enemy power that later will be destroyed. As a texture, we use two graphics with 128 × 128 pixels each.

We model both objects in 3ds Max and export them as Obj files including texture coordinates, as shown in the screen shots (Figure 6.15).

Having brought the Obj files with our online formatter into proper form, we integrate the data into a new project called "OGL3D_obj_withTexture."

Figure 6.14 asteroid.png, obstacle.png.

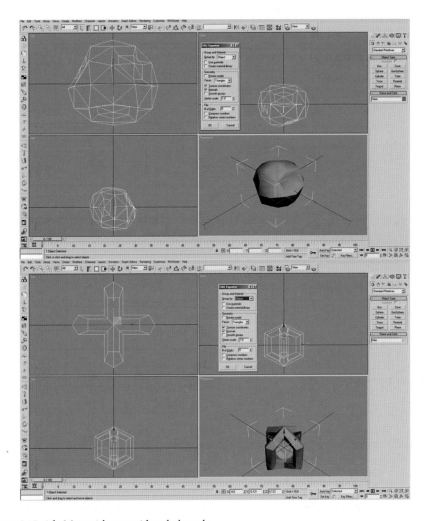

Figure 6.15 3ds Max with asteroid and obstacle.

There we create methods for rendering each model, which we call in the `playGame` method:

```
[self drawAsteroid];
[self drawObstacle];
```

Listing 6.2 drawAsteroid-Method

```
- (void) drawAsteroid {
    Tex *tex = [[GameManager getInstance] getTex: @"asteroid.png"
                                         isImage: YES];
    GLuint textureID = [tex getTextureID];

    //data come from obj file,
    //oonverted with www.qioo.de/objformatter/
    GLfloat vertices[] = {
        -0.207126, -0.066316, 17.863581, 23.264721, -1.502157,
        -0.192209, -0.207126,...
    };

    GLfloat textureCoords[] = {
        0.511933, 0.499667, 0.000000, 0.753190, 0.915463, 0.000000,
        0.054368, 0.673368,...
    };

    GLfloat normals[] = {
        0.003697, -0.091516, 0.995797, 0.960635, -0.009128, 0.277662,
        0.000000, 0.960620,...
    };

    GLushort faces[] = {
        0, 6, 8, 56, 57, 30, 56, 30, 58, 58, 30, 59, 7, 1, 22, 57, 60,
        30, 30, 60, 61, 30, 61,...
    };

    //number of array elements
    //int verticesLength = sizeof(vertices)/sizeof(GLfloat);
    int facesLength = sizeof(faces)/sizeof(GLushort);

    //render obj model
    glEnable(GL_TEXTURE_2D);//all surfaces are now textured
    glEnableClientState(GL_NORMAL_ARRAY);//activate normal arrays
    glEnable(GL_NORMALIZE);

    glEnable(GL_CULL_FACE);//ignore invisible faces
    glCullFace(GL_BACK);

    glVertexPointer(3, GL_FLOAT, 0, vertices);
    glBindTexture(GL_TEXTURE_2D, textureID);
    glTexCoordPointer(3, GL_FLOAT, 0, textureCoords);
    glNormalPointer(GL_FLOAT, 0, normals);

    glColor4f(1, 1, 1, 1);//no extra color
```

```
        //matrix operations
        glPushMatrix();
        glTranslatef(0, 0, -200);
        static int angle = 0; angle + = 2;
        glRotatef(angle, 1, 1, 0);
        glDrawElements(GL_TRIANGLES, facesLength, GL_UNSIGNED_SHORT,
        faces);
        glPopMatrix();

        //clean-up
        glDisable(GL_TEXTURE_2D);
        glDisable(GL_NORMALIZE);
        glDisable(GL_CULL_FACE);
}
```

**Listing 6.3** drawObstacle-Method

```
- (void) drawObstacle {
    Tex *tex = [[GameManager getInstance] getTex: @"obstacle.png"
                                     isImage: YES];
    GLuint textureID = [tex getTextureID];

    //data come from obj file,
    //converted with www.qioo.de/objformatter/
    GLfloat vertices[] = {
        17.474174, -0.120721, -9.998633, 14.994154, 3.820796,
        -8.566791, 10.981397,...
    };

    GLfloat textureCoords[] = {
        0.462371, 0.457327, 0.000000, 0.366348, 0.421955, 0.000000,
        0.274115, 0.367637,...
    };

    GLfloat normals[] = {
        0.469522, -0.010598, -0.882857, 0.423198, 0.532556, -0.732999,
        -0.160498,...
    };

    GLushort faces[] = {
        34, 1, 0, 0, 38, 34, 2, 60, 61, 62, 35, 2, 23, 3, 63, 23, 64,
        65, 21, 3, 23, 20, 4, 3,...
    };

    //number of array elements
    //int verticesLength = sizeof(vertices)/sizeof(GLfloat);
    int facesLength = sizeof(faces)/sizeof(GLushort);

    //render obj model
    glEnable(GL_TEXTURE_2D);//all surfaces are now textured
    glEnableClientState(GL_NORMAL_ARRAY);//activate normal arrays
```

```
    glEnable(GL_NORMALIZE);

    glEnable(GL_CULL_FACE);//ignore invisible faces
    glCullFace(GL_BACK);

    glVertexPointer(3, GL_FLOAT, 0, vertices);
    glBindTexture(GL_TEXTURE_2D, textureID);
    glTexCoordPointer(3, GL_FLOAT, 0, textureCoords);
    glNormalPointer(GL_FLOAT, 0, normals);

    glColor4f(1, 1, 1, 1);//no extra color

    //matrix operations
    glPushMatrix();
    glTranslatef(0, 0, -100);
    static int angle = 0; angle + = 2;
    glRotatef(angle, 1, 1, 1);
    glDrawElements(GL_TRIANGLES, facesLength, GL_UNSIGNED_SHORT,
    faces);
    glPopMatrix();

    //clean-up
    glDisable(GL_TEXTURE_2D);
    glDisable(GL_NORMALIZE);
    glDisable(GL_CULL_FACE);
}
```

Of course, it makes sense to write an importer that reads in an Obj file directly from the resources folder, but that would mean that we have already decided on the Obj format; here we want instead to show a universal way of proceeding.

Now that we have integrated and displayed the data of the 3D model, we note that the obstacle model is to be found *before* the asteroid model. Both models do not move, but rather rotate about the xyz-axes. What if we could fly through both objects? Instead of moving the models toward the viewer with glTranslatef() (corresponding optically to flying through), it would be more elegant if we could change the camera position and move ourselves forward with the camera—in first-person perspective, as it were.

## ▌ 6.10  First-Person Perspective: Setting and Deploying the Camera

Every reasonable 3D API has an implementation of a camera function. For OpenGL as well there exists such a function, though it is outsourced to the GLU library and the gluLookAt() method. The reason for this is clear: The implementation of a camera takes place purely in software, and since OpenGL is set up as a hardware interface, the implementation of such functionality is not really suited to the concept. There is also the fact that a variety of implementations are possible and, depending on the concrete situation, the type of implementation can have an effect on performance.

Since the GLU library is unavailable for the mobile variant of OpenGL, we must take care of the implementation ourselves. Beginning with iOS 5, developers have an alternative in the GLKit.

By a camera we understand the eye of the viewer, which can be located at various places in our 3D world and can look in various directions. We must satisfy two criteria:

1. The camera should be able to be placed at any xyz-position.

2. From that position, we would like to fix the viewing direction in the x-, y-, and z-directions.

Moreover, the position and the viewing direction should be able to be changed at each frame so that we can call the camera method over and over with various values. In this way, all perspectives that are typical of games can be realized—from first-person perspective, in which the camera represents the viewer, to third-person perspective, in which the camera is slightly offset behind the game figure.

These requirements can be worked out mathematically with matrix operations; the idea is to transform the entire 3D scene in such a way that the coordinate origin is shifted. Thus, instead of the camera moving through the scene, it is the 3D objects that are moving.

The implementation of such a camera is a typical application in 3D mathematics, and therefore you can find a number of implementations on the Internet. We will orient ourselves here with an algorithm that is taken from the free Mesa 3D graphics library (*http://www.mesa3d.org*).

Listing 6.4 Camera Implementation

```
- (void) setCameraX: (GLfloat) camX
           cameraY: (GLfloat) camY
           cameraZ: (GLfloat) camZ
           lookAtX: (GLfloat) atX
           lookAtY: (GLfloat) atY
           lookAtZ: (GLfloat) atZ {

    glLoadIdentity();

    GLfloat matrix[16];//multiplication matrix

    //Vektoren
    GLfloat forward[3];//viewing direction
    GLfloat upward[3];//normal to the viewing direction
    GLfloat sideward[3];//normal to the plane of forward and upward

    //camera rotation, standard setting is "stationary"
    upward[0] = 0;//x
    upward[1] = 1;//y
    upward[2] = 0;//z
    //[self normalizeVector: upward];//if upward, no unit vector

    //determine forward vector from camera position and viewing
    direction
```

```
forward[0] = camX - atX;
forward[1] = camY - atY;
forward[2] = camZ - atZ;
[self normalizeVector: forward];

//sideward results from the cross product:
//upward vector x forward vector
sideward[0] =  upward[1] * forward[2] - upward[2] * forward[1];
sideward[1] = -upward[0] * forward[2] + upward[2] * forward[0];
sideward[2] =  upward[0] * forward[1] - upward[1] * forward[0];

//recompute upward from forward vector x sideward vector
upward[0] =  forward[1] * sideward[2] - forward[2] * sideward[1];
upward[1] = -forward[0] * sideward[2] + forward[2] * sideward[0];
upward[2] =  forward[0] * sideward[1] - forward[1] * sideward[0];

[self normalizeVector: sideward];
[self normalizeVector: forward];

//create 4*4 multiplication matrix
matrix[0] = sideward[0];
matrix[1] = sideward[1];
matrix[2] = sideward[2];
matrix[3] = 0;

matrix[4] = upward[0];
matrix[5] = upward[1];
matrix[6] = upward[2];
matrix[7] = 0;

matrix[8] = forward[0];
matrix[9] = forward[1];
matrix[10] = forward[2];
matrix[11] = 0;

matrix[12] = 0;
matrix[13] = 0;
matrix[14] = 0;
matrix[15] = 1;

//shift the entire "world"
glMultMatrixf(matrix);

//"position" camera
glTranslatef(-camX, -camY, -camZ);
}

- (void) normalizeVector: (GLfloat [3]) v {
    //length of the vector
    float length = sqrt(v[0] * v[0] + v[1] * v[1] + v[2] * v[2]);

    //normalize to unit length
    if (length ! = 0) {
        v[0] /= length;
        v[1] /= length;
        v[2] /= length;
    }
}
}
```

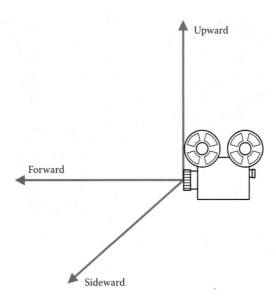

Upward

Forward

Sideward

**Figure 6.16** Camera with the vectors forward, upward, and sideward.

Since we have to normalize vectors repeatedly, we have added the auxiliary function `normalizeVector:`. We add both methods to the `GameManager` (Figure 6.16).

From the camera position and viewing direction we obtain, if we assume an upward camera position (`upward`), a plane that is spanned by two vectors (`forward` and `upward`). The cross product gives us a vector perpendicular to this plane (`sideward`). After all three vectors have been normalized, we can finally use the `glMultMatrix()` function to multiply the current matrix by the matrix formed from the three unit vectors and translate opposite to the current camera position. The camera is thereby established, and the world has been moved to a new position from the camera's point of view.

As you can tell, only a single matrix calculation comes into play here; you can look up the terms cross product, matrix, and so on in any book on linear algebra. For us at this point, what is important is that we apply this method. The use of the new method is fortunately very straightforward:

```
- (void) playGame {
    static float z = 0;
    z - = 0.5;
    [self setCameraX: 0 cameraY: 0 cameraZ: z
            lookAtX: 0 lookAtY: 0 lookAtZ: z-1];

    [self drawAsteroid];
    [self drawObstacle];
}
```

The camera's xyz-values determine the position, while we specify the viewing direction with `lookAtX:lookAtY:lookAtZ:`; the xyz-values represent, on the one hand, a vector and, on the other, a point in space on which the viewer's eye is fixed. We use the `playGame` method to change the z-position of the camera continually, flying along

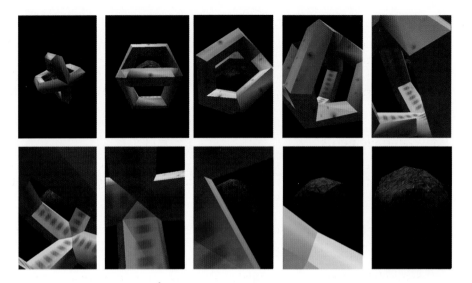

Figure 6.17 Screen shots: flight through the obstacle and the asteroid.

the z-axis into the screen. The viewing direction is determined by z-1, so we are always looking in the direction of flight. In any case, it makes no difference whether you call the camera before or after the objects are rendered. The camera shifts the entire world in relation to itself. Here "world" means the coordinate system and everything that is in it or not yet in it (Figure 6.17).

# ■ 6.11  Spaceflight: A 3D Game Is Born

We now have assembled the necessary ingredients for 3D games (camera, 3D models, textures, transformations); now let us create some action! Our next 3D game project will emphasize, among other things, how you can navigate a player through the 3D world in first-person perspective. Various objects are to be placed in the world. Some can be collected, others must be avoided, and still others should be destroyed with a laser bullet. With this game plan, we can show the mechanisms that are valid for almost all types of 3D games: positioning of elements in three-dimensional space, setting up a camera, and collision checking with the elements of the 3D world—in other words, precisely what we have already learned. In addition, what we have to consider here is the proper interaction of these elements. So let us not waste any time; we begin by defining the general framework for our game.

## 6.11.1  Game Concept: Spaceflight

*As the pilot of a reconnaissance spacecraft you have the task of clearing the enemy satellites from an asteroid belt in front of the moon of the planet Jarson. Your spaceship is equipped with unlimited firepower. You must avoid collisions with the asteroids and also with the satellites. Your craft can withstand three hits; a fourth terminates your mission. If you pick up energy capsules, you can undo previous damage to your spaceship.*

## 6.11.2 Control

The game is controlled from a first-person perspective. The screen is divided diagonally into four regions and, by touching a region, the spaceship can be steered upward, downward, to the right, and to the left. Such motion takes place without rotation parallel to the xy-axes. The spaceship automatically flies forward at a constant speed (along the negative z-axis).

## 6.11.3 Game Elements

- **Player:** The player takes over the control of the camera perspective and the representation of the cockpit as a 2D billboard graphic that is aligned parallel to the xy-plane and handles sustained fire.

- **Bullet:** Laser bullets are fired at regular intervals by the player to the right and left beneath its current position. The direction of flight is parallel to the z-axis.

- **Asteroid:** The asteroid is generated randomly in space just in front of the zFar clipping pane as a function of the player's position. All asteroids move toward the player along the z-axis.

- **Spy satellite:** This must be destroyed by the player with laser bullets.

- **Energy capsules:** Capsules can be gathered to repair recent damage.

- **Text messages:** Damage is announced by text message, as are other announcements during the game.

Let us begin with the implementation. We construct the game on the basis of the previous section, so the framework already has the texture class, a camera, and textures for the asteroids and satellites.

We model the laser bullets with 3ds Max based on a stretched pyramidal form without texture. For the energy capsules, we choose the basic shape "capsule." We export the model in Obj format, also without texture (Figure 6.18).

The two files `bullet.obj` and `capsule.obj` can be found in the project folder (the complete project has the name "Spaceflight").

By the way, if you are not working with 3ds Max, the Obj files can be imported via almost any other 3D editor and then customized as necessary; the Obj format contains the necessary data, so any editor should be able to cope with these files.

Our framework has the following (familiar) classes:

- `MyGameAppDelegate`

- `MainView`

- `GameManager`

- `Tex`

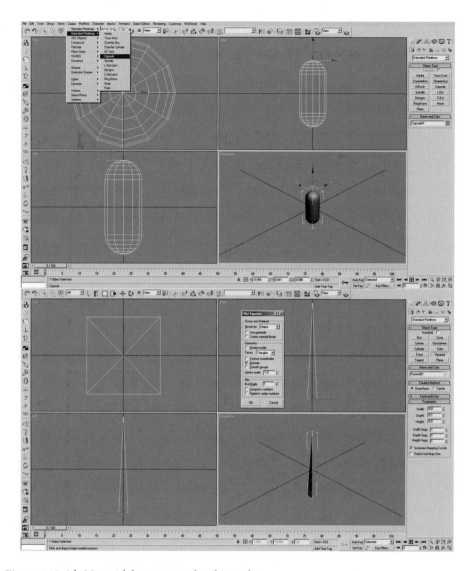

Figure 6.18  3ds Max with laser pyramid and capsule.

In addition to the `Sprite` class, which we want to use as the superclass for all 3D objects, we shall create the following derived classes:

- **Sprite:** parent class of all sprites

- **Player:** the player

- **Bullet:** laser bullet

- **Asteroid:** spherical indestructible object

- **Obstacle:** spy satellite

- **Capsule:** energy capsule

- **Text:** all text messages output to the screen as textures; for ease of use, `Text` will also be realized as a `Sprite`

This results in the following `Sprite` constants, which we can now place in the header of the otherwise empty `Sprite` class.

```
//sprite types
enum types {
    PLAYER,
    ASTEROID,
    OBSTACLE,
    CAPSULE,
    BULLET,
    TEXT
};
```

Then we add a vertex structure to the `Sprite` class:

```
struct Vertex {
    float x, y, z;
};
typedef struct Vertex Vertex;
```

The reason is that all 3D sprites have a position (or a directional vector or a rotational vector) in 3D space. Since here we can no longer work with the `CGPoint` structure, we now create a structure for the xyz-values.

For example, we could create a new vertex structure as follows:

```
Vertex position;
position.x = 20; position.y = 111; position.z = -45871;
```

With these preparations completed, we can now begin to implement the game concept in the `GameManager`. Then we shall fill the `Sprite` classes with life.

First, we complete the manager using the `Sprite` control that we already used for the 2D OGL shooter; 3D objects can be conveniently managed in this way for the third dimension as well:

```
NSMutableArray *sprites; //active sprites
NSMutableArray *newSprites; //new sprites
NSMutableArray *destroyableSprites; //inactive sprites
NSMutableDictionary* dictionary; //resource hash table
```

In the `preloader` method, we load into memory the textures to be used later:

```
- (void) preloader {
    sprites = [[NSMutableArray alloc] initWithCapacity:20];
    newSprites = [[NSMutableArray alloc] initWithCapacity:20];
    destroyableSprites = [[NSMutableArray alloc] initWithCapacity:20];

    //preload OGL textures
    [self getTex: @"asteroid.png" isImage: YES];
```

```
[self getTex: @"obstacle.png" isImage: YES];
[self getTex: @"cockpit.png" isImage: YES];

[self setOGLProjection];
state = LOAD_GAME;
}
```

And with the loadGame method, which is invoked before every game is launched, we ensure that outer space is supplied with its initial complement of randomly generated game elements:

```
- (void) loadGame {
    [sprites removeAllObjects];
    [newSprites removeAllObjects];
    [destroyableSprites removeAllObjects];
    [self createSprite: PLAYER];

    //start state
    for (int i = 0; i<20; i++) {
        [self createSprite: ASTEROID];
    }
    for (int i = 0; i<10; i++) {
        [self createSprite: OBSTACLE];
    }
    for (int i = 0; i<5; i++) {
        [self createSprite: CAPSULE];
    }
}
```

For this game, we can use a very simply constructed createSprite: method signature; the specification of the type to be generated suffices since, this time, the assignment of individual characteristics is handled later by setters and getters. Parameters such as position, speed, and rotation are generated before the initialization of the sprite:

```
- (id) createSprite: (int) type {
    Player *p = [self getPlayer];
    Vertex posPlayer = [p getPos];

    Vertex pos;
    pos.x = [self getRndBetween: posPlayer.x - zFar/4
                            and: posPlayer.x + zFar/4];
    pos.y = [self getRndBetween: posPlayer.y - zFar/2
                            and: posPlayer.y + zFar/2];
    pos.z = [self getRndBetween: posPlayer.z + zFar+10
                            and: posPlayer.z + zFar+50];

    Vertex speed;
    speed.x = 0; speed.y = 0; speed.z = 0;

    Vertex rotation;
    rotation.x = 1; rotation.y = 1; rotation.z = 1;

    if (type = = ASTEROID) {
        Asteroid *asteroid = [[Asteroid alloc] init];
        [asteroid setPos: pos];
```

```
      speed.z = -20;
      [asteroid setSpeed: speed];
      [asteroid setRotationStep: [self getRndBetween: -10 and: 10]
                  aroundAxis: rotation];
      [newSprites addObject: asteroid];
      [asteroid release];
      return asteroid;
   } else if (type = = OBSTACLE) {
      Obstacle *obstacle = [[Obstacle alloc] init];
      [obstacle setPos: pos];
      [obstacle setSpeed: speed];
      [obstacle setRotationStep: [self getRndBetween: -5 and: 5]
                  aroundAxis: rotation];
      [newSprites addObject: obstacle];
      [obstacle release];
      return obstacle;
   } else if (type = = CAPSULE) {
      Capsule *capsule = [[Capsule alloc] init];
      [capsule setPos: pos];
      speed.z = 2;
      [capsule setSpeed: speed];
      [capsule setRotationStep: [self getRndBetween: -10 and: 10]
                  aroundAxis: rotation];
      [newSprites addObject: capsule];
      [capsule release];
      return capsule;
   } else if (type = = PLAYER) {
      Player *player = [[Player alloc] init];
      [newSprites addObject: player];
      [player release];
      return player;
   } else if (type = = BULLET) {
      //parameters for a bullet
      pos.y = posPlayer.y-40;
      pos.z = posPlayer.z;
      speed.z = 100;

      //left bullet
      Bullet *bulletL = [[Bullet alloc] init];
      pos.x = posPlayer.x+20;
      [bulletL setPos: pos];
      [bulletL setSpeed: speed];
      [newSprites addObject: bulletL];
      [bulletL release];

      //right bullet
      Bullet *bulletR = [[Bullet alloc] init];
      pos.x = posPlayer.x-20;
      [bulletR setPos: pos];
      [bulletR setSpeed: speed];
      [newSprites addObject: bulletR];
      [bulletR release];
   } else {
      NSLog(@"ERROR: unknown sprite type:%i", type);
      return nil;
   }
   return nil;
}
```

In addition, we obtain the current player instance, which we have already created in the loadGame method, using a getPlayer method:

```
- (Player *) getPlayer {
    for (Sprite *sprite in sprites) {
        if ([sprite isActive]) {
            if ([sprite getType] = = PLAYER) {
                return (Player *) sprite;
            }
        }
    }
    return nil;
}
```

We need the current player instance within the createSprite: method to determine the current position of the player. When we have it, we create a new Vertex structure with random xyz-values. (For the generation of the player itself, this is unnecessary; recall that calls to nil are allowed in Objective-C.)

The z-value of a sprite should lie at the end of the visible region. This is derived from the z-position of the player and the zFar distance plus a random value:

```
pos.z = [self getRndBetween: posPlayer.z + zFar+10
                        and: posPlayer.z + zFar+50];
```

We proceed similarly for the xy-position; here, we have no clear limit to the visible region and we divide the region on both sides proportionally to zFar.

If you wish to examine the generation mechanism of the current sprite more closely, then set the following properties:

- **Asteroid:** moves with a speed of 20 units along the z-axis toward the player. The speed of rotation is between –10° and 10° per frame.

- **Satellite/obstacle:** is a fixed position. Rotational velocity is between –5 and 5 degrees.

- **Energy capsule:** moves with a velocity of two units along the z-axis in the same direction as the player. To reach a capsule, the player has to move faster than the capsule. Rotational velocity is between –10° and 10°.

- **Player:** in the createSprite: method, no parameters are set for the player, since there is, after all, only one Player instance.

- **Laser bullet:** the starting position is 40 units below the player. The velocity is 100 units in the same direction as the player along the z-axis. Two shots are always fired, both of which are 20 units away along the x-axis from the player's midpoint, one to the right and one to the left.

Touch handling takes place in the GameManager class, as was the case in our earlier games; the touch point is passed to the setTouch: and touchEnded: methods of the Player class.

The game has three states (LOAD_GAME, PLAY_GAME, GAME_OVER), which are handled as follows in the drawStatesWithFrame: method:

```
- (void) drawStatesWithFrame: (CGRect) frame {
    W = frame.size.width;
    H = frame.size.height;
    switch (state) {
        case LOAD_GAME:
            [self loadGame];
            [self createOGLText: @"GOOD LUCK"
                        offsetX: 2
                        offsetY: 2
                     selfDestroy: YES];
            state = PLAY_GAME;
            break;
        case PLAY_GAME:
            [self playGame];
            break;
        case GAME_OVER:
            [self playGame];
            break;
        default: NSLog(@"ERROR: unknown game state:%i", state);
            break;
    }
}
```

The playGame method deals only with the continual creation of new sprites, for which it uses the modulo operator. Moreover, the familiar manageSprites and renderSprites methods are called:

```
- (void) playGame {
    timer++;

    if (timer% 5 = = 0) {
        [self createSprite: ASTEROID];
    }
    if (timer% 20 = = 0) {
        [self createSprite: OBSTACLE];
    }
    if (timer% 80 = = 0) {
        [self createSprite: CAPSULE];
    }

    [self manageSprites];
    [self renderSprites];
}
```

The viewport changes with a change in the player's position, which in turn corresponds to the camera position and thereby represents the center of the screen:

```
- (Vertex) getViewportOrigin {
    Vertex v = [[self getPlayer] getPos];
    return v;
}
```

```objc
- (void) checkSprite: (Sprite *) sprite {
    Player *player = [self getPlayer];
    if ([sprite getType] = = ASTEROID || [sprite getType] = = OBSTACLE) {
        if ([player checkColWithSprite: sprite]) {
            [self createOGLText: @"DAMAGED!!"
                        offsetX: 2
                        offsetY: 1
                     selfDestroy: YES];
            [sprite hit];
            [player hit];
        }
    }
    if ([sprite getType] = = OBSTACLE) {
        for (Sprite *bullet in sprites) {
            if ([bullet getType] = = BULLET) {
                if ([bullet checkColWithSprite: sprite]) {
                    [self createOGLText: @"DESTROYED"
                                offsetX: 2
                                offsetY: 1
                             selfDestroy: YES];
                    [sprite hit];
                    [bullet hit];
                }
            }
        }
    }
    if ([sprite getType] = = CAPSULE) {
        if ([player checkColWithSprite: sprite]) {
            [self createOGLText: @"GOOOOOD!!"
                        offsetX: 2
                        offsetY: 1
                     selfDestroy: YES];
            [sprite hit];
            [player hitCapsule];
        }
    }
}
```

All asteroids and satellites (`Obstacle`) are checked for collision with the player; collision with an energy capsule (`Capsule`) is checked separately. All `Bullet` instances are in turn checked for collision with a satellite, since only the satellites can be destroyed.

For displaying text messages, we use the new `createOGLText:offsetX:offset Y:selfDestroy:` method:

```objc
- (id) createOGLText: (NSString *) txt
            offsetX: (float) x
            offsetY: (float) y
         selfDestroy: (bool) destroy {

    Text *text = [[Text alloc] init];

    [text setText: txt
        offsetX: x
        offsetY: y
     selfDestroy: destroy];
```

```
[newSprites addObject: text];
[text release];
return text;
}
```

Since we have realized text output as a sprite this time, this method serves simply as a helper for a simplified generation of text messages. The Text is derived from the Sprite class, since the text is to be rendered to the display in relation to the viewpoint origin; nevertheless, a Text is a texture without physical extension but with a fixed position in space. This gives us optionally the possibility of employing additional text effects—for example, having the text slowly vanish into the depths of space, such as you may have seen in the famous *Star Wars* introduction. So that we can more easily leave the Text sprites to the release handling of the sprite manager, the destroy parameter (when true) ensures that the text will be automatically deactivated after a timeout defined in the class.

We do this with all texts, with one exception: The "GAME OVER" announcement is displayed permanently—that is, until the player begins a new game; meanwhile, the loadGame method clears all the sprites from memory.

Since we create a Text object as a texture and know only the texture width rather than the actual width of the text in 3D space, we can adjust the center position of the text by means of the offsetXY parameter.*

To prevent a text message from being hidden behind other sprites, we ensure in the renderSprites method that the text is rendered only after the other sprites, just as we did for the Player in our previous game.

Note that we have to create the Text only once and then put it in the Sprite pipeline using the preceding method. We shall look at what precisely goes on in the Text class when we introduce the game elements (= sprites).

The last adjustment that we make in the GameManager class relates to the setLight method. Here, we add a second light source in order to illuminate the cockpit from behind:

```
glEnable(GL_LIGHT1);
GLfloat color1[] = {1, 1, 1, 1};
glLightfv(GL_LIGHT1, GL_DIFFUSE, color1);
GLfloat light_position1[] = {0, 0, -1, 0};//light comes from behind
glLightfv(GL_LIGHT1, GL_POSITION, light_position1);
```

The cockpit is simply a plane surface with no z-depth. Since the first light source shines constantly on the scene from above, the cockpit would otherwise be difficult to see.

## 6.11.4 Three-Dimensional Sprites

We have already seen in the GameManager class that we manage our 3D model for the Spaceflight game as Sprite objects. Therefore, we must now adapt the Sprite class for use in 3D space. First, let us introduce the complete class:

---

* The text solution implemented here demonstrates only a possible approach to creating texts with OpenGL ES. For more frequent use of texts, you would certainly be better off using individually rendered bitmap fonts (also as a texture), thereby assembling arbitrary texts from individual letters. Creating such a text-rendering engine would, however, exceed the scope of this book.

## Listing 6.5  Sprite.h

```objc
#import <UIKit/UIKit.h>
#import <OpenGLES/ES1/gl.h>
#import "Tex.h"

//sprite types
enum types {
    PLAYER,
    ASTEROID,
    OBSTACLE,
    CAPSULE,
    BULLET,
    TEXT
};

struct Vertex {
    float x, y, z;
};
typedef struct Vertex Vertex;

@interface Sprite : NSObject {
    GLuint textureID;  //texture ID
    Vertex pos;        //current xyz-position
    Vertex speed;      //movement per frame in the xyz-direction
    Vertex rotation;   //rotation about the xyz axes
    float angle;       //current rotation angle
    float angleStep;   //change in the angle per frame
    float radius;      //radius of the bounding sphere
    int type;          //sprite type
    bool active;       //inactive sprites are deleted by the GameManager
    bool autoDestroy;  //!tolerance limit -> active = false


    //arrays with.obj data
    GLfloat *vertices;
    GLfloat *textureCoords;
    GLfloat *normals;
    GLushort *faces;

    //length of arrays
    int verticesLength;
    int facesLength;
}

- (void) additionalSetup;
- (int) getType;
- (Vertex) getPos;
- (float) getRadius;
- (void) setPos: (Vertex) newPos;
- (void) setSpeed: (Vertex) newSpeed;
- (void) setRotationStep: (float) newAngleStep
            aroundAxis: (Vertex) newRotation;
- (bool) isActive;
```

```
- (void) draw;
- (void) move;
- (void) setColor;
- (void) renderSprite;
- (void) hit;
- (bool) checkColWithSprite: (Sprite *) sprite;
- (void) setVertices: (GLfloat *) verticesObjData
                size: (int) sizeVerts
       setTexCoords: (GLfloat *) textureCoordsObjData
                size: (int) sizeTex
         setNormals: (GLfloat *) normalsObjData
                size: (int) sizeNorms
           setFaces: (GLushort *) facesObjData
                size: (int) sizeFaces;
@end
```

## Listing 6.6 Sprite.m

```objc
#import "Sprite.h"
#import "GameManager.h"

@implementation Sprite

-(id) init {
    if (self = [super init]) {
        textureID = -1;
        pos.x = 0;
        pos.y = 0;
        pos.z = 0;
        speed.x = 0;
        speed.y = 0;
        speed.z = 0;
        rotation.x = 0;
        rotation.y = 0;
        rotation.z = 0;
        angle = 0;
        angleStep = 0;
        radius = 1;
        type = -1;
        active = true;
        autoDestroy = true;
        [self additionalSetup];
    }
    return self;
}

- (void) additionalSetup {
    //override for individual setup
}
```

```
- (int) getType {
    return type;
}

- (Vertex) getPos {
    return pos;
}

- (void) setPos: (Vertex) newPos {
    pos = newPos;
}

- (float) getRadius {
    return radius;
}

- (void) setSpeed: (Vertex) newSpeed {
    speed = newSpeed;
}

- (void) setRotationStep: (float) newAngleStep
           aroundAxis: (Vertex) newRotation {
    angleStep = newAngleStep;
    rotation = newRotation;
}

- (bool) isActive {
    return active;
}

- (void) draw {
    if (active) {
        [self renderSprite];
    }
}

- (void) renderSprite {
    glEnable(GL_NORMALIZE);
    glEnable(GL_CULL_FACE);
    glCullFace(GL_BACK);

    if (textureID > 0) {
        glEnable(GL_TEXTURE_2D);//all surfaces are now textured
        glBindTexture(GL_TEXTURE_2D, textureID);
        glTexCoordPointer(3, GL_FLOAT, 0, textureCoords);
    }
    glVertexPointer(3, GL_FLOAT, 0, vertices);
    glNormalPointer(GL_FLOAT, 0, normals);

    [self setColor];

    glPushMatrix();
    [self move];
    if (facesLength = = 0) {
        glDrawArrays(GL_TRIANGLE_STRIP, 0, verticesLength/3);
    } else {
```

```
        glDrawElements(GL_TRIANGLES, facesLength, GL_UNSIGNED_SHORT,
            faces);
    }
    glPopMatrix();

    glDisable(GL_TEXTURE_2D);
    glDisable(GL_NORMALIZE);
    glDisable(GL_CULL_FACE);
}

- (void) setColor {
    //override for individual colors
    glColor4f(1, 1, 1, 1);
}

- (void) move {
    pos.x + = speed.x;
    pos.y + = speed.y;
    pos.z + = speed.z;
    angle + = angleStep;

    glTranslatef(pos.x, pos.y, pos.z);
    glRotatef(angle, rotation.x, rotation.y, rotation.z);

    if (autoDestroy) {
        Player * p = [[GameManager getInstance] getPlayer];
        Vertex posPlayer = [p getPos];
        if (pos.z < posPlayer.z) {
            active = false;//sprite behind the player
        }
    }
}

- (void) hit {
    //override for individual collision handling
    active = false;
}

//collision sphere <-> sphere
- (bool) checkColWithSprite: (Sprite *) sprite {

    //sphere 1
    //midpoint: MP1 (x1, y1, z1), Radius: r1
    Vertex v = [sprite getPos];
    float x1 = v.x;
    float y1 = v.y;
    float z1 = v.z;
    float r1 = [sprite getRadius];

    //sphere 2:
    //midpoint: MP2 (x2, y2, z2), Radius: r2
    float x2 = pos.x;
    float y2 = pos.y;
    float z2 = pos.z;
    float r2 = radius;
```

```
    if (((x2 - x1) * (x2 - x1) + (y2 - y1) * (y2 - y1)
        + (z2 - z1) * (z2 - z1))
        < (r1 + r2) * (r1 + r2)) {
        return true;
    }

    return false;
}

- (void) setVertices: (GLfloat *) verticesObjData
              size: (int) sizeVerts
       setTexCoords: (GLfloat *) textureCoordsObjData
              size: (int) sizeTex
        setNormals: (GLfloat *) normalsObjData
              size: (int) sizeNorms
          setFaces: (GLushort *) facesObjData
              size: (int) sizeFaces {

    verticesLength = sizeVerts/sizeof(GLfloat);
    facesLength = sizeFaces/sizeof(GLushort);

    //create local arrays as members
    vertices = malloc (sizeVerts);
    memcpy(vertices, verticesObjData, sizeVerts);

    textureCoords = malloc (sizeTex);
    memcpy(textureCoords, textureCoordsObjData, sizeTex);

    normals = malloc (sizeNorms);
    memcpy(normals, normalsObjData, sizeNorms);

    faces = malloc (sizeFaces);
    memcpy(faces, facesObjData, sizeFaces);
}

- (void) dealloc {
    [super dealloc];
}

@end
```

The class contains little that is new; we have merely adapted it to our new requirements for managing 3D models. Therefore, all sprites now have a Vertex structure (as already shown) for storing the position (pos), velocity (speed), and rotation axis (rotation). In addition, for rotation we have the current angle (angle) and the amount by which the angle is changed each frame (angleStep).

Since we are now moving the rendering process for the texture into the Sprite class, we store in the class only the texture ID instead of a Tex instance.

In addition to a texture, a 3D model also has four arrays for the vertices of the model (vertices), the texture coordinates (textureCoords), the normals (normals), and the faces (faces).

If you look at the renderSprite method, you will see that we have made the rendering process somewhat more flexible by means of two if statements—if, for example, a model has no texture coordinates (`Capsule`, `Bullet`) or no faces (`Text`). Since we use at least one light source, the model must have a `normals` array. Therefore, the client state `GL_NORMAL_ARRAY`, just like the `GL_VERTEX_ARRAY`, will be permanently activated in the `setOGLProjection` method.

In analogy with our previous examples, we have placed the transformation of the models in the `move` method. Here, a model is rotated about itself and shifted in the xyz-direction. Moreover, the method checks whether a sprite can be deactivated if it has left the visible region. Since all sprites are either fixed or move toward the player along the z-axis, we merely check whether the sprite is behind the player's current z-position (here we can ignore the `zNear` pane):

```
if (autoDestroy) {
    Player * p = [[GameManager getInstance] getPlayer];
    Vertex posPlayer = [p getPos];
    if (pos.z < posPlayer.z) {
        active = false;
    }
}
```

To check for a collision between 3D models, this time we implement a sphere <-> sphere collision check. We have already discussed the algorithm for this. To carry out the check, we need only the radius of an imaginary sphere around the sprite and the current position. This radius is an approximate value that we will assign individually to a sprite with our formatter script.

Finally, take note of the `setVertices:size:setTexCoords:size:setNormals:size:setFaces:size:` method. As we shall soon see, we shall place the model data within the appropriate `Sprite`. Since these are C arrays, we cannot directly initialize the member already declared in the header. Therefore, we pass the (at most) four arrays via this setter, taking care to note that C arrays are passed via call by reference, while the setter method contains only a pointer to the first element of the array. The length of the array must therefore be passed explicitly (`size`). With the `malloc()` function, we set the memory region for the `Sprite` member and use the `memcpy()` function to copy the array, which is created only locally in the subclass.

## 6.11.5 The Implementation of the Game Elements

Using the `Asteroid` class as a first example, let us see how a `Sprite` class and one of its child classes interact.

---

**Listing 6.7** Asteroid.h

```
#import "Sprite.h"

@interface Asteroid : Sprite {
}

@end
```

---

## Listing 6.8 Asteroid.m

```objc
#import "Asteroid.h"
#import "GameManager.h"

@implementation Asteroid

/*
 Vertex x-Range from: -23.678974 to: 23.264721
 Vertex y-Range from: -21.068602 to: 21.969690
 Vertex z-Range from: -20.450109 to: 17.863581

 Suggested radius for bounding sphere: 22.032924333333
*/

- (void) additionalSetup {
    type = ASTEROID;
    Tex *tex = [[GameManager getInstance] getTex: @"asteroid.png"
                                        isImage: YES];
    textureID = [tex getTextureID];
    radius = 22.032924333333;

    //data come from an obj file,
    //converted with www.qioo.de/objformatter/
    GLfloat verticesObjData[] = {
        -0.207126, -0.066316, 17.863581, 23.264721, -1.502157,
        -0.192209, -0.207126,...
    };

    GLfloat textureCoordsObjData[] = {
        0.511933, 0.499667, 0.000000, 0.753190, 0.915463, 0.000000,
        0.054368, 0.673368,...
    };

    GLfloat normalsObjData[] = {
        0.003697, -0.091516, 0.995797, 0.960635, -0.009128, 0.277662,
        0.000000,...
    };

    GLushort facesObjData[] = {
        0, 6, 8, 56, 57, 30, 56, 30, 58, 58, 30, 59, 7, 1, 22, 57, 60,
        30, 30, 60, 61, 30,...
    };

    [self setVertices: verticesObjData
                 size: sizeof(verticesObjData)
           setTexCoords: textureCoordsObjData
                 size: sizeof(textureCoordsObjData)
            setNormals: normalsObjData
                 size: sizeof(normalsObjData)
              setFaces: facesObjData
                 size: sizeof(facesObjData)];
}

@end
```

In its one method `additionalSetup`, the `Asteroid` class sets only the type, the texture ID, and the radius. Then, the four arrays are filled with content using the data from the Obj file.

The `Obstacle` for the satellites is constructed just as simply.

---

Listing 6.9  Obstacle.h

```
#import "Sprite.h"

@interface Obstacle : Sprite {
}

@end
```

---

Listing 6.10  Obstacle.m

```
#import "Obstacle.h"
#import "GameManager.h"

@implementation Obstacle

/*
 Vertex x-Range from: -17.474178 to: 17.474174
 Vertex y-Range from: -17.594904 to: 17.353456
 Vertex z-Range from: -18.822365 to: 18.679285

 Suggested radius for bounding sphere: 17.963815666667
 */

- (void) additionalSetup {
    type = OBSTACLE;
    Tex *tex = [[GameManager getInstance] getTex: @"obstacle.png"
                                        isImage: YES];
    textureID = [tex getTextureID];
    radius = 17.963815666667;

    //Data come from the obj file,
    //converted with www.qioo.de/objformatter/
    GLfloat verticesObjData[] = {
        17.474174, -0.120721, -9.998633, 14.994154, 3.820796,
        -8.566791, 10.981397,...
    };

    GLfloat textureCoordsObjData[] = {
        0.462371, 0.457327, 0.000000, 0.366348, 0.421955, 0.000000,
        0.274115, 0.367637,...
    };
```

```
    GLfloat normalsObjData[] = {
        0.469522, -0.010598, -0.882857, 0.423198, 0.532556, -0.732999,
        -0.160498,...
    };

    GLushort facesObjData[] = {
        34, 1, 0, 0, 38, 34, 2, 60, 61, 62, 35, 2, 23, 3, 63, 23, 64,
        65, 21, 3, 23, 20, 4, 3,...
    };

    [self setVertices: verticesObjData
               size: sizeof(verticesObjData)
         setTexCoords: textureCoordsObjData
               size: sizeof(textureCoordsObjData)
         setNormals: normalsObjData
               size: sizeof(normalsObjData)
           setFaces: facesObjData
               size: sizeof(facesObjData)];
}

@end
```

Also, the `Capsule` class, for the energy capsules, holds no further secrets. Note that here we have stored no texture coordinates and have specified the color explicitly via the `setColor` method.

---

**Listing 6.11** Capsule.h

---

```
#import "Sprite.h"

@interface Capsule : Sprite {
}

@end
```

---

**Listing 6.12** Capsule.m

---

```
#import "Capsule.h"
#import "GameManager.h"

@implementation Capsule

/*
Vertex x-Range from: -3.6 to: 3.5
Vertex y-Range from: -3.5 to: 3.6
Vertex z-Range from: -8.7 to: 8.6
```

```
Suggested radius for bounding sphere: 5.3
*/

- (void) additionalSetup {
    type = CAPSULE;
    radius = 5.3;

    //data come from the obj file,
    //converted with www.qioo.de/objformatter/
    GLfloat verticesObjData[] = {
        -0.1, 0.0, 8.6, 0.9, 0.0, 8.5, 0.7, 0.5, 8.5, 0.4, 0.8, 8.5,
        -0.1, 1.0, 8.5, -0.5,...
    };

    GLfloat normalsObjData[] = {
        -0.0, -0.0, 1.0, 0.3, 0.0, 1.0, 0.2, 0.1, 1.0, 0.1, 0.2, 1.0,
        -0.0, 0.3, 1.0, -0.1,...
    };

    GLushort facesObjData[] = {
        0, 1, 2, 0, 2, 3, 0, 3, 4, 0, 4, 5, 0, 5, 6, 0, 6, 7, 0, 7, 8,
        0, 8, 9, 0, 9, 10, 0,...
    };

    [self setVertices: verticesObjData
                 size: sizeof(verticesObjData)
          setTexCoords: nil
                 size: 0
            setNormals: normalsObjData
                 size: sizeof(normalsObjData)
              setFaces: facesObjData
                 size: sizeof(facesObjData)];
}

- (void) setColor {
    glColor4f(0.5, 0.5, 0.5, 1);
}

@end
```

For the Player class, on the other hand, we have to implement a bit more code. We have to place the cockpit precisely on the screen, and we also have to process the touch input and use it to control the camera.

Listing 6.13 Player.h

```
#import "Sprite.h"

@interface Player : Sprite {
    CGPoint touchPoint;
    bool touchAction;
    float speedOffset;
```

```
    int w, h;//dimensions of the cockpit texture
    int hitCnt;//number of hits
    int timer;
}

- (void) setTouch: (CGPoint) p;
- (void) touchEnded;
- (void) hitCapsule;

@end
```

## Listing 6.14 Player.m

```objc
#import "Player.h"
#import "GameManager.h"

@implementation Player

- (void) additionalSetup {
    type = PLAYER;
    Tex *tex = [[GameManager getInstance] getTex: @"cockpit.png"
                                        isImage: YES];
    textureID = [tex getTextureID];
    radius = 15;
    speedOffset = 0;
    hitCnt = 0;

    //do not use the original size, so that the texture can be
       positioned
    //directly in front of the camera (otherwise too big)
    //and maintain aspect ratio at a height of 1
    w = [tex getWidth]/[tex getHeight];
    h = 1;

    GLfloat verticesObjData[] = {//cockpit
        0,   h,  0, //upper left
        w,   h,  0, //upper right
        0,   0,  0, //lower left
        w,   0,  0  //lower right
    };

    GLfloat textureCoordsObjData[] = {
        1, 0, 0, //lower right, warning: y-axis points upward
        0, 0, 0, //lower left
        1, 1, 0, //upper right
        0, 1, 0  //upper left
    };

    GLfloat normalsObjData[] = {
        0, 0, 1, //front
```

```
            0, 0, 1,
            0, 0, 1,
            0, 0, 1
        };

        [self setVertices: verticesObjData
                       size: sizeof(verticesObjData)
            setTexCoords: textureCoordsObjData
                       size: sizeof(textureCoordsObjData)
              setNormals: normalsObjData
                       size: sizeof(normalsObjData)
                 setFaces: nil
                       size: 0];
}

- (void) draw {

    timer++;
    if (timer% 15 = = 0 && [[GameManager getInstance]
            getState] ! = GAME_OVER) {
        [[GameManager getInstance] createSprite: BULLET];
    }

    if (touchAction) {
        speedOffset + = 1;
        if (speedOffset > 10) speedOffset = 10;

        //midpoint M
        int x = W/2;
        int y = H/2;

        //equation of a line y = mx + n, slope m = 1 resp. -1
        int n1 = y - x;
        int n2 = y + x;
        int np1 = touchPoint.y - touchPoint.x;
        int np2 = touchPoint.y + touchPoint.x;

        //the slopes of the midpoint diagonals determine the touch area
        //warning: y-axis is inverted
        if (np1 < n1 && np2 < n2) {pos.y + = speedOffset;}//UP
        if (np1 > n1 && np2 > n2) {pos.y - = speedOffset;}//DOWN
        if (np1 > n1 && np2 < n2) {pos.x + = speedOffset;}//LEFT
        if (np1 < n1 && np2 > n2) {pos.x - = speedOffset;}//RIGHT
    } else {
        speedOffset = 1;
    }

    pos.z+ = 5;//fly forward automatically

    //z+1 -> always look along the z-axis
    [[GameManager getInstance] setCameraX: pos.x
                                   cameraY: pos.y
                                   cameraZ: pos.z
                                   lookAtX: pos.x
                                   lookAtY: pos.y
                                   lookAtZ: pos.z+1];
```

```
        [super renderSprite];//render cockpit texture
}

- (void) move {//position cockpit
    glTranslatef(pos.x - 0.5, pos.y - 0.752, pos.z + 1.59);
}

- (void) hit {
    hitCnt++;
    if (hitCnt = = 3) {
        [[GameManager getInstance] setState: GAME_OVER];
        [[GameManager getInstance] createOGLText: @"GAME OVER"
                                        offsetX: 2.1
                                        offsetY: 2
                                     selfDestroy: NO];

    }
}

- (void) hitCapsule {
    hitCnt- ;
    if (hitCnt < 0) hitCnt = 0;
}

- (void) setTouch: (CGPoint) p {
    touchAction = true;
    touchPoint = p;
}

- (void) touchEnded {
    touchAction = false;
}

@end
```

The cockpit is set up as a billboard over a 2D surface, and therefore we do not need any Obj data here. Nor do we need to specify any faces. For illuminating the cockpit, we should not forget about the normals at each vertex point in the direction of the viewer $(0, 0, 1)$.

The $512 \times 512$ pixel cockpit texture is laid on the 2D model with width and height of one unit each. There is no sense in using the original dimensions of the texture template, which would be much too big and therefore have to be positioned too far from the camera. This would cause them to be hidden by sprites located farther forward along the z-axis.

We accomplish the positioning of the cockpit with the glTranslatef() function in the overwritten move() method, using as reference the current position of the player (pos = origin). Per parameter, we translate the cockpit minimally to align it properly on the display. The amount of the shift depends on the size of the model ($1 \times 1$) and also on the chosen perspective ($45°$ viewing angle).

## 6.11.6  Control

We process touch input (touchPoint) in the draw() method of the Player class. We simply change the player's xy-position and move it continuously forward parallel to

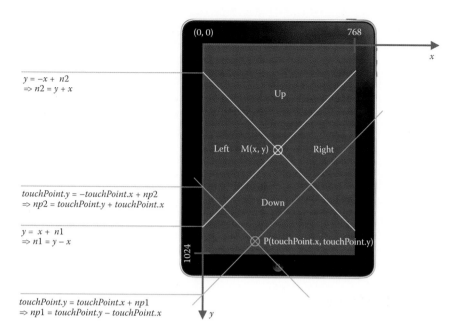

The figure contains the following labels:

(0, 0)    768    x

$y = -x + n2$
$\Rightarrow n2 = y + x$

Up

Left    M(x, y) ⊗    Right

$touchPoint.y = -touchPoint.x + np2$
$\Rightarrow np2 = touchPoint.y + touchPoint.x$

Down

$y = x + n1$
$\Rightarrow n1 = y - x$

⊗ P(touchPoint.x, touchPoint.y)

1024

$touchPoint.y = touchPoint.x + np1$
$\Rightarrow np1 = touchPoint.y - touchPoint.x$

y

**Figure 6.19** Control overview with the regions UP, DOWN, LEFT, RIGHT. To the left, the equations of the lines and the determination of the intersection points.

the z-axis. The velocity is five units (and is thus faster than an energy capsule; otherwise, it would be impossible to collect one).

With the increasing speedOffset parameter we ensure that movement is not too jerky and that the speed increases only with the time of touch contact.

In accord with our established control concept, the screen is to be divided into four regions (see Figure 6.19). But how do we determine in which region the touch point is located? To do this, we turn to the equation of a straight line: $y = mx + n$, where $m$ is the slope, which for the diagonals has the value 1 or –1. The intersection with the y-axis is denoted by $n$. And please do not forget that the y-axis runs from above to below—opposite to what you learned in school.

We may also imagine two diagonals running through the touch point. We thus have four lines, with $n$ determining whether the line runs above or below another line. This enables us to determine the region in which the touch point is located by comparing the four $n$-values (n1, n2, np1, np2). This simple procedure could be used, for example, to simulate a four-way arcade joystick.

## 6.11.7  First-Person Perspective

Since the camera's position should be that of the viewer, we likewise change the camera position in the draw method based on the current position of the player:

```
[[GameManager getInstance]
    setCameraX: pos.x cameraY: pos.y cameraZ: pos.z
    lookAtX: pos.x lookAtY: pos.y lookAtZ: pos.z+1];
```

The viewing direction (lookAt) is always parallel to the z-axis so that the xy-values correspond to the current position and the z-value (pos.z+1) determines the direction.

## 6.11.8  Laser

From the current position of the player, the origin is also determined, and therefore we do not need to set any position for the creation of new bullets via the createSprite: method of the GameManager. We simply use a timer to determine the frequency of the sustained fire.

## 6.11.9  Notification of a Strike

Finally, in the hitCnt member of the Player class, we store the number of collisions with asteroids and obstacles. If the critical value is reached, the game shifts to the GAME_ OVER state in the hit method, and a suitable text message is output to the display. The hitCapsule method makes it possible to repair damage from hits: Here we simply decrease the hitCnt parameter by 1.

## 6.11.10  Other Sprites

Now let us look again at the Bullet class. As was the case with the energy capsules, here no texture data are necessary; instead, we specify the color of the model via the setColor method. Since the bullets are moving fairly quickly away from the player, we check in the draw method whether the bullets are located behind the zFar clipping pane. If that is the case, then the Sprite object is deactivated. If you implement a number of sprites that move away from the player, you could, of course, do this check more universally in the Sprite class itself (see autoDestroy).

**Listing 6.15  Bullet.h**

```
#import "Sprite.h"

@interface Bullet : Sprite {
}

@end
```

**Listing 6.16  Bullet.m**

```
#import "Bullet.h"
#import "GameManager.h"

@implementation Bullet

/*
```

```
Vertex x-Range from: -2.5 to: 2.5
Vertex y-Range from: -2.5 to: 2.5
Vertex z-Range from: -22.6 to: 27.4

Suggested radius for bounding sphere: 10.8
*/

- (void) additionalSetup {
    type = BULLET;
    radius = 10.8*2;

    //data come from the obj file,
    //converted with www.qioo.de/objformatter/
    GLfloat verticesObjData[] = {
        0.0, -0.0, 27.4, -2.5, -2.5, -22.6, 2.5, -2.5, -22.6, 2.5,
        2.5, -22.6, -2.5, 2.5, -22.6, 0.0, -0.0, -22.6
    };

    GLfloat normalsObjData[] = {
        0.0, -0.1, 0.0, 0.0, -1.5, 0.1, 0.0, -1.5, 0.1, 1.5, 0.0, 0.1,
        0.0, 1.5, 0.1, 0.0, 0.0, -1.0
    };

    GLushort facesObjData[] = {
        0, 1, 2, 0, 2, 3, 0, 3, 4, 0, 4, 1, 1, 5, 2, 2, 5, 3, 3, 5, 4,
        4, 5, 1
    };

    [self setVertices: verticesObjData
                 size: sizeof(verticesObjData)
           setTexCoords: nil
                 size: 0
             setNormals: normalsObjData
                 size: sizeof(normalsObjData)
               setFaces: facesObjData
                 size: sizeof(facesObjData)];
}

- (void) setColor {
    glColor4f(0, 0.7, 1, 1);
}

- (void) draw {
    Player * p = [[GameManager getInstance] getPlayer];
    Vertex posPlayer = [p getPos];
    if (pos.z > posPlayer.z + [[GameManager getInstance] getzFar]) {
        active = false;//sprite outside of field of view
    }
    [super draw];
}

@end
```

We have now introduced all the Sprite classes except the Text class. We shall make up for this now.

---

## Listing 6.17  Text.h

```
#import "Sprite.h"

@interface Text : Sprite {
    int timer;
    int w, h;//dimensions of text texture
    float offsetX;//offset from the origin
    float offsetY;
    bool selfDestroy;//object is deleted when timer runs out
}

- (void) setText: (NSString *) text
        offsetX: (float) x
        offsetY: (float) y
     selfDestroy: (bool) destroy;

@end
```

## Listing 6.18  Text.m

```
#import "Text.h"
#import "GameManager.h"

@implementation Text

//Note: the text color is set when the texture is created

- (void) additionalSetup {
    type = TEXT;
}

- (void) setText: (NSString *) text
        offsetX: (float) x
        offsetY: (float) y
     selfDestroy: (bool) destroy {

    Tex *tex = [[GameManager getInstance] getTex: text isImage: NO];
    textureID = [tex getTextureID];

    //maintain aspect ratio at a height of 1
    w = [tex getWidth]/[tex getHeight];
    h = 1;

    //text length does not necessarily correspond to the texture width
    //therefore left-justified alignment at the origin
    GLfloat verticesObjData[] = {
        0, h, 0,//upper left
        w, h, 0,//upper right
        0, 0, 0,//lower left
```

```
            w, 0, 0 //lower right
        };

        GLfloat textureCoordsObjData[] = {
            1, 0, 0,//lower right
            0, 0, 0,//lower left
            1, 1, 0,//upper right
            0, 1, 0 //upper left
        };

        GLfloat normalsObjData[] = {
            0, 0, 1,//front
            0, 0, 1,
            0, 0, 1,
            0, 0, 1
        };

        [self setVertices: verticesObjData
                     size: sizeof(verticesObjData)
                setTexCoords: textureCoordsObjData
                     size: sizeof(textureCoordsObjData)
                setNormals: normalsObjData
                     size: sizeof(normalsObjData)
                  setFaces: nil
                     size: 0];

        offsetX = x;//texture wider than text, therefore manual alignment
        offsetY = y;
        selfDestroy = destroy;
    }


- (void) move {//position text
        Vertex o = [[GameManager getInstance] getViewportOrigin];
        glTranslatef(o.x - w + offsetX, o.y - h + offsetY, o.z + 10);

        if (selfDestroy) {
            timer++;
            if (timer > 30) {
                active = false;
            }
        }
    }
}

@end
```

We have already gone into the functionality of the class and its implementation. Since we are dealing with a 2D surface, as with the cockpit, onto which the Text texture will be mapped, we specify the object data directly and do not need any faces. The alignment of the text is done in the move() method, using the origin and offsetX, offsetY parameters. If the flag selfDestroy has been set to true, the Text object will be deactivated in the if statement after more than 30 frames and thereby removed from memory by the

**Figure 6.20** Screen shots of the completed game.

sprite manager. As mentioned earlier, you can regenerate text messages with the same content without having to regenerate the texture. This is managed by the texture manager of the GameManager. This means also, conversely, that you can delete unneeded text components explicitly via

```
[[GameManager getInstance] removeFromDictionary: @"my text"];
```

This removes the texture as well, rather than only the Text object (Figure 6.20).

# 7 On the Trail of Angry Birds—Physics Engine Box2D

## ▉ 7.1 Introduction

The success of iOS has resulted in numerous additional libraries being created to help developers in their work by encapsulating frequently used functionalities in a universally implementable way. Thus, for example, we have Sparrow and, from Apple itself, the GLKit. In addition, there are interesting frameworks that provide developers with entirely new possibilities. In this category can be found, for example, the physics engines, which make possible the realistic simulation of objects in their environment. Here we shall introduce one of the best known examples of such libraries: Box2D.

You most likely are familiar with the game Angry Birds (Rovio 2009, Figure 7.1). Small birds are shot with a slingshot onto tower-like buildings in order to kill the piglets concealed inside. The flight paths of the birds and the collapsing buildings seem quite realistic despite the 2D perspective, since each of these objects behaves realistically with respect to its mass and geometric form. Such a scenario could be achieved only with a great deal of programming effort. Velocity, direction of motion, and angle of rotation must be calculated for each frame using Newton's laws applied to the gravitational force that is operational in the game world. In addition, one must consider momentum-inducing forces that act on the objects from without—for example, through user interaction. Or imagine other game scenarios, such as a game of marbles, in which a marble has to be maneuvered through a labyrinth, or a classical pinball game. Such game concepts can be realized in a relatively short time with a physics engine such as that we would now like to demonstrate.

Figure 7.1 Angry Birds (Rovio).

Box2D is one of the best known and most widely used such engines. It allows one to create impressive physical effects with a few lines of code. While OpenGL ES is conceived as a pure graphics library, Box2D, in contrast, is a pure 2D physics simulator without any reference to the graphical representation of a game.

## 7.1.1 What Should I Expect from a Physics Engine for 2D Games?

As game developers, we are usually working with a variety of moving objects that interact with one another. For a physics engine, it is important that such interactions take place under realistic physical conditions. For this, we ideally should need to specify the position of our game object only once. Then, the physics engine should tell us the current position of the object at each frame along with the current rotation angle:

- Definition of the 2D world with respect to gravitation

- Definition of the objects (position/shape, rotation angle)

- Dynamic creation of new objects

Once the game has started, the current positions of the bodies and their current rotation angles are obtained for each frame, and then the objects are rendered. This means that the engine also takes over for us the task of collision checking for the objects.

This all seems rather simple, does it not it? It is rather simple, in fact, and, fortunately, Box2D meets all of our requirements, which is certainly a reason for its popularity on a number of platforms. Of course, this engine offers many additional possibilities. For example, you can define the properties of materials such as frictional coefficient and elasticity (consider the difference between a superball and a steel bearing). You can also define ropes and bodies hanging from them (a prominent example here is Cut the Rope, ZeptoLab 2010) or a composite body, such as a rag-doll figure, consisting of individual rectangles. But first things first. Before we move to a more complex example, let us begin with something simple—say, a couple of blocks that behave just like, well, real blocks in real life, as if you had a set of blocks inside your iPhone.

## 7.1.2 A First Test

The documentation for the Box2D API is satisfyingly brief. At *http://box2d.org/documentation.html* you will find a 66-page PDF that explains all your options with coded examples. Since Box2D uses a C++ framework on a variety of platforms (including Windows Phone, Android, and iOS), the code is platform independent—for example, it does not implement an STL container—to avoid unwanted dependencies. The API has been developed since 2006, primarily by Erin Catto, and can be used for all kinds of projects thanks to the free software licensing (zlib license, a slightly modified form of the well-known MIT license).

From the Box2D homepage, *http://box2d.org,* you can find the free distributions under *Downloads.* For this book we used Box2D Release 2.2.1 from September 17, 2011. If you unpack the zip file, you will find in the Build folder, along with a Visual Studio project, an example project that is executable directly under Xcode. You can execute it with a double click on `\Box2D_v2.2.1\Build\xcode4\Box2D.xcodeproj`. The project opens in Xcode. The test-bed project is a Unix executable that you can launch as a stand-alone project (PRODUCTS > SHOW IN FINDER) (Figure 7.2).

Since the source code for the examples is included, you can use it as a source of inspiration for your own game ideas. It is amazing how little code it takes to produce a game that seems relatively complex. You surely recall the countless Flash versions on the web in which a skier (or sledder, or bobsledder, or …) rushes down a slope. A similar example can be found in the "Car" project.

# ▮ 7.2 How Do I Integrate Box2D?

Although example code is provided and the documentation focuses on all the important questions, how we achieve our most important goal has not been clarified. An iOS 5 project is not included and, in any case, how do we best integrate the API into our own

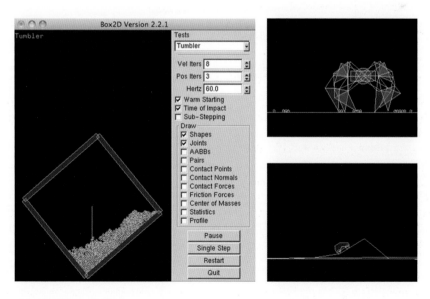

**Figure 7.2** Box2D test-bed app.

projects? To answer this question, let us create a simple test app—say, an empty Xcode project—into which we integrate the familiar parts of our OpenGL ES (AppDelegate, Sprite class, GameManager, MainView). The framework is initially no different from that in our previous examples. The complete test project can be found under the name "Box2dCubeTest" in the download archive.

Since Xcode and iOS 5 support not only Objective-C and C, but also C++, we can use the project's original code. For other languages such as Flash, Java, C#, and Python, you can find ports in the Internet; however, they are not directly supervised and hosted by Erin Catto.

So let us copy manually the entire folder "Box2D" into our project directory. The folder is found directly at the top level of the unpacked archive—that is, Box2D_v2.2.1\ Box2D. In this folder you will find the entire source code of the API. All parts of the library are integrated and referenced via Box2D.h. Copy the folder into the top level of the Xcode project—that is, in the folder in which xcodeproj lies.

In Xcode we now add the folder as well as other resources to the project by a right-click. Now click in the folder view to the left on the project folder and then on ADD FILES TO…. Make sure that the box under *Destination* is unchecked: We have already placed the folder in the project and do not want to make this known in the project as a reference. The Box2D folder now appears next to the other folders of the project (Figure 7.3).

To get started now with Box2D, you have to execute the following steps for each project:

1.  To find the Box2D header, we have to enlarge the header search path to the project directory, since we have added Box2D to the project's top level. Go to "Build Settings" and select SEARCH PATHS > HEADER SEARCH PATHS. There, add ${PROJECT_ DIR} as a variable, which always contains the current path to the project.

2.  Since Box2D is a C++ API, the compiler must be informed of this. Normally, this is visible at the creation of a class from the file type (*.cpp). If we wish to use Box2D,

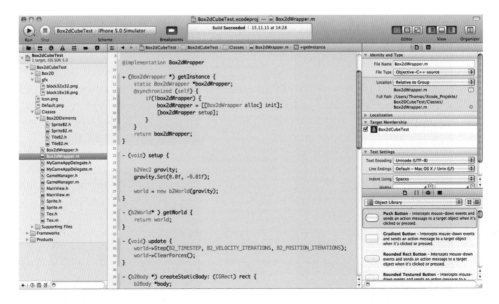

**Figure 7.3** File type for Box2dWrapper.m.

Block 32×32.png

Block 16×16.png

Figure 7.4 The two block graphics.

we have to access the C++ classes in our classes written in Objective-C. Thus, we usually alter the file type from *.m to *.mm. But there is a simpler way: If it has not been done already, open, via the view menu, the right-hand window and there select "Identity and Type." Here you can specify the file type for every class. Under "File Type," instead of "Objective-C source," choose the combined solution "Objective-C++ source." Now all classes with this file type can contain both Objective-C and C++ code. But do not worry: No deep knowledge of C++ will be necessary.

3. Finally, in the affected classes you have to import the Box2D header—that is, #import <Box2D/Box2D.h>.

So that we can use the test project later more easily for other games, we make only minimal changes in the code. To show that everything works as expected, we simply add two block graphics to the project (Figure 7.4).

- The large block (32 × 32) represents a dynamic body.

- The small block (16 × 16) represents a static body.

From the point of view of Box2D, the physical world is divided into two types of bodies. The first are "dynamic" and can move and are subject to physical forces such as gravitation, impulses, and collisions with other objects. In addition, Box2D offers static bodies, which remain fixed at a given position. In contrast to the real world, these bodies cannot be moved, no matter how great the force. For game development, these bodies are ideally implemented as tiles—for example, as level borders, fixed platforms, or walls. The advantage here is obvious: Since these bodies are fixed, collision checking is made easy, and that saves a whole lot of computation time, particularly in complex worlds.

# ▍ 7.3 What Goes Up Must Come Down

Newton certainly understood the principle on which Box2D functions. The central force is gravitation, and all bodies that we add to the world will fall downward unless acted on by some outside force, such as an obstacle. For our example, this will be the bottom of the display, for which we must create a static body.

But let us take things one at a time. First, of course, we have to define a world in which this static body will be placed. To this end, we create a central helper class that will encapsulate for us the access to Box2D.

Listing 7.1 Box2dWrapper.h

```
#import <Foundation/Foundation.h>
#import <Box2D/Box2D.h>
#import "TileB2.h"
#import "SpriteB2.h"

extern int32 B2_VELOCITY_ITERATIONS;
extern int32 B2_POSITION_ITERATIONS;
extern float32 B2_TIMESTEP;
extern int32 B2_RATIO;

@interface Box2dWrapper : NSObject {
    b2World* world;
}

+ (Box2dWrapper *) getInstance;
- (void) setup;
- (b2World*) getWorld;
- (void) update;
- (b2Body *) createStaticBody: (CGRect) rect;
- (b2Body *) createDynamicBody: (CGRect) rect;

@end
```

Listing 7.2 Box2dWrapper.m

```
#import "Box2dWrapper.h"

int32 B2_VELOCITY_ITERATIONS = 8;
int32 B2_POSITION_ITERATIONS = 8;
float32 B2_TIMESTEP = 1.0f/33.0f;
int32 B2_RATIO = 60.0f;//box2d computes in meters, not in pixels

@implementation Box2dWrapper

+ (Box2dWrapper *) getInstance {
    static Box2dWrapper *box2dWrapper;
        @synchronized (self) {
            if(!box2dWrapper) {
                box2dWrapper = [[Box2dWrapper alloc] init];
                [box2dWrapper setup];
        }
    }
    return box2dWrapper;
}
```

```
- (void) setup {
    //gravity is implemented as a vector
    b2Vec2 gravity;
    gravity.Set(0.0f, -9.81f);

    world = new b2World(gravity);
}

- (b2World*) getWorld {
    return world;
}

- (void) update {
    world->Step(B2_TIMESTEP, B2_VELOCITY_ITERATIONS,
        B2_POSITION_ITERATIONS);
    world->ClearForces();
}

- (b2Body *) createStaticBody: (CGRect) rect {
    ...
}

- (b2Body *) createDynamicBody: (CGRect) rect {
    ...
}

@end
```

Do not forget, as described earlier, to set the file type for the implementation to "Objective-C++ source." Later we shall discuss the two methods—createStaticBody: and createDynamicBody:.

There will be only one Box2D world for each game, and therefore it makes sense to create our wrapper as a singleton. With the getInstance class method, we obtain access to the world from every class. If the wrapper instance has been created, we return it; otherwise, a unique new one is created. With this instance we can access the Box2D world via getWorld, which we return as a b2World instance.

To create this instance, the setup method must be called. In it, we set the gravitational constant for the world. After all, our game could be taking place on the Moon. However, in this example, we shall choose to mimic Earth's gravitation, which acts as a downward vector, so we create a vector of type b2Vec2, which is initialized via gravity.Set(0.0f, -9.81f).

We can pass this gravitation vector directly to the b2World constructor, so that, with a mere two lines of code, we have created an entire world:

```
world = new b2World(gravity);
```

We do not know how complex the conditions were at the time of the Big Bang, but to create a new world in two lines of code is no mean feat. To be sure, the b2World constructor has done some of the work for us, but as with any creator, we must give consideration to another important factor: time. This was not created automatically with the Big Bang, but has to be specified by us more precisely. We know already what it is all about: In every game, a clock is ticking in the form of a game loop. At each iteration, we have to compute the game state and render the graphics in a prescribed tempo. We have to bring this into line with Box2D. We have defined the following values as constants:

```
int32 B2_VELOCITY_ITERATIONS = 8;
int32 B2_POSITION_ITERATIONS = 8;
float32 B2_TIMESTEP = 1.0f/33.0f;
```

These are passed as a world step in the wrapper's `update`. That sounds more complicated than it actually is; at each iteration of the loop, we call the `update` method once and ensure that the bodies in the Box2D world move according to the parameters that have been set for them. Since eight iterations are set, Box2D will recalculate the bodies eight times per frame. More physically realistic results are obtained if, for example, the flight paths of bodies are calculated more frequently than they are to be seen on the screen. A very fast body will seem optically to fly through other bodies, but the collision will nevertheless be recognized by Box2D and will have an effect on the "flown-through" bodies in subsequent frames. Too many iterations lead, of course, to greater computation cost. Therefore, adjust this value as necessary. Now we inform Box2D via `B2_TIMESTEP` about the tempo at which our game loop generally operates: 33 times per second.

Finally, let us look at the `B2_RATIO` constant. We are not using this at present, but it is worthwhile to prepare for conversion between pixels and meters. As is suitable for a physics simulation, Box2D represents the world in the MKS (meter–kilogram–second) system. We therefore require a scaling factor to convert meters into pixels. We can experiment with this value to customize the representation of the world on the display. We have chosen the value 60, which means that one image point on the screen is equivalent to 1/60 of a meter in the real world. For a game in landscape view, there are 480 image points, which is equivalent to

```
1/60 × 480 = >8 meters
```

Our world is therefore 8 meters wide. Box2D recommends that for realistic effects, the world not be made too big and that objects move between 0.1 and 10 meters. We are therefore well within these limits. Change this ratio if you want a proportionally large world on the display.

## 7.3.1  Defining Bodies

Box2D uses not only the MKS system, but also the well-known coordinate system that you learned in school, the one with the y-axis pointing upward. Furthermore, the position of a simple body is determined by the location of its center and not, as with Core Graphics, with respect to its upper left-hand corner. We must take all of this into account when we create a new body:

```
- (b2Body *) createStaticBody: (CGRect) rect;
- (b2Body *) createDynamicBody: (CGRect) rect;
```

You can see already from the method signatures that we wish to create only rectangular forms. Of course, Box2D supports other forms as well, such as circles and polygons with arbitrarily many sides. You can see examples of these in the Box2D documentation. Here, our goal is simply to show how Box2D creates bodies and how to integrate them into your game.

Sprite graphics often have a rectangular form, which we pass to the `create` methods as `CGRect` structures. Here, the upper left-hand point of the rectangle refers to the actual screen position of the object. We obtain in return a `b2Body` instance, which represents the body and therefore also its current position in the world. We can query this body about such things as the forces acting on it, collisions with other bodies, and, above all, its current position in the simulated world—but more on this later. Let us first look at the implementation of a static body.

Listing 7.3  createStaticBody: method

```
- (b2Body *) createStaticBody: (CGRect) rect {
    b2Body *body;
    b2BodyDef bodyDef;
    b2PolygonShape itemShape;

    int x = rect.origin.x,
        y = rect.origin.y,
        w = rect.size.width,
        h = rect.size.height;

    bodyDef.type = b2_staticBody;

    //body definition, box2d uses an inverted y-axis
    bodyDef.position.Set((x + w/2.0f)/B2_RATIO, -(y + h/2.0f)/
        B2_RATIO);

    //call box2d factory method to create a new body
    body = [[Box2dWrapper getInstance] getWorld] ->
        CreateBody(&bodyDef);

    //set the shape of the body; box2d proceeds from the center of the
        body
    float32 j = w/2;
    float32 k = h/2;
    itemShape.SetAsBox(j/B2_RATIO, k/B2_RATIO);

    //bind the properties to the body
    body->CreateFixture(&itemShape, 0.0f);
    return body;
}
```

To each `b2Body` there belong at least a body definition (`b2BodyDef`) and a shape (`b2PolygonShape`). The decision that we make concerns the type of body. To define a static body, we have only to set `b2_staticBody` as a `type` property of the body definition. In determining the desired position, we must be careful. Our rectangular body should appear on the screen at position xy. Box2D expects the midpoint as the position. We can determine this easily from w and h. Now we have only to consider the conversion factor B2_RATIO set by us and the inverted y-axis (for this it suffices to insert a minus sign):

```
bodyDef.position.Set((x + w/2.0f)/B2_RATIO, -(y + h/2.0f)/B2_RATIO);
```

Now, to create the body, we have only to pass the just determined body definition as a parameter to the `CreateBody` method of the `b2world` instance.

With this, a body of size `1/B2_RATIO` has appeared in the world. We can determine the shape via the `b2PolygonShape` structure; for rectangular bodies, we use the `SetAsBox` method, which takes as parameter the distances from the midpoint to the upper and side edges. For this, we again must use the scaling factor. With the `CreateFixture()` method, the shape can finally be linked to the just created object. With the second parameter, we can determine the density and hardness of the body; for impenetrable tiles, the value 0 is given.

We proceed similarly in the creation of a dynamic body.

---

Listing 7.4 createDynamicBody: method

---

```
- (b2Body *) createDynamicBody: (CGRect) rect {
    b2Body *body;
    b2BodyDef bodyDef;
    b2PolygonShape itemShape;
    b2FixtureDef fixtureDef;

    int x = rect.origin.x,
        y = rect.origin.y,
        w = rect.size.width,
        h = rect.size.height;

    bodyDef.type = b2_dynamicBody;

    //body definition, box2d uses an inverted y-axis
    bodyDef.position.Set((x + w/2.0f)/B2_RATIO, -(y + h/2.0f)/
        B2_RATIO);

    //call box2d factory method to create a new body
    body = [[Box2dWrapper getInstance] getWorld] ->
        CreateBody(&bodyDef);

    //set the shape of the body;, box2d proceeds from the center of
        the body
    float32 j = w/2.0f;
    float32 k = h/2.0f;
    itemShape.SetAsBox(j/B2_RATIO, k/B2_RATIO);

    //set the properties of the body
    fixtureDef.shape = &itemShape;
    fixtureDef.density = 1.0f;//density (kg/m^2) - from 0 to 1 (0 is
        default)
    fixtureDef.friction = 0.103f;//friction - from 0 bis 1 (0.2 is
        default)
    fixtureDef.restitution = 0.03f;//elasticity - from 0 bis 1 (0 is
        default)

    //bind the properties of the body
    body->CreateFixture(&fixtureDef);

    return body;
}
```

The implementation proceeds similarly to the creation of a static body. As type we set the constant b2_dynamicBody. Position and shape are determined as previously in terms of the midpoint. To bind the properties to the body, this time we use an overloaded version of the CreateFixture method, to which we pass a reference to a b2FixtureDef structure; it is useful for dynamic bodies to set additional properties such as elasticity (restitution) and friction (friction). This time, we can set the shape directly with the shape property of the Fixture structure. Finally, once again the body's properties are linked to the body instance via CreateFixture.

## ▌ 7.4  Sprites under Box2D

We thus now have two methods for creating objects, though they exist only in the Box2D world without any visualization and are therefore (as of now) invisible. So we have to create some sprites. One of the most common pitfalls in the use of Box2D is a lack of agreement between the position of a body within the box2D engine and its representation on the screen. This has as its origin above all the fact that Box2D uses an inverted y-axis and positions objects at their midpoints. We have already taken care of this: Both methods contain a rectangle as template for positioning the body. Within the methods, this is then incorporated according to the Box2D coordinate system and passed back as a return parameter. We can obtain the current position within the Box2D world at any time from the body. Then, we must, of course, again calculate this position on the screen. For this, we are going to create a new Sprite class.

But, first, our Box2DWrapper must be joined to the GameManager. In the preloader method of the GameManager, we call the getInstance method of the wrapper once and create a static body as the ground:

```
[Box2dWrapper getInstance];//init box2d
[[Box2dWrapper getInstance]
    createStaticBody: CGRectMake(-100, H+1, W+200, 1)];
```

The ground corresponds to the bottom edge of the screen and keeps our Box2D bodies from falling downward without limit. We have added 100 pixels to the right and left of the screen so that objects cannot tumble down beyond the edges of the screen. The thickness of the ground is 1 pixel, which is sufficient since the ground simply represents a border and does not have to be visible.

Our Box2D example app should simply create a box at the touch position on the screen, which then falls downward until it hits the ground. To set up a few obstacles for our box as it falls, we also create static bodies using a simple rule: Dynamic bodies are created above the center of the screen (a block of size 32 × 32), while below this point are the static bodies (a block of size 16 × 16). Let us anticipate a bit and act as though we had already created the new Box2D sprite class(es) and add the following code to the touchBegan: method of the GameManager:

```
- (void) touchBegan: (CGPoint) p {
    [self handleStates];

    if (state = = PLAY_GAME) {
        if (p.y < H/2) {
            //dynamic box2d body
```

```
        SpriteB2 *sprite = [[SpriteB2 alloc] initWithPic: @"block32x32.png"
                                                 frameCnt: 1
                                                frameStep: 0
                                                    speed: CGPointMake(0, 0)
                                                      pos: p];
        [newSprites addObject: sprite];
        [sprite release];
    } else {
        //static box2d body
        TileB2 *tile = [[TileB2 alloc] initWithPic: @"block16x16.png"
                                               pos: p];
        [tiles addObject: tile];
        [tile release];
    }
  }
}
```

As you can see, we have derived a new sprite type for dynamic bodies (SpriteB2), which can be created on the basis of the previous examples. In addition to the specification of the PNG, the init method takes the number of frames, the frame playback rate, and the position at which the body is to appear for the first time on the screen. We can forget about the frame rate here, since the body is going to fall according to the law of gravity. We will show later how you can assign a direction vector and thereby a velocity and momentum to a body under Box2D.

Since a static body does not require a direct collision check with other sprites, we create for it a separate class called TileB2. Static bodies act as immovable elements, just as you would do, for example, for 2D Jump'n'Run Tiles.

As you can see as well, we treat SpriteB2 objects just like usual sprites and integrate them into the game architecture via the newSprites array. For the tiles, we have created a new array, which has to be iterated explicitly.

To complete the demo, we have only to adapt the game loop:

```
- (void) playGame {
    timer++;

    [self manageSprites];
    [self renderSprites];

    [self drawOGLLineFrom: CGPointMake(0, H/2) to: CGPointMake(W, H/2)];

    [[Box2dWrapper getInstance] update];

    for (TileB2 *tile in tiles) {
        [tile draw];
    }
}
```

At each iteration, we must call the update method of the wrapper to bring the Box2D body up to date. Moreover, we draw a center line and iterate through all tiles, which are then rendered via the draw method. We thereby prevent the tiles from undergoing unnecessary checks within checkSprite and manageSprite (which we shall use for our next Box2D example). We have now only to present the implementation of the two new classes.

## Listing 7.5  SpriteB2.h

```objc
#import "Sprite.h"
#import <Box2D/Box2D.h>
#import "GameManager.h"
#import "Box2dWrapper.h"

@interface SpriteB2 : Sprite {
    b2Body *body;
}

- (void) removeBody;

@end
```

## Listing 7.5.1  SpriteB2.m

```objc
#import "SpriteB2.h"

@implementation SpriteB2

- (void) additionalSetup {
    type = CUBE;
    body = [[Box2dWrapper getInstance]
        createDynamicBody: CGRectMake(pos.x, pos.y, frameW, frameH)];
    }

- (void) renderSprite {
    b2Vec2 position = body->GetPosition();
    pos.x = position.x * B2_RATIO - frameW/2.0f;
    pos.y = -position.y * B2_RATIO - frameH/2.0f;

        float32 angleRad = body->GetAngle();
        angle = -angleRad/(b2_pi/180.0);

        [super renderSprite];

        if (!active) {
            [self removeBody];
    }
}

- (void) removeBody {
    [[[Box2dWrapper getInstance] getWorld]->DestroyBody(body);
}

- (void) dealloc {
    [self removeBody];
    [super dealloc];
}

@end
```

As expected, the `SpriteB2` class is derived from `Sprite`. Within it, we have defined `CUBE`, a new `Sprite`-enum type. We allocate this in the `additionalSetup` method and instantiate the Box2D body in the `createDynamicBody:` method of the wrapper. Via the wrapper we also obtain the Box2D world instance so that in the `removeBody` method we can ensure that the sprite does not simply vanish from the screen and also lose its place in the Box2D world as soon as the `SpriteB2` object is deallocated.

Furthermore, we must overwrite the `renderSprite` method and there query the current position and current rotation angle of the B2 body. The parent class then takes care of the rest for us. Note that the B2 position must be recalculated in terms of the coordinate system used by us. Moreover, the rotation angle must be converted into degrees.

Since we implement no parent class (other than `NSObject`) for the `TileB2` class, we must take care of the rendering process and creation of textures here. We rely, as we did already in the `Sprite` class, on the `Tex` helper class.

Listing 7.6  TileB2.h

```
#import <Foundation/Foundation.h>
#import <Box2D/Box2D.h>
#import "Tex.h"

@interface TileB2 : NSObject {
    b2Body *body;
    Tex *tex;
    int x, y, w, h;
}

- (id) initWithPic: (NSString *) picName
              pos: (CGPoint) pxy;
- (void) draw;
- (void) removeBody;

@end
```

Listing 7.6.1  TileB2.m

```
#import "GameManager.h"
#import "Box2dWrapper.h"

@implementation TileB2

- (id) initWithPic: (NSString *) picName
              pos: (CGPoint) pxy {
    self = [super init];

    x = pxy.x;
    y = pxy.y;

    tex = [[GameManager getInstance] getTex: picName isImage: YES];
    w = [tex getWidth];
```

```
        h = [tex getHeight];

        body = [[Box2dWrapper getInstance]
            createStaticBody: CGRectMake(x, y, w, h)];

        return self;
}

- (void) draw {
    [tex drawAt: CGPointMake(x, y)];
}

- (void) removeBody {
    [[Box2dWrapper getInstance] getWorld]->DestroyBody(body);
}

- (void) dealloc {
    [self removeBody];
    [super dealloc];
}

@end
```

A further difference with the SpriteB2 class is that in the init method, in addition to creating textures, we create the body using the createStaticBody: method of the wrapper. Finally, the tiles are not going to move and will therefore be static. This means also that we do not have to concern ourselves further with the position conversions between Box2D and UIView, since this takes place already within the createStaticBody: method and is used only once. Of course, tile objects must be removed from the Box2D world once the object has been deleted from the array of the GameManager. As before, this job is handled by the removeBody method, which is called by the dealloc method when the retain count of the tile object has the value 0 (Figure 7.5).

## 7.4.1 Possible Extensions

Do you recall the skier game mentioned earlier? In it, a line is drawn with the finger (or with the mouse) along which the skier goes downhill. Up till now, B2 tiles could be added in our app only by a click or touch. But if you want to create an effect similar to that in the skier game, you have to undo the commenting out of the touchMoved: method in the GameManager class. Now a new block is added at each finger movement. If you choose a smaller graphic for the block of 2 × 2 pixels, you will give the impression that you are drawing a line on the display. The line consists of many small, static bodies and creates a sort of track along which the dynamic bodies can slide.

Of course, in addition to rectangles, Box2D offers other 2D shapes, so you can find a more suitable alternative, such as b2EdgeShapes, which have no extent and simply represent one or more lines that can be tested for collision with other bodies (other than lines). Another simple extension would be to replace the falling blocks with polygonal shapes (b2PolygonShape) or balls (b2CircleShape). For this, you would have simply to create a new body form in the wrapper.

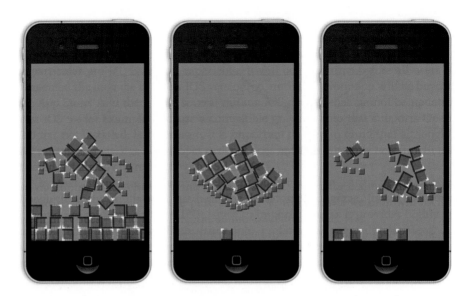

Figure 7.5 The completed Box2D-Cube-Test app.

# ■ 7.5 A Box2D Game: Free the Birds

Now that we have gained some insight into the workings of the physics engine Box2D, we shall hesitate no longer and begin a new game project. As we mentioned earlier, we shall look at some of the techniques that can be used in games like Angry Birds. Our main focus is the interplay between Box2D and the GameManager architecture. Furthermore, we will see how the interaction with Box2D objects can take place in a game, how objects can be moved by providing an impulse, and how the position of an object can be queried during a game. Finally, we shall show how you can create an OpenGL ES game in landscape mode.

Taking inspiration from the hit game Angry Birds, we will name our game Free the Birds (Figure 7.6). As the name suggests, this game is not going to be about using birds to kill piglets. Instead, we will set three little blue chicks the task of freeing their yellow siblings. Furthermore, the chicks are not going to be shot with a slingshot but instead catapulted in the proper direction with a swipe of the finger. The game figure will be the chick sprite that graced the first edition of this book.

The game concept involves the following:

- *Three yellow chicks are being held prisoner in a red stone tower.*

- *The player has three blue chicks that can be catapulted in a given direction by swiping the finger. Each chick can be catapulted only once. Once the chick has flown off in a given direction, its eyes begin to blink to indicate that the chick has already been deployed. Once all three blue chicks have been deployed, the game must be restarted by pressing a button.*

- *The yellow chicks are held in a tower constructed of red blocks. When a blue chick is thrown against the tower, the individual blocks collapse in a way that depends on the velocity and direction of the blue chick.*

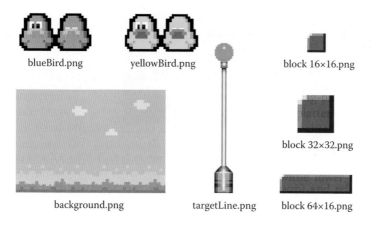

blueBird.png    yellowBird.png          block 16×16.png

                                        block 32×32.png

background.png    targetLine.png    block 64×16.png

**Figure 7.6** The graphics for Free the Birds.

- *The game is won when all the yellow chicks have passed the lantern at the right-hand edge of the picture. This is indicated by a speech bubble ("Yippie!") above the chicks and by blinking eyes. In addition, a congratulatory message appears on the display.*

As a basis for the game we use the Box2D app that we created earlier in this chapter. However, we can do without the `TileB2` class, since our level design does not specify any tiles at this point. Of course, they could be added later as a game extension—for example, to limit the chicks' flight path. The two Box2D-specific classes `Box2dWrapper` and `SpriteB2` remain unchanged. Only for the two chick types do we develop new classes (`BlueBird`, `YellowBird`). All other changes relate, as before, only to changes in the `GameManager` class.

## 7.5.1 Landscape versus Portrait Mode

Earlier, portrait mode was typically used for games, but nowadays landscape mode has established itself as a preferred game format. Contributing to this change were the 16:9 cinema format as well as mobile game consoles such as the Sony PSP and Nintendo DS (Figure 7.7).

First, the splash screen must be customized. This remains upright, but the displayed motif must be rotated by 90°. There are two basic ways of playing a game sideways: The home key can be located on the left or the right of the display. This setting can be made in Plist.info. For the "Initial interface orientation," choose here the entry "Landscape (right home button)" and, under "Supported interface orientations," delete all the entries except "Landscape (right home button)" (Figure 7.8).

The next changes affect primarily the adaptation of the OpenGL perspective and viewport. In the implementation of the `GameManager`, interchange the global constants W and H, so that W = 480 und H = 320. This automatically adjusts the perspective, which accesses these constants.

Next, the viewport has to be customized. This is set by the `MainView` class, our OpenGL view, after we have passed via `MyGameAppDelegate` the dimensions

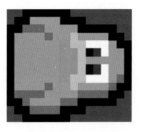

Figure 7.7 Default.png (320 × 480 pixels, landscape mode).

| Bundle version | String | 1.0 |
|---|---|---|
| Application requires iPhone environment | Boolean | YES |
| Application does not run in background | Boolean | YES |
| ▼ Required device capabilities | Array | (1 item) |
| Item 0 | String | armv7 |
| Status bar is initially hidden | Boolean | YES |
| ▼ Supported interface orientations | Array | (1 item) |
| Item 0 | String | Landscape (right home button) |
| Main nib file base name | String | MainWindow |
| Application Category | String | Games – Arcade Games |
| Initial interface orientation | String | Landscape (right home button) |

Figure 7.8 The Plist with the settings for landscape orientation.

of the view as a parameter to the view's `init` method. To interchange the values for width and height, we modify the creation of the `MainView` class in the delegate as follows:

```
mainView = [[MainView alloc] initWithFrame: CGRectMake(0,0,W,H)];
mainView.backgroundColor = [UIColor grayColor];

//landscape orientation
mainView.transform = CGAffineTransformMakeRotation(M_PI * 90/180.0);
mainView.center = CGPointMake(H/2, W/2);

[mainView setupOGL];
```

Instead of setting the dimensions of the screen via [UIScreen mainScreen]. applicationFrame], we rely directly on the constants set in the GameManager. This causes the previous ApplicationFrame to be overwritten with the new values so that, later, it can be accessed as usual in the game loop ([mainView drawRect:[UIScreen mainScreen].applicationFrame];).

Finally, the view must be rotated, as shown before, by a transformation, so that the coordinate system has its origin in the customary upper left-hand corner. Since the view is rotated by 90° (= pi * 90/180 radians) to the left, the home button is now on the right side of the display. The center property specifies the point at which the rotation is to be made; therefore, here, W and H must be interchanged, since the rotation is in reference to the portrait screen, while the constants have already been modified in the GameManager.

Figure 7.9 Landscape orientation with right-hand home button.

To test whether everything works properly, let us render the background image at position $(0, 0)$. To do this, add the following line in the playGame method of the GameManager:

```
[self drawOGLImg: @"background.png" at: CGPointMake(0, 0)];
```

If you now start the emulator, it will automatically rotate into landscape mode based on the information given in the Plist. In addition, our background, as expected, is shown on the display; the position $(0, 0)$ denotes the upper left-hand corner of the screen, while the home button is located on the right (Figure 7.9).

## 7.5.2 The New Sprite Classes

Since the stone building in which the yellow chicks are imprisoned is composed of three types of block, the game uses five Sprite types altogether, which we add to the enum list in the Sprite class:

```
//sprite types
enum types {
    CUBE16x16,
    CUBE32x32,
    CUBE64x16,
    BLUEBIRD,
    YELLOWBIRD
};
```

It makes sense to construct the house out of individual sprites, since each separate building block must behave physically correctly when it is struck by another object. It is only thus that we can cause the birdhouse to collapse effectively on being struck by the blue chicks.

While we can rely directly on the SpriteB2 class for the three building blocks, we have a bit more in mind for the birds, and therefore we give them their own classes.

Listing 7.7 YellowBird.h

```
#import "SpriteB2.h"

@interface YellowBird : SpriteB2

- (void) twinkle;

@end
```

Listing 7.8 YellowBird.m

```
#import "YellowBird.h"

@implementation YellowBird

- (void) additionalSetup {
    type = YELLOWBIRD;
    [super additionalSetup];
}

- (void) twinkle {
    frameStep = 4;
}

@end
```

The yellow chicks are constructed basically like the blocks and have a rectangular basic form. The only additional property is that the chicks are able to blink their eyes when they have passed the goal line (in the form of a lantern). We have therefore only to set the `Sprite` type via the `additionalSetup` method of the parent class and implement the `twinkle` method. The blinking animation consists of two frames, which will be played with a frame rate of four images. After initialization, this distance is 0 frames. To make the birds blink, we have to increase this value to 4.

We can create the `BlueBird` class in exactly the same way and worry later about the swipe gesture. We can thus already integrate the existing `Sprite` types into the `GameManager`. With the `addB2Sprite:at:` method, we can finally render the sprites to the display.

Listing 7.9 addB2Sprite:at: implementation

```
- (void) addB2Sprite: (int) type at: (CGPoint) p {
    if (type = = CUBE16x16) {
        SpriteB2 *sprite = [[SpriteB2 alloc] initWithPic:
            @"block16x16.png"
                                        frameCnt: 1
                                       frameStep: 0
                                           speed: CGPointMake(0, 0)
                                             pos: p];
        [newSprites addObject: sprite];
        [sprite release];
    } else if (type = = CUBE32x32) {
        SpriteB2 *sprite = [[SpriteB2 alloc] initWithPic:
            @"block32x32.png"
                                        frameCnt: 1
                                       frameStep: 0
                                           speed: CGPointMake(0, 0)
                                             pos: p];
```

```
            [newSprites addObject: sprite];
            [sprite release];
        } else if (type = = CUBE64x16) {
            SpriteB2 *sprite = [[SpriteB2 alloc] initWithPic:
                @"block64x16.png"
                                        frameCnt: 1
                                        frameStep: 0
                                            speed: CGPointMake(0, 0)
                                            pos: p];
            [newSprites addObject: sprite];
            [sprite release];
        } else if (type = = BLUEBIRD) {
            BlueBird *sprite = [[BlueBird alloc] initWithPic:
                @"blueBird.png"
                                        frameCnt: 2
                                        frameStep: 0
                                            speed: CGPointMake(0, 0)
                                            pos: p];
            [newSprites addObject: sprite];
            [sprite release];
        } else if (type = = YELLOWBIRD) {
            YellowBird *sprite = [[YellowBird alloc] initWithPic:
                @"yellowBird.png"
                                        frameCnt: 2
                                        frameStep: 0
                                            speed: CGPointMake(0, 0)
                                            pos: p];
            [newSprites addObject: sprite];
            [sprite release];
        } else {
            NSLog(@"ERROR: Unkown sprite type: %i", type);
        }
    }
}
```

## 7.5.3 Building the Tower

This time, we will put the call to the `addB2Sprite:at:` method to create new
sprites in a separate class. We fix the level architecture once and for all, and at any
time, we can return the game to its initial state or reload additional levels with
more buildings. But first we have to determine where the sprite elements should be
placed. For this you can use an external level editor such as Tile Studio or an image-
processing program such as Photoshop or Freehand. Freehand offers the advantage
that you can place the sprites on the screen as you wish and then export the resulting
"painting" in XML format. This then contains all the placed graphics along with the
pixel positions.

Since our birdhouse does not have a complex structure, we can construct it using an
image-processing program like Photoshop. Create a new file in landscape format with the
dimensions of the display (320 × 480 pixels). Now place the graphics as you like and note
their xy-positions. Since we already know the heights of the three house components, it
suffices to note only the x-values. With these values, we can define the level by means of a
new class.

---

Listing 7.10 Level.h

```
@interface Level : NSObject

- (void) setLevel;

@end
```

Listing 7.11 Level.m

```
#import "Level.h"
#import "GameManager.h"

@implementation Level

- (void) setLevel {
    int x = 50;

    [[GameManager getInstance] addB2Sprite: BLUEBIRD
                                        at: CGPointMake(24, H-32)];
    [[GameManager getInstance] addB2Sprite: BLUEBIRD
                                        at: CGPointMake(70, H-32)];
    [[GameManager getInstance] addB2Sprite: BLUEBIRD
                                        at: CGPointMake(118, H-32)];

    [[GameManager getInstance] addB2Sprite: YELLOWBIRD
                                        at: CGPointMake(323-x,
                                            H-32*2-16)];
    [[GameManager getInstance] addB2Sprite: YELLOWBIRD
                                        at: CGPointMake(386-x,
                                            H-32*3)];
    [[GameManager getInstance] addB2Sprite: YELLOWBIRD
                                        at: CGPointMake(356-x,
                                            H-32*5)];

    [[GameManager getInstance] addB2Sprite: CUBE32x32
                                        at: CGPointMake(261-x, H-32)];
    [[GameManager getInstance] addB2Sprite: CUBE32x32
                                        at: CGPointMake(435-x, H-32)];
    [[GameManager getInstance] addB2Sprite: CUBE32x32
                                        at: CGPointMake(286-x,
                                            H-32*3-16)];
    [[GameManager getInstance] addB2Sprite: CUBE32x32
                                        at: CGPointMake(286-x,
                                            H-32*2-16)];
    [[GameManager getInstance] addB2Sprite: CUBE32x32
                                        at: CGPointMake(421-x,
                                            H-32*2-16)];
    [[GameManager getInstance] addB2Sprite: CUBE32x32
                                        at: CGPointMake(417-x,
                                            H-32*3-16)];
    [[GameManager getInstance] addB2Sprite: CUBE32x32
```

```
                                                at: CGPointMake(351-x,
                                                    H-32*7)];
[[GameManager getInstance] addB2Sprite: CUBE32x32
                                    at: CGPointMake(326-x, H-32)];
[[GameManager getInstance] addB2Sprite: CUBE32x32
                                    at: CGPointMake(388-x, H-32)];

[[GameManager getInstance] addB2Sprite: CUBE64x16
                                    at: CGPointMake(269-x,
                                        H-32-16)];
[[GameManager getInstance] addB2Sprite: CUBE64x16
                                    at: CGPointMake(335-x,
                                        H-32-16)];
[[GameManager getInstance] addB2Sprite: CUBE64x16
                                    at: CGPointMake(399-x,
                                        H-32-16)];
[[GameManager getInstance] addB2Sprite: CUBE64x16
                                    at: CGPointMake(304-x,
                                        H-32*4)];
[[GameManager getInstance] addB2Sprite: CUBE64x16
                                    at: CGPointMake(370-x,
                                        H-32*4)];
[[GameManager getInstance] addB2Sprite: CUBE64x16
                                    at: CGPointMake(332-x,
                                        H-32*6)];

[[GameManager getInstance] addB2Sprite: CUBE16x16
                                    at: CGPointMake(360-x,
                                        H-16*4)];
[[GameManager getInstance] addB2Sprite: CUBE16x16
                                    at: CGPointMake(360-x,
                                        H-16*5)];
[[GameManager getInstance] addB2Sprite: CUBE16x16
                                    at: CGPointMake(360-x,
                                        H-16*6)];
[[GameManager getInstance] addB2Sprite: CUBE16x16
                                    at: CGPointMake(360-x,
                                        H-16*7)];
[[GameManager getInstance] addB2Sprite: CUBE16x16
                                    at: CGPointMake(392-x,
                                        H-16*4)];
[[GameManager getInstance] addB2Sprite: CUBE16x16
                                    at: CGPointMake(325-x,
                                        H-16*9)];
[[GameManager getInstance] addB2Sprite: CUBE16x16
                                    at: CGPointMake(325-x,
                                        H-16*10)];
[[GameManager getInstance] addB2Sprite: CUBE16x16
                                    at: CGPointMake(325-x,
                                        H-16*11)];
[[GameManager getInstance] addB2Sprite: CUBE16x16
                                    at: CGPointMake(389-x,
                                        H-16*9)];
[[GameManager getInstance] addB2Sprite: CUBE16x16
                                    at: CGPointMake(389-x,
                                        H-16*10)];
```

```
    [[GameManager getInstance] addB2Sprite: CUBE16x16
                                        at: CGPointMake(389-x,
                                            H-16*11)];
    }

@end
```

To make the house more easily movable horizontally, we have added another variable along with x that allows for the definition of an offset. You can try out various values until you are satisfied with the level architecture. Of course, it is a good idea with larger projects to automate the input of the level data with a parser (adapted to the output format of the level editor used) (Figure 7.10).

To integrate a new Level class, we add the following implementation to the GameManager class in the loadGame method:

```
//level setup
level = [[Level alloc] init];
[level setLevel];
[level release];
```

After the setLevel method has been called, the Level instance can be released directly, since the required sprites have already been added to the game.

The swipe gesture for the blue chicks is now implemented using the same pattern that we employed for the zombie game.

---

**Listing 7.12  BlueBird.h**

---

```
#import "SpriteB2.h"

@interface BlueBird : SpriteB2 {
    bool touchAction;
    bool used;
}

- (void) touchBegan: (CGPoint) touchPoint;
- (void) touchEnded: (CGPoint) touchPoint;

@end
```

---

**Listing 7.13  BlueBird.m**

---

```
#import "BlueBird.h"

@implementation BlueBird

- (void) additionalSetup {
    type = BLUEBIRD;
```

```
        [super additionalSetup];
}

- (void) touchBegan: (CGPoint) point {
    if ([self checkColWithPoint: point] && !used) {
        touchAction = true;
    }
}

- (void) touchEnded: (CGPoint) point {
    if (touchAction) {
        touchAction = false;
        used = true;
        frameStep = 4;//eyes begin to blink

        //xf < 0 to the left, xf > 0 to the right
        float xf = (point.x - pos.x - frameW/2.0f) * 50;
        //yf < 0 downward, yf > 0 upward (inverted y-axis)
        float yf = (point.y - pos.y - frameH/2.0f) * -1 * 50;

        body->ApplyForceToCenter(b2Vec2(xf/B2_RATIO, yf/B2_RATIO));
    }
}

@end
```

As soon as a finger touches a bird, the touchAction flag is set to true. For this, we need only carry out a collision check with the finger position (TP) in the touchBegan: method. In addition, we check whether the current bird instance has previously been used (used), since according to our game concept, each bird can be used only once.

In the touchEnded method, we are informed where the finger has left the display. This point, together with the midpoint of the chick, forms a vector whose length and direction determine the force with which the chick is hurled against the tower (Figure 7.10). The longer the arrow is, the greater is the force. For purposes of debugging, you can, of course, draw in the line between the chick and the touch end point. The slingshot in Angry Birds works in the opposite way: The bird is pulled back and then flies in the opposite direction. Since the force vector consists of an x- and a y-component, we can pass the vector directly

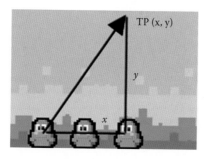

**Figure 7.10** Positioning of the level graphics. The touch point represents a direction vector.

to the `ApplyForceToCenter()` method of the Box2D object, and the chick begins to fly in the given direction. Since the force is applied to the midpoint of the object, a negative x-value indicates a flight to the left, 0 upward, and x > 0 to the right. Since the y-axis under Box2D runs in the opposite direction, we multiply the y-component by –1. As you can see, you can also make the force act downward—namely, when the y-value is negative. To enhance the bird's flight path, we multiply the x-direction by the factor 50. Of course, you are free to experiment with other values.

Of course, we still have to ensure that the touch point is passed to the blue chicks. As is usual under iOS, this is processed via the `UIView`. Since we have to process the touch end point for the Free the Birds game, we complete the `touchesEnded:withEvent:` interface in the `MainView` class.

```
- (void) touchesEnded: (NSSet *) touches withEvent: (UIEvent *) event {
    CGPoint p = [[touches anyObject] locationInView: self];
    [gameManager touchEnded: p];
}
```

Now we can make the necessary modifications in the GameManager.

Listing 7.14  Touch Handling in the GameManager

```
- (void) touchBegan: (CGPoint) p {
    [self handleStates];
    if (state = = PLAY_GAME) {
        for (Sprite *sprite in sprites) {
            if ([sprite isActive]) {
                if ([sprite getType] = = BLUEBIRD) {
                    [(BlueBird *) sprite touchBegan: p];
                }
            }
        }
    }
}

- (void) touchMoved: (CGPoint) p {
}

- (void) touchEnded: (CGPoint) p {
    if (state = = PLAY_GAME) {
        for (Sprite *sprite in sprites) {
            if ([sprite isActive]) {
                if ([sprite getType] = = BLUEBIRD) {
                    [(BlueBird *) sprite touchEnded: p];
                }
            }
        }
    }

    if (p.x > W-130 && p.y < 30) {
        state = LOAD_GAME;
    }
}
```

7. On the Trail of Angry Birds—Physics Engine Box2D

Aside from the [Restart] button, the touch points are of relevance only for the blue chicks. When a touch occurs, the sprite array is iterated until an active blue chick is discovered. The touch information is then passed to the chick. The touch-moved information is not needed for the game.

## 7.5.4 Winning Ending

The game is won when all the yellow birds have landed to the right of the lantern. We can reverse this condition and check whether there are still chicks located to the left of the lantern and continue the game until that condition is no longer satisfied. With the flag (gameWon), we can shift the game into the GAME_WON state.

Listing 7.15  Game Loop

```
- (void) playGame {
    timer++;

    [self drawOGLImg: @"background.png" at: CGPointMake(0, 0)];
    [self drawOGLString: @"[RESTART]" at: CGPointMake(W-130, 0)];

    [self manageSprites];
    [self renderSprites];

    [[Box2dWrapper getInstance] update];

    //winning condition
    [self drawOGLImg: @"targetLine.png" at: CGPointMake(targetLineX-8,
                                                        H-128)];
    bool gameWon = true;
    for (Sprite *sprite in sprites) {
        if ([sprite getType] = = YELLOWBIRD) {
            if ([sprite getPos].x < targetLineX) {
                gameWon = false;
            }
        }
    }
    if (gameWon) {
        state = GAME_WON;
    }
}
```

Since the winning condition must be checked at each frame, we can implement the necessary logic directly in the game loop. Optionally, you could also integrate the code into the renderSprites method and thereby save an additional iteration, since this is also iterated in each frame for all sprites, and the winning condition depends only on the sprite state. In addition, in the game loop we draw the finish line in the form of a lantern graphic.

To illustrate that a yellow bird has passed the lantern, it should give a cry of joy and blink its eyes. For this, we can use the checkSprite method to write "Yippie!" above the sprite as soon as its x-position is beyond the goal line (Figure 7.11).

**Figure 7.11** Screen shots of the game.

```
- (void) checkSprite: (Sprite *) sprite {
    if ([sprite getType] = = YELLOWBIRD) {
        CGPoint pos = [sprite getPos];
        if ([sprite getPos].x > = targetLineX) {
            [(YellowBird *) sprite twinkle];
            [self drawOGLString: @"Yippie!"
                            at: CGPointMake(pos.x-20, pos.y-25)];
        }
    }
}
```

## 7.5.5 Outlook

Of course, Free the Birds represents only a small slice of what is possible with Box2D. Indeed, one could write a whole book on this topic. On the other hand, the fundamentals are not too difficult to understand, so you should now have the necessary tools for your own experiments.

With a few modifications, you could change the game in a number of ways. For example, you could deactivate the used flag to allow the player additional swipes with the blue chicks; as soon as a chick hits a tower, it can be hurled again at the birdhouse. You could vary the definitions of the objects in Box2D: With the Density property, for example, you could increase or decrease the stability of the birdhouse. You could give each yellow chick its own flight characteristics by introducing a random force. Of course, Box2D also offers the possibility of querying the collision points of an object (b2Contact). In this way you could determine, for instance, whether a bird can fly upward (without causing the tower to collapse).

And, of course, you can change the nature of the levels. Since the screen, with its $320 \times 480$ image points, does not offer a lot of space, you could create a higher level and allow the player to scroll or zoom the picture by a pinch or pan gesture (or, alternatively, with zoom buttons or a pan D-pad). Thanks to OpenGL ES, it is easy to scale or shift an entire game scene. To scale the entire screen, for example, call the `glScalef()` function in the `drawRect:` method of the `MainView` before the `GameManager` renders the game elements. With the combination of `glTranslatef()` and `glScaleF()`, you can determine the zoom midpoint, as was shown earlier for rotation in the `Tex` class. Of course, scaling is suitable as well for dynamic zoom changes during the flight of a blue chick. Also make sure that you adapt the touch point with respect to the shifting or scaling factor if you want to allow interaction with the game at various zoom levels or pan positions.

# $8$ The GLKit Framework—OpenGL ES Made Easy

## ■ 8.1 Introduction

For iPhone developers, iOS 5, released in fall 2011, not only represents one of the most extensive updates so far, but also closes a significant hole in relation to OpenGL ES: Even though games are among the most successful apps, a technology that does *not* come from Apple is the preferred one. Moreover, the OpenGL ES framework from the Khronos Group is lacking important functionalities, such as the implementation of a 3D camera. Apart from that, as we have already seen, the integration of the library into the UIView-based iOS architecture is anything but elegant.

With the GLKit, Apple has introduced for the first time an Objective-C-based framework that is supposed to unify and simplify working with OpenGL ES. Not least, in relation to OpenGL ES 2.0, it lowers the learning curve for beginners, since the change from ES 1.1 to ES 2.0 can be carried out without much adaptation. Since the GLKit has been available only since iOS 5 and since the update can be installed only on the newer devices—that is, from iPhone 3GS/iPod Touch 2 and iPad—it is impossible that an ES 1.1 device not be able optionally also to support ES 2.0.

### 8.1.1 Pros and Cons

Nevertheless, the GLKit framework is no substitute for ES 1.1/2.0. For many uses, it remains necessary to know the basics of OpenGL. With the help of the GLKit, textures of numerous image formats can be read in with no difficulty; however, there is still no importer for 3D models. Looked at in its entirety, the GLKit represents a step in the right direction, but it is not (yet) a substitute for game frameworks such as Cocos2D, Sparrow, and Unity, which make knowledge of OpenGL ES almost completely unnecessary.

You should also consider the extent to which the use of the GLKit makes sense for your particular project. Based on experience, it will be some time before all users have implemented the upgrade to a new iOS version, so, until then, your app will be boycotted in the App Store. And there exist several million iOS devices that cannot be updated to at least iOS 5—for example, because a compatible graphics chip that supports OpenGL ES 2.0 was not installed. Furthermore, it is important to keep in mind that although the GLKit makes your work as a developer easier, it does not offer any truly new functionality that could not already be realized with ES 1.1/2.0.

Why, then, should we, as game developers, bother at all to learn a new framework? Although the focus of this book has been the development of games for all iOS devices, you should not miss out on the GLKit, since in important areas it provides highly optimized solutions that also facilitate entry into professional game development. And, finally, you already know how you can support older iOS devices as needed. If you wish to go more deeply into ES 2.0 development, the GLKit represents your first choice, since many ES 1.1 functions are simply missing for ES 2.0, but are again available through GLKBaseEffects. In sum, you still have the choice to use the GLKit exclusively for ES 1.1 or ES 2.0, even if Apple itself sees the actual purpose of the API as facilitating the use of ES 2.0. For every view, you can determine which variant you wish to use, though a mixture of both APIs in the same view is not possible.

Documentation of the framework can be found at the Apple Developer Center under *http://developer.apple.com/library/ios/#documentation/GLkit/Reference/GLKit_Collection/_index.html*.

## 8.1.2 Overview

The number of new classes is relatively straightforward and can be divided into four types:

- **View support:** GLKit supports the creation of an OpenGL view using a standalone GLKView or a view controller (GLKitViewController) with integrated view, update/render loop, and support for various display orientations.

- **Texture support:** OpenGL ES requires the raw pixel data of an image to create a texture. GLKit offers various methods for creating textures directly from various image output formats. Textures can also optionally be loaded asynchronously via a background thread.

- **Math library:** Many matrix and vector routines for calculating perspective or implementing a camera are available for OpenGL through the GLU supplementary libraries. For the mobile ES version, however, these are missing. Their equivalents can be found, optimized for iOS, through Apple's GLMath library.

- **Effects:** While ES 1.0 offers the programmer ready-made functions for such things as setting light, color, and material properties ("fixed pipeline"), these are lacking in ES 2.0, so they must be created. The missing ES 1.0 functions are available under ES 2.0 through GLKBaseEffects. You will also find additional effects such as fog, skyboxes, and various light/material reflections.

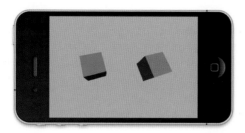

**Figure 8.1** The new "OpenGL Game" example app (Xcode template from iOS 5).

New effects such as the skybox effect (GLKSkyboxEffect) and reflection maps (GLKReflectionMapEffect) are available only under ES 2.0 due to the special connection to the graphics chip (Figure 8.1).

## 8.2 A First Example

Once you have downloaded iOS 5 together with Xcode from the Apple Dev Center, you will find under the template projects a new OpenGL ES example project (NEW PROJECT > OPENGL GAME). This demonstrates how you can simplify shader programming under ES 2.0; the blue cube is traditionally created with the help of shaders, while the red cube is implemented simply with the GLKit framework and therefore requires much less code.

But it can be done with even fewer lines! We would like to show this through our first GLKit example. Let us create a new empty Xcode project and begin by adding the requisite libraries (the complete project can be found in the download folder under "GLKitBasics"):

- GLKit.framework
- OpenGLES.framework

If you plan to add to an existing project in an older version of Xcode with the GLKit, you should, without fail, remove all old frameworks from the project and add new ones. Under iOS 5, parts of the libraries were modified, so you should bring everything up to date.

The simplest architecture includes a view controller. In the GLKit version, this also offers a sort of integrated game loop, which is precisely what we as game developers need. We shall now show how to use the GLKit for 2D games. An example for 3D will come later.

Till now, our app has consisted simply of the AppDelegate, which Xcode has already created for us. The project uses a total of two classes and no additional resources. So let us now add the second class, the GLKitViewController.

---

**Listing 8.1** GLKitViewController.h

```
#import <UIKit/UIKit.h>
#import <GLKit/GLKit.h>

@interface GLKitViewController : GLKViewController

- (void) setOGLProjection;
- (void) drawOGLTriangle;

@end
```

---

Listing 8.2 GLKitViewController.m

```objc
#import "GLKitViewController.h"

@implementation GLKitViewController

#pragma mark - Initialization

- (id) initWithNibName: (NSString *) nibNameOrNil
               bundle: (NSBundle *) nibBundleOrNil
{
   self = [super initWithNibName: nibNameOrNil bundle: nibBundleOrNil];
   if (self) {
       GLKView *view = (GLKView *) self.view;
       view.context = [[EAGLContext alloc]
           initWithAPI: kEAGLRenderingAPIOpenGLES1];
       self.preferredFramesPerSecond = 33;
   }
   return self;
}

#pragma mark - GLKView and GLKViewController delegate methods

- (void) update
{
    //update game logic
}

- (void) glkView: (GLKView *) view drawInRect: (CGRect) rect
{
    static float b = 0;
    b + = 0.001;

    //render game
    glClearColor(0.1, 0.5, 0.1 + b, 1.0);
    glClear(GL_COLOR_BUFFER_BIT);

    [self setOGLProjection];
    [self drawOGLTriangle];
}

#pragma mark - OpenGL

- (void) setOGLProjection {
   glLoadIdentity();
   int w = self.view.bounds.size.width;
   int h = self.view.bounds.size.height;
   glOrthof(0, w, h, 0, 0, 1);//2D perspective
}

- (void) drawOGLTriangle {
    static int x = 0; x++;
    GLshort vertices[] = {
        x + 0, 250,
        x + 250, 250,
```

```
         x + 0, 0,
    };

    glMatrixMode(GL_MODELVIEW);
    glEnableClientState(GL_VERTEX_ARRAY);
    glVertexPointer(2, GL_SHORT, 0, vertices);
    glColor4f(1, 0, 0, 1);
    glDrawArrays(GL_TRIANGLES, 0, 3);
}

#pragma mark - Touch handling methods

//...

#pragma mark - Lifecycle

//...

#pragma mark - Orientation

- (BOOL) shouldAutorotateToInterfaceOrientation:
    (UIInterfaceOrientation) interfaceOrientation {
    return YES;
}

@end
```

To use the GLKit API, you must first import the <GLKit/GLKit.h> header. Although in some places we call OpenGL functions, you do not need to specify the required OpenGL explicitly, since it is already linked via the GLKit header. Nevertheless, you must also add the OpenGL ES framework to the project in addition to the GLKit framework since, for some classes, the GLKit needs access to the OpenGL ES library as well.

Since we do not want to use the Interface Builder, there is no need to create a nib file, and the controller can be created directly via the ppDelegate. To do this, add the following initialization in the application:didFinishLaunchingWithOptions: method:

```
self.window.rootViewController = [[GLKitViewController alloc] init];
```

Done! The OpenGL ES project can already be run; it displays a red triangle moving in front of a background whose blue value changes slightly at each frame—not bad if we compare the amount of work it would have taken under OpenGL ES without the help of the GLKit to initialize the render and frame buffers and designate the UIView as a CAEAGLLayer. The magic is accomplished by the GLKViewController, from which our controller is derived and which is again the OpenGL version of a view controller.

All of the GLKit code that is needed can be found in the controller's init. We have only to take care that the desired OpenGL ES context is set; in our case, this is the kEAGLRenderingAPIOpenGLES1 variant. For the 2.0 API, you would instead pass kEAGLRenderingAPIOpenGLES2 as a parameter. The context is set as a parameter for the GLKView, which was already created via the controller and serves as the actual

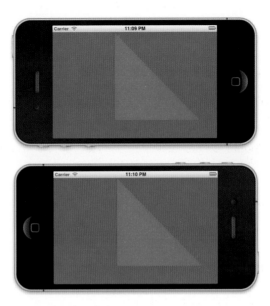

**Figure 8.2** An initial GLKit test: the display automatically rotates (above, the home button is to the right; below, it is to the left).

drawing area. As a further convenience, the controller also offers us a rendering loop consisting of the delegate methods update and glkView:drawInRect:. We have merely to set the desired frame rate via preferredFramesPerSecond, which in the present case is 33 frames per second. This is not a fixed rate, but rather an ideal value that is adhered to as closely as possible.

In addition, the integrated loop offers the advantage of separating the game logic and the graphical output according to the MVC (model–view–controller) model. The two methods update and glkView:drawInRect: are called alternately, once per frame each. Position calculations and collision checks are ideally placed in the update method, while only the actual rendering calls of the content take place in the glkView:drawInRect: method. The two methods are called by different threads and thus can be internally optimized since, for example, the game logic can be computed in a background thread by the CPU while the glkView:drawInRect: can contain nothing but code that is passed to the GPU (UI thread) (Figure 8.2).

As you can see from the code sample, the OpenGL source code used previously can be used again without any problem. The determination of the 2D perspective and the implementation of the red 2D triangle correspond precisely to the previously discussed OpenGL code.

## 8.2.1 Setting the Perspective with the GLKit

Alternatively, you can also access the relevant functions in the GLKit library. To set the 2D perspective, for example, you have the GLKMatrix4MakeOrtho function at your disposal. However, it returns, like all math helper functions, just a matrix. To apply the 2D perspective to the model data of the scene, you must pass the 16 values of the matrix to the glMultMatrixf() function. Only then will all vertices be multiplied by the new matrix and thus ensure the desired view on the display:

```
GLKMatrix4 m4 = GLKMatrix4MakeOrtho(0, w, h, 0, 0, 1);
glMultMatrixf(m4.m);
```

As for any UIView, you have available the familiar interfaces touchesBegan: withEvent:, touchesMoved:withEvent:, etc. so that you can process the touch input as you did previously.

A very useful bonus is provided by the shouldAutorotateToInterface Orientation: method, which is available for every view controller and now can be used for an OpenGL or GLKit view:

```
- (BOOL) shouldAutorotateToInterfaceOrientation:
    (UIInterfaceOrientation) interfaceOrientation {
    return YES;
}
```

For each of the four possible orientations, we return the value YES so that the display is automatically rotated when the user turns the device. Thus, the triangle and the status bar are always located at the upper edge of the screen and, via self.view.bounds. size, the perspective is automatically adjusted so that the triangle maintains its proportions. For a game, you would generally allow only one perspective in order to avoid accidental rotations during a game.

# ▋ 8.3  GLKitView and Game Loop

However, it is also possible to do without a controller and work just with a view and the obligatory delegate. You thereby obtain more control over the game loop and more easily keep the source code backward compatible with older iOS models. Using such an example, we would now like to look more closely at working with textures. You can find the complete project under the name "GLKit2D."

The delegate is included according to the familiar pattern; it has a game loop using NSTimer or, optionally, the CADisplayLink version. A call to the drawRect: method of the view is triggered in the loop selector method via setNeedsDisplay.

The addition of GLKitView is done just as for any other UIView and is implemented in the delegate as follows:

```
glKitView = [[GLKitView alloc]
    initWithFrame: [UIScreen mainScreen].applicationFrame];
glKitView.backgroundColor = [UIColor grayColor];
[glKitView setupOGL];
[self.window addSubview: glKitView];
```

The setupOGL method takes care of setting the EAGLContext context in the GLKitView class:

```
- (void) setupOGL {
    eaglContext = [[EAGLContext alloc] initWithAPI:
        kEAGLRenderingAPIOpenGLES1];
    if (!eaglContext || ![EAGLContext setCurrentContext: eaglContext]) {
        [self release];
    } else {
```

```
        self.context = eaglContext;

    if (!gameManager) {
        gameManager = [GameManager getInstance];
    }
    }
}
```

We also check this time whether the context can be initialized and only then link the OpenGL context with the view and initialize the GameManager, which is to contain all the game-related tasks. With this, the drawRect: method of the GLKitView contains only a clear call to delete the content of the screen, followed by [gameManager drawStatesWithFrame: rect]. You can see that the GLKitView behaves up to the assignment of the context just like a garden-variety view. You can now, just as before, control all the OpenGL code via the GameManager and additional helper classes.

To see that we can also still render in a reasonable way with the GLKit, we draw 100 randomly positioned blue rectangles using the playGame method of the GameManager, which is called in the tempo of the game loop (Figure 8.3):

```
for (int i = 0; i < 100; i++) {
    int x = [self getRndBetween: 0 and: W];
    int y = [self getRndBetween: 0 and: H];
    [self drawOGLRect: CGRectMake(x, y, 30, 30)];
}
```

We would now like to try the same thing with textures. For this, we add an additional helper class called Tex, which takes care of rendering a given image to the display. It is necessary only that the dimensions of the image be powers of 2, as was the case earlier.

**Listing 8.3 Tex.h**

```
#import <GLKit/GLKit.h>
#import <OpenGLES/ES1/gl.h>

@interface Tex : NSObject {
    GLKTextureInfo *textureInfo;
    GLKEffectPropertyTexture *textureProperty;
    GLuint textureID;
    int width;
    int height;
}

//initializer
- (void) createTexFromImage: (NSString *) picName;

//render the texture
- (void) drawAt: (CGPoint) p;

//getter
- (GLuint) getTextureID;
- (int) getWidth;
- (int) getHeight;

@end
```

Figure 8.3 Randomly generated blue squares on a yellow background.

The class expects the specification of an image name, and then the texture can be rendered via the drawAt: method of OpenGL. Since the class GLKTTextureInfo contains information such as width and height about the texture that has been read in, we store the texture ID required by OpenGL in the GLKEffectPropertyTexture instance.

Listing 8.4 Tex.m

```
#import "Tex.h"

@implementation Tex

- (void) createTexFromImage: (NSString *) picName {
    //load texture
    NSError *error;
    NSString *path = [[NSBundle mainBundle] pathForResource: picName
                                                     ofType: @"png"];
    textureInfo = [GLKTextureLoader textureWithContentsOfFile: path
                                                      options: nil
                                                        error: &error];

    if (textureInfo && !error) {
        width = textureInfo.width;
        height = textureInfo.height;
        if ((width & (width-1)) ! = 0 || (height & (height-1)) ! = 0
            || width > 2048 || height > 2048) {
            NSLog(
                @"ERROR:%@ width and/or height is
                not a power of 2 or is > 2048!", picName);
        }

        //generate texture
        textureProperty = [[GLKEffectPropertyTexture alloc] init];
        textureProperty.name = textureInfo.name;
        textureID = textureProperty.name;

        //activate texture-related states globally
        glEnable(GL_BLEND);
        glBlendFunc(GL_ONE, GL_ONE_MINUS_SRC_ALPHA);
        glEnableClientState(GL_TEXTURE_COORD_ARRAY);
    } else {
```

```
            NSLog(@"ERROR:%@ not found, texture%@ not created.",
                  [error localizedDescription], picName);
       }
}

- (void) drawAt: (CGPoint) p {
      //... as before
}

- (GLuint) getTextureID {
      return textureID;
}

- (int) getWidth {
      return width;
}

- (int) getHeight {
      return height;
}

- (void) dealloc {
      NSLog(@"Delete texture, ID:%i", textureID);
      glDeleteTextures(1, &textureID);
      [textureProperty release];
      [textureInfo release];
      [super dealloc];
}

@end
```

Once the texture has been created, it can be rendered at any time using the standard tools of OpenGL (depending on the version ES 1.1/2.0). Access to OpenGL ES is necessary to delete a texture from memory, since the GLKit does not (yet) encapsulate this task for us. The main new feature is contained in the createTexFromImage: method. The GLKTextureLoader class contains a number of ways to load textures. Here, we choose the textureWithContentsOfFile:options:error: option, to which we have only to pass an NSBundle path to our figure. As an option, various constants for texture generation can be specified along the way via a dictionary, such as the desired orientation. In this case, we can do without this, since the texture vertices within the drawAt: method follow the UIView convention, so that here no modifications are required (as was the case in the previous examples as well).

The texture has now been read in via the GLKit, but it remains in the graphics memory as a not explicitly usable texture. This task is accomplished implicitly for us by the GLKTextureInfo instance, to which we pass the name—that is, the ID—of the currently input image. Via the GLKTextureLoader, the most common required flags for texture behavior are set, such as GL_CLAMP_TO_EDGE and GL_LINEAR instead of GL_NEAREST, so here we have only to worry about the desired blend function, which causes the images to be rendered, as expected, together with their transparency setting (alpha channel). After all, in our example we are dealing with 2D textures rather than a completely textured 3D model without transparent surfaces (Figure 8.4).

Figure 8.4 A flock of birds.

In order to be able to render many different textures simultaneously to the screen, as is generally necessary in games, we again use a dictionary within the `GameManager`. The figure can be rendered directly via

```
- (void) drawGLKitImage: (NSString*) name at: (CGPoint) p {
    Tex *tex = [[self getDictionary] objectForKey: name];
    if (!tex) {
        tex = [[Tex alloc] init];
        [tex createTexFromImage: name];
        [[self getDictionary] setObject: tex forKey: name];
        NSLog(@"%@ placed as a Tex in the dictionary.", name);
        [tex release];
    }
    [tex drawAt: p];
}
```

without our having to worry about initialization or memory management. If the figure is already loaded, the stored texture is used; otherwise, a new texture is created.

All that is now missing is the code to create 100 small chicks randomly:

```
for (int i = 0; i < 100; i++) {
    int x = [self getRndBetween: 0 and: W];
    int y = [self getRndBetween: 0 and: H];
    [self drawGLKitImage: @"blueBird" at: CGPointMake(x, y)];
}
```

An advantage of the current GLKit library is that it provides great freedom in the implementation of your ideas. You can reuse existing source code without major modifications, and you also have easy access to additional functionalities.

## ▮ 8.4 GLKit and 3D—Using a Camera according to the GLU Model

Our last example will clarify the use of the GLKit in three-dimensional space. We begin with the architecture from the previous example and extend it with a 3D perspective. (You will find the source code in the download folder under "GLKit3D.") As you know, under OpenGL, we need an additional buffer for this, the so-called depth buffer, which we can add with an additional line of code in the GLKitView:

```
self.context = eaglContext;
self.drawableDepthFormat = GLKViewDrawableDepthFormat16;
```

In the GameManager we create the 3D perspective just as in the previous 3D examples via the glFrustumf() function. Alternatively, we could use the new GLKit version GLKMatrix4MakeFrustum(), which takes the same parameters but returns a matrix that, in a further step, must be multiplied by the model data of the scene. Under ES 2.0, you can use the matrix of the scene directly as an effect.

We also implement a rotating cube using the drawOGLCube method, whose code is identical to that in the previous examples. For this we use directly the OpenGL glRotatef() function, although you have an alternative in GLKMatrix4Make Rotation from the extensive mathematics arsenal of the GLKit, which as a bonus returns a matrix with the result of the rotation (Figure 8.5).

What is of interest now is to show how easily the rotating cube can be viewed from a variety of perspectives with a camera. We have implemented this in the playGame method of the GameManager as follows:

```
//camera
static float z = 0; z + = 0.1;
glLoadIdentity();
GLKMatrix4 glm = GLKMatrix4MakeLookAt(0, 0, z,//camera position
                                      0, 0, z-1,//look-at
                                      0, 1, 0);//"stationary"
glMultMatrixf(glm.m);

[self drawOGLCube];
```

The GLKMatrix4MakeLookAt() function is also to be found in the math library of the GLKit. It returns a camera implementation based on the gluLookAt() function. If, in Xcode, you right-click on JUMP-TO-DEFINITION, you can see the implementation

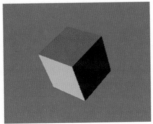

Figure 8.5 A cube that gradually becomes smaller.

of the camera. Similarly to our own camera version, this one's first two vectors give the position and the point at which the camera is pointing. The third vector, (0, 1, 0), defines how the camera is set up. Since the vector points upward, we are looking at the display in portrait mode. With this vector you could, for example, cause the camera to rotate.

Since the cube is located one unit from the coordinate origin and the z-axis is pointing toward us, the cube will grow smaller continuously if we shift the camera 0.1 units along the positive z-axis at each frame. On the device, it seems, of course, as though the cube were moving away from us, though in reality it is the GLKit camera that is moving along with us—the viewers of the scene—away from the midpoint.

# 9 Complete Control: Game Sounds with OpenAL

## ▌ 9.1 Introduction

In addition to OpenGL, Apple provides another interface that comes from a third party. The OpenAL framework (Open Audio Library) has been distributed since 1999 by Creative Labs. Not only was the library used in the Sound Blaster Live sound cards for hardware acceleration of audio reproduction, but it also was used, in addition to the Apple Mac OS, in Microsoft's Xbox/Xbox 360.

Like OpenGL, OpenAL consists of a number of C-based functions that support direct use of audio buffers. This gives you maximum control over the sound being played, and you can even make changes in real time. In addition, the use of the API is the first choice when it comes to game sounds since different sounds or the same sounds can be played with no latency.

Recall the sequencer app from Section 3.11 in Chapter 3, which was able to play several music files simultaneously, but always stopped like sounds before playback, and only then were they output. In addition, with the use of Apple's own AVFoundation framework, the performance is not quite as crisp and optimized as under OpenAL. On the other hand, the use of the OpenAL library requires a bit more effort to learn.

But the effort is worth it. In addition to the hesitation-free reproduction and (optional) control over the sound data at playback time, OpenAL is suited above all as a complement to OpenGL and is advertised by Creative Labs as a 3D sound API. Thus, in addition to buffers for each sound, one can define a listener and as many sound sources as desired, distributed in the space. The listener defines, so to speak, the position at which the player is located, and the sources represent the game objects in 3D space, which can be associated with any buffer. The result is a realistic audio playback that updates the audio sources in stereo panorama depending on the positions of the listener and the source. For mobile devices, which are typically played without headphones, we can usually dispense with 3D audio effects and concentrate on the reproduction of latency-free and polyphonic sounds.

You will find further information on this topic at the OpenAL homepage: *http://connect.creativelabs.com/openal/default.aspx*. Among other things, you will find the OpenAL specification 1.1 of the framework: *http://connect.creativelabs.com/openal/Documentation/OpenAL%201.1%20Specification.htm#_Toc199835880*.

This has been used since iOS 2.1 and is based on the Core Audio interface from Apple. This means as well that, in principle, you should use uncompressed audio files (PCM), either already transformed into *.caf format or as WAV files. For playing polyphonic sounds, Apple recommends a sample rate of 22 kHz. OpenAL, however, is fast enough to enable you to obtain clean sounds in monoformat at the CD-quality rate of 44.1 kHz.

## ■ 9.2  Encapsulation of the OpenAL API

To create the most easily reusable OpenAL components as possible, we begin a new project based on the sequencer app of Section 3.11 in Chapter 3. We use the same sounds, but encapsulate the playback in a new singleton class called SoundOAL. If you want to use OpenAL for your own games, you have merely to integrate this class. You can find the complete project in the downloads folder under the name "OpenALSounds" (Figure 9.1)

Listing 9.1  SoundOAL.h

```
#import <Foundation/Foundation.h>
#import <OpenAL/al.h>
#import <OpenAL/alc.h>
#import <AudioToolbox/AudioToolbox.h>

@interface SoundOAL: NSObject {
    ALCcontext *context;
    ALCdevice *device;
    NSMutableArray *soundIDs;
    NSMutableDictionary *soundIDDictionary;
    NSMutableDictionary *soundBufferIDDictionary;
}

+ (SoundOAL *) getInstance;
- (void) setupOpenAL;
- (void) logErrors: (OSStatus) status;
- (NSUInteger) findFreeSoundID;

- (void) loadSound: (NSString*) soundName
               Hz: (NSUInteger) sampleRate;
- (void) playSound: (NSString*) soundName;
- (void) loopSound: (NSString*) soundName;
- (void) stopSound: (NSString*) soundName;

@end
```

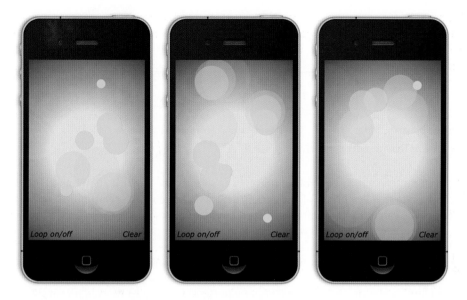

Figure 9.1 The sequencer app with yellow sound circles.

To be able to use the OpenAL framework in an app, you have to add the OpenAL. framework to the project via the link libraries dialog, as well as the AudioToolbox. framework. We will use this later to read in the sound files. Let us first look at the header interface.

In addition to importing the required header, we see that we can use the same interface as for the sequencer app; that is, we can play, loop, and stop sounds through the file name. We also need a loading method and a couple of setup methods.

# ▌ 9.3  How Is Sound Formed?

From the perspective of OpenAL, a sound consists mainly of two components. The first is the actual audio data, which can be referenced in memory in the form of a buffer ID. The second is a sound ID, which in turn represents the concrete sound source. From the sound IDs, you can begin playback, provided that the sound ID was linked to a buffer containing the actual audio data. IDs can be linked to any buffer; a buffer is, so to speak, a container for the raw data that make up the sound.

But what is meant by the raw data of a sound, and why is the use of buffers so important for hesitation-free sound playback?

In order for us to hear music, the membranes of the loudspeakers have to be set vibrating. For example, the "A" of concert pitch has a frequency of 440 Hz.

The values of the sound can be computed in terms of the sine function: $y = a*\sin(2*Pi*f*t)$.

The x-axis represents the time over which the tone sounds (t), while the y-axis gives the amplitude, which is a measure of the sound's intensity—the degree to which the membrane of a loudspeaker moves outward (positive y-value) and inward (negative y-value). The movement of the loudspeaker sets the air vibrating, and our ears receive

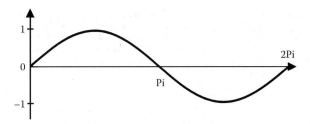

Figure 9.2 The sine curve (one cycle).

these vibrations, which our brain interprets as sound. The factor *a* allows us to increase (or decrease) the amplitude of the pure sine curve, which, as is well known, oscillates between the values –1 and 1, making the sound louder (or softer).

One cycle of the sine curve, as shown in Figure 9.2, runs from 0 to 2*Pi, where the value 2*Pi will by convention represent 1 second of time. The unit of frequency is the hertz (Hz), which means that our sine curve vibrates at a frequency of 1 Hz per second. A frequency of 1 Hz is inaudible to the human ear. If we want to create a sound at "concert A," we will need a sine curve that vibrates 440 times per second. We obtain this by multiplying the time value t by the factor f = 440. This means that only every 440th value of the sine curve is sample output. In other words, we obtain a vibration that changes sign exactly 440 times per second. Therefore, the membrane of the loudspeaker vibrates not 1 time, but 440 times per second.

The greater the amplitude is, the greater is the volume of air that is moved and hence the louder the sound is. What we actually hear (a newscaster or a Mozart sonata) is determined entirely by the amplitudes of the samples that constitute the waveform. And it is the sign that determines whether the membrane is moving forward or backward. In the case of an electrical signal, such as one created by an analog synthesizer, we do not need a sine function. The oscillation is created by the circuit, and the current brings the loudspeaker membrane exactly into the "rhythm" of the current.

However, if we are using a digital oscillator, then we must rely on the sine function and the vibration is less "fluid," since the amplitude can be detected only at discrete intervals of time. The same holds for all digital music, CDs, and, of course, for iOS playback devices. Let us suppose that we have a sound wave whose maximum amplitude is 128 y-units in one direction and –127 in the other. The audio raw data are then a sequence of numbers, such as the following:

```
82, 97, 108, 51, 73, 22, -27, -31, -25, -47, -68, -45, 10, 27, etc.
```

This could represent, for example, a digitized voice, a piece of music, or some random sequence of numbers generated by a computer program. To make this audible, we must know in what format the data are to be output and what the sampling rate is. The individual numbers in the sequence are known as "samples."

- **Format:** The format determines how precisely the amplitude fluctuations were recorded. Usually, a distinction is made between 8 and 16 bits. The former means that there is 1 byte available per sample, which makes the maximum amplitude values equal to 128 and –127 units. The format must be taken into account by the digital-to-analog (DA) converter, since it must reconcile these units with the maximum fluctuation of the loudspeaker.

- **Sample rate:** The sample rate determines how many times a second the sound source was sampled. Typical values are 8,000; 22,500; and 44,100 Hz. The last of these represents CD quality. Whereas in the case of a long-playing record the vibration is defined directly by the grooves in the vinyl platter (analog), which is then passed to the amplifier and thence to the loudspeakers, a CD contains only numerically coded samples—precisely 44,100 samples per second. For the human ear, such a sample rate is completely satisfactory. It is clear that with higher sample rates, larger data sets are involved, while lower sample rates detect the original sound source at greater intervals and therefore yield a less precise result.

To record music or other sound digitally, the analog signal must be digitized and stored in a particular audio format. The MP3 format is particularly space saving, but it cannot be directly played back through a DA converter without the compressed files first being decoded. Things are different with the PCM format. For example, if a piece of music is stored in WAV format, then the individual samples appear in the file in exactly the sequence in which they can be passed to the loudspeaker or DA converter. The format and sample rate appear before the data in a header definition so that every WAV file can be played back just as it was recorded.

As we have shown, this sequence of individual samples can be converted directly into sound. Through its buffers, OpenAL gives the possibility of storing samples in memory, and we can determine at any time when we want to direct the sample data to the loudspeaker.

This gives us maximal control over the sound, since we sit very close to the hardware and can output numbers to the loudspeaker whenever we want. Thus, for example, you can create random columns of numbers and listen to them. Of course, it would sound like radio static, but if played for a brief period of time, it could represent a suitable game sound for an explosion or a gunshot.

# 9.4 Creating a Polyphonic Sound Engine

For our sequencer example, we have created five WAV sounds with 16-bit samples and a sample rate of 44.1 kHz. To enable us to play them back without latency, the raw data in each file must be written to an OpenAL buffer. Furthermore, we define a certain number of sound sources to provide the desired polyphony. This means that we can link the columns of figures in a particular buffer with a sound source, and then we have only to inform OpenAL to move this sound source to the audio output.

Polyphony results mathematically from a simple addition of sounds or, more precisely, by adding the sampled values. Suppose we have two different sounds. At time t1, the first sound has the value 42, while the second sound has at this time the value –7. If the two sounds are added, the resulting sample value at time t1 will be 35. This is the principle of a digital mixer, and we will not concern ourselves with it any further, since OpenAL takes care of sound mixing for us.

## 9.4.1 Sound IDs and Buffers

For the OpenAL sound engine, we can define a maximum of 22 sound sources, which means that we need 22 sound IDs. In the header of the SoundOAL class we have already created an array for storing the respective sound IDs. Moreover, we would like to play the sounds based only on the file name. To be able to map the file names and the sound IDs dynamically, we create a dictionary called soundIDDictionary. We would also like to assign the respective audio raw data to the sound IDs. For this, we create the dictionary soundBufferIDDictionary, which also contains a mapping of file names and buffer data, so that we can find a corresponding audio buffer for every file name.

For our example, we shall use only five sound effects, but we would like to play them polyphonically. With 22 sound sources, the maximal polyphony is 22 voices, where theoretically, we could begin Sound1 eight times at different points in time, and Sound2 ten times so that, say, for Sound3, only four sound sources would be available.

In this way, we avoid the staccato effect, since a gun sound will be played at any point in time, even when the player presses the firing button several times per second. Although there is only one buffer for the gun sound, the sample data can be read at any time from the buffer and a sound ID can be assigned and then added in the mixer; the sound seems instantaneous, though with different start times, as with a canon (not a cannon!), but not so melodious.

The remaining methods of the SoundOAL header serve in the setup of OpenAL, and we would like to look at them now more closely.

Listing 9.2 SoundOAL.m

```
#import "SoundOAL.h"

@implementation SoundOAL

+ (SoundOAL *) getInstance {
    static SoundOAL *sound;
    @synchronized (self) {
        if(!sound) {
            sound = [[SoundOAL alloc] init];
            [sound setupOpenAL];
        }
    }
    return sound;
}

- (void) setupOpenAL {
    soundIDs = [[NSMutableArray alloc] init];
    soundIDDictionary = [[NSMutableDictionary alloc] init];
    soundBufferIDDictionary = [[NSMutableDictionary alloc] init];

    device = alcOpenDevice(NULL);

    if (device) {
        context = alcCreateContext(device, NULL);
        alcMakeContextCurrent(context);
```

```
        int maxSounds = 22;//polyphony: we have more slots than sounds
        for (int i = 0; i < maxSounds; i++) {
                NSUInteger soundID;
                alGenSources(1, &soundID);//create sound IDs
                [soundIDs addObject: [NSNumber numberWithUnsignedInt:
                                            soundID]];
        }

        [self logErrors: 0];
    }
}

- (void) loadSound:(NSString*) soundName
               Hz:(NSUInteger) sampleRate {
    //...
}

- (void) playSound: (NSString*) soundName {
    //...
}

- (void) loopSound: (NSString*) soundName {
    //...
}

- (void) stopSound: (NSString*) soundName {
    //...
}

- (NSUInteger) findFreeSoundID {
    //...
}

- (void) logErrors: (OSStatus) status {
    //...
}

- (void) dealloc {
    //...
}

@end
```

With the getInstance method, we implement the familiar singleton pattern, so only one instance of the class can be created. In the setupOpenAL method, which is automatically called once during initialization of the class, we create the array and dictionaries for the sound IDs and the buffers.

## 9.4.2 Audio Context

As was the case for OpenGL, we must next define the context in which we find ourselves. For this, we first obtain access to the audio device via alcOpenDevice() and determine with it the current context using the alcCreateContext() function and alcMakeContextCurrent(). Then we can create the previously discussed sound sources and sound IDs in a loop. This is an integer value that is incremented by OpenAL via the alGenSources() function. We store the available sound IDs in an array so that, later, we can iterate through the available sound sources.

With the logErrors: method, we arrange for the output of error messages:

```
- (void) logErrors: (OSStatus) status {
    ALenum err = alGetError();
    if (err ! = 0) {
        NSLog(@"ERROR OpenAL:%d", err);
    }

    if (status ! = 0) {
        NSLog(@"ERROR OSStatus:%ld", (long) status);
    }
}
```

We can do this by querying the alGetError() function, which at any time returns the error that most recently occurred. As a parameter we optionally pass OSStatus, which gives us error messages of the audio file API (audio toolbox). This is necessary in the input of WAV files, as we shall soon see.

### 9.4.3 Loading Sounds

OpenAL behaves like a platform-independent API with respect to the supported file formats, similarly to how OpenGL behaves with respect to textures. There we needed the pixel raw data in the form of RGBA values. Now we need sample data of the individual WAV files. To read these in and evaluate them, Apple provides the Audio Toolbox framework, a description of which you can find at *http://developer.apple.com/library/mac/#documentation/ MusicAudio/Reference/CAAudioTooboxRef/_index.html*. In particular, here we need the Audio File Services for loading the samples:

```
- (void) loadSound:(NSString*) soundName
              Hz:(NSUInteger) sampleRate {

    //open sound file and assign fileID
    OSStatus status;
    AudioFileID fileID;
    NSString *path = [[NSBundle mainBundle] pathForResource: soundName
                                                    ofType: nil];

    NSURL *afUrl = [NSURL fileURLWithPath: path];
    status = AudioFileOpenURL(
        (CFURLRef) afUrl, kAudioFileReadPermission, 0, &fileID);

    //determine file size (fileSize)
    UInt64 outDataSize = 0;//file size in bytes
    UInt32 thePropSize = sizeof(UInt64);
    status = AudioFileGetProperty(
        fileID,
        kAudioFilePropertyAudioDataByteCount, &thePropSize, &outDataSize);
    UInt32 fileSize = (UInt32) outDataSize;

    //temporarily read in sound data
    unsigned char *tempData = malloc(fileSize);
```

```
status = AudioFileReadBytes(fileID, FALSE, 0, &fileSize, tempData);
status = AudioFileClose(fileID);

//create a new audio buffer
NSUInteger bufferID;
alGenBuffers(1, &bufferID);

//write sound data as raw bytes into the buffer (without header
information)
alBufferData(bufferID, AL_FORMAT_MONO16, tempData, fileSize,
sampleRate);

//store the buffer in a dictionary
[soundBufferIDDictionary setObject:
    [NSNumber numberWithUnsignedInt: bufferID] forKey: soundName];

if(tempData) {
    free(tempData);
    tempData = NULL;
}

[self logErrors: status];
}
```

Before we get at the sample data that are stored in the WAV file, we first have to read in the file using the `AudioFileOpenURL()` function. Moreover, we need the file size, which is given to us by `AudioFileGetProperty()`. As you can see from the parameters, the `loadSound:Hz:` method must also be given the sample rate. As we have seen already, you can alter the sounds considerably using other sample rates (in case you are interested in sound experiments).

We obtain the actual sample data using the `AudioFileReadBytes()` function of the Audio Toolbox framework, with which we read the samples into the `tempData` variable. For each call to the `loadSound:Hz:` method, a new buffer is created via `alGenBuffers()` and filled with the `tempData` data of the samples via `alBufferData()`. Finally, we store the `bufferID` and the file name in a dictionary. In addition to the `FORMAT_MONO16` format, OpenAL supports `AL_FORMAT_MONO8`, `AL_FORMAT_STEREO8`, and `AL_FORMAT_STEREO16`.

Alternatively, the `alBufferData()` function is available through an OES extension from Apple as a static variant that under certain conditions offers better performance. You can find the extension `alBufferDataStaticProc` in the `OpenAL/oalStaticBufferExtension` header file.

## 9.4.4  Digression: Synthetic Sounds

OpenAL gives us control over the actual sample data to be played. For example, you can fill a buffer with values in real time and immediately send them to the sound output. Here, the latency depends only on the size of the buffer and the time that it takes to fill the buffer. The smaller the chosen buffer is, the smaller is the latency.

Using the sine function, we can easily create a synthetic sound. Instead of reading in a WAV file, we create the audio data programmatically. The higher the frequency is, the higher is the pitch. The amplitude has its highest value at +128 and –127 units, and values outside this range will lead to a distorted sound. The easiest way to produce synthetic sounds—that is, artificially generated sounds that are not recorded by a microphone from real-world noises—is with 8 bits and 8 kHz.

The values of the sine function that we will later write to the OpenAL buffer are stored in an `unsigned char` array that contains numbers in the range 0 to 256. In assigning values to the sine functions, we add 128 units, so that we comply with the range of values, and convert the values of the sine function that oscillate between –100 and 100 (given an amplitude a = 100) into the format required by OpenAL:

```
int sampleRate = 8000;//8 kHz
int a = 100;//amplitude
int f = 440;//frequency (concert pitch 'A', 440 Hz)
unsigned char *sinusTable = malloc(sampleRate);
static int currentSample = 0;
float TWO_PI = 2.0f * M_PI;

//create sine-wave table
for (int i = 0; i < sampleRate; i++) {//1 cycle with f = 1 (inaudible)
    sinusTable[i] = (a * sin(TWO_PI * i/sampleRate)) + 128;
}

//frequency
for (int i = 0; i < fileSize; i++) {
    if (currentSample > sampleRate - 1) {
        currentSample = currentSample - sampleRate;
    }
    tempData[i] = sinusTable[currentSample];
    currentSample + = f;
}

alBufferData(buffer, AL_FORMAT_MONO8, tempData, fileSize, sampleRate);
```

The sine values consist of one complete cycle (frequency = 1), which results from the sample rate. Recall that the sample rate gives the number of samples per second. Since our sound can remain audible for more than a second or could contain another frequency, we iterate in a second loop over the sine values and include every 440th sample. Now the wave oscillates at the desired frequency. But in practice, the sample rate is in fact lower: at 2 Hz, the sine wave would complete two cycles per second, and only every second sample would be evaluated. The sample rate has thereby decreased by half. The higher the frequency is, the smaller is the number of samples per cycle.

## 9.4.5 Playing Sounds

With the `SoundOAL` class, we can play sounds once they have been loaded. This is accomplished by the `playSound:` method, which takes the file name as parameter:

```
- (void) playSound: (NSString*) soundName {
  NSUInteger bufferID =
      [[soundBufferIDDictionary objectForKey: soundName] unsignedIntValue];
  NSUInteger soundID = [self findFreeSoundID];
  [soundIDDictionary setObject:
      [NSNumber numberWithUnsignedInt: soundID] forKey: soundName];

  alSourcei(soundID, AL_BUFFER, 0);//delete old buffer data
  alSourcei(soundID, AL_BUFFER, bufferID);//bind new buffer data
```

```
    //sound characteristics
    alSourcef(soundID, AL_PITCH, 1.0);
    alSourcef(soundID, AL_GAIN, 1.0);
    alSourcei(soundID, AL_LOOPING, AL_FALSE);

    alSourcePlay(soundID);
    [self logErrors: 0];
}
```

Using the file name, the appropriate buffer ID, which gives us access to the sound samples, is identified via the dictionary. Now we must find a free sound source—that is, a sound ID that is not currently being played. This is given to us by the findFreeSoundID method, which we present next. Once we have found a free ID, we can link the desired buffer with the ID via alSourcei(). In addition, we store the sound ID and the file name in a dictionary, so that we can later determine which file name is currently bound to which sound ID.

Via alSourcef() we can also set various sound characteristics. In addition to the pitch, which we leave at the original value via AL_PITCH, you have parameters such as AL_POSITION, AL_DIRECTION, and AL_VELOCITY, which allow for the positioning of the sound source in 3D space. You can optionally set an explicit listener using alListener3f(AL_ORIENTATION, x, y, z). Using the new Apple spatial audio extension and the oalMacOSX_OALExtensions header, you also have, since iOS 5, effects such as reverb.

We have set the parameter AL_LOOPING to false. For the implementation of the loopSound: method, you must simply set this to true, and the sound will be played until you stop it.

To control the playback behavior of a sound, you have the following functions:

```
alSourcePlay(ALuint sid);//playback
alSourceStop(ALuint sid);//stop
alSourceRewind(ALuint sid);//rewind to the beginning
alSourcePause(ALuint sid);//pause
```

To play a sound, it suffices to call alSourcePlay(soundID). Similarly, we use the alSourceStop() function to stop a looped sound:

```
- (void) stopSound: (NSString*) soundName {
    id obj = [soundIDDictionary objectForKey: soundName];
    if (obj ! = NULL) {
       NSUInteger soundID = [obj unsignedIntValue];
       alSourceStop(soundID);
       [self logErrors: 0];
    }
}
```

The following parameters apply to the playback functions with which you can query the current state of a sound via AL_SOURCE_STATE:

```
AL_INITIAL
AL_PLAYING
AL_PAUSED
AL_STOPPED
```

The status information helps us to find a free sound slot:

```
- (NSUInteger) findFreeSoundID {
    for (NSNumber *aSoundID in soundIDs) {
        NSInteger idState;
        alGetSourcei([aSoundID unsignedIntValue], AL_SOURCE_STATE, &idState);
        if(idState ! = AL_PLAYING) return [aSoundID unsignedIntValue];
        }

        //When all sounds have been played, the oldest is replaced
        NSUInteger soundID = [[soundIDs objectAtIndex:0]
            unsignedIntegerValue];
        alSourceStop(soundID);
        [self logErrors: 0];
        return soundID;
}
```

We iterate through the soundID array until we find an ID that is currently not being played. If all 22 slots are occupied and no free ID was found, we stop the sound source located at index position 0 and in its place start a new sound:

```
- (void) dealloc {
    //delete sound IDs
    for(NSNumber *soundID in soundIDs) {
        NSUInteger sID = [soundID unsignedIntValue];
        alDeleteSources(1, &sID);
    }

    //delete buffer data
    NSEnumerator *enumerator = [soundBufferIDDictionary keyEnumerator];
    id key;
    while ((key = [enumerator nextObject])) {
        NSNumber *bufferID = [soundBufferIDDictionary objectForKey: key];
        NSUInteger bID = [bufferID unsignedIntValue];
        alDeleteBuffers(1, &bID);
    }

    [soundIDDictionary release];
    [soundBufferIDDictionary release];
    [soundIDs release];

    alcMakeContextCurrent(NULL);
    alcDestroyContext(context);
    alcCloseDevice(device);
    [self logErrors: 0];

    [super dealloc];
}
```

Of course, we can explicitly delete buffers and sound IDs that are no longer needed. You can see how that is done via the functions alDeleteBuffers() and alDelete Sources() in the dealloc() method. In addition, we provide here manually for the release of the two dictionaries and the sound ID array. If you have activated ARC (since iOS 5), you can ignore this step. Finally, we release the audio context and close the audio device.

# 10 Waiting to Be a Millionaire

## 10.1  Your Gateway to the World—iTunes Connect

So far, so good. We now know how to bring a game to life in the emulator. But to send a game out into the world (and make yourself a millionaire) requires a few additional steps, all defined by Apple and therefore well documented on the Apple developer web pages. Here, the focus is on the following two items:

- Deployment to a device

- Distribution through the App Store

A requirement for both of these tasks is access to the Apple developer program, for which you have to pay. You can arrange for this at the home page of the developer program (*http://developer.apple.com/iphone/program*).

Access will cost you $99 per year and must be renewed annually; otherwise, your account will lapse and all your uploaded games will vanish from the App Store.

Once you have obtained access, you can accomplish all the remaining steps through the Apple Dev Center and iTunes Connect. There you will find weekly updated sales figures by country and by game.

## 10.2 Test, Test, Test: But How Does a Game Get into My Device?

It should go without saying that you should test every game that you publish in the App Store on a device in the iPhone family. As the weakest link in the chain, it is recommended to test on the original iPhone of 2007; you can still obtain used ones through the Internet. If your game runs on this device, then you can be fairly certain that your program will run on all models. As a basic version, you can choose a version of iOS as low as possible as your deployment target in order to increase the market for your game.

Before your application can be transferred to the test device, you must sign the application. Furthermore, you must also create a local certificate on your computer. Then the app can be transferred via Xcode to the device, which is attached by a USB cable. The individual steps are rather complicated, but are well laid out in the "Development Provisioning Assistant." Apple provides a straightforward step-by-step introduction, which you can find at *http://developer.apple.com/iphone/manage/overview/index.action* and then through the button "Launch Assistant."

## 10.3 Release and Distribution

Before the game can be placed in the App Store and thereby made available for sale world-wide, you must put your game through an approval process, whereby the app is tested by Apple employees for quality, functionality, and security. In addition to accompanying resources such as screen shots, contact website, and description, you must prepare the game project for release:

- Change the Xcode setting for your project from "debug" to "release" and test it again on the device. If all goes well, you will need an additional certificate. The previous developer certificate serves only for deployment, while the required distribution certificate can be obtained from the Provisioning Center at *https://developer.apple.com/iphone/manage/distribution/index.action*.

- For building the app, choose "Distribution" mode. But beware: since your project is no longer available locally on a device but is to be sold exclusively through the App Store, choose the release schema under Xcode.

- To verify the build, you can look at the build logs. You will find these if you click on the *Succeeded* message on the lower edge. Note that the app was signed with the distribution certificate.

- To create the final binary, you have simply to zip the app files in the build folder.

- You can now upload the app via iTunes Connect (Figure 10.1).

The actual upload process of the binary takes place via a program installed on your Mac, the "Application Loader." This can be found (since iPhone SDK 3.2) at */Developer/Applications/Utilities/Application Loader.app*.

This app provides for the binary being validated before the upload. It is important that the app has obtained the status "Waiting for Upload" in iTunes Connect before the upload.

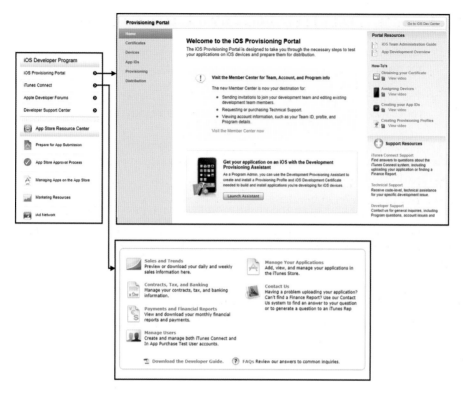

Figure 10.1 The road to the provisioning portal and to iTunes Connect leads through the Dev Center home page. (An account for which you must pay is required for access.)

# ▥ 10.4 Marketing Plans?

All right, then, you have done it. Your game has gone through the approval process and now can be found in the App Store through a search. It is of crucial importance to choose suitable search terms. Since the key words can be set only once, they should be as specific as possible and avoid common phrases. However, these are not the only steps you should take in making potential buyers aware of your product:

- Consider a "lite" version. A free app is more likely to be downloaded and will increase your market penetration.

- Alternatively, you can offer a free version of the game and then make higher levels available for sale through In-App Purchases. (In-App Purchases are also processed wholly by Apple through the App Store.)*

---

* Do you remember the 3D classic Doom? In 1993, the first two levels could be downloaded over the Internet for free. Fifteen million people did so, and 150,000 users bought the full version, which represents a conversion rate of only 1%, but 150,000 purchases was enough to make John Romero, the founder of id Software, a millionaire.

- The price of an app can be changed at any time. During the start-up phase, you can offer your app at a discount price or even for free in order to generate more reviews. Even a start-up discount of 50% can encourage fence-sitters to make the purchase.

- You can earn extra money by integrating advertising. With the iAd framework (since iOS 4.0), developers can integrate this feature into their apps.

Of course, you can also take the classical path through the Internet and send marketing materials to webzines and blogs or create a video to post on YouTube. Apple offers three ways of linking your game:

- iTunes Direct Link to an app via *http://itunes.com/apps/appname*

- iTunes Direct Link with developer name via *http://itunes.com/apps/developername/ appname*

- iTunes Direct Link to all your apps via *http://itunes.com/apps/developername*

If iTunes is not installed on the user's computer, a link opens with an installation guide.

# Bibliography

Aarnio, T., and K. P. Ville Miettinen. 2007. *Mobile 3D graphics with OpenGL ES and M3G.* San Diego, CA: Academic Press.

Feldman, A. 2000. *Designing arcade computer game graphics.* Plano, TX: Wordware Publishing, Inc. Available without charge at http://wiki.yoyogames.com/index.php/Ari_Feldman%27s_Book_on_Game_Graphics

Fournier, A., and D. Fussell. 1988. On the power of the frame buffer. *ACM Transactions on Graphics* 7 (2): 103–128.

Gamma, E., R. Helm, R. Johnson, and J. Vlissides. 2000. *Design patterns: Elements of reusable object-oriented software.* Boston: Addison–Wesley.

Kochan, S. G. 2011. *Programming in Objective-C,* 4th ed. Boston: Addison–Wesley.

Lengyel, E. 2003. *Math for 3D game programming and computer graphics.* Boston: Course Technology.

Neuburg, N. 2012. *Programming iOS 5: Fundamentals of iPhone, iPad, and iPod touch development,* 2nd ed. Cambridge, MA: O'Reilly Media.

NFGman. 2006. *Character design for mobile devices.* Florence, KY: Focal Press.

Richter, K. 2011. *Beginning iOS Game Center and Game Kit For iPhone, iPad, and iPod touch.* New York: Apress.

Rideout, P. 2010. *iPhone 3D programming. Developing graphical applications with OpenGL ES.* Cambridge, MA: O'Reilly Media. Available without charge at http://iphone-3d-programming.labs.oreilly.com

Stark, J. 2010. *Building iPhone apps with HTML, CSS, and JavaScript.* Cambridge, MA: O'Reilly Media.

Strougo, R., and R. Wenderlich. 2011. *Learning Cocos2D: A hands-on guide to building iOS games with Cocos2D, Box2D, and Chipmunk.* Boston: Addison–Wesley.

# Index

# R